Peachtree
Made Easy

Fifth Edition

JOHN HEDTKE AND CONNIE BRENDEN

Osborne McGraw-Hill

Berkeley New York St. Louis San Francisco
Auckland Bogotá Hamburg London Madrid Mexico City Milan Montreal
New Delhi Panama City Paris São Paulo Singapore Sydney Tokyo Toronto

Osborne/**McGraw-Hill**
2600 Tenth Street
Berkeley, California 94710
U.S.A.

For information on translations or book distributors outside the U.S.A., or to arrange bulk purchase discounts for sales promotions, premiums, or fund-raisers, please contact Osborne/**McGraw-Hill** at the above address.

Peachtree Made Easy, Fifth Edition

1234567890 VFM VFM 019876543210

ISBN 0-07-212507-1

Publisher
Brandon A. Nordin

**Associate Publisher and
Editor-in-Chief**
Scott Rogers

Acquisitions Editor
Megg Bonar

Acquisitions Coordinator
Stephane Thomas

Project Editor
Jody McKenzie

Technical Editors
Monty Dillavou
Elise Taylor

Copy Editor
Lunaea Weatherstone

Proofreader
Susie Elkind

Indexer
Karin Arrigoni

Computer Designers
Gary Corrigan
Roberta Steele

Illustrators
Beth Young
Bob Hansen
Brian Wells

Series Designer
Peter F. Hancik

Cover Designer
Woods & Woods
Design Communications

This book was composed with Corel VENTURA™ Publisher.

To David McTarnahan.

— John

For my mom, Ana.

— Connie

Contents At a Glance

Contents

Acknowledgments

Creating a book is a rewarding process involving team participation. As the co-author, I have had the pleasure of working with the wonderful staff at Osborne/McGraw-Hill (who are listed below in detail). John, thank you for giving me this fabulous opportunity. Monty Dillavou and Elise Taylor of e-controller.com, thanks for your technical expertise. And lastly, to Ashley, my daughter, thanks for being patient while I was tying up the phone line sending files in the evenings.

To all the wonderful folks at Osborne/McGraw-Hill:

- Brandon A. Nordin and Scott Rogers for their continued support.
- Megg Bonar, Acquisitions Editor, for guidance throughout the project.
- Stephane Thomas, Acquisitions Coordinator, who always knows where to track down information.
- Jody McKenzie, Project Editor, who gently kept the project on track.
- Lunaea Weatherstone, Copy Editor, for catching technical errors and improving readability.
- Susie Elkind, Proofreader.
- Karin Arrigoni, Indexer.
- Roberta Steele and Gary Corrigan, Designers, for doing the page layout, and Beth Young, Bob Hansen, and Brian Wells, Illustrators, for the art, all of whom are working under Lisa Bandini, Production Manager.

Thanks also to Constance Maytum for her sage project management advice to John, and to Brad MacAfee of Peachtree Software, who graciously provided copies of the Peachtree 7.0 software.

To all of these people and many more, thank you for making this book possible.

John Hedtke and Connie Brenden
Seattle, 2000

Introduction

Welcome to *Peachtree Made Easy, Fifth Edition*. This book tells you how to use Peachtree Accounting for Windows Release 7.0 and Peachtree Complete Accounting for Windows Release 7.0. These are the latest versions of general accounting software produced by Peachtree Software. Both Peachtree Accounting for Windows and Peachtree Complete Accounting for Windows offer a number of advantages over other accounting packages:

- **The software is easy to use and understand.** In Peachtree Accounting for Windows and Peachtree Complete Accounting for Windows, the functions are clearly defined, and there are online help and wizards to guide you.
- **The software is flexible.** You don't have to tailor your business's accounting practices to fit the shortcomings of your software.
- **The software grows with you.** When you buy Peachtree Accounting for Windows or Peachtree Complete Accounting for Windows, you are receiving the complete program. You don't have to buy a number of different modules when you want to add capabilities—they're all part of the basic package.
- **The software is inexpensive.** Peachtree Accounting for Windows and Peachtree Complete Accounting for Windows can handle all the accounting requirements for most small businesses. To get the same number of functions and modules, you would have to spend anywhere from two to ten times as much for other software.

Why This Book Is for You

Peachtree Made Easy, Fifth Edition is written for anyone who wants a fast introduction to the many features of Peachtree Accounting for Windows and Peachtree Complete Accounting for Windows. If you haven't used Peachtree before, the book discusses each of the features in simple terms. Only minimal accounting experience is required. If you have used Peachtree before, the process-oriented approach makes this an excellent book for easy reference and a handy guide to features you have not used before. Experienced users will also find discussions on how features can be used together to make a truly integrated accounting system.

Peachtree Made Easy, Fifth Edition is the perfect choice for a brief, self-contained introduction to this vast accounting system.

About This Book

This book is meant to be a fast introduction to the latest versions of Peachtree Accounting for Windows and Peachtree Complete Accounting for Windows. After giving an introduction to the software, each feature is discussed by taking you through the menus and explaining how to use the feature. Each chapter begins by showing you how to set defaults for the feature, then leads you through setting up entries for the feature (such as customers, vendors, and employees). "Putting It to Work" sections give tips on how you can take advantage of Peachtree Accounting's features to greater effect. Finally, the chapter shows you how to perform tasks associated with that feature and how to print reports and forms. Screens with sample data are plentiful so you can follow along on your computer. Experienced users will find it quite simple to look up the techniques they will need to run and adapt their system. New users will find instructions on setting up features and the options available to them.

You don't need to be familiar with Peachtree to use this book, but you should know some basic accounting concepts and understand how to operate your computer. If you are not an accountant yourself and are setting up Peachtree Accounting for Windows and Peachtree Complete Accounting for Windows for your business, you may occasionally want to ask an accountant for advice on setting options and defaults. Most of the information you need to set up and run Peachtree is already in your company's files. All you will need to do is take some time to plan what you want and then organize the information for entering into the program.

How This Book Is Organized

This book is divided into thirteen chapters. Each chapter discusses one or two features of Peachtree Accounting for Windows and Peachtree Complete Accounting for Windows in detail. The chapters are organized in the order in which you might set up and use the various features: general accounting concepts, setting up the General Ledger, accounts receivable, accounts payable, payroll, and so on.

Chapter 1, "The Basics of Accounting," describes the differences between accounting and bookkeeping. It also explains the basic accounting process and shows how automating this process with Peachtree will give you greater control.

Chapter 2, "Basics of Peachtree Accounting Software," shows you how to install Peachtree Accounting for Windows and Peachtree Complete Accounting for Windows, and introduces you to the various general options and features in the software. If you're already familiar with the previous versions of Peachtree, this chapter will also identify some of the major enhancements in the current version.

In Chapter 3, "Setting Up Your Business in Peachtree Accounting," you will see how to set up the general options and defaults using the New Company Setup Wizard in Peachtree for Big Business, Inc., a fictitious sample firm used throughout this book.

Chapter 4, "Setting Up Your General Ledger," sets up the General Ledger by entering the chart of accounts and account balances for Big Business, Inc. You will also learn how to print General Ledger reports such as the transaction register, the trial balance, and a balance sheet, and how to set up passwords.

With your business and General Ledger set up, you are introduced to the receivables side of accounting in Chapter 5, "Accounts Receivable and Invoicing." You will see how to enter accounts receivable defaults and options, create sales tax codes, and set up and enter customers and payment terms. After this, you will learn about entering sales and receipts, creating and printing invoices and credit memos, and posting Accounts Receivable transactions. The Time & Billing feature of Peachtree Complete Accounting for Windows shows users how to use time and expense tickets to charge time and expenses back to clients.

Chapter 6, "Accounts Payable and Purchase Orders," introduces you to the Accounts Payable feature. In this chapter, you'll see how to set up and use Accounts Payable functions: add and edit vendor information, print vendor reports, enter vendor invoices and purchase orders, select bills for payment, print checks and assorted Accounts Payable reports, and post Accounts Payable transactions. The Time & Billing feature of Peachtree Complete Accounting for Windows shows users how to apply vendor costs as time and expense items.

Chapter 7, "Payroll," deals with setting up and using Peachtree's Payroll feature. In this chapter, you'll learn how to set up payroll and employee defaults using the new Payroll Wizard, edit payroll tax tables, enter and maintain employee and sales rep records, run payroll checks, print reports, and post payroll transactions.

Chapter 8, "Inventory," introduces Peachtree's Inventory features. You'll start by setting up inventory item defaults for such things as the sales price for an item, stocking requirements, and how it is used in a bill of materials. You will then see how to enter inventory items, build and break down assemblies, make adjustments to inventory, and print inventory reports.

Chapter 9, "Job Costing," teaches you how to set up and use jobs to track and identify time, materials, and costs for a specific project for a client. Peachtree Complete Accounting for Windows users will also see how to subdivide jobs into phases and cost codes for tighter, more detailed tracking of the financial information for a project.

Chapter 10, "Time & Billing," discusses the time and expense ticket feature found only in Peachtree Complete Accounting for Windows. You will see how to enter daily and weekly time sheets, enter expenses, and print time and expense reports.

Chapter 11, "Fixed Asset Management," addresses the Peachtree Fixed Assets module. After setting up fixed assets, you will learn how to calculate depreciation, post depreciation to the General Ledger, and print a wide variety of fixed asset reports.

Peachtree's reporting features are discussed in Chapter 12, "Customizing Reports." You'll see how to plan and make changes to the standard reports in Peachtree, how to print financial statements, and where to go for more information on customizing financial statements and forms.

Finally, Chapter 13, "Management Tools and Procedures," shows you how to perform a wide range of management tasks, such as how to back up your data and programs, purge old transactions and inactive records using the Purge Wizard, reconcile your accounts against your bank statements, and close payroll and financial periods. You will then see how to use the various management tools in the Peachtree Complete Manager Series to plan and track your accounting information. You will also see how to import and export data.

A glossary of accounting terms is also included.

Conventions Used In This Book

This book has several standard conventions for presenting information.

Characters or words you are to type appear in **bold**.

Defined terms are in *italics*.

Keyboard names appear in SMALL CAPITALS. If you are supposed to press several keys together, the keys are joined with a hyphen. For example, "Press CTRL-F1" means to hold down the control key (CTRL) and press F1.

There are three types of note in the text:

NOTE: A note is simply a comment related to the material being discussed.

TIP: A tip is a technique for doing things faster, easier, or better in Peachtree.

CAUTION: A caution is a warning to prevent you from doing something that could result in a loss of data or cause you problems with the way you run your business.

The screen shots in this book show you how Peachtree looks on a standard Pentium computer using an SVGA monitor with a standard $800 \times 600 \times 256$ color display in Microsoft Windows 98. What you see on your screen may be slightly different, depending on the configuration of your hardware.

Other Books by the Authors

If you enjoy *Peachtree Made Easy, Fifth Edition*, you may also enjoy some other books by John Hedtke, including the following:

Peachtree Made Easy, Fourth Edition (Osborne/McGraw-Hill, 1998), focuses on Peachtree Accounting for Windows v5.0 and Peachtree Complete Accounting for Windows v6.0 (the previous versions of general accounting software produced by Peachtree Software). This book describes how to install the software, set up your company, set up and maintain your General Ledger, set up and process accounts receivable, accounts payable, and payroll, maintain your company's inventory, use job costing, enter time and expense tickets, use Peachtree Fixed Assets to track fixed assets and depreciation, and perform system tasks such as backing up and closing years.

Peachtree Complete Business Toolkit (Osborne/McGraw-Hill, 1998) covers some of the add-on products and features for Peachtree Accounting for Windows and Peachtree Complete Accounting for Windows. This book and CD cover the Peachtree Report Writer, an add-on product that lets you create custom reports and labels, PeachLink, a product included on the Peachtree Accounting for Windows 5.0 and Peachtree Complete Accounting for Windows 6.0 CDs that helps you set up your own Web page in about an hour, and the Electronic Bill Payment feature, which lets you transmit check information to ADP via modem. In addition, the CD accompanying *Peachtree Complete Business Toolkit* has a number of reports, programs, and utilities to enhance Peachtree Accounting in your business.

Peachtree Complete Accounting for Windows Made Easy (Osborne/ McGraw-Hill, 1997) focuses on Peachtree Complete Accounting for Windows v4.0 (the previous release of Peachtree Complete Accounting for Windows). This book describes how to install Peachtree Complete Accounting for Windows v4.0, set up your company, set up and maintain your General Ledger, set up and process accounts receivable, accounts payable, and payroll, maintain your company's inventory, use job costing, enter time and expense tickets, use Peachtree Fixed Assets to track fixed assets and depreciation, and perform system tasks such as backing up and closing years.

Peachtree Accounting for Windows Made Easy (Osborne/McGraw-Hill, 1995) is written for Peachtree Accounting for Windows v3.0. (Because there were relatively few changes in the subsequent release, this book is also applicable to Peachtree Accounting for Windows v3.5.) This book describes how to install Peachtree Accounting for Windows, set up your company, set up and maintain your General Ledger, set up and process accounts receivable, accounts payable, and payroll, maintain your company's inventory, use job costing, and perform system tasks such as backing up and closing years. There are also a number of forms in the back of the book to assist you in converting your accounting data from another accounting system into Peachtree Accounting for Windows v3.0.

The Basics of Accounting

1

B A S I C S

- Differences between accounting and bookkeeping
- Role of accounting in business operations
- Elements of the accounting process

B E Y O N D

- How to increase your efficiency with Peachtree Accounting
- How to take advantage of Peachtree's built-in flexibility

In this chapter, you'll learn about the basics of accounting and the accounting process. You'll also learn how to automate your business's accounting process with Peachtree Accounting software.

Accounting is a fundamental part of running your business. Of course, selling is also very important. What good is a sale, however, if you can't bill accurately or on time, if your payroll costs are digging you in deeper each day, or if you don't know the cost of the goods you are selling? If you can't measure your business, you can't manage it. Accounting is the yardstick you need to measure, and manage, every aspect of your business.

This chapter is intended for those who know little or nothing about accounting. It covers the basic concepts of accounting in a simple, straightforward way. You don't have to be an accountant to use Peachtree Accounting for Windows or Peachtree Complete Accounting for Windows, but knowing something about accounting helps. If you already know accounting basics, feel free to skim this chapter or go directly to Chapter 2.

 NOTE: This book discusses the options and features of both Peachtree Accounting for Windows and Peachtree Complete Accounting for Windows. Unless otherwise noted, both products will be referred to as "Peachtree Accounting" throughout this book.

Accounting Versus Bookkeeping

All businesses do bookkeeping, but not all do accounting. Bookkeeping is the process of recording information on business transactions. If you have a checking account, you do bookkeeping. Accounting requires bookkeeping, but encompasses much more, including the design of the bookkeeping system, analysis of accounting data, creating financial reports, and making business decisions. Peachtree Accounting unifies the bookkeeping and accounting processes, providing for journal entries, posting to accounts, financial reporting, and business analysis.

The Importance of Accounting

Accounting weaves its way into every aspect of a business. When the salesperson on the road fills out an expense form, that involves accounting. When you cut a payroll check to an employee, that also involves accounting. Even the chair you sit in and the rugs and lamps in your office involve accounting. Accounting plays four major roles in any business: financial control, operations, reporting, and planning.

Financial Control

Financial control is the accounting function most people are familiar with. Television has popularized the image of a funny little guy with a green eyeshade who keeps track of every pencil and paper clip. While it makes for good television, this character has little to do with accounting in the real world. Managing overhead and production costs can make the difference between profit and loss. You may not care about paper clips, but you probably do care what your business spends on rent, electricity, personnel, office equipment, and materials.

Controlling costs is a key factor to the success of any business. Consider this example: A business builds a machine at a cost of $50 and sells it for $100. After deducting the cost of sales, advertising, overhead, and other business costs, the company keeps only $10 of the original $100. In other words, the company had to sell $100 to keep $10.

Suppose that the company, by doing things a little differently, finds a way to reduce costs by just $10 per week. While this cost reduction may seem small, it is the equivalent of a $100 sale. Without good accounting practices, however, you won't know where to start cutting costs. Maybe your salespeople are spending too much on their trips, or your production costs are out of line. Perhaps your advertising dollars aren't pulling their weight. A good accounting system helps you identify the problem areas, giving your company the financial control it needs.

Operations

If you run a business, you know that accounting is a part of your company's day-to-day operations. You are constantly billing customers, generating a payroll, paying bills, and tracking inventory, and each task has a role in the accounting process.

For the operational aspects of accounting, companies have varying approaches. The one-person consulting firm, for example, can simply track billings and expenses. The needs of a dress manufacturer with 50 employees, on the other hand, are far more extensive, involving payroll, inventory, cost estimation, receivables, and payables.

Peachtree Accounting is split into modules. This lets your company use only the modules it needs today, adding the others as the company grows. Peachtree Accounting also makes learning the system easy. This is a major consideration when you factor in the cost of training personnel.

Reporting

Every business person wants to know periodically how his or her company is doing. Accounting reports, including balance sheets and income statements, provide you with the information you need to assess your company's performance.

Surprisingly, many businesses operate without the benefit of timely accounting reports. It is not uncommon for a company to find itself in a cash crunch months after the problem could have been identified. With Peachtree Accounting, you can have reports on a daily or weekly basis. You never have to be in the dark about where your company stands.

For publicly held companies, financial reporting takes on special significance. Investors and analysts rely on your financial statements to guide them in taking positions and making recommendations. Accurate financial statements are critical to a market economy, which is why the government and the accounting profession spend millions each year to root out fraud and enforce proper accounting methods.

Planning

Accounting has an important role in charting your company's future, which is often reflected in the accounting data you've accumulated day by day, yet not enough companies take the time to review their progress over time.

Planning means setting goals and putting together a step-by-step approach for reaching those goals. Setting reasonable goals is a key component of this process. Aiming for the moon won't do you or your business any good. At the same time, setting your sights too low won't produce the results you want. If your business has a good accounting system, you will have the information you need to set attainable goals.

For example, suppose your inventory system shows, on average, that you have a 60-day supply of parts on hand. Since inventory ties up cash, you want to reduce this unnecessary cost. In reviewing your accounting data, you find that the lowest point your inventory ever fell to was a 30-day supply. With this information, you decide to set a reasonable goal of reducing your average inventory level to 45 days but never letting it fall below 30 days. If you are successful in reaching this goal, you will improve the profitability of your business.

Having set the goal of reducing inventory, you must also define how to achieve that goal. Referring once again to data provided by your accounting system, you find that the fluctuations in inventory are caused by a lack of timely information about current stock levels. Your plan, then, is to computerize the inventory process so that you only order what you really need.

Fluctuation = เปลี่ยนแปลงอยู่เรื่อย

It is clear that a good accounting system is essential to successful business practices. Peachtree Accounting and your personal computer are all you need to improve your operations, get the information you need, and improve your company's profitability.

Accounting Fundamentals

You don't have to be an accountant to use Peachtree Accounting, but it does help if you understand some accounting basics. Fortunately, accounting relies on some fairly simple rules known as *generally accepted accounting principles*. Learn these rules and you will know all you need to get the most from Peachtree Accounting.

Accounts

The *account* is the basic building block of accounting. In fact, from an accounting point of view, your entire business is little more than many accounts, each one serving a specific purpose. One account tells how much cash you have on hand, another records how much you've paid your employees so far this year, still another tracks your inventory.

All the accounts belonging to a business, taken together, form the *chart of accounts*. Setting up the chart of accounts is the first step in creating an accounting system. You organize the chart of accounts by major account categories, such as assets, liabilities, capital, income, cost of sales, and expenses. Within the categories, you divide accounts further. For example, the asset category might include the current assets account that, in turn, contains the cash and accounts receivable accounts.

Transactions

While accounts are used for different purposes, they all have balances that are increased or decreased by *transactions*. A transaction is any business operation that has a monetary impact. Examples include selling merchandise, purchasing inventory, paying bills, and amortizing an asset.

A transaction consists of two parts: *debits* and *credits*. Debits are recorded on the left side of an account, and credits are recorded on the right side. Debits increase the balance of the cash account, and credits decrease the cash balance. Figure 1-1 shows an account used to record cash transactions. The first item listed in the account is a debit of $5,000. Also listed are two credits for $500 and $200, leaving a net balance of $4,300.

```
                          Cash
    _____

              5,000         |
                            |   500
                            |   200
                            |
                            |
                            |
                            |
                            |
                            |
    _____  •
```

FIGURE 1-1   A typical cash account

Notice that the credits and debits listed in the cash account do not tell the whole story. The account in Figure 1-1 does not tell you where the $5,000 came from or what the $700 was spent on. In practice, transactions are recorded in a transaction journal before they are posted to their accounts. A transaction journal entry contains all the accounting information for a specific transaction. A typical journal entry might look like this:

```
Debit Cash                   $5,000.00
Credit Accounts                               $5,000.00
Receivable
```

The journal entry indicates that the $5,000 debit to the cash account resulted from a credit to the Accounts Receivable account. In other words, someone paid a bill. Often an entry in an account will include an identification number indicating which journal entry the number came from. With Peachtree Accounting, the computer keeps track of this process for you.

The preceding example demonstrates the concept of _double entry accounting_. The double entry concept is quite simple: any transaction contains both credits and debits that, when summed, are equal. This is true even when the transaction affects more than one account at a time, as shown here:

```
Debit Inventory              $5,000.00
Credit Cash                                   $3,000.00
Credit Accounts Payable                       $2,000.00
```

In this transaction, the company increases inventory by $5,000, decreases cash by $3,000, and increases accounts payable by $2,000. The sum of the credits equals the sum of the debits, and the accounts are in balance.

If all your entries hold to the rule that debits equal credits, your books will always balance. Unfortunately, companies that use manual bookkeeping methods often find their books out of balance due to clerical errors. These errors can be difficult to track down and can waste valuable time and energy. With Peachtree Accounting, you can ensure that debits will always equal credits.

Assets, Liabilities, and Equity

While all accounts operate in the same fashion, they differ in one important respect. For some accounts, such as the cash account, debits increase the balance and credits decrease the balance. For other accounts, debits decrease the balance while credits increase it. The rule you use depends on whether the account is an asset account, a liability account, or an equity account.

Assets are the resources a company uses to generate revenue. Examples of assets include buildings, property, equipment, cash, accounts receivable, securities, trademarks, copyrights, patents, and more. When a transaction increases an asset—for example, purchasing a new building—it is recorded as a debit to the asset account.

Whereas assets represent a company's resources, liabilities and equity represent claims on those resources. *Liabilities* represent the economic obligations of a firm to outsiders. *Equity* represents the value allocated to ownership of the firm. These claims can take many forms, including the equity claimed by the owners of the firm, accounts payable, taxes payable, retained earnings, and so on. Liability and equity accounts are increased by credit entries.

For example, if inventory is purchased on credit, the transaction is reflected by a debit to inventory and a credit to accounts payable. Both accounts are increased by the amount of the transaction. Note that some transactions might involve only assets or only liabilities. If inventory is purchased for cash, the transaction consists of a debit to inventory and a credit to cash; one asset account is increased while the other is decreased.

In other words, asset account balances are increased by debits and decreased by credits. Liability and equity account balances, on the other hand, are decreased by debits and increased by credits.

Revenues and Expenses

Two groups of accounts that deserve special attention are *revenue accounts* and *expense accounts*. Revenue is any proceeds from business activities (such as rental or sales income). Expenses are the cost of doing business (such as rent, depreciation expense, professional fees, heat, light, and so on). You determine *income* by subtracting expenses from revenues. To record revenue, you credit a revenue account; to record an expense, you debit an expense account. If revenues exceed expenses, the company makes a profit and equity is increased. If expenses exceed revenues, the company books a loss and equity is decreased.

Accrual Versus Cash Accounting

Accounting methods can be broadly categorized into *accrual accounting* and *cash accounting*. Most people are comfortable with cash accounting because it reflects the way they lead their lives. For example, if you perform work this year, but get paid for it next year, that income will go on next year's tax return, not this year's. The rule for cash accounting is that revenues and expenses are recognized *when they are received or paid*.

Many small businesses operate on a cash basis. This works well when revenues and expenses tend to be small or are booked close to the time they are incurred. For larger companies, however, cash accounting does not adequately reflect their financial situation. These businesses do their accounting on an accrual basis.

In *accrual accounting,* revenues and expenses are recognized in the accounting period in which they are incurred, regardless of when the money comes in or goes out. For example, suppose a company earns $100,000 this year, but will not receive payment until next year. The revenue is booked (or accrued) this year through a credit to a revenue account and a debit to accounts receivable. Next year, when the payment is made, accounts receivable is credited and an offsetting debit is made to the cash account. The income is recognized before the money is collected.

The accrual principle also applies to expenses. Your company may incur an expense, perhaps for a sales trip, in one accounting period and pay the expense in another accounting period. Under accrual accounting, the expense is booked in the period in which the sales trip was made by debiting a travel expense account and crediting accounts payable. In the next period, when payment is made, you debit accounts payable and credit the cash account.

Despite its complexities, accrual accounting better reflects your company's financial position. For example, suppose that Company A performs some work, but will not be paid for it in the current accounting period. The work was done for a reputable client, and Company A knows that it will collect the revenue. Company B, on the other hand, performed no work during the current accounting period.

Clearly, given the choice, you would prefer to be Company A. Yet, under the rules of cash accounting, both companies would show the same revenue for the current accounting period. The difference between the two would not appear until the next accounting period, when Company A is paid. Using accrual accounting, however, the difference between the two companies would be evident in the current accounting period. For this reason, all companies of significant size use accrual accounting.

Depreciation and Materiality

One aspect of accounting that confuses many people is the distinction between assets and expenses. Both can be increased by expenditures. However, an expense is an expenditure that benefits the company in the current accounting period only, while an asset is a resource that will benefit the company in the current *and* future accounting periods.

Distinguishing between assets and expenses is important because many assets can be depreciated while expenses cannot. *Depreciation* spreads the cost of an asset over many accounting periods. In the case of a building, each year your company will take a depreciation expense representing the amount of use the building received that year. In other words, assets are turned into expenses over time by means of depreciation.

In some cases, the distinction is obvious. If you spend money to purchase a building, the building should be viewed as an asset since it will provide value to the company over many years. Paying the electric bill, however, is clearly an expense since its benefit is derived only during the current accounting period.

Sometimes the distinction between an asset and an expense is less clear. Strictly speaking, a screwdriver could be viewed as an asset if it is expected to last more than one accounting period. Of course, depreciating something so small as a screwdriver is silly. To deal with these situations, accountants use the rule of *materiality*. An asset is treated as an expense if the financial impact is so small that it will have no material effect on the firm's financial picture.

In practice, the materiality principle requires the accountant to use good judgment to determine when an asset should be treated as an expense. Because expensing an asset reduces current taxes more than depreciating assets, companies have an incentive to expense everything in sight. The best advice is to be prudent: overindulging in the expensing of assets can leave you open to unhappy audits.

The Accounting Process

Peachtree Accounting handles all the details of posting transactions, linking journal entries to account entries, and summarizing account information. Even so, you will get more out of Peachtree Accounting if you understand the manual methods it was designed to replace. The accounting process consists of three elementary steps: journal entry, posting to the ledger, and account summarization.

Journal Entry

The *journal* is a register in which you record every transaction that affects your firm. A typical journal format contains space for a date, the account affected and an explanation, a post reference (used during posting), and spaces for debits and credits. Figure 1-2 shows a typical journal entry for a transaction involving the purchase of supplies for cash.

The journal is an important part of the accounting process for two reasons. First, it provides a chronological history of all transactions affecting your business. If you want to see transactions that occurred on June 15, you can do so easily. Second, the journal puts together all debits and credits associated with a particular transaction. If you just had the chart of accounts, it would be difficult or impossible to match credits and debits from the same transaction.

Posting to the Ledger

Periodically, you must *post* journal transactions to their appropriate accounts. Posting brings your accounts up to date, adding new debits and credits and changing balances. When you post a journal entry, the account number of the posted account is written in the post reference field. This reference simplifies error checking. The transaction in the journal affects two accounts, cash and supplies, both of which are asset accounts. Posting the transaction updates the general ledger information for these two accounts. Figure 1-3 shows these accounts with the items already posted.

Date	Account and explanation	PR	Debits		Credits	
2/1/2000	Supplies		123	34		
	Cash				123	34
	General office supplies					

FIGURE 1-2   A typical journal format

Date	Account and explanation	PR	Debits		Credits	
2/1/2000	Supplies	10345	123	34		
	Cash	10100			123	34
	General office supplies					

FIGURE 1-3 Using the post reference field

As shown in Figure 1-4, the cash account started the month with a balance of $1,532.06 carried over from the previous month. The posted transaction is a credit of $123.34, which reduces the cash balance. Notice that the post reference field contains J-1. This tells the bookkeeper that this transaction originated from page 1 in the journal. This reference completes the link between the account and the journal entry. Also shown in Figure 1-4 is the supplies account. The debit to the supplies account increases the supplies balance.

Cash   Account: 10100

Date	Explanation	PR	Debits		Credits		Balance	
2/1/2000	Balance						1,532	06
	Purchase supplies	J-1			123	34	1,408	72

Supplies   Account: 10345

Date	Explanation	PR	Debits		Credits		Balance	
2/1/2000	Balance						3,221	87
2/1/2000	Purchase supplies	J-1	123	34			3,345	21

FIGURE 1-4 A typical ledger format

Entering and posting transactions manually is time-consuming and error-prone. For many companies, automating this process alone is worth the price of computerizing. With Peachtree Accounting, you simply enter transaction information. The software makes sure that the debits and credits are equal when they are entered, and later posts are made to the correct accounts automatically.

Account Summarization

After posting, all accounts are up to date. You can now summarize your accounts in the form of financial statements. All financial statements, including balance sheets and income statements, are nothing more than summaries of account balances. In the balance sheet, the accounts are summarized by assets, liabilities, and equity. In the income statement, accounts are summarized by revenues and expenses. These financial statements are discussed in detail in the next section.

Once you know the format of your financial statements, creating them just requires taking account balances and entering them in the right place on the statement. Consider the simplified balance sheet shown in Figure 1-5. The asset, liability, and equity categories are simply the names of the respective accounts. The numbers to the right are the balances in those accounts.

```
                    XYZ Company
                   Balance Sheet
                 December 31, 2000


        Assets

            Cash                    100
            Inventory               500
            Equipment             1,000

            Total Assets          1,600

        Liabilities

            Accounts payable        200
            Equity                1,400

            Total Liabilities     1,600
```

FIGURE 1-5   A simple balance sheet

Financial Statements

Financial statements are the signposts by which businesses measure their progress. These statements are so important, especially to publicly held corporations, that scores of books have been written on their analysis and interpretation.

While financial statements come in various forms, the two types that most businesspeople recognize are the *balance sheet* and the *income statement.* These statements summarize, for a specific period of time, every bit of accounting information available to the firm.

The Balance Sheet

The balance sheet, also known as the *statement of financial condition,* is a snapshot summary of your company's asset, liability, and equity accounts as of a specific date. The ironclad rule of the balance sheet is:

Assets = Liabilities + Equity

If you have entered all your transactions correctly, so that debits equal credits, this equation will always hold. As a precaution, businesses often run a *trial balance* before generating the balance sheet. A trial balance is simply a sum of all accounts to ensure that credits precisely offset debits. Trial balances were more important when accounting was manual and creating a balance sheet was time-consuming. Even with the use of computers, however, trial balances are still widely used as an interim step.

Balance sheets always list assets first, liabilities second, and equity last. Figure 1-6 shows a typical complete balance sheet. Of course, your balance sheet will contain account categories that make sense for you. Typical asset categories include:

- Cash
- Securities and investments
- Notes receivable
- Accounts receivable
- Accrued receivables
- Merchandise inventory
- Prepaid expenses
- Long-term investments
- Land

⑩ • Buildings
⑪ • Equipment
⑫ • Intangible assets

Typical liabilities include:

① • Notes payable
② • Accounts payable
③ • Accrued expenses payable
④ • Income received in advance
⑤ • Long-term liabilities
⑥ • Long-term debt
⑦ • Income tax payable

The balance sheet groups assets, liabilities, and equity into categories, the most common being current assets, prepaid expenses, fixed assets, current liabilities, long-term liabilities, income received in advance, retained earnings, and stockholders' equity.

- **Current assets**   These include cash and assets that will normally be converted into cash within one year or within the company's normal *operating cycle,* whichever is longer. The operating cycle is the length of time between the purchase of inventory or merchandise and the sale of the finished product. Current assets are also known as liquid assets or working assets.
- **Prepaid expenses**   These are expenses that are paid in advance and provide benefit over a period of time. A common example is insurance or rent paid in advance. Prepaid expenses are also known as *deferred expenses* or *deferred assets.*
- **Fixed assets**   These are assets that will provide lasting value to the firm beyond the current accounting period. Because fixed assets "wear out" over a number of years, each year a portion of their cost is taken as a depreciation expense.
- **Current liabilities**   Liabilities that mature (become payable) within one year or one operating cycle are called current liabilities. They typically include accounts payable, wages payable, and taxes payable. In addition, long-term liabilities become current liabilities during the year in which they become due.
- **Long-term liabilities**   Any liability not due within the current accounting period is referred to as a long-term liability. These are sometimes referred to as fixed liabilities or long-term debt, and include mortgages.

```
                        Big Business, Inc.
                          Balance Sheet
                       December 31, 2000

                             ASSETS
Current Assets
  Cash                                            11,200
  Marketable securities                           23,030
  Accounts receivable                   54,000
    Less estimated uncollectible accounts   540   53,460
  Accrued interest receivable                      1,030
  Merchandise inventory                           65,100
  Supplies on hand                                   520
  Prepaid insurance                                  650

  Total current assets                                      154,990

Fixed Assets
  Land                                            54,330
  Building                              150,230
    Less accumulated depreciation        25,340  124,890
  Equipment                              56,300
    Less accumulated depreciation        13,180   43,120

  Total fixed assets                                        222,340
                                                            -------
Total Assets                                                377,330

                       LIABILITIES AND EQUITY

Current Liabilities

  Accounts payable                                34,510
  Accrued wages payable                           13,400
  Taxes payable                                   13,000
  Rent received in advance                        43,220

  Total current liabilities                                 104,130

Long-Term Liabilities
  Mortgages payable                               34,200
  Long-term notes payable                         15,000

  Total long-term liabilities                                49,200
                                                            -------
Total Liabilities                                           153,330

Equity
  Common stock                                   201,000
  Retained earnings                               23,000

  Total equity                                              224,000
                                                            -------
Total Liabilities and Equity                                377,330
```

FIGURE 1-6 A typical complete balance sheet

- **Income received in advance** When a customer pays for something in advance, the amount is recorded as income received in advance. A magazine publisher, for example, would include paid subscriptions in this category.
- **Retained earnings** This amount represents accumulated net income retained by the firm. When a corporation makes a profit, the proceeds can be distributed as dividends or reinvested in the company, in which case they are added to retained earnings.
- **Stockholders' equity** Owners invest in a company by purchasing capital stock. The amount they pay for the stock is recorded as stockholders' equity. The sum of stockholders' equity and retained earnings represents the owners' value in the company.

The balance sheet is important not just in itself, but also as a means of measuring corporate change. Companies often report balance sheets with data for up to five years, making it easy to spot important changes.

The Income Statement

When people talk about income, they often mean revenue—the amount of money they take in. In accounting, income is very clearly defined as revenue minus expenses. There are even different types of income: income from operations, income before interest and taxes, income before extraordinary items, net income, and so forth. A commonly used term that fits the accounting definition of income is "the bottom line"—what is left over after everything is taken out.

The term "the bottom line" originated from the income statement. An income statement starts out by listing revenues. Expenses are listed next. When expenses are deducted from revenues, the result is income, which appears on the bottom line of the income statement.

The income statement is arguably the most important financial statement because it indicates directly how profitable your company has been over a specific period of time. Most companies are more concerned about profits than about the specific levels of assets, liabilities, and equity. Analysts often use information from both the income statement and balance sheet. For example, dividing net income by total assets yields *return on assets,* a primary indicator of a company's performance.

A typical income statement (Figure 1-7) begins with revenues. In this case, gross revenues are reduced by returns, allowances for returns, and discounts given, yielding net sales.

After revenue, all expenses are listed. Expenses are often categorized into *cost of goods sold* and *operating expenses.* Cost of goods sold refers to expenses incurred directly in the production of something to be sold. In the example

```
                            Big Business, Inc.
                            Income Statement
                     Year Ending December 31, 2000


Revenue from sales
   Sales                                          215,920
   Sales returns and allowances      2,500
   Discounts                        13,410         15,910
   Net sales                                                200,010

Cost of goods sold
   Beginning inventory (1/1/2000)                  45,320
   Purchases                                       73,230
   Less ending inventory (12/31/2000)              35,320
Cost of goods sold                                          83,230
                                                           -------
Gross profit on sales                                      116,780

Operating expenses
   Selling expenses
      Salaries and commissions                    10,000
      Advertising                                 23,000
      Insurance                                    4,560
      Supplies                                     1,240
   Total selling expense                                    38,800

   Administrative and general expenses
      Office salaries                             45,000
      Depreciation                                10,450
      Utilities                                    7,660
   Total general expenses                                   63,110
                                                           -------
   Total operating expenses                               101,910

Net income from operations                                 14,870
                                                           -------
Taxes                                                       6,690

Net income                                                  8,180
```

FIGURE 1-7   A typical income statement

income statement, cost of goods sold is determined by taking beginning inventory, adding all purchases, and deducting the inventory remaining at the end of the accounting period.

Operating expenses are expenses not directly related to the production of something for sale. This category includes selling expense and general administrative expense. By categorizing expenses in this way, you can tell if expenses are out of line in any area.

The bottom of the income statement shows *net income from operations* (net sales less cost of goods sold and operating expenses). Taxes are then deducted, yielding net income—the amount the business retains at the end of the accounting period. Net income can be reinvested in the business by adding it to retained earnings, or it can be distributed to the owners as dividends.

Automating with Peachtree Accounting

Automating your accounting with Peachtree Accounting can be the most valuable investment you make in your business. Peachtree Accounting not only automates the most tedious aspects of bookkeeping, it completely integrates all accounting functions into one program. You may buy Peachtree Accounting just to do your payroll and then later learn how easily it meets all your business needs. You can use any or all of the modules, depending on your needs.

TIP: Both Peachtree Accounting for Windows and Peachtree Complete Accounting for Windows handle all the basic accounting functions; however, Peachtree Complete Accounting for Windows has additional modules such as advanced job costing, time and expense tracking, advanced password security, audit trail, and fixed assets management. Talk to your accountant to determine which product best fits your accounting needs.

Many businesses still do their accounting by hand, from journal entries to posting and payroll. If you are among these diehards, Peachtree Accounting can change the way you do business forever. For a modest investment in the Peachtree Accounting software and a personal computer, you will save thousands of dollars lost in manual processing, tracking down errors, producing financial reports, and accounting fees. You'll get a more efficient business, better control over your finances, and the flexibility to expand your accounting system as your business grows.

On the other hand, if you are switching to Peachtree Accounting from another accounting program, you can *import* your accounting information using Peachtree Accounting's Import feature. From the File menu, select the Select Import/Export option and follow the directions. You can import information from other accounting programs, spreadsheets, and even word-processor and database files. You can also import data from Peachtree Complete (the DOS version of Peachtree Accounting) using the built-in data conversion features.

Increasing Your Efficiency

Do you have any idea how much your present accounting system costs? In addition to the bookkeeper's salary and your accountant's fees, there are hidden costs. For example, consider the cost of losing out on new business because you're tied up writing checks, or the cost of paying overtime or penalties because you can't get your financial statements and tax payments out on time.

Would you hesitate to use a new piece of equipment that could increase your sales staff's efficiency by 100 percent (or more) or increase production by 100 percent? This is the kind of increase in efficiency you will get from using Peachtree Accounting.

Too many businesspeople hesitate to improve their accounting systems. Sometimes it's a fear of computerization. Sometimes it's a fear of fixing something that is working or concern about alienating a trusted bookkeeper. There are a hundred reasons not to improve an accounting system, all stemming from one fear or another. As difficult as the transition to computerization may be, the rewards are well worth it.

Increased Control

Managing a business means controlling expenses, cash, and corporate assets. When your business was small, you probably had all the control you needed in your checkbook register. But growth means more complex accounting: financial reports, government regulations, payroll, and so on. You simply can't control a growing business if you don't automate.

With Peachtree Accounting, you can get up-to-the-minute reports on a daily basis. Do you want to know who owes you money? The Aged Receivables report will tell you all you need to know, in greater detail than you ever thought possible. Do you need to know how your inventory levels are doing? The Inventory Reorder Worksheet will tell you what items need to be restocked. Do you want to see what you're paying in wages? The Current Earnings Report will provide the answers. Once you get used to Peachtree Accounting, you'll wonder how you made decisions without it.

Built-in Flexibility

It's easy to start using Peachtree Accounting. The software is completely modular, so you can use just the parts you need. Many businesses start by automating their payroll function, one of the most time-consuming tasks when done manually. From there, you can move easily into accounts receivable and inventory. When you're ready, add accounts payable, invoicing, fixed asset management, and job costing. However you use Peachtree Accounting, you'll spend less time on accounting and more time on building your business.

For More Information

If you'd like more information on the basics of accounting, Peachtree Accounting comes with an accounting primer in the Help file. You can access this by selecting Contents and Index from the Help menu in Peachtree Accounting, then clicking the Contents folder tab, double-clicking the Reference icon, and then double-clicking the Accounting Primer icon. You can click the individual topic you'd like to read about or just start with the overview and work your way through the lessons and descriptions.

2

Basics of Peachtree Accounting Software

In this chapter, you'll decide which Peachtree product you should use, you'll learn how to install Peachtree Accounting for Windows and Peachtree Complete Accounting for Windows, and you'll learn the basic elements and features of the Peachtree Accounting software.

This chapter shows you how to install Peachtree Accounting for Windows Release 7.0 and Peachtree Complete Accounting for Windows Release 7.0, how to identify the elements of the Peachtree Accounting window, and how to get help and use the tutorials. You'll also learn how to access the Internet through Peachtree Accounting online help and how to use keyboard shortcuts. If you're already familiar with the previous version of Peachtree Accounting for Windows or Peachtree Complete Accounting for Windows, this chapter will also identify some of the major enhancements in the current product versions.

Deciding Which Peachtree Product to Use

When deciding which Peachtree product to use, consider the size of your business and the features you need. Generally, if your business has fewer than ten employees, Peachtree Accounting for Windows will be fine. Peachtree Complete Accounting for Windows has additional features such as advanced job costing, time and expense tracking, advanced password security, audit trail, and fixed asset management. Refer to Table 2-1 for a quick summary of the features of Peachtree Accounting and Peachtree Complete Accounting.

N O T E : Discussion of Web site/Web storefront creation tools is beyond the scope of this book. For information on using PeachLink 2.0, refer to the *Peachtree Complete Business Toolkit* (Osborne/McGraw-Hill, 1998).

Installing Peachtree Accounting for Windows and Peachtree Complete Accounting for Windows

Both Peachtree Accounting for Windows and Peachtree Complete Accounting for Windows are easy to install. Both products are shipped on CD-ROM.

Before you install Peachtree Accounting, be sure to close all programs, including your screensaver program and remember to disable your virus protection program. Load the CD in your CD-ROM drive. Peachtree Setup will display the Welcome menu. Click Install Peachtree Accounting. Follow the instructions to complete the installation program, or select the Run command from the Windows Start menu, type the drive letter of the CD-ROM followed by :SETUP and click OK to start the installation program. For example, if your CD-ROM drive is drive F, you would type **F:SETUP** and click OK. Follow the instructions on the screen.

FEATURES	PEACHTREE ACCOUNTING	COMPLETE ACCOUNTING
Accounts Receivable / Accounts Payable	✓	✓
Customizable Checks, Invoices, and Statements	✓	✓
Customizable Reports and Financials	✓	✓
Payroll, 401(k), Cafeteria Plans, Print W2, W3, 940-EZ, 1099	✓	✓
Integrates with Microsoft Excel	✓	✓
Web Site / Web Storefront Creation Tools	✓	✓
Integrates with Microsoft Office 2000 Small Business Financial Manager	✓	✓
Business Analysis for Financial Status, Collection, and Payments	✓	✓
Inventory, POs, Sales Orders	Basic	Advanced
Job Costing	Basic	Advanced
Time and Expense Tracking		✓
Password Security	Basic	Advanced
Audit Trail		✓
Fixed Assets		✓

TABLE 2-1 Which Product Is Right for You?

CAUTION: As part of the installation process, Peachtree Accounting will convert any data files from the previous versions of Peachtree Accounting software. It's a good idea to back up your data files before you begin installing a new version of Peachtree Accounting, just in case anything goes wrong.

Once you've installed the software, Peachtree Accounting will ask you for registration information. The serial number is located on the title page of the Getting Started Guide. You'll also need to get your registration unlock code from Peachtree by phoning Peachtree Software toll-free at (800) 718-1592 (international customers should call [770] 492-6333) or by visiting the Peachtree Software Web site at http:/www.peachtree.com/register/. When you call, make sure to have your serial number. The customer service representative will provide you with your registration unlock code. This code is your personalized registration number. Type in the serial number and your registration unlock code number in the fields provided onscreen. Your copy of Peachtree Accounting is now registered!

 N O T E : The PeachLink software on the CD requires a separate installation procedure. For detailed information on installing and running PeachLink to create and maintain a Web site for your company that uses your Peachtree Accounting information, see *Peachtree Complete Business Toolkit* (Osborne/McGraw-Hill, 1998).

Understanding the Peachtree Accounting Window

The Peachtree Accounting window, as shown in Figure 2-1, has features that are common to most windows in Windows 98 based application programs.

Window Border   The window border is the thin beveled edge around the window. Clicking and dragging the mouse on the window border expands or contracts the window.

Control Menu   The Control menu is accessed by clicking the small Peachtree icon in the upper-left corner. The Control menu allows you to restore, move, size, minimize, maximize, or close the window. You can also access the Control menu by pressing ALT-SPACEBAR. Use your mouse or the up and down arrow keys to select the appropriate option. You can close the window by double-clicking on the small Peachtree icon.

Title Bar   The title bar is at the top of the window. It contains the name of the company you're working with. You can move the window by clicking the mouse button on the title bar and dragging the window to the desired position.

Minimize, Maximize, and Close   The Minimize, Maximize, and Close buttons are the buttons in the upper-right corner of the window. Clicking Minimize (the underscore character) shrinks the window down to an icon-sized button on the Windows 98 taskbar. Clicking Maximize (the square) expands the window to fill the desktop. Clicking Close (the X) closes the window and exits the program.

Menu bar — Control menu icon   Title bar   Minimize, Maximize, and Close buttons

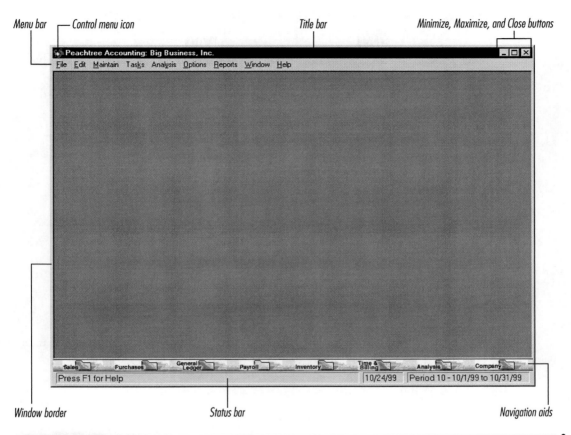

Window border   Status bar   Navigation aids

FIGURE 2-1   Peachtree Accounting window

 N O T E : After you have maximized a window, the Maximize button becomes the Restore button, and the single square on the Maximize button is replaced by two overlapping squares, as shown here:

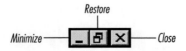

                                    Restore

            Minimize   Close

Clicking Restore restores the window to its original size.

Menu Bar   The menu bar lists the available menus. To display the options within a particular menu, click the menu item on the menu bar. To access a menu using the keyboard instead of the mouse, hold down the ALT key and press the underlined letter in the menu item (refer to Figure 2-1); for example, to select the File menu, press ALT-F.

The Peachtree Accounting window also contains some features specific to the Peachtree Accounting program:

Navigation Aids   Navigation aids give you a visual means of navigating in Peachtree Accounting. For more information, see the discussion of navigation aids under the "Getting Help" section later in this chapter. You can hide the navigation aids if you want by deselecting the View Navigation Aids option on the Options menu.

Status Bar   Most windows have a status bar of some kind. The Peachtree Accounting status bar shows information about the field you are working with, the current date, and the current accounting period. If you set up "alerts" with the Action Items option on the Tasks menu, an alarm clock will appear on the status bar as well. You can hide the status bar if you want by deselecting the View Status Bar option on the Options menu.

N O T E :   If you are using Windows 95 or NT 4.0, the screen elements are almost identical to those for Windows 98, but there will be a few minor differences in the buttons at the top of the screen.

Getting to Know Peachtree Accounting

When you start Peachtree Accounting for the first time, you'll see a startup window like the one shown in Figure 2-2.

From the startup window, you can do the following:

- **Open an existing company**   Use this option to open the files for a company you've already set up. When you first install Peachtree Accounting, you will have two companies, Bellwether Garden Supply and Pavilion Design Group, already set up.
- **Set up a new company**   Select this option when you want to set up a new company. You'll see how this option works in Chapter 3 when you set up the files for Big Business, Inc.
- **Learn about Peachtree Accounting through an online tutorial**   Select this option if you want to view the online tutorials.

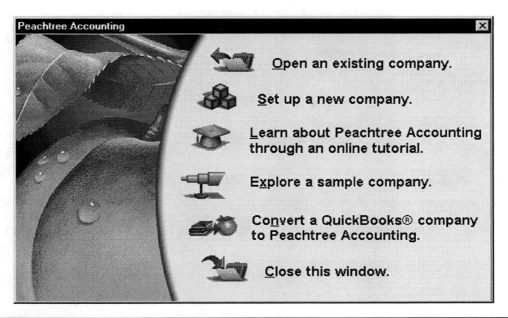

FIGURE 2-2 Peachtree Accounting startup window

- **Explore a sample company**   Select this option to view Bellwether Garden Supply, a retail and service company that uses the inventory and job tracking capabilities, or view Pavilion Design Group, a service company that uses the time and billing feature.
- **Convert a QuickBooks company to Peachtree Accounting**   Use this option if you are converting files created in QuickBooks to Peachtree Accounting.
- **Close this window**   Use this option if you want to close the window.

Getting Help

Peachtree Accounting offers several ways to get help:

- Status bar
- General help from the Help menu
- Context-sensitive help
- Wizards
- Navigation aids

Status Bar

The simplest form of help is available on the window's status bar, which is the line of information at the bottom of the window. Point to any button or field in the Peachtree Accounting window that you want information on, then press and hold the left mouse button. A description of that feature appears on the status bar. The status bar also shows help for the currently selected menu option, as shown in Figure 2-3.

General Help from the Help Menu

You can always get help through the Help menu in the Peachtree Accounting window. Choose the Contents and Index option from the Help menu and then choose the Contents tab to display the Contents screen as shown in Figure 2-4. This is a standard Windows 98 contents screen. From here, you can click on one of the book icons to find specific information, or you can search for topics

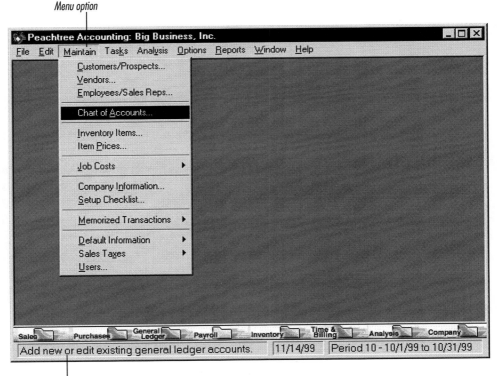

Menu option

Status bar help for menu option

FIGURE 2-3   Status bar with help for highlighted menu option

Main topics in Help   Index tab   Ask a Question tab

Contents tab   Find tab

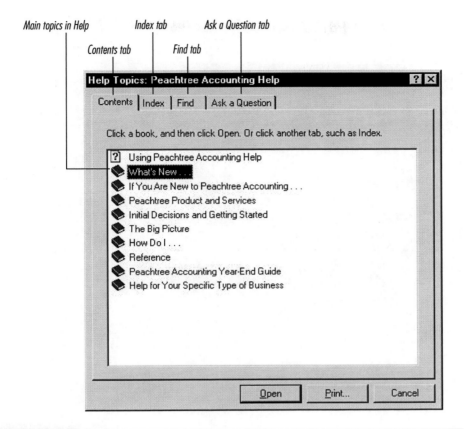

FIGURE 2-4   Help Contents screen

using the Index, Find, or Ask a Question tab. From the Ask a Question tab, type your question, and then click Search.

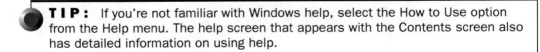

TIP: If you're not familiar with Windows help, select the How to Use option from the Help menu. The help screen that appears with the Contents screen also has detailed information on using help.

In addition to navigation methods common to most Windows 98 help files, the help files for Peachtree Accounting also have graphical help. Many help screens have buttons labeled The Big Picture. Clicking The Big Picture gets you to a menu of tasks that lets you see an entire process in graphic form. From there, you can jump to other places in the help file for more specific information. Figure 2-5 shows an overview of the General Ledger navigation aid. You can click any of the pictures on the screen for more information on that topic.

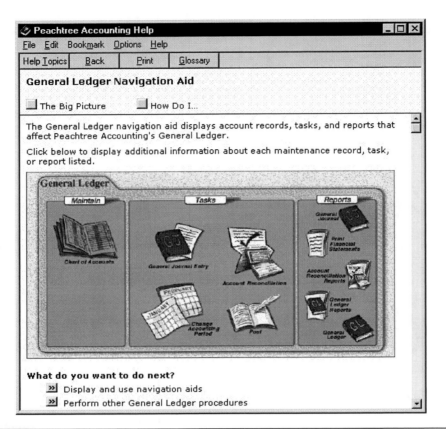

FIGURE 2-5 Overview of the General Ledger navigation aid

You can also access the Internet from Peachtree Accounting online help, which we will discuss in the "Putting It to Work" section.

Context-Sensitive Help

For context-sensitive help on a field or a task you are performing, press F1. Peachtree Accounting will display help from the online help file relating to the field or task.

Wizards

Peachtree has implemented the New Company Setup Wizard and the Payroll Setup Wizard. The New Company Setup Wizard walks you quickly through the process of setting up your company. The Payroll Setup Wizard walks you through setting up most defaults and standard payroll fields.

Putting It to Work

Accessing the Internet from Peachtree Accounting Online Help

One of the most powerful features of Peachtree Accounting online help is the ability to access the Internet for more information directly from the help file. To do this, you must already be able to access the Internet through your company's network or via a dial-up connection from your computer. You must also have an Internet browser set up on your computer. When you click on an Internet link in the help file, Windows starts your Web browser and goes to the URL (Uniform Resource Locator; the Internet address) of the specified Web page and displays the page in your browser.

Figure 2-6 shows an example of how to do this.

1 *Start by accessing an online help screen with an Internet link.*

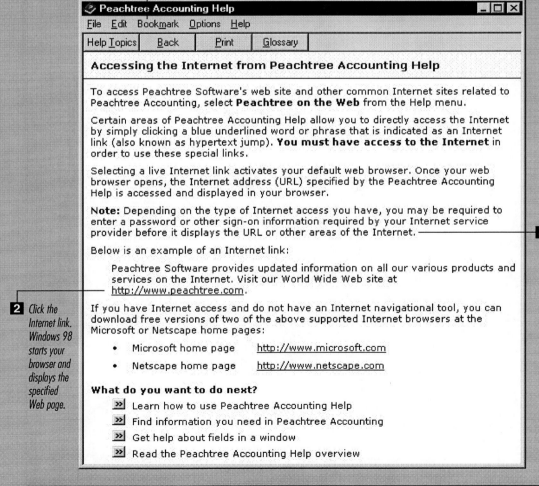

2 *Click the Internet link. Windows 98 starts your browser and displays the specified Web page.*

3 *You can exit the browser when you are finished and return to the online help file.*

FIGURE 2-6 Accessing the Internet from online help

Navigation Aids

One of the hottest features of Peachtree Accounting for Windows and Peachtree Complete Accounting for Windows is the navigation aids. (The navigation aid for Sales is shown in Figure 2-7).

When you click one of the Navigation Aid tabs at the bottom of the Peachtree Accounting window (such as Sales or Purchases), Peachtree Accounting displays a navigation aid—a graphic representation of the flow of tasks involved in that particular process. It contains icons representing the various journals and ledgers and indicates their relationship to one another. To go directly to a specific task (such as the General Ledger or Receipts), you click the icon in the navigation aid.

If you don't want to see the Navigation Aid tabs at the bottom of the screen, you can deselect the View Navigation Aid option from the Options menu.

Using the Tutorials

As mentioned earlier, Peachtree Accounting comes with extensive tutorials. You can start the tutorials directly from the startup window (shown earlier in

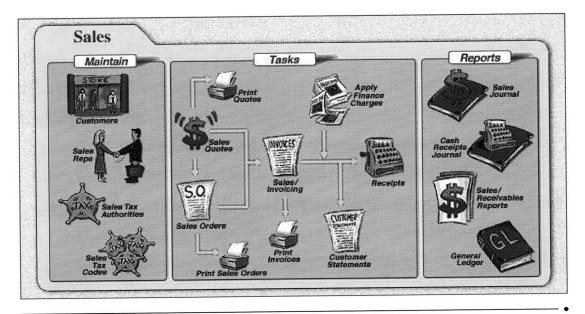

FIGURE 2-7   Navigation aid for Sales

Figure 2-2), or you can start the tutorials by selecting the Peachtree Accounting Tutorial option from the Help menu.

 NOTE: If you're not already familiar with Windows online help programs, you should go through the How to Use tutorial to learn Windows basics.

Keyboard Shortcuts

Peachtree Accounting has extensive mouse options. However, you may prefer to use the keyboard to issue commands and move between windows. Table 2-2 shows a list of keyboard shortcuts you can use.

SHORTCUT	DESCRIPTION
F1	Displays online help topic for the current window.
SHIFT-F1	Changes the mouse pointer to the What's This help selector.
F5	In certain windows, this command saves records and posts (or saves) transactions.
F10	Toggles between the open window and the menu bar.
CTRL-F4	Closes the current document window.
ALT-F4	Closes the application.
CTRL-F6	Moves to the next window.
SHIFT-CTRL-F6	Moves to the previous window.
CTRL-X	Cuts the selected text to the Windows clipboard.
CTRL-C	Copies the selected text to the Windows clipboard.
CTRL-V	Pastes text from Windows clipboard to current cursor location.
CTRL-E	Deletes the current record.
CTRL-F	Finds a record.
CTRL-D	Finds the next record matching the search specifications.
CTRL-N	Starts a new company.
CTRL-O	Opens an existing company.
CTRL-B	Backs up a company's data.
CTRL-R	Restores a company's data from an existing backup.
CTRL-P	Prints the displayed report or record.

TABLE 2-2 Keyboard Shortcuts in Peachtree Accounting

What's New in Peachtree Accounting?

If you've used previous versions of Peachtree Accounting for Windows or Peachtree Complete Accounting for Windows, you'll be pleased with the new and enhanced features in Peachtree Accounting for Windows Release 7.0 and Peachtree Complete Accounting for Windows Release 7.0.

New Features in Peachtree Accounting

The features in this section appear in both Peachtree Accounting for Windows Release 7.0 and Peachtree Complete Accounting for Windows Release 7.0.

Payment Status Tracking

Peachtree Accounting now lets you track purchases or invoices. In an instant, you can check to see if invoices are paid in full, partially paid, or unpaid. You can easily keep track of who owes you and who you owe. Plus, this feature provides partial payment information and net total due on specific sales invoices and purchase screens.

Customize the Way You Work

You can customize templates to suit the industry you are in. You can also modify customer IDs, record IDs, and inventory IDs.

Task Window Templates   Some data fields may not be appropriate for your type of industry, considering the amount of detail you want to appear in the purchase and sales task windows. By hiding certain fields, you can simplify your data-entry process. You can customize templates for the following task windows: Quotes, Sales Orders, Sales/Invoicing, Purchase Orders, Purchases/Receive Inventory. To customize a template, you must first create a new one or edit an existing customized template. Peachtree provides professional quote and sales invoice templates, which you are free to customize or delete.

Change Record IDs   You can change the way you identify data records by modifying certain IDs. When you change a customer's, vendor's, or inventory item's ID, all data records, including historic transactions and transactions associated with the changed record, will reflect the new ID.

Payroll Enhancements

Several payroll enhancements have been made to Peachtree Accounting and Peachtree Complete Accounting.

More Pay Levels   In employee defaults, you can now set up to 20 salary and hourly payment levels.

401(k) Plan Setup   To quickly set up 401(k) defaults and payroll tax adjustments, use the Payroll Setup Wizard. You will be asked what type of 401(k) plan your company offers, which General Ledger accounts to associate with the contributions, and whether your company will match employee contributions. Then, in their individual records, you can specify the percentages of gross pay each employee wants to contribute to the 401(k) plan.

N O T E : If you set up a 401(k) plan in Peachtree Accounting Release 6 (or lower), you must manually update your 401(k) payroll fields and tax tables.

Employee 401K % Field   Use the Payroll Setup Wizard to quickly set up 401(k) defaults and payroll tax adjustments. In their individual records, you can then enter the percentages of gross pay each employee wants to contribute to your company's 401(k) plan.

Employee Special 1 and Special 2 Fields   You can use these fields, located in the Withholding Information table of the Maintain Employees/Sales Reps window, to customize your payroll setup. Use these fields when you want to set up labor and industry taxes, workers' compensation taxes, and union dues.

Pre-Check Register Before Printing Checks   Before checks are actually posted and printed, you can examine payment detail, approve selected checks, and prepare the check order. Click the Report button in the Select for Payment or Select for Payroll Entry window to print a pre-check register listing all payments currently selected to process.

Enhanced Payroll Check Forms   You can print up to 15 payroll fields on each stub using the two enhanced payroll check forms:

- Use MultiP 2 Stub with preprinted multipurpose two-stub check forms.
- Use PR MultiP 1 Stub with preprinted multipurpose seven-inch check forms with only one stub.

Inventory

In the Maintain Inventory Items window, Peachtree has added a Last Unit Cost field.

Last Unit Cost Field   The last Unit Cost Field value indicates the latest unit cost amount associated with this item. The last unit cost is updated when a purchase, payment, or adjustment (including beginning balances) is made for an item.

For new stock items you can enter a cost amount. After a purchase, payment, or adjustment is made for the item, the field becomes disabled and is automatically updated based on the item's costing method.

For non-stock, service, and labor items, enter the estimated cost or change the displayed unit here. At the time of sale, a cost entry is generated based on the cost you enter. When you are trying to generate a direct labor fee based on service or labor that is performed, this feature can be handy.

Business Analysis

The Financial Manager has been added to the Business Analysis tools.

Financial Manager   The Financial Manager displays an overall financial picture of how your business is performing. The Financial Manager summarizes business data and key account balances within a specific time period. It is based on two levels of business analysis:

- **Numeric level**   Includes business summary data or account balances, which can be viewed in a numeric table, referring to a specified point in time.
- **Spreadsheet level**   Includes a set of business summary data or account balances, used for comparison purposes, projected for the end of sequential periods.

Sales and Purchase Enhancements

A few sales and purchase enhancements have been made to Peachtree Accounting and Peachtree Complete Accounting.

Taxable Freight   This feature computes sales tax on freight charges you apply to customer orders. Check with your local sales tax authority, as sales tax varies from state to state.

Invoice Payment Status   The Sales/Invoicing and Purchase/Receive Inventory task windows now display the payment status of invoice transactions. Status may be Unpaid, Partially Paid, or Paid in Full, and it appears in the task window after the invoice is posted (or saved) or until a payment is applied to it.

Enhanced Sorting when Applying Tickets on Sales Invoices   When entering a sales invoice, you can now sort the recorded time and expense tickets and reimbursable expenses listed in the Apply Tickets/Reimbursable Expenses window. As there are several methods for sorting tickets and expenses, this feature can be useful when consolidating information on the invoice line items.

Reports and Forms

Several reports and forms enhancements have been made to Peachtree Accounting and Peachtree Complete Accounting. Each report can be customized to fit your needs.

Statement of Retained Earnings   The Statement of Retained Earnings shows the beginning and ending retained earnings amounts, adjustments made to retained earnings within the reporting period, and dividends paid within the reporting period.

Statement of Income and Retained Earnings   The Statement of Income and Retained Earnings shows income and expense activity for a specified period of time and retained earnings information. For accurate results, run this report for one month or from the beginning of the year through the current date.

Customer Sales History Report   Sales totals for each of your customers are listed in the Customer Sales History report. Recorded invoices in the Sales/Invoicing window and cash sales entered using the Apply to Revenues tab in the Receipts window are used to derive the Sales amounts.

Items Sold to Customers Report   Quantity, amount, cost of sales, gross profit, and the gross margin of items sold to customers are listed in the Items Sold to Customer report.

Mailing Labels   You can now get customer, vendor, and employee mailing labels in a standard 3 × 10 label format. Sort labels by customer ID, customer name, customer ship-to address zip code, or customer's bill-to address zip code.

Forms Design Enhancements

A few design enhancements have been made to Peachtree Accounting and Peachtree Complete Accounting.

Forms Design Window   You can easily customize your company forms using the Forms Design window:

- Reverse the last action performed on certain design tasks using the New Undo menu option.
- Perform common design tasks by selecting multiple form objects at one time using the Selection tool.
- Align form objects horizontally and vertically using the alignment option.
- Select background color and borders for text and data objects.
- Autosize data fields to the default field width.
- Display a ruler or grid by using the Design options in the design window.

Object Order List Report   Click the Print button in the Edit Object Order window to print an ordered list of all objects included on your form. This may be helpful when troubleshooting design errors.

Back Up Customized Forms   Peachtree Accounting's backup file stores each form customized in the Forms Design window. This feature makes it easy for you to copy or restore customized forms.

Company Administration Enhancements

Some company administration enhancements have been made to Peachtree Accounting and Peachtree Complete Accounting.

Peachtree Accounting Backup Format   This feature allows you to back up company data and customized forms to a single compressed file. In case you need to restore information at a later date, save your backup to a hard disk, floppy disk, or other data storage device.

Backup Reminder   You can specify how often you want to be reminded to back up. If the specified number of days elapses since your last Peachtree Accounting backup, Peachtree displays a message reminding you to back up.

Other New Features in Peachtree Accounting

Additional administrative features have been added to Peachtree Accounting and Peachtree Complete Accounting.

Exporting to Microsoft Excel   You can export report data into a new Microsoft Excel spreadsheet by simply clicking the Excel toolbar button. Peachtree will open the Microsoft Excel program and export the report data into a new worksheet while retaining most of the report's original formatting. To complete this procedure, you must have Microsoft Excel 97 or a later version installed on your computer.

Pick from 75 Sample Companies   Get started quickly by selecting from 75 sample companies. Select the company that is most similar to yours and then modify the accounts.

Microsoft Small Business Customer Manager (SBCM)   The SBCM helps you gain a better understanding of your customers by analyzing certain customer factors such as which customers have increased their purchases in the last three months or which customers have stopped buying in the last three months.

PeachLink 2.0   You can create and manage an electronic storefront on the Internet using PeachLink 2.0. For information about PeachLink 2.0, refer to *Peachtree Complete Business Toolkit* (Osborne/McGraw-Hill, 1998).

New Features in Peachtree Complete Accounting for Windows

In addition to the general features described in the preceding section, Peachtree Complete Accounting for Windows has some additional features, including advanced screen-level password security, audit trail, the ability to change item prices globally, in-depth job costing, a time and billing system, and fixed assets.

Inventory

Peachtree Complete Accounting has added a Change Item Prices window.

Change Item Prices   Use the Maintain Item Prices window to change sales and billing prices for a single item, a range of items, or all inventory items. For example, you can mark up sales prices for all your stock items by 10 percent.

Time and Billing

Peachtree Complete Accounting has added enhanced sorting from the Apply Tickets/Reimbursable Expenses window (see the previous section "Sales and Purchase Enhancements" for an explanation).

Summary

In this chapter, you've decided which Peachtree product to use, and learned how to install Peachtree Accounting and Peachtree Complete Accounting, how to identify the elements of the Peachtree Accounting window, and how to navigate through the accounting program. You also learned how to get help in Peachtree Accounting, how to use keyboard shortcuts, and what the new features are in Peachtree Accounting for Windows and Peachtree Complete Accounting for Windows. In the next chapter, you'll learn how to create a new company in Peachtree Accounting and how to set global options.

Setting Up Your Business in Peachtree Accounting

In this chapter, you'll learn how to set up your business on Peachtree Accounting. You'll also see how to set global options and how to use Peachtree Accounting's security features.

B A S I C S

- How to add a company to Peachtree Accounting
- How to enter general company information
- How to specify business type
- How to select a basic chart of accounts
- How to specify an accounting method
- How to specify a posting method
- How to set up accounting periods

B E Y O N D

- How to set global options
- How to set up user IDs and passwords

To computerize your accounting functions with Peachtree Accounting, you must first set up your business on the software. This process can be simple or complicated, depending on the options you select and how involved your business is. Peachtree Accounting offers many options that let you customize the software to meet your needs. This chapter takes you through the setup process step by step, so you can start using Peachtree Accounting right away.

Adding a Company to Peachtree Accounting

To learn about Peachtree Accounting, you will set up a company called Big Business, Inc., a firm that develops coin-operated software and personal computers. Big Business has been growing lately and is going to computerize its accounting using Peachtree Accounting. The software is already installed on the office PC in a subdirectory named PEACHW on the C drive.

To start Peachtree Accounting, click Start on the Windows 98 taskbar, then select Programs. From the Peachtree Accounting group folder, click the Peachtree Accounting icon shown here. (Or simply double-click the Peachtree Accounting program icon on your desktop.)

Peachtree
Accounting

When you start Peachtree Accounting, you will see the following startup window. (The various options were described in Chapter 2).

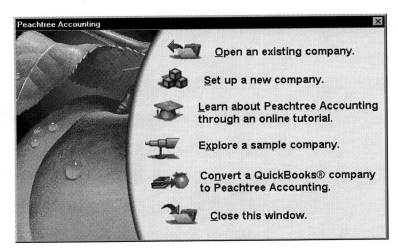

Follow these steps to set up your company:

1. Choose the second option, Set Up a New Company, to display the New Company Setup window. As you work through the process of setting up your company, Peachtree Accounting gives you a number of helpful hints along the way. In addition to the descriptions in the windows themselves, you can get online help at any time by pressing F1.

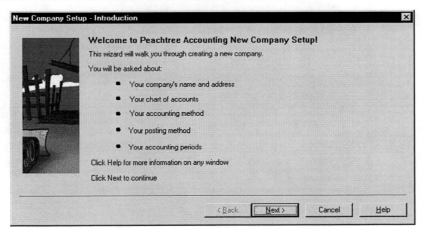

2. The New Company Setup Wizard will walk you through the new company setup process. Click the Next button to move to the first window. In this window you will enter basic information about the company.

3. After you've begun the company setup process, the first step in setting up your company is to enter company information—company name, address, type of business, and tax ID numbers. Click Next to move to the first window in which you enter data, the Company Information window. Fill in the appropriate fields. A sample of this window is shown here, filled in with information for Big Business, Inc.

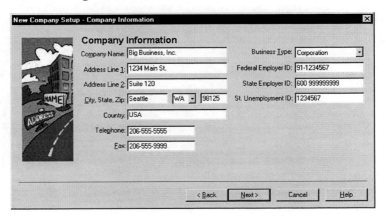

For Business Type, select one of the following options:

- Corporation
- S Corporation
- Partnership
- Sole Proprietorship
- Limited Liability Company

The type of business you select tells Peachtree Accounting how to determine the equity for your company. Equity is the value of a company to its owners—what is left after you subtract the company's liabilities from its assets. In sole proprietorships and partnerships, the equity belongs to the business owners, whereas in corporations the equity is divided among the stockholders.

 C A U T I O N : Once you have completed the new company setup, you shouldn't change the business type you've selected, as it will affect the equity accounts in your chart of accounts. If you're not sure what type of business you should select in this window, talk to your accountant.

You will be asked to enter your Federal Employer ID, State Employer ID, and State Unemployment ID.

One of the most important steps in setting up your company is to set up the chart of accounts. As mentioned in Chapter 1, the chart of accounts identifies the major account categories, such as assets, liabilities, capital, income, cost of sales, and expenses.

4. Click Next to go to the first Chart of Accounts window. This window describes what a chart of accounts is. From this window, you can select one of the following options for creating or copying your company's chart of accounts:

OPTION	DESCRIPTION
Set up a New Company Based on One of Several Companies	Uses one of the predefined charts of accounts that come with Peachtree Accounting as the basis for the chart of accounts for your company.
Copy Settings from an Existing Peachtree Company	Copies an existing company set up in Peachtree. This is useful if you are setting up accounts for subordinate companies or divisions, or if you have a preferred model for a certain type of company, such as a nonprofit organization.

OPTION	DESCRIPTION
Convert a Company from Another Accounting Program	Creates a chart of accounts based on a company set up from another accounting program. The actual importation of data will happen after you complete Part 1 of the new company setup.
Build Your Own Company	Creates your own chart of accounts. (You probably won't want to use this option unless you're extensively familiar with setting up charts of accounts.)

By the way, unless you're converting from an existing accounting program or Peachtree Accounting for DOS, you're probably going to want to copy one of the sample charts of accounts supplied with Peachtree Accounting. Copying a chart of accounts is much easier than entering one from scratch.

5. Click Next to go to the new company setup Chart of Accounts window, which contains a list of general ledger accounts, as shown below.

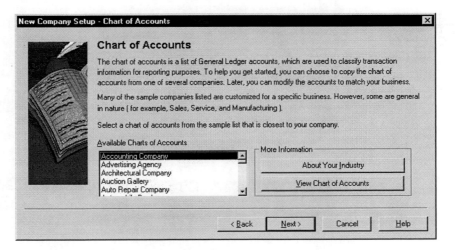

Click on the sample business that most closely matches your own business. You can view the types of accounts set up for that business by clicking View and scrolling through the accounts for the sample company. Peachtree Accounting will set up a default chart of accounts for your business based on the sample business you select. You can then add, modify, or delete accounts and account information as necessary. There is a wide variety of sample businesses you can use as models.

If you're not sure which chart of accounts to use, you can click About Your Industry under More Information. This will show you an overview of the selected industry. For example, if you select Manufacturing Company and click About Your Industry, the sample manufacturing company window appears, as shown below. Clicking Print at the top of the window will print the overview.

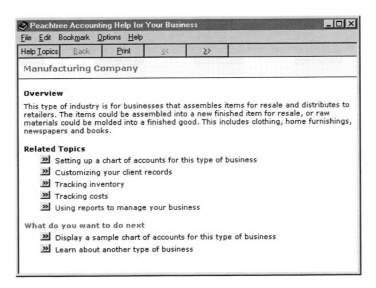

You can also review the sample charts of accounts in detail by selecting View Chart of Accounts under More Information. The sample Manufacturing Company Chart of Accounts contents window appears, as shown below. Clicking Print at the top of the window will print the chart of accounts.

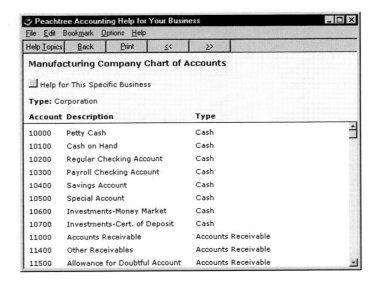

You don't need an exact match between the chart of accounts you choose and your company. Choose the closest one; you'll see how to make modifications to the chart of accounts in Chapter 4.

After you've established your chart of accounts, tell Peachtree Accounting which accounting method to use.

6. When you are satisfied with your selection for the chart of accounts you want, highlight the name of the chart of accounts in the window, then click Next. The New Company Setup - Accounting Method window appears. This window provides information describing the differences between cash and accrual accounting (as discussed in Chapter 1). Use this window to tell Peachtree Accounting if you want to use accrual or cash accounting. Check with your accountant if you're not sure which accounting method you should use.

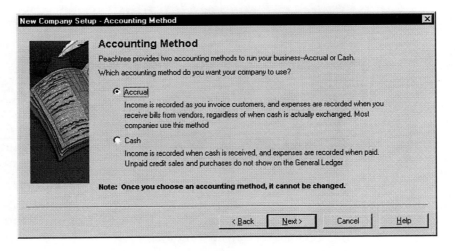

CAUTION: Once you have completed the new company setup, you can't switch between cash and accrual accounting at a later date. Talk to your accountant if you're not sure which option to choose.

7. In this step, you pick a posting method. Click Next to display the Posting Method window, where you select the posting method you want to use. Real-time posting immediately updates the company's financial information. Batch posting holds the entries in a temporary file you can review before you post them. If you're new to Peachtree Accounting or to accounting

software in general, you should choose batch posting at first, as it allows you greater opportunities to work with the data before posting it. You should also use batch posting if you're working on a network, as you can enter information without having to wait for other users on the network to complete transactions. Unlike cash or accrual accounting, you can switch between batch and real-time posting methods whenever you like by selecting the Company Information option from the Maintain menu, then choosing the posting method from the bottom of the window. (When you choose real-time posting, the Save button in the Task windows becomes a Post button.)

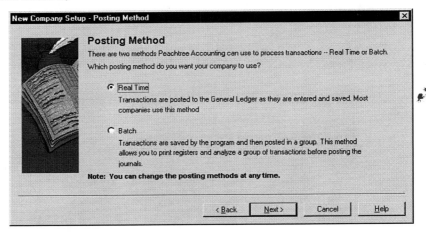

8. To conclude Part 1 of new company setup, you establish your accounting periods. Click Next to display the Accounting Periods window. This window provides some basic information on what accounting periods are. You will select from 12 monthly accounting periods or accounting periods that do not match the calendar months.

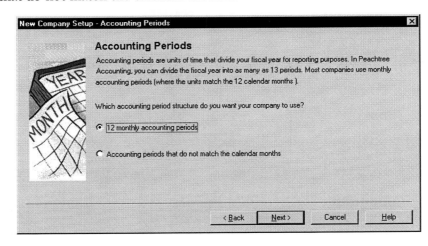

9. Click Next to display the Monthly Accounting Periods window. You use this window, shown below, to set up and confirm the accounting periods for the current and next fiscal year. You must enter both a start and an end date for each accounting period. Be sure to modify the first period in which you will be entering data to reflect the current accounting period.

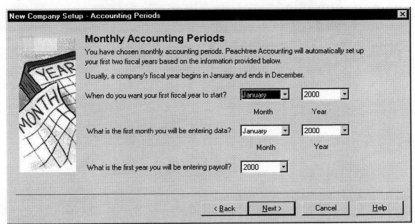

10. Click Next to display the Defaults window. Peachtree automatically sets up defaults for you based on the information you entered. You can modify any of these defaults by selecting Default Information from Peachtree Accounting's main menu.

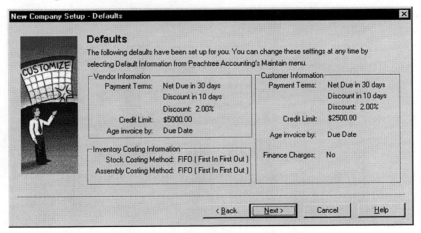

CAUTION: Once you have completed the new company setup, you can't change the accounting periods you've specified for two years. If you're not sure what to enter for accounting periods, talk to your accountant.

11. With Part 1 complete, you are ready to create the company. Click Next to view the Congratulations window, which looks like this:

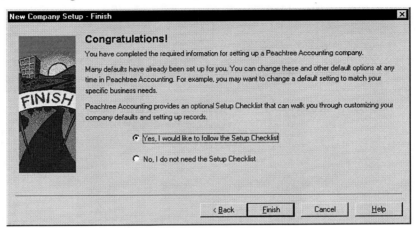

CAUTION: Once you create the company, you cannot change the accounting method (cash or accrual) or the accounting periods. Be sure the information you have entered in these windows is correct for your company.

When Peachtree Accounting has created the company, it opens the new company and displays the Setup Checklist, as shown here.

Setup Checklist

General Ledger
- ☑ Chart of Accounts
- ☑ General Ledger Defaults
- ☐ Account Beginning Balances

Accounts Payable
- ☑ Vendor Defaults
- ☐ Vendor Records
- ☐ Vendor Beginning Balances

Accounts Receivable
- ☑ Customer Defaults
- ☑ Statement and Invoice Defaults
- ☐ Customer Records
- ☐ Customer Beginning Balances

Payroll
- ☐ Employee Defaults
- ☐ Employee Records
- ☐ Employee Y-T-D Earnings and Withholdings

Inventory Items
- ☑ Inventory Defaults
- ☐ Inventory Items and Assembly Records
- ☐ Inventory Beginning Balances

Jobs
- ☑ Job Defaults
- ☐ Job Records
- ☐ Job Beginning Balances

Close   Help

Click the name of the area you want to set up

The various setup options on the checklist will be covered throughout this book. Click Exit to close the checklist for now. You'll be coming back to the checklist (via the Maintain menu) a little later, but first you need to set global options. Remember, the check mark is just a convenient way of keeping track of the things you've done. You can still modify items that are checked off on the list from options on the Maintain menu.

Maintaining Company Information

You enter company information as part of the new company setup procedure, but you also need to be able to maintain company information. For example, you may move, get a new area code, or even change a state employer ID. This section shows you how to maintain the company information.

Start by selecting the Company Information option from the Maintain menu. The Maintain Company Information window, shown below, appears with your company information.

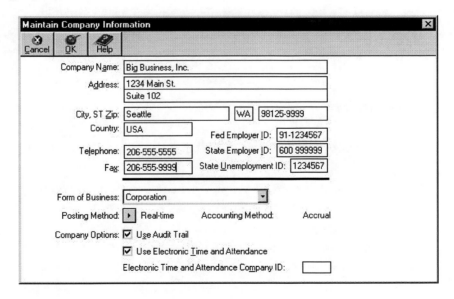

NOTE: This is the Maintain Company Information window for Peachtree Complete Accounting for Windows. It looks slightly different in Peachtree Accounting for Windows.

As you can see, the information displayed in this window was entered as part of the company setup process. You can modify most of the information and settings in this window as follows:

Company Name Enter changes to the company name. The name can be up to 39 characters long, but it can't start with a number or a space.

Address Enter changes to the company address. Each line can be up to 30 characters long.

City Enter changes to the company's city. This can be up to 20 characters long.

ST Enter changes to the company's state using the standard two-letter state abbreviations.

Zip Enter changes to the company's zip code. This can be up to 12 characters (including a hyphen). This can also accept Canadian postal codes and other formats.

Country Enter changes to the company's country. This field is optional. If you do not do business in other countries, you can leave it blank.

Telephone Enter the company's telephone number. This can be up to 10 characters.

Fax Enter the company's telephone number. This can be up to 10 characters.

Fed Employer ID Enter the company's federal employer ID number. This can be up to 11 characters.

State Employer ID Enter the company's state employer ID number. This can be up to 20 characters.

State Unemployment ID Enter the company's state unemployment ID number. This can be up to 20 characters.

Form of Business Select an entry from the drop-down list for the company's form of business: Corporation, S Corporation, Partnership, Sole Proprietorship, or Limited Liability Company.

Posting Method Click the arrow to display a small dialog box (not shown) for selecting real-time or batch posting. You may switch from one posting method to another whenever you like.

Accounting Method This display-only field shows the accounting method you chose during the setup process: cash or accrual. You cannot change the accounting method for your company.

Use Audit Trail   Check this box if you want to use audit trails. Peachtree Accounting will log user activity in an audit file. (This company option only appears in Peachtree Complete Accounting for Windows.)

Use Electronic Time and Attendance   Check this box if you want to use electronic time and attendance tracking. If you check this box, you will also be prompted for a three-character electronic time and attendance ID.

When you are satisfied with your entries, click OK. You can update company information at any time.

Setting Global Options

Although you won't be setting individual defaults for such things as payroll, accounts receivable, and job costing at this time, you will probably want to set global options for Peachtree Accounting. Global options determine such things as decimal point entry, line item entry, and Smart Data Entry options. They apply to all companies you use in Peachtree Accounting. (You'll see how to modify the General Ledger chart of accounts you copied from the sample company and enter beginning balance information in Chapter 4.)

Setting Global Options

Start by selecting Global from the Options menu. The Maintain Global Options window appears with the Accounting tab selected, as shown here.

Maintain Global Options
Accounting   _G_eneral
_D_ecimal Entry
⦿ Automatic ○ Manual
_N_umber of decimal places: 2 ▾
Hide General Ledger Accounts
☐ Accounts _R_eceivable (Quotes, Sales Orders, Sales/Invoicing, Receipts)
☐ Accounts _P_ayable (Purchase Orders, Purchases/Receive Inventory, Payments)
☐ Pay_r_oll Entry
Other Options
☑ _W_arn if a record was changed but not saved
☐ Warn if _i_nventory item is out of stock
☐ Hide inacti_v_e records
☐ Recalculate cash _b_alance automatically in Receipts and Payments

Buttons: _O_k, _C_ancel, _H_elp

Global options are the default options that affect such things as how data is displayed and entered, how reports are printed, and ways to improve performance.

Select the global accounting options you want, as described in Table 3-1.

The Maintain Global Options window appears with the General Tab selected, as shown below.

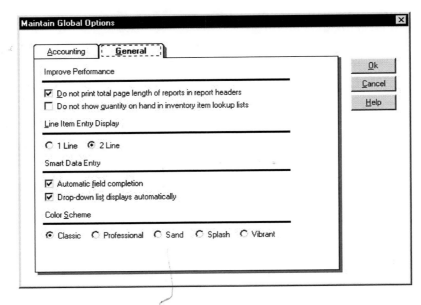

Select the global general options you want, as described in Table 3-2.

When you've made your selections, click OK. Your global options are now set up in Peachtree Accounting for Windows!

Setting Up Security

Accounting information is highly sensitive and confidential. If there is any chance of unauthorized people using your computer, you will probably want to protect yourself. Peachtree Accounting for Windows has password-level security, and Peachtree Complete Accounting has a full user-level security system. This section tells you how to set up security for each version of Peachtree Accounting.

OPTION	DESCRIPTION
Decimal Entry	Peachtree Accounting will enter a decimal point for you automatically (very much like setting a calculator for automatic decimal places), or you can enter the decimal point manually.
Number of Decimal Places	Enter the default number of decimal places. The default is 2, but you can enter from 0 to 5 decimal places.
Hide General Ledger Accounts	These three options let you hide the General Ledger account information on the transaction screens for each of the following classes of transactions: **Accounts Receivable** Hides the General Ledger account numbers on the Quotes, Sales Orders, Sales/Invoicing, and Receipts task windows. **Accounts Payable** Hides the General Ledger account numbers on the Purchase Orders, Purchases/Receive Inventory, and Payments task windows. **Payroll** Hides the General Ledger account numbers when doing payroll entry. You can still use the Accounting Behind the Screens feature to review and modify General Ledger account numbers for specific transactions.
Warn If a Data Record Was Changed But Not Saved	If you select this option (the default), Peachtree Accounting displays a warning when you try to exit a record that has not been saved.
Warn If Inventory Item Is Out of Stock	If you select this option, Peachtree Accounting will warn you if you try to sell inventory that is currently out of stock. You can still enter the transaction, but the warning will inform you that the item is not in stock at the moment.
Hide Inactive Records	If you select this option, Peachtree Accounting will not display inactive records.
Recalculate Cash Balance Automatically in Receipts and Payments	If you select this option, Peachtree Accounting automatically recalculates the cash balance each time you add a line item in the Receipts and Payments windows.

TABLE 3-1   Accounting Global Options in Peachtree Accounting for Windows

Setting Passwords in Peachtree Accounting for Windows

The security system in Peachtree Accounting for Windows uses passwords to control access to various features in the program. Peachtree Accounting for Windows allows you to set passwords for the various accounting functions as well as for access to the password function itself.

OPTION	DESCRIPTION
Do Not Print Total Page Length of Reports in Report Headers	Check this to suppress the total number of pages in the report headers when you generate reports and speed up report processing.
Do Not Show Quantity on Hand in Inventory Item Lookup Lists	Check this to suppress the quantity on hand for inventory items when generating lookup lists, which will speed up processing of those lists.
Line Item Entry Display	Peachtree Accounting lets you enter a second line of information in journal entries, as well as in the Cash Manager, Collection Manager, and Payment Manager detail windows. The second line is used for descriptions or notes.
Automatic Field Completion	Peachtree Accounting will look for potential matches with information you've entered before and fill in the field automatically.
Drop-Down List Displays Automatically	Drop-down lists give you a choice of options in a field. You just click on one of the options in the list to enter it rather than typing the data yourself. If you select this option, the drop-down list appears as soon as you move the cursor into the field.
Color Scheme	Select one of the five color schemes in this drop-down list (described earlier in Chapter 2) to determine how the windows and dialog boxes will appear. The options are Classic, Professional, Sand, Splash, and Vibrant. The color scheme will only affect the appearance of Peachtree Accounting. It will not affect the appearance of other applications or the Windows desktop. The color scheme can be different for each workstation on a network to suit the individual user's preferences. Peachtree Accounting applies the new color scheme when you start Peachtree Accounting again.

TABLE 3-2 General Global Options in Peachtree Accounting for Windows

Select the Users option from the Maintain menu. The Maintain Users window appears (shown here with a sample administrator password entered).

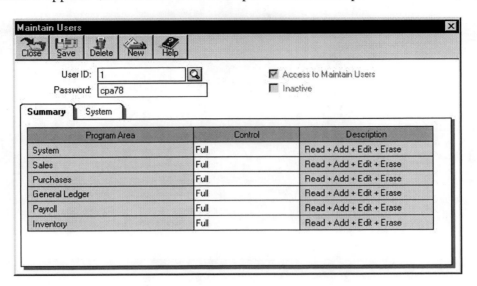

User ID   Enter a user ID of up to 13 alphanumeric characters. The user ID is case sensitive.

Password   Enter a password of up to 13 characters for the user. The password is case sensitive. Passwords must also be unique: one user can't have the same password as another.

Access to Maintain Users   Check this box if you want the user to be able to set up other users, including adding or changing passwords and access privileges. (The first user you set up has this privilege automatically to prevent you from turning on the security features and locking yourself out.) You can grant this privilege to other users as well, but you should be cautious about granting this privilege to too many users, as you can easily undermine your Peachtree Accounting security.

Inactive   Check this box to remove user access.

On the Maintain program item in the systems folder, you can choose from No Access, Read, Add, Edit, or Full. The password can be up to 13 characters.

Summary   The Summary tab shows a high-level view of all the tabs including: System, Sales, Purchases, General Ledger, Payroll, and Inventory. The Control column displays Full or No Access.

System   The System tab displays program areas for Analysis, File, Maintain, Options, Tasks, and Reports.

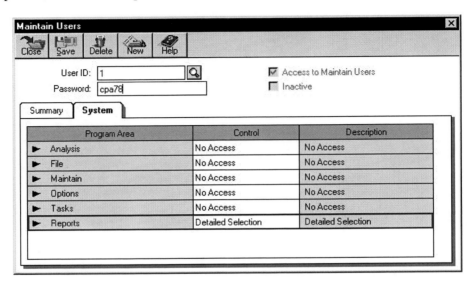

Double-click the triangle to the left of the program area to see the following settings:

- **Analysis**   Cash, Collection, Payment, Financial Managers
- **File**   Backup, Import/Export, All Files, Integrity Check, Restore
- **Maintain**   Company Information, Jobs
- **Options**   Action Items/Event Log Options, Change System Date
- **Tasks**   Action Items, Account Reconciliation, Change Accounting Period
- **Reports**   Jobs, Account Reconciliation

It's important that at least one user have access to the Maintain Users window. Be careful about granting access to this feature, as access to the Maintain Users window may be a major security breach.

You can create up to 50 different passwords, each with its own rights. You can also set up separate passwords that have overlapping rights. For example, you can set up individual passwords for separate accounting clerks, all of whom are able to access the General Ledger, but with separate additional rights, such as Accounts Receivable, Accounts Payable, or Inventory.

Once you've set up passwords, click OK. The next time you open the company, Peachtree Accounting prompts you for a password, as shown here.

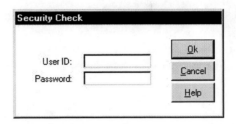

The password you enter determines which functions you can access. If your password doesn't let you access a function such as Payroll, the various Payroll options will be grayed out on the menus.

You can modify an existing password or privileges in the Maintain Users window by highlighting the password in the list, clicking OK, and then entering a new password in the Password field. You can delete a password and its associated privileges by highlighting the password and then clicking the Delete button from the menu bar. The password will be deleted.

Keep in mind the following tips when setting up passwords:

- Passwords can contain up to 13 characters.
- Passwords are case sensitive: *PASSWORD* is not the same as *password*.
- At least one user must have rights to the Maintain Users window. (Peachtree Accounting won't let you save changes in the Maintain Users window unless one user has password maintenance rights.)
- Avoid using passwords like "password," "security," "safety," your name, your spouse's name, your children's names, birthdays, anniversaries, or holiday dates.
- Avoid short passwords as well; use at least six characters in a password.
- Mix letters and numbers, and use both upper- and lowercase letters.
- When setting up a series of passwords, make sure they're all different.
- Remember that users who have AP, AR, or PR access can also get to the Accounts Reconciliation selection on the Tasks menu, from which they can view balances and outstanding checks.

• If you write down your password, store it in a safe place. Don't write down your password and then leave it in a desk drawer where anyone can find it. You should also write down the administrator password and store it in a safe place. A user with access to the Maintain Users window can look up passwords for other users, but if you forget the password for the administrator, you will lock yourself out of the program. Peachtree can unlock your files for you, but you will have to provide clear written authorization before this can happen.

Setting Up Users in Peachtree Complete Accounting for Windows

Peachtree Complete Accounting has an enhanced security system. In Peachtree Complete Accounting, you can set up detailed security for the various accounting functions, as well as for access to the password function itself, using a combination of user IDs and passwords.

To set up users, select the Users option from the Maintain menu. The Maintain Users window appears (as shown below with a sample administrator-level user entered).

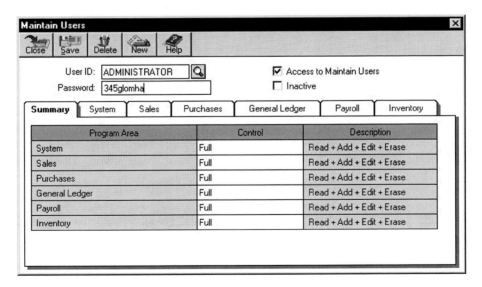

Enter information in this window as follows:

User ID   Enter a user ID of up to 13 alphanumeric characters. The user ID is case sensitive.

Password   Enter a password of up to 13 characters for the user. The password is case sensitive. Passwords must also be unique: one user can't have the same password as another.

Access to Maintain Users   Check this box if you want the user to be able to set up other users, including adding or changing passwords and access privileges. (The first user you set up has this privilege automatically to prevent you from turning on the security features and locking yourself out.) You can grant this privilege to other users as well, but you should be cautious about granting this privilege to too many users, as you can easily undermine your Peachtree Accounting security.

Inactive   Check this box to inactivate the user ID. (You must be logged on with a user ID that lets you maintain users to do this.) Inactivating a user ID is preferable to deleting the user ID if the user is going to return to the company. For example, if the user is out on vacation, inactivating the user ID prevents anyone from using the user's account inappropriately, but you wouldn't have to reenter all the permissions for that user when he or she returns.

The tabs let you set the permissions levels for the user ID. Table 3-3 lists the types of permissions you can set in each tab.

Each module, program area, or individual item has a corresponding Control field that identifies the access the user is allowed.

Summary   The Summary view shows a high-level view of all the tabs including: System, Sales, Purchases, General Ledger, Payroll, and Inventory. The Control column will display Detailed Selection if you specify more than one type of control access.

PERMISSION LEVEL	DESCRIPTION
No Access	The user has no access to this option.
Read	The user can look up information and read records, but can't add or change any information.
Add	All rights of Read access, plus the user can add records.
Edit	All rights of Read and Add access, plus the user can change records.
Full	The user has complete access to the feature and is able to read, add, edit, and delete information.

TABLE 3-3   Permission Levels

System   The System tab displays program areas for Analysis, File, Maintain, Options, Tasks, and Reports.

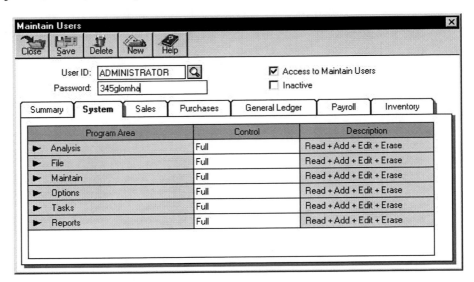

Double-click the triangle to the left of the program area to see the following settings:

- **Analysis**   Cash, Collection, Payment, Financial Managers
- **File**   Backup, Import/Export, All Files, Integrity Check, Restore
- **Maintain**   Company Information, Jobs
- **Options**   Action Items/Event Log Options, Change System Date
- **Tasks**   Action Items, Account Reconciliation, Change Accounting Period, Close Fiscal Year, Close Payroll Year, Post, Un-Post, Purge, Time and Expense Tickets, Link to Other Apps
- **Reports**   Audit Trail, Jobs, Account Reconciliation, Term/Expense, Report Groups

Sales   The Sales tab displays program area sections for Maintenance, Tasks, and Reports.

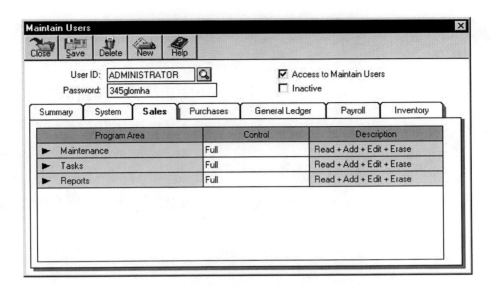

Double-click the triangle to the left of the program area to see the following settings:

- **Maintenance**   Customer and Customers/Prospects, Beginning Balances
- **Tasks**   Quotes, Sales Orders, Receipts, Sales/Invoicing
- **Reports**   Master Lists, Transaction Lists, Other Reports, Forms

Purchases   The Purchases tab displays program area sections for Maintenance, Tasks, and Reports.

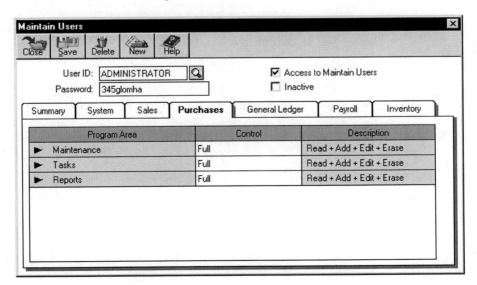

Double-click the triangle to the left of the program area to see the following settings:

- **Maintenance**   Vendors, Vendors, Beginning Balances
- **Tasks**   Payments, Purchase Orders, Purchases/Receive Inventory, Void AP Checks
- **Reports**   Master Lists, Transaction Lists, Other Reports and Forms

General Ledger   The General Ledger tab displays program area sections for Maintenance, Tasks, and Reports.

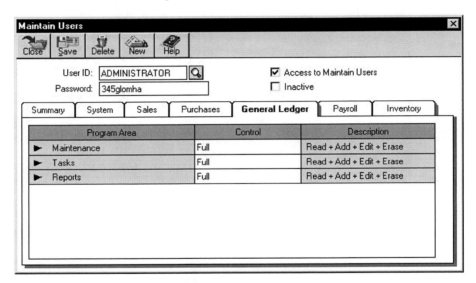

Double-click the triangle to the left of the program area to see the following settings:

- **Maintenance**   Chart of Accounts, Chart of Accounts, Beginning Balances
- **Tasks**   General Journal Entry
- **Reports**   Master Lists, Transaction Lists, Financial Statement

Payroll   The Payroll tab displays program area sections for Maintenance, Tasks, and Reports.

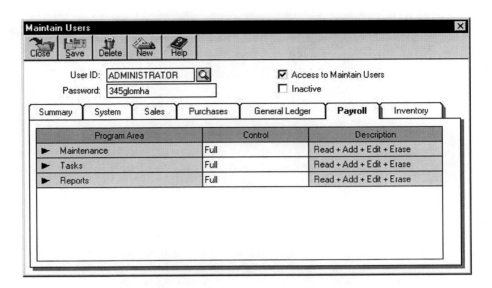

Double-click the triangle to the left of the program area to see the following settings:

- **Maintenance**   Employees/Sales Reps, Employees/Sales Reps, Beginning Balances, Payroll Tax Tables
- **Tasks**   Payroll Entry, Void Payroll Checks
- **Reports**   Master Lists, Transaction Lists, Other Reports and Forms

Inventory   The Inventory tab displays program area sections for Maintenance, Tasks, and Reports.

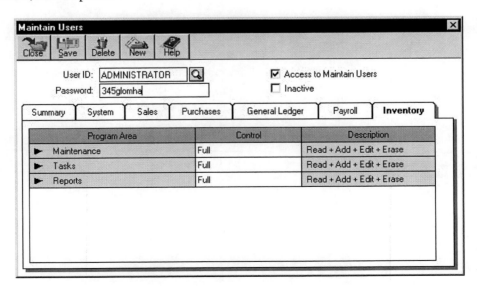

Double-click the triangle to the left of the program area to see the following settings:

- **Maintenance**   Inventory Items, Inventory Item/Beginning Balances, Multiple Item Prices
- **Tasks**   Inventory
- **Reports**   Master Lists

Items that have information you update and maintain (such as vendor or employee records) will have all the permission levels in Table 3-4. Note that some features, such as the module-level options on the Summary tab and the reports, are not maintainable. Access for these options is simply a choice of No Access or Full.

You can set permissions at several levels. The broadest level of security is for entire modules using the options on the Summary window. You can also set more detailed permissions within each module by going to the appropriate tab and double-clicking on the Control field for a specific program area, such as the Tasks program area in the Purchases tab. For precision control, you can even set the access levels for individual items within a program area by double-clicking the triangle to the left of the program area to display the subordinate items and then double-clicking the appropriate Control field and choosing one of the permission levels. The window shown below contains a sample user ID with some detailed permission levels set. As you can see, when

PERMISSION LEVEL	DESCRIPTION
No Access	The user has no access to this option.
Read	The user can look up information and read records, but can't add or change any information.
Add	All rights of Read access, plus the user can add records.
Edit	All rights of Read and Add access, plus the user can change records.
Full	The user has complete access to the feature and is able to read, add, edit, and delete information.

TABLE 3-4   Permission Levels

you make changes to a subordinate permission level, Peachtree Accounting displays Detailed Selection at the program area's control level.

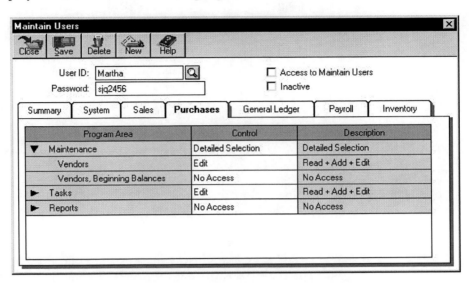

When you are satisfied with your permission level entries in each of the tabs, click Save. The first user you set up is automatically granted the Access to Maintain Users permission—this prevents you from locking yourself out of the company—so be sure to set up an administrator user ID first.

To set up additional users, click New on the toolbar and enter the new user ID and information. When you are done entering user IDs, click Close. If you need to delete a user ID, select the user ID from the preview window list and click Delete from the menu bar. (You can't delete a user ID if it is the only one with the Access to Maintain Users box checked.) Changes, additions, and deletions to the user IDs will take effect the next time you open the company.

Once you have even one user ID set up, Peachtree Accounting will require you to enter a valid user ID and password when you open the company. (For convenience, Peachtree Accounting displays the last user ID entered for the company.) Peachtree Accounting displays asterisks when you type the password to prevent anyone from seeing your password. When you open the company, Peachtree Accounting displays the Security Check window, shown

here. The user ID you enter determines the features you have access to.
(Any features that aren't allowed for that user ID are grayed out.)

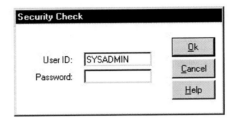

Keep in mind the following tips when setting up user IDs and passwords in
Peachtree Complete Accounting for Windows:

- User IDs should be reasonably easy to remember. If your company is small,
  using first names or first names and a last initial is fine, such as Martha or
  MarthaR. If many people are likely to be using Peachtree Accounting, using
  the first initial and last name is better, such as MRiegert or PMackintosh.
- A quick way to set up an administrative user is to enter the user ID and
  password and then set the control levels for all the program areas in the
  Summary tab to Full Access.
- Obvious choices for a system administrator ID are user IDs such as
  SYSADMIN, ADMINISTRATOR, or MANAGER, but for security reasons, it
  is better to have the actual administrator user ID be something unexpected,
  such as S3b4alq51 or a user ID that looks like just another user. You can
  even have a dummy administrator set up with an obvious user ID and few
  or no permissions as a decoy. If someone is trying to crack the security on
  your system, they will try the obvious user IDs first and not look at the
  individual users.
- User IDs and passwords only apply to the company you set them up for.
  If you have multiple Peachtree Accounting companies maintained by the
  same people, consider if you want your users to have separate user IDs and
  passwords—for example, having an Accounts Receivable clerk have the
  same user ID and password on both systems. Regardless of the general user
  levels, any administrator user IDs and passwords should be different from
  one company to the next to minimize the possibility of security breaches.
- Minimize the number of users who have Access to Maintain Users. It is
  almost always preferable that only one user have access to this feature.

- Although you can set up an unlimited number of user IDs, you may have trouble monitoring activity on them if you have too many, particularly where you have user IDs that are used only for one specific task. Where you have a group of user IDs that will have identical or similar access privileges, you may want to name them to show a relationship to the group, such as Payroll1, Payroll2, Payroll3, and so on.
- User IDs and passwords are case sensitive: *BONNIER* is not the same as *BonnieR* or *bonnier*; *PASSWORD* is not the same as *password*.
- Passwords can contain up to 13 characters. Avoid short passwords (which are easier to crack); use at least six characters in a password. Mix letters and numbers, and use both upper- and lowercase letters.
- Avoid using passwords like "password," "security," "safety," your name, your spouse's name, your children's names, birthdays, anniversaries, or holiday dates.
- If you write down your password, store it in a safe place. Don't write down your password and then leave it in a desk drawer where anyone can find it. You should also write down the administrator password and store it in a safe place. A user with Access to Maintain Users can get into the Maintain Users window and look up passwords for other users, but if you forget the password for the administrator, you will lock yourself out of the program. Peachtree can unlock your files for you, but you will have to provide clear written authorization before this can happen.

Summary

In this chapter, you've seen how to create a new company in Peachtree Accounting, how to create a basic chart of accounts from the sample charts of accounts, how to set global options for your version of Peachtree Accounting, and how to set up security. In the next chapter, you'll learn how to modify the chart of accounts (and enter new accounts), print General Ledger reports, enter beginning account balances, and use audit trails.

Setting Up Your General Ledger

4

B A S I C S

- How to set up the chart of accounts
- How to enter beginning balances and prior period adjustments
- How to enter General Journal entries
- How to print General Ledger reports

B E Y O N D

- How to enter budget amounts
- How to use audit trails

In this chapter, you'll learn how to customize your chart of accounts, how to make entries to the General Journal, and how to print General Ledger reports. You'll also learn how to enter budget amounts and how to use audit trails.

The previous chapter showed you how to start a new company named Big Business, Inc., in Peachtree Accounting and how to set global options. In this chapter, you'll learn how to modify the chart of accounts, print the chart of accounts and Working Trial Balance reports, set General Ledger defaults, and enter beginning account balances and prior period adjustments. You'll also learn how to add, modify, and delete entries in the General Journal, print other General Ledger accounts, and enter budget amounts.

The focus of this chapter is setting up the General Ledger for your business. The General Ledger is the central component of your accounting system. It is the summary of all financial activity for your company. The General Ledger accepts information from Accounts Receivable, Accounts Payable, Payroll, and Inventory. The General Journal is comprised of entries to the General Ledger that do not come in from any of the other ledgers.

Setting Up the Chart of Accounts

The chart of accounts is the list of account IDs and descriptions you use for your company. In Chapter 3 you copied a basic chart of accounts from the sample company. The next step in setting up your General Ledger is to modify the chart of accounts as necessary and enter beginning balances. (If you are not sure how to modify the charts of accounts according to your business, ask your accountant for assistance.)

The chart of accounts is the heart of your whole financial system. A well-planned chart of accounts is worth the time it takes to plan it through. The steps for setting up your chart of accounts are as follows:

1. Print a Chart of Accounts report to see the chart of accounts you copied from the sample company.
2. Add, modify, and delete accounts for a better fit with the way your company does business.
3. Print another Chart of Accounts report to verify your entries.
4. Print a Working Trial Balance report to enter beginning balances.
5. Enter the beginning balances.

Before you begin making changes to the chart of accounts, you should understand how Peachtree Accounting handles accounts.

Understanding Accounts

For a general idea of what the chart of accounts looks like, you can review the various sample charts of accounts you copied from the sample company. Click Start on the Windows 98 taskbar and then select Programs. Select the Peachtree Accounting group, then click the Peachtree Accounting icon. Select Contents and Index from the Help menu, and then click the Help for Your Specific Type of Business icon. Double-click the List of Sample Chart of Accounts icon.

From the Sample Charts of Accounts Contents window, you can select any of the sample charts of accounts. Figure 4-1 shows the chart of accounts for the sample manufacturing company. Clicking Print at the top of the window will print the sample chart of accounts.

FIGURE 4-1   Chart of Accounts for the sample manufacturing company

You can see that each account in the chart of accounts has an account ID, a description, and an account type. The following sections give you basic information on account IDs, account types, descriptions, and creating an account ID system using a technique known as masking.

Account IDs

Peachtree Accounting sets up initial account ranges as specified by the sample company information you copied. According to these definitions, asset accounts use a range of account IDs from 10000 to 19999, liability and equity accounts use 20000 to 29999, and so on. You can use these ranges if you like, as it makes searching for and selecting account IDs easiest when all accounts of one type are in a contiguous range of numbers. If you decide to modify the default account ID ranges, keep the following in mind:

- Make sure that the account range you define has ample room for growth.
- The Current Earnings account ID is created and maintained internally by Peachtree Accounting. It is defined as the last posting account in Liability & Equity—that is, the account with the highest number. You can't post to this account. The Current Earnings account holds the total profit or loss for the period, calculated as the total of all income, cost of sales, and expenses. The Current Earnings account should always be equal to the net income amount on the bottom line of the income statement.
- Peachtree Accounting lets you have only one account with an account type of Retained Earnings. (The Retained Earnings account holds the total profit or loss for the company for the year.) To follow good accounting practice, the Retained Earnings account should have the account ID *immediately* preceding the Current Earnings account ID.

Peachtree Accounting allows you considerable flexibility when creating account IDs. However, there are a few rules:

- Account IDs can contain any characters except question marks, plus signs, and asterisks. For example, *123456789, 1-2-3-4, A21COMM,* and *ABCDEF* are all valid account IDs, but *A?B?C?, 1+2+3+4,* and *A*1*B* are not.
- Account IDs are case sensitive. For example, *CASH, Cash,* and *cash* are all different account IDs.
- Account IDs cannot have leading or trailing spaces, but you can have spaces in the middle. For example, you could have accounts called *CASH 1, CASH SALES,* and *PETTY CASH.*

- Account IDs are sorted in ASCII order: numbers before letters and from the left. If you have the account IDs 1, 13, 27, 49, 124, and 200, Peachtree Accounting will sort these numbers as follows: 1, 124, 13, 200, 27, 49. To ensure proper sorting, your account IDs should have the same number of characters, and all numeric account IDs should be preceded with zeros. Using preceding zeros to fill a 5-character account ID, the previous account IDs become, in sorted order, 00001, 00013, 00027, 00049, 00124, and 00200. Although Peachtree Accounting allows you to enter accounts in any order, it is easier to read reports and financial statements if all the accounts of a similar type (see the upcoming "Account Types" section) are grouped together with account IDs within a range.

Peachtree Accounting allows you complete flexibility in setting up your account IDs, but it is usually a good idea to start out with the standard chart of accounts from the closest sample company and modify it as your needs dictate. The default chart of accounts you copied uses a 5-character account ID, but you can enter up to 15 alphanumeric characters for an account code. Any accounts you create should be consistently named and easily understood by anyone who uses them. You should also be aware that the predefined financial statements have a default selection range of 1 to zzzzzzzzzz for account IDs. If your account IDs use preceding zeros, you will need to modify the financial statements to select from 0 to zzzzzzzzzz, as described in Chapter 12.

In general, the charts of accounts in the sample companies are fairly complete. You may not need to add accounts in the chart of accounts you copied. You also don't need to make every modification to the chart of accounts all at once; you can always add accounts to the chart later as you need to. Be careful, though: if you make entries to an account, you cannot delete it.

Account Types

Peachtree Accounting recognizes 16 categories, known as account types, for General Ledger accounts. These account types are listed in Table 4-1.

When setting up accounts, keep these account types in mind. GAAP (Generally Accepted Accounting Principles) expects that the Asset accounts and the Liability and Equity accounts make up the balance sheet; Income, Cost of Goods, and Expense Accounts make up the profit-and-loss statement or income statement. If you have the account types in an order other than Assets, Liability, Equity, Income, Cost of Goods, and Expenses, it will be difficult for auditors or bank officers to review your financial statements. These reports are the final summary of all your financial activities. Finance committees, banks, reports to loan officers, and stockholders' annual reports use these financial statements in this format. Look at the examples in the financial reports later in this chapter and use the sample client data included with Peachtree Accounting for further information on how this will affect your company's account structure.

Descriptions

The description is an important part of the account information. It should be clear, unambiguous, and easy to understand when it appears on invoices, receipts, and reports. Examples of account descriptions are "Office Supplies," "A/R—Royalties," and "A/P—Rent for Hardware."

Account ID Masking

As you set up your chart of accounts, you may want to use masking in your account IDs. Masking is the creation of IDs to allow filtering of specific divisions, departments, and locations when printing financial reports. Because Peachtree Accounting also lets you select accounts by account type, you can use a combination of account types and account ID masking to select accounts for reporting.

ACCOUNT TYPE	FINANCIAL CATEGORY
Accounts Payable	Liability
Accounts Receivable	Asset
Accumulated Depreciation	Expense and Asset (offset)
Cash	Asset
Cost of Sales	Cost of Goods/Expense
Equity—doesn't close	Equity
Equity—gets closed	Equity
Expenses	Expense
Fixed Assets	Asset
Income	Revenue/Income
Inventory	Asset
Long Term Liabilities	Liability
Other Assets	Asset
Other Current Assets	Asset
Other Current Liabilities	Liability
Retained Earnings	Equity

TABLE 4-1   General Ledger Account Types

The following example shows you one way you might set up account IDs for a company with divisions containing locations that, in turn, contain units.

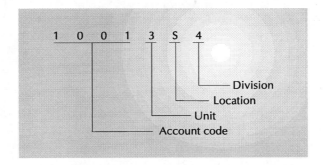

Here, the account ID breaks down into four parts: the specific account code (the first four digits), a unit ID, a location ID, and a division ID. When you select data for reports, you can use wildcards to select for any unit, location, division, or account code. Wildcards can represent any other character. For example, to select all accounts for division 4, you would specify ******4. Similarly, for all accounts in unit 3, you would specify ****3**.

Masking is also a useful technique for creating customer, vendor, and employee ID codes. For example, you might set up customer codes that identify the customer's location, vendor codes that identify the type of merchandise you purchase, and employee codes that identify the employee's division or classification. You can then select groups of customers, vendors, and employees when you print reports. (You'll learn how to create customer IDs in Chapter 5, vendor IDs in Chapter 6, and employee IDs in Chapter 7.)

Printing the Chart of Accounts Report

The chart of accounts is the basic financial structure of your company. You may need to modify the chart of accounts you copied from the sample by adding unit, division, or department codes as described earlier. A printed chart of accounts will help you set up and delete accounts to fit your needs. Look carefully at the accounts you may not need at this time. If you delete an account now and find later that you need it after all, you can always add it back in, but you cannot delete an account once activity has been posted to it.

The first step in customizing your chart of accounts is to print a Chart of Accounts report to see the accounts you copied from the sample company. The Chart of Accounts report lists the General Ledger account ID, the description, and the account type. (Printing the other General Ledger reports is covered later in the "Printing the Working Trial Balance" and "Printing Other General Ledger Reports" sections of this chapter.)

To print the Chart of Accounts report, start by selecting the General Ledger option from the Reports menu. The Select a Report window appears with the Chart of Accounts option selected, as shown in Figure 4-2.

The Select a Report window is used for selecting reports throughout Peachtree Accounting. Take a moment to familiarize yourself with the features on the Select a Report window.

- The Report Area lets you select the class of reports to print: Accounts Receivable, Accounts Payable, and so on.
- The Report List shows the specific reports within a class. As you can see in Figure 4-2, Peachtree Accounting has five General Ledger reports: the Chart of Accounts, the Working Trial Balance, the General Ledger Trial Balance, the General Journal, and the General Ledger.
- The Description of Report gives a brief description of the report highlighted in the Report List (in this example, the Chart of Accounts report).

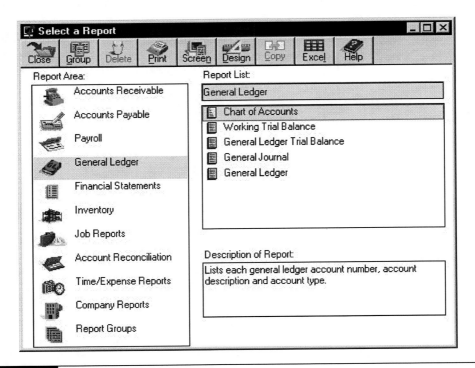

FIGURE 4-2   Select a Report window

The toolbar at the top of the window also has some buttons you haven't seen before, described in Table 4-2.

You'll usually just use the Print and Screen buttons for printing and displaying standard reports. Grouping, deleting, designing, and copying reports are discussed in Chapter 12.

To print or display a report, highlight the report in the Report List and click either Print or Screen. The Report Options window appears, as shown in Figure 4-3. (Note that the name appearing in the title bar of this window is the name of the report you selected in the Select a Report window—in this case, Chart of Accounts.)

 TIP: If you don't already have a default printer set up in Windows, or if you want to change the default printer, select Print from the File menu in Peachtree Accounting. You'll see a list of printers you can choose from. Select the printer you want to use and click OK, or click Help for more information.

BUTTON	NAME	DESCRIPTION
Close	Close	Close the window without running the report.
Group	Group	Create or edit a group of reports.
Delete	Delete	Delete the current report.
Print	Print	Print the selected report on the printer.
Screen	Screen	Display the selected report on the screen.
Design	Design	Design forms and statements or reformat existing reports.
Copy	Copy	Copy financial statements.
Excel	Excel	Insert a copy of the selected report into a Microsoft Excel spreadsheet.
Help	Help	Display the online help.

TABLE 4-2   Toolbar Buttons in the Select a Report Window

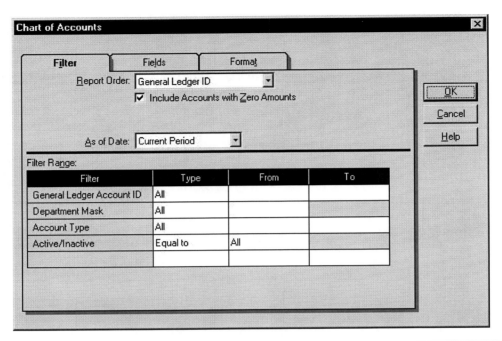

FIGURE 4-3 Report Options window

The Report Options window has three tabs that let you customize your reports. You'll see how to change report options later in the "Printing the Working Trial Balance" section. For right now, click OK to use the defaults for printing the Chart of Accounts report. The report starts printing on the printer or the screen, depending on whether you clicked Print or Screen. You used the sample manufacturing template for the Big Business chart of accounts, which creates a two-page Chart of Accounts report. Figure 4-4 shows the beginning of the first page of the Chart of Accounts report for Big Business, Inc.

The report lists accounts in numerical order, beginning with Petty Cash (10000), Cash on Hand (10100), Regular Checking Account (10200), and Payroll Checking Account (10300). The report also contains the account description, the current status of the account (active or inactive), and the account type. Note that Peachtree Accounting lists the filter criteria (set using the Filter tab in the Report Options window) at the top of the report.

Big Business, Inc.
Chart of Accounts
As of Apr 30, 2000

Filter Criteria includes: Report order is by ID. Report is printed with Accounts having Zero Amounts and in Detail Format.

Account ID	Account Description	Activ	Account Type
10000	Petty Cash	Yes	Cash
10100	Cash on Hand	Yes	Cash
10200	Regular Checking Account	Yes	Cash
10300	Payroll Checking Account	Yes	Cash
10400	Savings Account	Yes	Cash
10500	Special Account	Yes	Cash
10600	Investments-Money Marke	Yes	Cash
10700	Investments-Cert. of Depos	Yes	Cash
11000	Accounts Receivable	Yes	Accounts Receivable

FIGURE 4-4 Chart of Accounts report

A good idea is to first display the report on the screen (by clicking Screen on the toolbar of the Select a Report window) and then print it on the printer by clicking Print. You don't have to return to the Select a Report window; just click Print on the toolbar above the report after the report has been displayed on the screen. This method is useful if you're experimenting with a report format and don't want to waste paper.

When you have viewed a report, you can return to the Select a Report window by clicking Close on the toolbar. Click Close on the Select a Report window to close the window.

You are now ready to set the General Ledger defaults.

Setting General Ledger Defaults

Setting the General Ledger defaults is very easy. Start by selecting the Setup Checklist option from the Maintain menu. The Setup Checklist (which you saw earlier in Chapter 3) appears, as shown in Figure 4-5.

As you can see, the first section of the Setup Checklist window deals with General Ledger information. Click the box for the second item, General Ledger

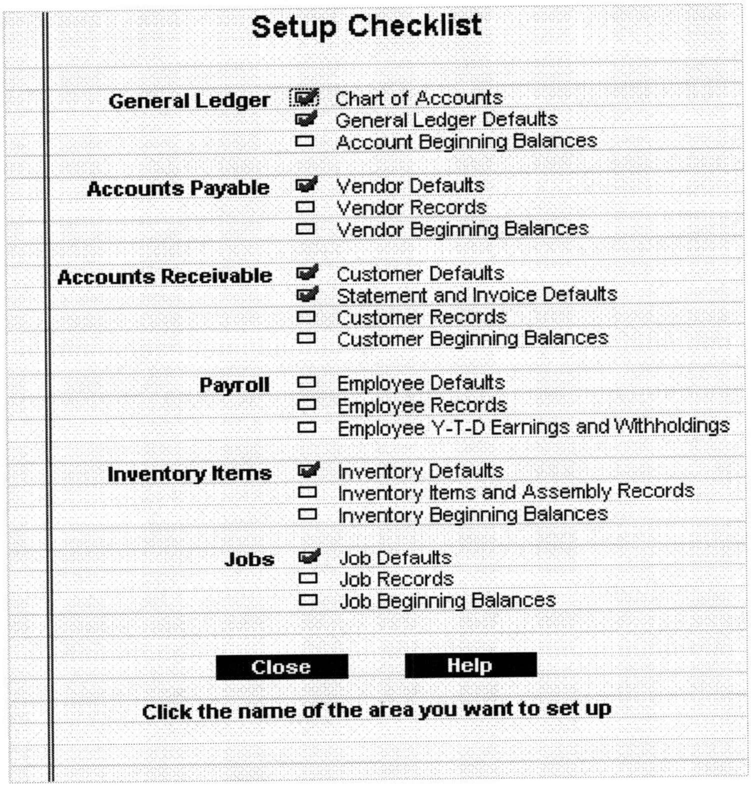

FIGURE 4-5 Setup Checklist window

Defaults. Peachtree displays the General Ledger Defaults window, shown in Figure 4-6, and prompts you for the rounding account number. (Peachtree Accounting supplies a default account number in this window.)

The rounding account is a General Ledger account that collects rounding differences from other accounts. This is used for rounding totals on financial statements. Note that the rounding account is a holding account Peachtree Accounting uses only for calculations. This account cannot be posted to, printed from, or used in a report, nor can you transfer the information in the rounding account to another account. You need to specify a rounding account even if you calculate to the penny, as Peachtree Accounting also uses the rounding account for some tax calculations and per-unit cost extensions, and you might get an out-of-balance error later when posting sales or purchase journals.

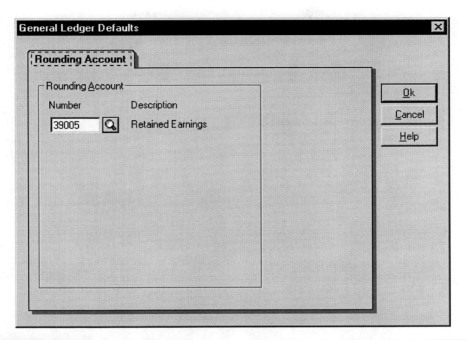

FIGURE 4-6 General Ledger Defaults

When you click OK or Cancel, you return to the Setup Checklist window. Peachtree then asks if you want to mark the task as completed on the checklist. Choose Yes for Peachtree to put a check mark next to the item, but don't exit the checklist yet. You are now ready to start entering and modifying account information.

 REMEMBER: You can always modify items that are checked off on the Setup Checklist. The check mark is just a convenient way of keeping track of the things you've done.

Entering and Modifying Your Account Information

Once you've printed a Chart of Accounts report and have examined it to see what changes you need to make, you can add, modify, and delete accounts for a better fit with the way your company does business.

You saw how to select an option from the Setup Checklist when you entered the General Ledger defaults. Now use the Setup Checklist to enter a new account or modify an existing account by clicking the Chart of Accounts item on the Setup Checklist. The Maintain Chart of Accounts window, shown in Figure 4-7, appears.

Adding New Accounts

Although the chart of accounts templates are reasonably complete, you will probably need to add a few new accounts to customize the chart of accounts you copied for your business. As you can see in Figure 4-7, there are two tabs in the Maintain Chart of Accounts window, General and Budgets. You'll enter general account information through the General tab for right now. (Later in this chapter, you'll see how to use the Budgets tab to enter budget amounts.)

Account ID Enter the account ID in this field. If you're not sure a similar account exists, you can see the accounts you've already set up by clicking the magnifying glass icon next to the Account ID field. A list of accounts drops down from the Account ID field, as shown in Figure 4-8.

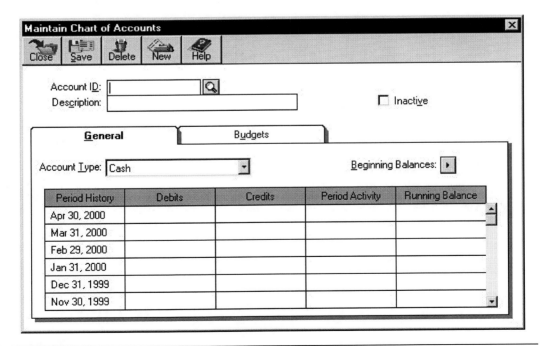

FIGURE 4-7   Maintain Chart of Accounts window

Maintain Chart of Accounts

Close | Save | Delete | New | Help

Account ID:
Description:

10000	Petty Cash	Cash
10100	Cash on Hand	Cash
10200	Regular Checking Account	Cash
10300	Payroll Checking Account	Cash
10400	Savings Account	Cash
10500	Special Account	Cash
10600	Investments-Money Market	Cash
10700	Investments-Cert. of Deposit	Cash
11000	Accounts Receivable	Accounts Receivable
11400	Other Receivables	Accounts Receivable
11500	Allowance for Doubtful Account	Accounts Receivable
12000	Raw Materials Inventory	Inventory

Gen

Account Type:

Period History

OK | Cancel | Find | Next | Help

Apr 30, 2000			
Mar 31, 2000			
Feb 29, 2000			
Jan 31, 2000			
Dec 31, 1999			
Nov 30, 1999			

FIGURE 4-8 Account ID list in the Maintain Chart of Accounts window

You can scroll through the list of accounts using the arrow keys on your keyboard or the scroll bar on the right side of the list, but this may be impractical if you have a large chart of accounts. Peachtree Accounting lets you search for accounts using Find at the bottom of the list. When you click Find, Peachtree Accounting displays a window that lets you enter the text or number to search for. When you click OK, Peachtree Accounting starts looking through the chart of accounts for accounts that match the information. For example, if you enter **Sales**, Peachtree Accounting will match accounts that have the word "Sales" in the account ID, account description, or the account type. Once you find the first match, click Next to find the next occurrence in the chart of accounts. You can search for an account ID (or a part of one) or text from the description or account type.

 T I P : The Find and Next buttons appear on drop-down lists throughout Peachtree Accounting. They can make searching for information in long lists much easier.

Description   The description you enter here appears on most windows and reports where General Ledger accounts are listed. The description also appears on the General Ledger account drop-down list (shown earlier in Figure 4-8). Account descriptions can have up to 30 characters.

Inactive   Click the Inactive check box to inactivate an account. You inactivate accounts because they are not currently needed; for example, you might inactivate an account set up for a promissory note when the note is paid off. You might also inactivate an obsolete account that has entries—Peachtree Accounting won't let you delete an account with entries. When you try to use an inactive account in a transaction, Peachtree Accounting warns you that the account is inactive. Inactive accounts with zero balances are closed during year-end processing (accounts with zero balances that have not been flagged as inactive are not purged). To tidy up a chart of accounts, review the accounts with no activity or a zero balance and set the accounts to inactive before year-end closing.

N O T E : Peachtree Accounting lets you purge accounts at any time. This is preferable to automatically deleting inactive accounts as part of the year-end processing, as the account purge is a separate process. Purging accounts is discussed in Chapter 13.

Account Type   You can select an account type by clicking on the down arrow to the right of the Account Type field to drop down a list of the 16 available types. Click the one you want. You can also type the first few characters of the account type you want in the Account Type field. Peachtree Accounting fills in the account type for you.

When you're satisfied with the information you've entered, click Save at the top of the window. Peachtree Accounting saves the account information but doesn't clear the fields. Click New to clear the fields so you can enter a new account. You'll see how to use the period history on the lower half of the window later in this chapter in the "Entering Beginning Balances and Prior Period Adjustments" section.

Modifying Accounts

You can also use the General tab in the Maintain Chart of Accounts window to modify an existing account. Simply display the information for an existing account, then modify the account description and account type. Click Save when you are satisfied with the changes. You can modify everything about an account except the account ID. Although you can enter a new account ID, Peachtree Accounting simply creates a new account with the account ID and other information, but it does not delete the old account. If you want to change an account ID for a specific purpose (such as changing your account ID structure), you would have to delete the account and reenter it. Remember, you cannot delete an account that has a non-zero balance. Peachtree Accounting lets you delete only accounts with zero balances and no activity.

 T I P :   If you're entering a number of accounts with similar information, you can save data entry time: enter and save the first account, but don't click New. You can then enter a new Account ID, leave the rest of the information unchanged, and click Save.

Deleting Accounts

To delete an account from the chart of accounts, display the account by entering the account ID in the Account ID field (you can use the drop-down list to select an account ID). After you have displayed the account you want to delete, click Delete. Peachtree Accounting asks if you're sure you want to delete this record. Click Yes to delete the account. If you want to delete an account that has outstanding transactions against it, you should simply change the account to inactive and wait until year-end close, then purge the account using the purging process described in Chapter 13.

When you have finished modifying the chart of accounts, click Close in the Maintain Chart of Accounts window to return to the Setup Checklist. Peachtree then asks you if you want to mark the task as completed on the checklist. If you choose Yes, Peachtree puts a check mark next to the item to indicate that you've completed this portion of the setup. (Remember, you can modify the chart of accounts at any time regardless of whether the chart of accounts item is checked off on the Setup Checklist.)

When you've made your modifications to the chart of accounts, exit the Setup Checklist by clicking Close. Print another Chart of Accounts report to verify your entries (select the General Ledger option from the Reports menu, then select the Chart of Accounts report from the Report List). Take time now to save yourself time later. Save the final Chart of Accounts report as the first record of your company's financial structure.

Printing the Working Trial Balance

You've now seen how to print the Chart of Accounts report, add accounts to the chart of accounts, and modify and delete existing accounts. Now you need to enter all the account balances and prior period information to bring it up-to-date. The Working Trial Balance is a worksheet for entering and adjusting amounts in the General Ledger. It lists the General Ledger accounts and amounts and provides spaces for entering amounts. You've already seen the basics of selecting a report when you printed the Chart of Accounts report. Printing a Working Trial Balance is equally easy.

Start by selecting the General Ledger option from the Reports menu. The Select a Report window appears with the General Ledger option selected, as shown earlier in Figure 4-2. Select Working Trial Balance in the Report List. Click Printer or Screen. The Report Options window appears, as shown in Figure 4-9.

The Report Options window has three tabs: Filter, Fields, and Format. The default tab for this window is Filter. The Filter folder lets you select the range of information that appears on the report. You can also specify the report order and the date. (As you print other reports in Peachtree Accounting, you'll see

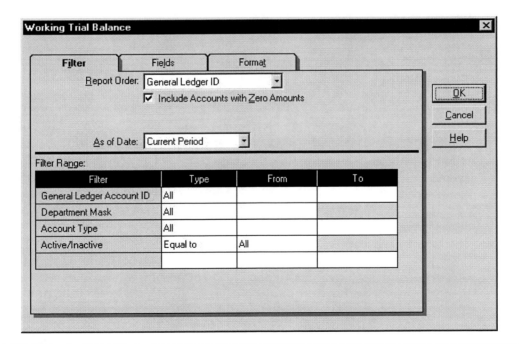

FIGURE 4-9   Report Options with the Filter folder showing

that the specific selection options in the various folders are different from report to report, but the general types of information for each Report Options tab are the same.)

Report Order   Click the down arrow to the right of the Report Order field for a drop-down list of sort criteria. The default for the Working Trial Balance is to sort by General Ledger account ID.

Include Accounts with Zero Amounts   Check this box to include accounts with zero amounts. (For the first Working Trial Balance, all your accounts will have zero amounts.)

As of Date   Click the down arrow to the right of this field for a drop-down list of the period to include. The default for the Working Trial Balance is the current period.

The lower half of the screen contains the Filter Range section. In this section are line items for the various items you can select. In the Working Trial Balance, you can select for the General Ledger account ID, the department mask, the account type, and active or inactive accounts.

The default selection for each of the four line items is All. You can change this by clicking in the Type field. A down arrow appears to the right of the field; clicking on this lets you view the various options for the field.

Peachtree Accounting gives you several different ways to select information. For example, you can select all General Ledger account IDs or a range. If you choose to select a range, clicking in the From and To fields on the line will display the standard magnifying glass icon for selecting accounts from a drop-down list. You can also look for all account types, a range of account types, or select account types equal or not equal to a specific selection (which you enter in the From field).

When you are satisfied with the information you've entered, click the Fields tab. The Fields folder appears, as shown in Figure 4-10.

As you can see, the Fields folder lets you specify the fields you want to display, set report breaks, and specify the order in which data appears.

There are several items that do not appear in the default setup for the Working Trial Balance: the account type, active/inactive status, the current balance, and budget amounts for previous, current, and future periods.

Show   Check this field to select a field for inclusion on the report. You can prevent a field from appearing on a report by clicking this field so the check mark is removed.

Field   This displays the description of the field. This field is display-only.

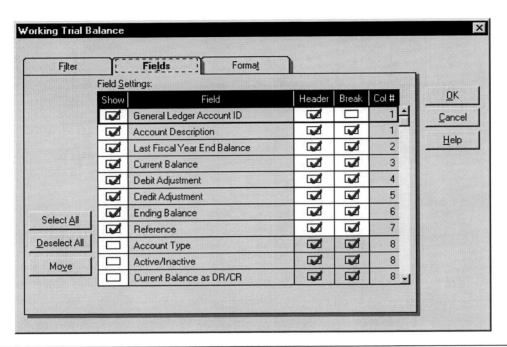

FIGURE 4-10 Report Options window with Fields folder showing

Header   Check this field to display the field name as the title of a report column. You can prevent the field name from appearing as the title of a report column by clicking this field so the check mark is removed.

Break   Check this field to put the information in its own column, as opposed to stacking fields of information one over another in a single column. (You stack information to save space and to group related information.) You can prevent a report break by clicking this field so the check mark is removed.

Col #   The column number is the number of the column where the information appears. You can change the order of columns of data by clicking Move and then clicking the line where you want the information to appear.

When you are satisfied with the information you've entered, click the Format tab. The Format folder appears, as shown in Figure 4-11.

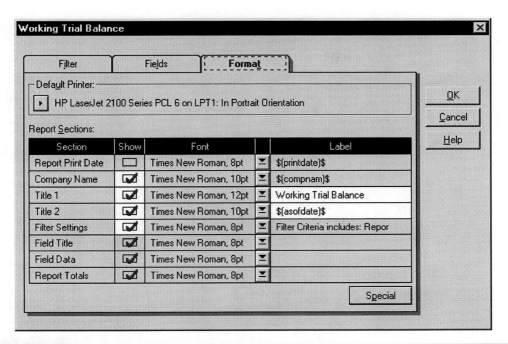

FIGURE 4-11 Report Options window with Format folder showing

The Format folder lets you set headings, specify font sizes for report headers and fields, and add special information, such as the current period and the company name. You can also pick an alternate printer.

Default Printer You can pick an alternate printer for the report by clicking the button. The standard Windows Print Setup dialog box appears. Make any changes to the printer options and click OK.

Number of Copies Enter the number of copies you want to print. The default is 1.

The Report Sections area in the lower portion of the window lets you specify the headings that appear on the report.

Section This is the data item to create a heading for. This field is display-only.

Show   Check this field to show a heading for the field on the report. You can prevent a field from having a heading on a report by clicking this field so the check mark is removed.

Font   Enter the font for the heading by clicking on the down arrow to the right of the field. The standard Windows Font dialog box appears. Select the font, style, size, effects, and color for the heading. Click OK when you're done.

Label   Enter the heading that will appear on the report. There are some predefined variables, such as $(**compnam**)$, which prints the company name from the company information and $(**printdate**)$, which prints the system date. Some reports also let you select from a list of predefined variables by clicking Special at the bottom of the window. A list of variables to choose from appears. (Predefined variables are discussed in detail in Chapter 12.)

When you are satisfied with the information you've entered in the three folders, click OK to start printing the Working Trial Balance. Figure 4-12 shows a portion of the Working Trial Balance report.

After you print the Working Trial Balance and write in the balances, you're ready to start entering beginning balances into the empty chart of accounts.

If you are in the middle of an accounting period, you will have to gather account balances as of the beginning of the period as well as all transactions to date. As you can imagine, the farther along in your accounting period you are, the more tedious and time-consuming this task becomes. For this reason, most

Big Business, Inc.
Working Trial Balance
As of Apr 30, 2000

Filter Criteria includes: Report order is by ID. Report is printed with Accounts having Zero Amounts and in Detail Format.

Account ID Account Description	Last FYE Bal	Current Bal	Debit Adj	Credit Adj	End Bal	Reference
10000 Petty Cash	0.00	0.00				
10100 Cash on Hand	0.00	0.00				
10200 Regular Checking Account	0.00	0.00				
10300 Payroll Checking Account	0.00	0.00				
10400 Savings Account	0.00	0.00				

FIGURE 4-12   Working Trial Balance report

people computerize their accounts at the beginning of a new accounting period since they have a clean slate to work with.

Entering Beginning Balances and Prior Period Adjustments

You enter beginning balances for the initial entries to accounts. You make prior period adjustments to correct or adjust entries in the General Journal made to accounts that already have transactions posted against them. This section shows you how to enter beginning balances as well as prior period adjustments. If you're entering beginning balances, Peachtree Accounting will display the Chart of Accounts Beginning Balances window. If you're making prior period adjustments, the Chart of Accounts Prior Year Adjustments window will be displayed. The data and fields in both windows are the same. If there are no transactions for the account, you will post beginning balances; otherwise, you will be posting prior period adjustments.

To enter beginning balances or prior period adjustments, follow this procedure:

1. Click the Account Beginning Balances item on the Setup Checklist (shown earlier in Figure 4-5). You can also enter beginning balances by clicking Beginning Balances on the Maintain Chart of Accounts window (shown earlier in Figure 4-7). The Select Period window appears, as shown in Figure 4-13.

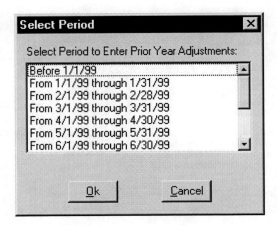

FIGURE 4-13 Select Period window

2. Select the accounting period from the list and click OK. For beginning balances, you can select previous, current, or future periods (but only if there are no entries for the account in any of the journals). Prior period adjustments can only be made to prior periods. If you selected an account with no entries, the Chart of Accounts Beginning Balances window will appear, shown in Figure 4-14 with sample beginning balances being entered to the accounts. Beginning balances should be entered in the earliest period for which you have activity.

3. If you're using batch posting rather than real-time posting, Peachtree Accounting unposts all journal entries from the current period forward so that the journal entries are available for editing. For example, after Payroll posts to the General Ledger, the batch is entered but unposted in the General Ledger.

4. Select an account from the list. The account ID, description, and account type appear in the fields. The original balance is always zero for new accounts.

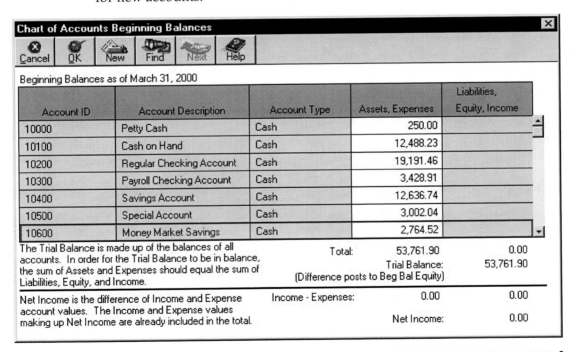

FIGURE 4-14   Chart of Accounts Beginning Balances window

5. Enter the beginning balance or prior period adjustment amount in the Assets, Expenses field (if the amount is for an asset or expense), or in the Liabilities, Equity, Income field (if the amount is for a liability, equity, or income) and press ENTER. You will enter all amounts as positive numbers unless one of the following applies: you are making an entry on a contra account; you have a negative retained earnings account; or you are converting to Peachtree Accounting mid-year and you have already recorded dividends paid. The highlight moves down the list and the next account appears in the fields in the top half of the window, so you can enter a series of desired balances fairly easily.

You can't enter a beginning balance to an account if you've already posted a transaction to it. If you need to enter a beginning balance for an account that already has transactions posted—for example, if you are switching to Peachtree Accounting mid-year and don't have all the beginning balance information available—you can unpost the information through the System option on the Task menu, enter the beginning balances, then repost the journals when you're done. For more information on unposting and posting journals, see Chapter 13.

TIP: The Trial Balance display in the bottom-right corner of the window keeps a running total of the balance for the entries. If you are entering amounts from a written chart of accounts, you can use the Trial Balance display to check your work against running subtotals.

You should be aware that when you are entering beginning balances to the General Ledger, you must be particularly careful that the amount entered here matches the amount of your beginning balance in each of the other ledgers. The beginning balance feature for Accounts Receivable, Accounts Payable, Payroll (with accrued tax liability), and Inventory are *not* posted to the General Ledger as later batches of transactions are. Details from these ledgers are not maintained in the General Ledger, only the summary amounts. Take the time to proof these numbers as you enter each ledger's beginning balance. Run reports for your opening transactions at each stage so there is a complete set of transitional records. This is especially important if you are installing your Peachtree Accounting software in the middle of your fiscal year.

CAUTION: Although you can add a new account while you are entering beginning balances by clicking New on the toolbar, this has been known to cause an "out of balance" condition in the software that is not correctable at this time. It is better, therefore, to enter new accounts normally through the Maintain Chart of Accounts window's General folder.

If you are entering many beginning balances or prior period adjustments at once, you should take precautions to avoid errors. You may want to break up your inputs into small balanced groups to make it easier to track down entry errors. Alternately, you can create subtotals in your list of entries and check the Trial Balance against the subtotals. (Using the Working Trial Balance report will make it easy to verify your totals before you enter them.) If you have entered all your account data and the Net Balance is not zero, you will need to check your entries to make sure they are correct. You should also make sure that the source data you entered is actually in balance.

When you have completed entering your amounts and the Trial Balance is zero, click OK. (If you want to cancel the changes you've made without saving them, click Cancel.) Peachtree Accounting posts the information to the General Journal and returns you to the Setup Checklist window. Peachtree then asks you if you want to mark the task as completed on the checklist. If you choose Yes, Peachtree puts a check mark next to the item. Click Exit to close the Setup Checklist. (If you are entering beginning balances and prior period adjustments from the Maintain Chart of Accounts window by clicking Beginning Balances, clicking OK returns you to the Maintain Chart of Accounts window rather than to the Setup Checklist.)

If you click OK while the Trial Balance is not zero, you will see a warning message telling you that Peachtree Accounting will create or update the Beginning Balance Equity account with the out-of-balance amount. Since you cannot enter a beginning balance for the Beginning Balance Equity account, it does not appear on the Beginning Balances window, although this account does show up on reports and in the list of accounts.

It is good accounting practice to find out why the accounts are out of balance *before* you post the beginning balances. The most common reasons are an entry error (such as transposed numbers in an amount) or missing an entry entirely. To search for an amount, select Cancel when the warning message appears and scroll through the accounts on the Beginning Balances window.

Although it is not recommended that you do so, if you want to proceed without identifying where the accounts are out of balance, you can select OK at the warning message and post the beginning balances. Because a balancing amount has been posted to the Beginning Balance Equity account (with an account type of Equity—Doesn't Close), your company's financial reports will balance and you will be able to enter transactions and set up other information. However, if you post transactions and then find the error, you will need to make an adjusting entry in the Prior Period Adjustments window rather than in the Beginning Balances window. (Peachtree Accounting checks for posted transactions and automatically displays the appropriate window for you.) When you have found the balance errors and zeroed the Beginning Balance Equity account, you should delete this account.

C A U T I O N : Reversing entries to clear the books of misposted amounts can form the basis of an audit query later on, particularly if you are converting to Peachtree Accounting from another accounting system. Moreover, you will not be able to trust the financial statements of your company until the error is identified and eliminated because you won't know if the out-of-balance amount is masking a single error or several errors. It is always better to start in balance, even if it takes you longer in the setup process.

6. You can now check your entries for individual accounts by selecting Chart of Accounts from the Maintain menu to display the Maintain Chart of Accounts window. The beginning balances and prior period adjustments you entered are now displayed in the Period History section of the window. Figure 4-15 shows an example of the Period History section with financial data displayed for the Cash on Hand account.

The Debits and Credits fields show the total debits and credits for the period. The Period Activity field is the total of the debits and credits fields. The Running Balance field is the total of the previous running balance and the current period activity. As you enter transactions in this account, the information displayed in the Period History section will change. (Peachtree Accounting records this as the end-of-month balance regardless of your system date.)

Using the General Journal

The General Journal is the summary of all the other parts of the accounting system: Accounts Receivable, Accounts Payable, Payroll, Inventory, and so on. The beginning balances in the General Journal are the opening amounts for each account you just entered. You will add to these later by processing transactions in the normal course of business.

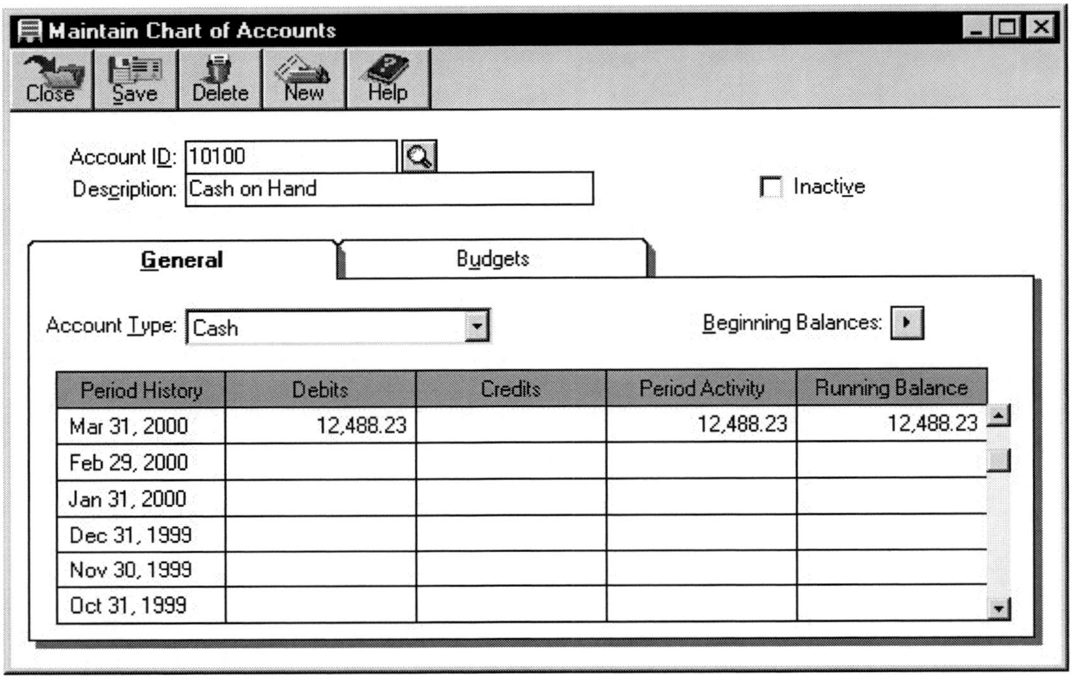

FIGURE 4-15 Maintain Chart of Accounts window with sample Period History data

The General Journal is used to post one-time transactions. These could include bank service charges, cash transfers between accounts—such as checking to savings or checking to checking—and paying down a line of credit or loans. The General Journal is the only journal you must keep in balance yourself. All other parts of the accounting system are set up to post to the General Ledger in an "in-balance" condition.

The General Journal is also used to reclassify a transaction or part of a transaction from one account to another. For example, a payment is made on an invoice through Accounts Receivable. After posting is complete, you discover that an overpayment of shipping charges and an underpayment of taxes was applied to the open invoice. A General Journal entry would correct the original entry by applying a debit to taxes and a credit to shipping. You can also use General Journal entries to reclassify misposted job-cost entries by debiting and crediting the same account, but debiting one job and crediting another.

To make entries to the General Journal, select General Journal Entry from the Tasks menu. The General Journal Entry window appears (shown in Figure 4-16 with a sample transaction being entered).

The toolbar at the top of the window has some buttons you haven't seen before, described in Table 4-3.

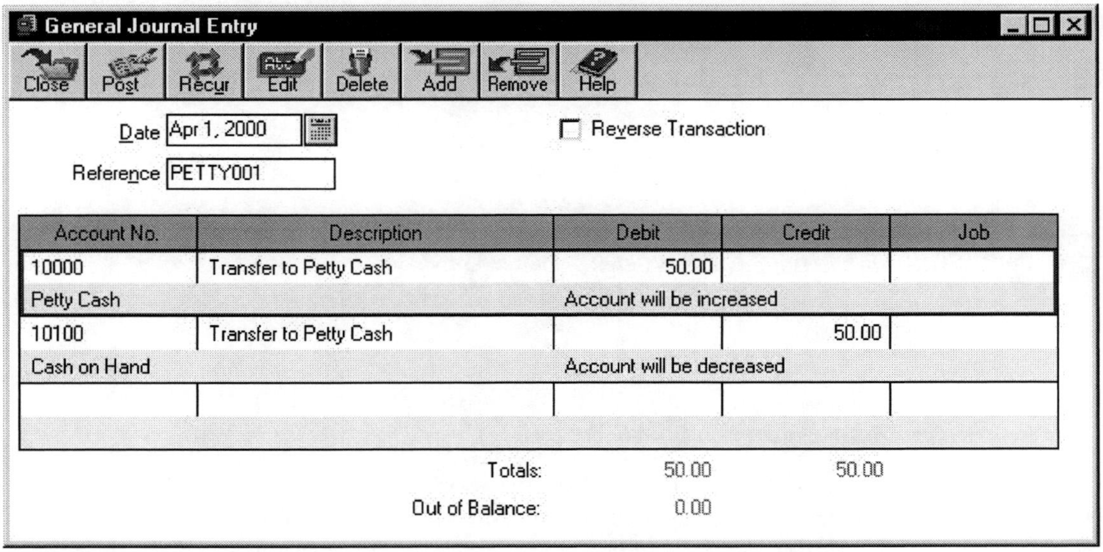

FIGURE 4-16 General Journal Entry window

BUTTON	NAME	DESCRIPTION
Close	Close	Close the window without running the report.
Post	Post	Post (save) the information in the fields.
Recur	Recur	Create a recurring journal entry.
Edit	Edit	Edit the General Journal entry.
Delete	Delete	Delete the current journal entry.
Add	Add	Add a journal entry.
Remove	Remove	Remove a journal entry.
Help	Help	Display the online help for the General Journal Entry window.

TABLE 4-3   Toolbar Buttons in the General Journal Entry Window

To make a journal entry, fill in the information for the entry (detailed instructions follow) and click Post.

Date   Enter the actual date of the transaction in this field. (The default entry is the first day of the current account period if the system date is not in the current period; otherwise, it is the system date.) The transaction date must fall within the current period or a future period. Click Calendar or right-click in this field to display the Peachtree Accounting date-selection calendar.

Reference   Enter up to 20 alphanumeric characters for a unique reference number. This field is optional, but will help you track General Journal entries. If you enter a number, Peachtree Accounting adds 1 to the number each time you make an entry in the General Journal window during this session.

Reverse Transaction   Check this box to tell Peachtree Accounting to make a reversing transaction. A reversing transaction reverses the debits and credits of an adjusting entry, but keeps the accounts and the amounts the same. You use a reversing transaction to reverse an accrual entry. (For more information, see Chapter 1.)

Account No.   Enter the account ID for the first General Ledger account you want to debit or credit. You can click the magnifying glass or right-click in the field for a drop-down list of General Ledger accounts. Enter a + or double-click in the field to add a new General Ledger account.

Description   Enter up to 160 characters describing the transaction.

Debit   Enter an amount for the transaction debit.

Credit   Enter an amount for the transaction credit.

Job   Enter a job ID. You can click the folder or right-click in the field for a drop-down list of jobs. (When you are first setting up Peachtree Accounting for your business, you will not have any jobs set up. For more information on setting up items, see Chapter 9.)

Totals   Peachtree Accounting displays the total debits and credits. These fields are display-only.

Out of Balance   Peachtree Accounting displays the balance for the entry. This must be zero before you can save or post the entry.

Entering Recurring General Journal Entries

Recurring General Journal entries are entries that Peachtree Accounting posts to the General Journal on a regular basis. If you have regular General Journal transactions, such as transferring money from savings to petty cash at the start of every month, you can set up an automatic transaction.

When you set up a recurring General Journal entry, you tell Peachtree Accounting to perform a transaction with fixed amounts weekly, biweekly, monthly, per period, quarterly, or annually. At the predetermined time, Peachtree Accounting automatically generates these transactions. Setting up automatic transactions can free you from a considerable amount of repetitious work. The following example shows how to set up an automatic transaction for a postage expense every month.

Start by entering a General Journal entry in the General Journal Entry window, as shown in the preceding section. Instead of clicking Save or Post to enter the information, click Recur on the toolbar. The Create Recurring Journal Entries window appears (as shown in Figure 4-17).

You can set up the journal entry to recur up to 99 times, or as many times as there are open periods (but not past the end of the next year). Journal entries can recur weekly, biweekly, monthly, per period, quarterly, or annually. If you are creating recurring entries on a weekly or biweekly basis, make a note on a calendar when they'll have to be reset for the rest of the year.

Create Recurring Journal Entries ⊠

Ok	You can save this journal entry in this AND future accounting periods. Do this by entering the number of times (periods) to save this entry, the first one being the current period.
Cancel	
Help	Number of Times [1] When to Recur

When to Recur

○ Weekly
○ Bi-Weekly
● Monthly
○ Per Period
○ Quarterly
○ Yearly

FIGURE 4-17 Create Recurring Journal Entries window

Editing General Journal Entries

To edit a General Journal entry, you need to select the one you want to change. Start by clicking Edit Records on the toolbar. The Select General Journal Entry window appears, as shown in Figure 4-18.

The Select General Journal Entry window shows the General Journal entries. You can use the Sort By drop-down list to sort records by date, reference, or account ID. The period and date, reference number (if any), amount, account IDs, and General Journal entry appear in the window.

 T I P : You can edit real-time transactions even if they've already been posted. Peachtree Accounting edits the General Ledger and other ledgers the journal entry may affect.

Double-click the General Journal entry you want to edit. Peachtree Accounting displays the information in the General Journal Entry window. Make the changes to the General Journal entry. When you are satisfied, click Post on the toolbar to post your changes.

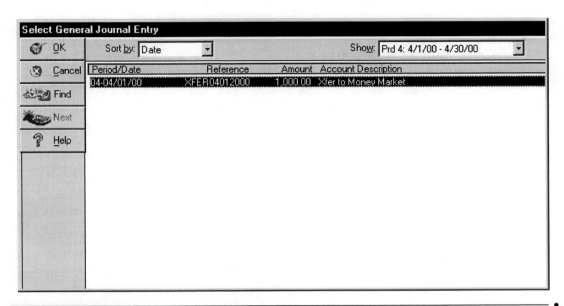

FIGURE 4-18   Select General Journal Entry window

If you're editing a recurring entry, a note will appear below the line item area on the General Journal Entry window. This note identifies the entry as a recurring entry and shows the number of remaining additional entries. Peachtree Accounting will also ask if you want to change all remaining entries.

*** The selected entry is a recurring entry.
There are 5 additional entries. ***

Deleting General Journal Entries

You can delete General Journal entries, even ones you've posted. To delete a General Journal entry, start by clicking Edit in the General Journal Entry window (shown earlier in Figure 4-16) to display the Select General Journal Entry window. Double-click the General Journal entry you want to delete. Peachtree Accounting displays the information in the General Journal Entry window. Click Delete on the toolbar. Peachtree Accounting asks if you are sure you want to delete the record. Click OK to delete the record.

Entering Memorized General Journal Entry Transactions

Peachtree Complete Accounting for Windows Release 7.0 has a feature called memorized transactions. This feature lets you create standard transactions that you use frequently, such as depreciation transactions, payments to vendors, standard orders from regular customers, and so on. The information in a memorized transaction can then be called up and used without having to reenter the standard information, rather like a template for entries. You can enter memorized transactions for General Journal entries, quotes, sales invoices, purchase orders, and payments.

Memorized transactions have many advantages over recurring transactions. For one thing, the memorized transactions let you set up the accounts and general information for a transaction without having to be sure of the exact amounts to be posted. Memorized transactions do not occur automatically and are therefore good for transactions that occur irregularly or even sporadically. By contrast, recurring transactions are set up to post automatically for specific amounts at specific times.

Creating a General Journal Memorized Transaction

To create a General Journal memorized transaction, select Memorized Transactions from the Maintain menu, then select General Journal Entries from the submenu. The Maintain Memorized General Journal Entries window appears (shown in Figure 4-19 with a sample memorized transaction entered).

The Maintain Memorized General Journal Entries window contains one new button, the Use button, shown here:

Clicking the Use button tells Peachtree to use the information in the Maintain Memorized General Journal Entries window to create an entry in the General Journal Entry window.

Enter information in the fields of the Maintain Memorized General Journal Entries window as follows:

Transaction ID   Enter a transaction ID of up to 20 alphanumeric characters (with the exception of the *, ?, or + character). This ID is used to identify the memorized transaction. You can click the magnifying glass or right-click in the field for a drop-down list of existing transaction IDs.

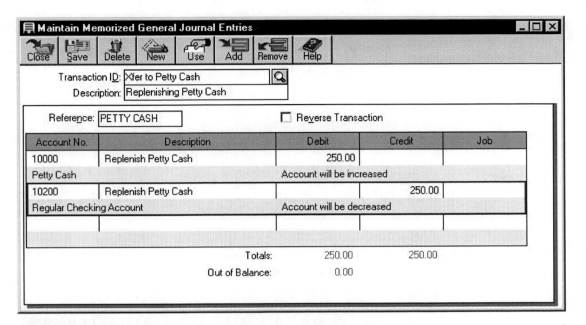

FIGURE 4-19 Maintain Memorized General Journal Entries window

Description   Enter a transaction description of up to 30 alphanumeric characters. Peachtree Accounting displays this description in the Memorized Transaction list box.

Reference   Enter a transaction reference of up to 20 alphanumeric characters. This field is optional, but will help you track General Journal entries. If you enter a number, Peachtree Accounting adds 1 to the number each time you make an entry in the General Journal window during this session. This reference can be a partial reference (such as CASHXFER) that you would then supplement with the date or other information when you use the memorized transaction.

Reverse Transaction   Check this box to tell Peachtree Accounting to make a reversing transaction. A reversing transaction reverses the debits and credits of an adjusting entry, but keeps the accounts and the amounts the same. You use a reversing transaction to reverse an accrual entry. (For more information, see Chapter 1.)

Account No.   Enter the account ID for the first General Ledger account you want to debit or credit. You can click the magnifying glass or right-click in the field for a drop-down list of General Ledger accounts. Enter a + or double-click in the field to add a new General Ledger account.

Description   Enter up to 160 characters describing the transaction.

Debit   Enter an amount for the transaction debit.

Credit   Enter an amount for the transaction credit.

Job   Enter a job ID. You can click the folder or right-click in the field for a drop-down list of jobs.

Totals   Peachtree Accounting displays the total debits and credits. These fields are display-only.

Out of Balance   Peachtree Accounting displays the balance for the entry. This must be zero before you can save or post the entry.

The information you enter here will be the same as you would enter for a regular General Journal entry except that you enter a transaction ID instead of a date. When you are satisfied with your entries, click Save. Saving a memorized transaction does not post the information to any of the journals or to the General Ledger; it merely saves the memorized transaction in Peachtree Accounting for future use.

Saving a Memorized Transaction While Entering a General Journal Entry

You may be able to identify some of the transactions you want to set up as memorized transactions when you're first setting up your company on Peachtree Accounting, but you're also going to have a number of additional memorized transactions. Sometimes, you'll be entering a transaction in the General Journal Entry window and will realize that this transaction is something you will want to use again. You can save a General Journal entry as a memorized transaction by entering the transaction information in the General Journal Entry window, then selecting the Save As Memorized Transaction option from the Edit menu. Peachtree Complete Accounting opens the Maintain Memorized General Journal Entries window and transfers all the relevant information from the General Journal Entry window to the Maintain Memorized General Journal Entries window. Make any entries or changes to the information on the Maintain Memorized General Journal Entries window and save the transaction, then close the Maintain Memorized General Journal Entries window and complete the transaction on the General Journal Entry window.

Using a Memorized General Journal Transaction

You can use a memorized General Journal transaction any time you want to enter a General Journal entry. Start by opening the General Journal Entry window as described earlier, then select the Save As Memorized Transaction option from the Edit menu. Peachtree Complete Accounting displays the memorized transactions in the Select Memorized Transaction window. The Select Memorized Transaction window is identical to the Select General Journal Entry window, except that there isn't a Status or a Show field. You can sort by the Transaction ID or the description.

When you select a memorized transaction from the window, Peachtree Complete Accounting displays the information in the General Journal Entry window. Enter the appropriate date for the transaction and make any changes to the entry's information. When you are satisfied with your entries, click Post. Peachtree Complete Accounting posts the information.

If you prefer, you can also select a memorized transaction by going to the Maintain Memorized General Journal Entries window as described earlier. Click the magnifying glass or right-click in the Transaction ID field for a drop-down list of existing transaction IDs. The transaction description appears to the right of the Transaction ID in the list. Select a transaction ID from the list. Peachtree Complete Accounting displays the transaction information in the window. Take a moment to review the details to make sure this is the right transaction. When you are satisfied, click Use. The information appears in the General Journal Entry window as before.

Deleting a Memorized General Journal Transaction

You can delete a memorized General Journal transaction by displaying the transaction in the Maintain Memorized General Journal Entries window, then clicking Delete. Peachtree Complete Accounting asks if you're sure you want to delete the record. Click OK to delete the record.

Printing Other General Ledger Reports

You've already seen how to print the Chart of Accounts report and the Working Trial Balance. Peachtree Accounting has three additional General Ledger reports: the General Ledger Trial Balance report, the General Journal report, and the General Ledger report.

General Ledger Trial Balance Report

The trial balance is one of the most commonly used accounting statements. You use it primarily to check that accounts are in balance. Because Peachtree Accounting automatically checks for out-of-balance conditions, trial balances are not usually necessary. However, they do provide a clear format for viewing account detail.

The General Ledger Trial Balance report lists the current balance for the General Ledger accounts. Figure 4-20 shows a portion of the General Ledger Trial Balance report after entering beginning balances.

General Journal Report

The General Journal report lists the transactions in the General Journal. Figure 4-21 shows a portion of the General Journal report after entering beginning balances. There is no reference number or transaction description for the journal entries on the report in this figure because these are beginning balances, but there are beginning balance transaction descriptions on the General Ledger report, which is described next.

Big Business, Inc.
General Ledger Trial Balance
As of Apr 30, 2000
Filter Criteria includes: Report order is by ID. Report is printed in Detail Format.

Account ID	Account Description	Debit Amt	Credit Amt
10000	Petty Cash	295.00	
10100	Cash on Hand	12,678.23	
10200	Regular Checking Account	20,156.46	
10300	Payroll Checking Account	3,428.91	
10400	Savings Account	12,536.74	
10500	Special Account	2,902.04	
10600	Investments-Money Marke	1,764.52	

FIGURE 4-20   General Ledger Trial Balance report

Putting It to Work

One way you can use memorized General Journal transactions is to make General Journal entries for amortized amounts. For example, you may pay your building insurance quarterly, semi-annually, or even annually, but you want to amortize the cost of the insurance on a monthly basis accrued daily. The cost of the insurance would vary from period to period depending on the number of days in the month.

You might also want to post interest expenses on a variable-rate loan. The memorized transaction would let you make changes to the amount for interest in the previous month.

Finally, there are many payroll taxes and expenses that are paid quarterly, and for your accounting purposes you will want to accrue these on a monthly or weekly basis. You would set up a memorized transaction for the basic allocations and accounts and then make adjustments based on the payroll totals as necessary.

Big Business, Inc.
General Journal
For the Period From Apr 1, 2000 to Apr 30, 2000

Filter Criteria includes: Report order is by Date. Report is printed with Accounts having Zero Amounts and with Truncated Transaction Descriptions and in Detail Format.

Date	Account ID	Reference	Trans Description	Debit Amt	Credit Amt
4/1/00	10000			100.00	
	10200				100.00
4/1/00	10100	XFER04012000	Xfer to Money Market		1,000.00
	10600		Xfer to Money Market	1,000.00	
4/8/00	10000			100.00	
	10200				100.00
4/15/00	10000			100.00	
	10200				100.00
		Total		**1,300.00**	**1,300.00**

FIGURE 4-21 General Journal report

One of Peachtree Accounting's convenient features is that you can usually double-click a line item of a report displayed on the screen and see the corresponding detail displayed in the appropriate window. (The cursor changes to a magnifying glass to signify when you are able to do this on a report.) This is known as "drilling down." For example, double-clicking on a line of the General Journal report shown in Figure 4-21 would bring up the General Journal window with the information. However, you can't drill down on a beginning balance entry as there is no additional information.

General Ledger Report

The General Ledger report shows you the General Ledger activity for each account for the selected period or periods. The General Ledger report gives the detailed information for the transactions summarized on the General Journal report. Figure 4-22 shows a portion of the General Ledger report after entering beginning balances.

For audit purposes, it's a good idea to print a General Ledger report after you have entered your beginning balances but before *any other* transactions are

Big Business, Inc.
General Ledger
For the Period From Apr 1, 2000 to Apr 30, 2000
Filter Criteria includes: Report order is by ID. Report is printed in Detail Format.

Account ID Account Description	Date Reference	Jrnl	Trans Description	Debit Amt	Credit Amt	Balance
10100 Cash on Hand	4/1/00		Beginning Balance			12,488.23
	4/1/00 XFER0401	GENJ	Xfer to Money Market		1,000.00	
			Current Period Change		1,000.00	-1,000.00
	4/30/00		**Ending Balance**			**11,488.23**
10200 Regular Checking Accoun	4/1/00		Beginning Balance			19,191.46
	4/1/00	GENJ			100.00	

FIGURE 4-22 General Ledger report

posted. This report is the beginning document of your Peachtree Accounting
records. It ties your prior accounting system to your new accounting system.
Keeping a copy of this report is particularly important if you are starting
Peachtree Accounting in the middle of your fiscal year.

Entering Budget Amounts

Peachtree Accounting has a budget feature that lets you enter budget amounts
for income and expense accounts. You may not need to enter budget amounts
the first year you are using Peachtree Accounting until you've built up enough
financial history to make predictions for the next year. Although you don't need
to set up budgeting for your company, you can use budgeting to track history
and measure your company's performance against expectations.

Enter budget amounts by first selecting the Chart of Accounts item on the
Setup Checklist. The Maintain Chart of Accounts window appears, as shown
earlier in Figure 4-7. Now click the Budgets tab to display the budget fields.
Figure 4-23 shows the Budgets fields of the Maintain Chart of Accounts window
with sample budget amounts for this year's and next year's payroll wages.

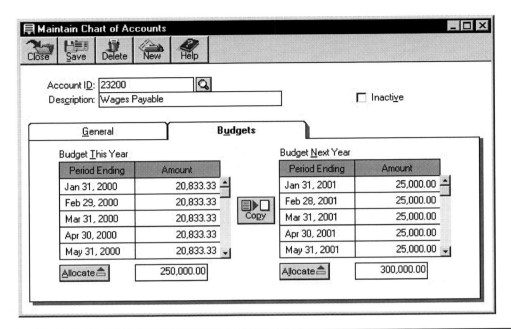

FIGURE 4-23 Maintain Chart of Accounts window with Budget fields displayed

To enter a budget amount for an account, enter an account ID in the Account ID field or select an account from the drop-down list. You can enter budget amounts individually in the period fields. This method of entering budget amounts is recommended if you have different amounts for each period.

If you have a yearly budget that you want to distribute evenly among the accounting periods, enter a single amount in the field to the right of the Allocate button and then click Allocate. Peachtree Accounting distributes the amount evenly between the periods.

Peachtree Accounting offers another budgeting shortcut. Once you have entered the budget amounts for the current year, click Copy to copy the budget amounts to the next year's fields. You can then adjust the fields manually if you want. When you are done entering budget information, click Save.

You can print a report showing the actual income compared to the budgeted income. Select Financial Statements from the Reports menu, then select the <Predefined> Income/Budgets report from the Report List.

Using Audit Trails

One of the new features of Peachtree Complete Accounting is the ability to audit user activity using audit trails. When you are using audit trails, Peachtree Complete Accounting tracks each action made by a user in a log file. You can print this log file whenever you like. Audit trail reports are useful for tracking and identifying:

- Transaction information for audit reports
- Entry errors
- User performance
- Possible security breaches

In general, the audit trails feature gives you and the accounting system an additional level of system and transaction tracking that will increase user accountability and make it simpler to identify errors and problems.

To start tracking user activity, check the Use Audit Trail box located in the Maintain Company Information window. When you are satisfied with your entries on this window, click OK.

If you are tracking user activity for more than a single user, you are strongly encouraged to set up user IDs as described in Chapter 3. This feature will provide greater security by tracking activity for individual user accounts as well as identify process or entry errors that may have occurred when two users entered conflicting or overlapping transactions.

Once you have started logging user activity, you can run an Audit Trail report at any time to list the user transactions that have occurred for a period. To print the Audit Trail report, start by selecting the Company option from the Reports menu. The Select a Report window (shown earlier in Figure 4-2 with General Ledger information) appears with the Audit Trail Report selected. Click Screen to display the Filter folder of the Options window. You can select specific transactions or dates for this report (the default is for all information to be printed for the current date). Figure 4-24 shows a sample Audit Trail report.

Big Business, Inc.
Audit Trail Report
For the Period From Nov 21, 1999 to Nov 21, 1999

Filter Criteria includes: 1) All Actions.

Date	Time	User ID	Action	Window Name	Transaction ID	Transaction Ref	Amount
11/21/99	6:05 PM	3	Change	Maintain Company Informatio	bigbusin	Big Business, Inc.	
11/21/99	6:09 PM	3	Change	Maintain Company Informatio	bigbusin	Big Business, Inc.	
11/21/99	6:10 PM	3	Add	Maintain Vendors	WAREV		
11/21/99	6:10 PM	3	Add	Maintain Vendors	KING		
11/21/99	6:11 PM	3	Add	Maintain Vendors	SEATTLE		
11/21/99	6:11 PM	3	Add	Maintain Vendors	BLVU		
11/21/99	6:11 PM	3	Add	Maintain Vendors	KIRKLAND		
11/21/99	6:12 PM	3	Add	Maintain Sales Tax Authorities	STATE		
11/21/99	6:16 PM	3	Change	Maintain Company Informatio	bigbusin	Big Business, Inc.	
11/21/99	6:17 PM	3	Change	Maintain Vendors	WAREV		
11/21/99	6:17 PM	3	Change	Maintain Vendors	KING		
11/21/99	6:17 PM	3	Change	Maintain Vendors	SEATTLE		
11/21/99	6:17 PM	3	Change	Maintain Vendors	BLVU		
11/21/99	6:17 PM	3	Change	Maintain Vendors	KIRKLAND		
11/21/99	6:18 PM	3	Change	Maintain Sales Tax Authorities	STATE		
11/21/99	6:18 PM	3	Add	Maintain Sales Tax Authorities	COUNTY		
11/21/99	6:21 PM	3	Change	Maintain Company Informatio	bigbusin	Big Business, Inc.	

FIGURE 4-24 Audit Trail report

Summary

Congratulations! In this chapter, you have set up your company's General Ledger in Peachtree Accounting. You saw how to modify the chart of accounts (and enter new accounts), set General Ledger defaults, enter beginning account balances and budget amounts, add, modify, and delete entries in the General Journal, and print General Ledger reports. In the next chapter, you'll see how to set up Accounts Receivable. You'll learn how to set up sales tax codes, set up and maintain customer accounts, create customer invoices and credit memos, receive, distribute, and post Accounts Receivable transactions and miscellaneous payments, apply finance charges, and print Accounts Receivable reports, statements, and collection letters.

Accounts Receivable and Invoicing

In this chapter, you'll learn how to set up Accounts Receivable defaults; enter sales tax information and customer records; create sales orders, invoices, quotes, and credit memos; and post receipts. You'll also see how to apply finance charges, write off bad debts, and print Accounts Receivable reports.

In Chapter 4 you set up your company's General Ledger in Peachtree Accounting. You modified the chart of accounts, entered new accounts, set General Ledger defaults, printed General Ledger reports, and entered beginning account balances and budget amounts. At this point, the General Ledger is completely set up and you can start entering transactions. This chapter will look at one specific type of transaction: Accounts Receivable.

Accounts Receivable is simply the money owed to you by your customers. Each time you sell a product or service to a customer on credit, the amount the customer owes you is charged to the Accounts Receivable account in the General Ledger. Its primary purpose is to create and post *invoices*, detailed bills you send to your customers that describe the exact terms, quantities, and prices relating to a transaction.

You could also use the Accounts Receivable to produce all your customers' bills as statements. Statements are a summary of invoiced amounts over time. They are particularly useful for billing your customers for services and other charges that don't have a tangible product associated with them. Furthermore, some activities, such as writing off bad debts, can only be done through Accounts Receivable. This chapter will show you how to set up Accounts Receivable: adding customer, statement, and invoice defaults, entering customer records and beginning balances, and entering sales and receipts.

 N O T E : By this time, you've seen how to use Peachtree Accounting's drop-down lists. For simplicity, you can assume that any time you see a magnifying glass to the right of a field or an I-beam-and-question-mark in a field, you can click the magnifying glass or right-click in the field for a drop-down list. You can also enter a **+** or double-click in the field to add a new entry in the field through the appropriate entry screen.

Setting Up Accounts Receivable Defaults

Accounts Receivable requires that you set up a great deal of information before you enter actual transactions and invoices. The setup process will be much easier if you spend some extra time organizing your information. If you haven't done so already, you should set up the business and the General Ledger (see Chapters 2, 3, and 4). You use Accounts Receivable to post information about receivables to the General Ledger automatically.

Setting Up Customer Defaults

The first step in setting up Accounts Receivable is to set up your customer defaults. Customer defaults determine such things as standard payment terms for your company, account aging, custom fields (with which you can track specific customer information), finance charges, and payment methods.

You've seen how to select an option from the Setup Checklist in Chapters 3 and 4. If the Setup Checklist is not already displayed, select the Setup Checklist option from the Maintain menu. From the Setup Checklist, click the Customer Defaults item. (You can also display this window by selecting the Default Information option from the Maintain menu, then selecting the Customers option from the submenu.) The Customer Defaults window appears with the Payment Terms folder already selected (shown in Figure 5-1).

Customer defaults can be overridden for any one customer or a specific invoice. You can also change the defaults for all customers that use the standard terms and information.

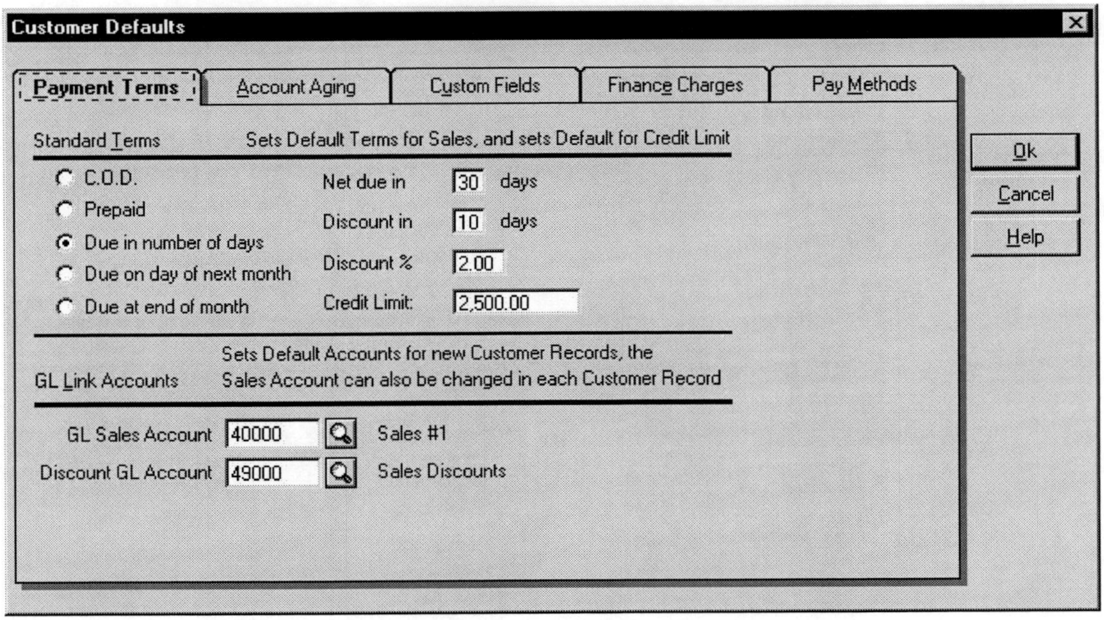

Customer Defaults

| Payment Terms | Account Aging | Custom Fields | Finance Charges | Pay Methods |

Standard Terms   Sets Default Terms for Sales, and sets Default for Credit Limit

- ○ C.O.D.
- ○ Prepaid
- ● Due in number of days
- ○ Due on day of next month
- ○ Due at end of month

Net due in   `30` days
Discount in   `10` days
Discount %   `2.00`
Credit Limit: `2,500.00`

[Ok] [Cancel] [Help]

Sets Default Accounts for new Customer Records, the
GL Link Accounts   Sales Account can also be changed in each Customer Record

GL Sales Account `40000` 🔍 Sales #1
Discount GL Account `49000` 🔍 Sales Discounts

FIGURE 5-1 Customer Defaults window showing the Payment Terms folder

Entering Default Payment Terms

Default payment terms include the payment terms such as C.O.D. or prepaid, when the balance is due, discount amounts (if any), the General Ledger link accounts, and the default credit limit.

Standard Terms   Select the default payment terms used by customers. You can select C.O.D., Prepaid, Due in number of days, Due on day of next month, or Due at end of month. If you select C.O.D. or Prepaid, you won't need to set up defaults for the other fields on the Payment Terms folder.

Net Due In ... Days   Enter the number of days after the date of the invoice before the invoice comes due. Typically, you will enter 0 (due immediately) or a number between 10 to 30 days.

Discount In ... Days   Enter the limit on discounts. This would typically be from 0 to 15 days.

Discount %   Enter the percentage allowed for the discount. Peachtree Accounting will calculate the default discount amount for you based on this percentage.

Credit Limit   Enter the default credit limit for your customers. For example, you may want everyone to have a nominal $500.00 credit limit. If you don't use or don't want to assign a credit limit, enter a large default, such as $10,000.00. This is a useful technique because whenever a customer exceeds the credit limit, Peachtree Accounting gives you a warning. If you entered a credit limit of $0.00, Peachtree Accounting would warn you every time you entered any activity for the customer.

GL Sales Account   Enter the default General Ledger sales account for the customer's sales activity. (You will normally want to use an Income account.)

Discount GL Account   Enter the General Ledger account used for Accounts Receivable discounts. For Big Business, Peachtree Accounting supplies a default entry (49000, Sales Discounts, with a Cost of Sales account type), but you can click the magnifying glass and view the entire chart of accounts.

Entering Account Aging Defaults

When you're satisfied with your entries, click the Account Aging tab to enter account aging defaults. The Account Aging folder appears, as shown in Figure 5-2.

The Account Aging folder lets you set the aging options for receivables.

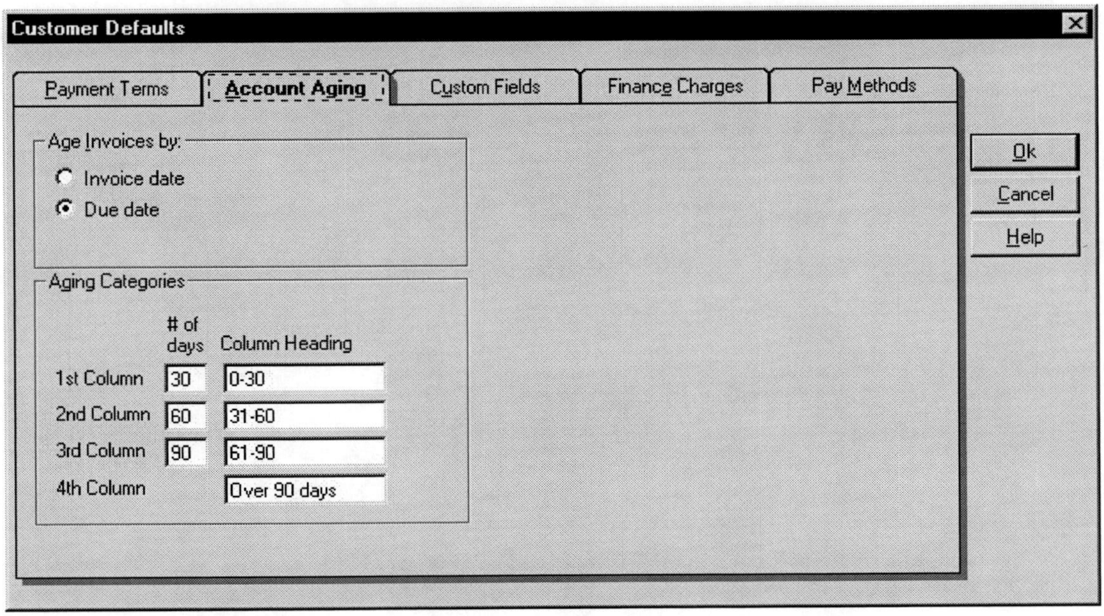

FIGURE 5-2   Customer Defaults window showing the Account Aging folder

Age Invoices By   Select either Invoice date or Due date for determining aging. You may want to set your customer aging by Invoice date, but your vendor aging (in Accounts Payable, discussed in Chapter 6) by due date. This will help get your receivables as quickly as possible and extend your payables to the limit.

Aging Categories   Set the number of days for each aging category and the appropriate heading for the column on the Aged Receivables report (discussed near the end of this chapter in the "Printing an Aged Receivables Report" section). Aging categories are typically set for 30, 60, and 90 days, but you can also enter other values; for example, entering 0 for the first field will show all current invoices. The fourth aging category should be set to whatever is older than the final aging category.

Entering Custom Field Defaults

When you're satisfied with your entries, click the Custom Fields tab to enter custom tracking information. The Custom Fields folder appears, as shown in Figure 5-3. (Sample data has been added to the fields.)

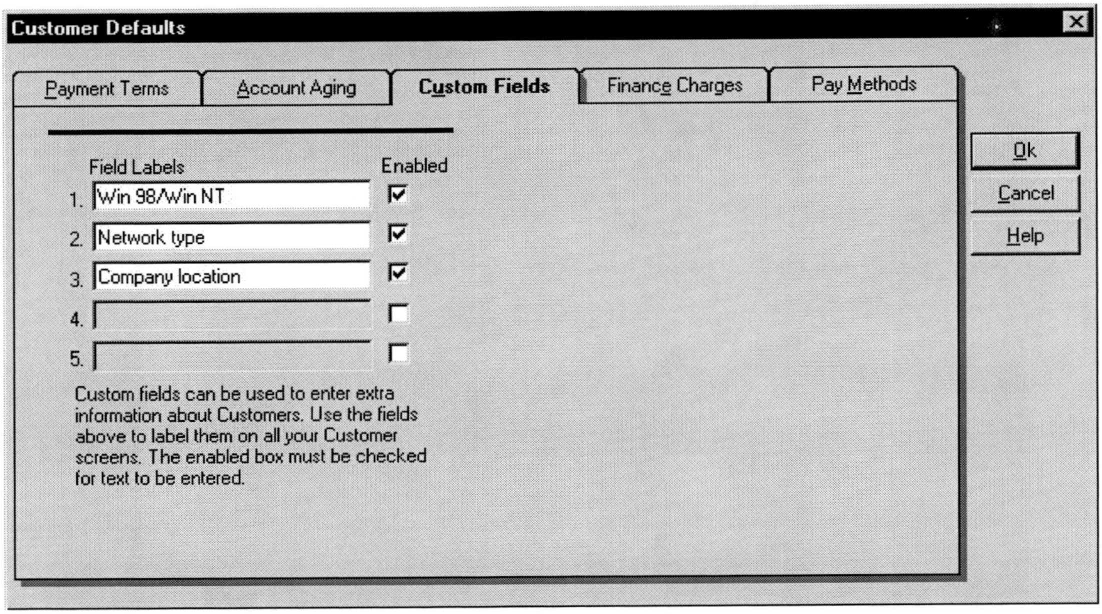

FIGURE 5-3 Customer Defaults window showing the Custom Fields folder

The Custom Fields folder lets you set default labels for tracking specific customer information that you enter in the Maintain Customers window for each customer. (The Maintain Customers window is discussed later in this chapter.) For example, you may want to set up custom fields for the number of sites a customer has, size of company, or anticipated annual sales.

Field Labels Enter as many as five headings or labels of up to 16 characters each in the fields here. The information in these fields is used for headings in the Maintain Customers window. For example, you might enter headings of "COMPANY SIZE" or "ANTICIPATED SALES."

Enabled Click the box to enable or disable the field label. If the Enabled box is not checked, the field label will not appear in the Maintain Customers window. (The Enabled box must be checked for you to enter text in the associated Field Labels field.)

Entering Finance Charge Defaults

When you're satisfied with your entries, click the Finance Charges tab to enter finance charge information. The Finance Charges folder appears, as shown in Figure 5-4.

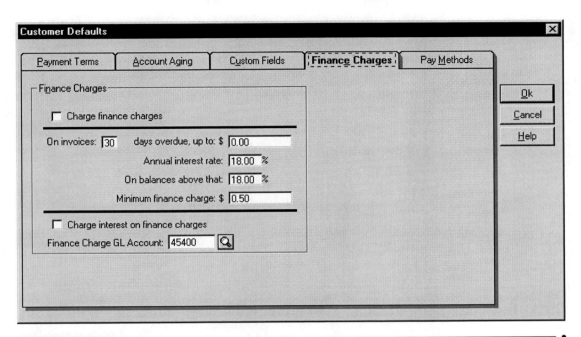

FIGURE 5-4 Customer Defaults window showing the Finance Charges folder

Finance charges are applied to overdue invoices on the terms you set up on this screen. You can override finance charges for a specific customer if you want.

Charge Finance Charges   Check the box to charge finance charges for customers. Even if this box is not checked, you can still apply finance charges for specific customers by changing the terms for that particular customer in the Maintain Customers/Prospects window.

On Invoices   Enter the number of days an invoice must be overdue before you start imposing finance charges. Be aware that even though finance charges will not be imposed until the invoice is overdue for the number of days you specify in this field, finance charges are calculated from the first day the invoice became overdue.

Days Overdue, Up To   Enter the maximum invoice amount for which the interest rate, set in the Annual Interest Rate field, will be charged. (Invoices over this amount will be charged the interest rate set in the On Balances Above That field.)

Annual Interest Rate   Enter the annual interest rate Peachtree Accounting will use for balances less than or equal to the amount in the Day Overdue, Up To field. You must enter an interest rate even if you are only going to charge a flat monthly fee for finance charges. In such cases, you should enter a very small percentage, such as .001%, so that Peachtree Accounting will apply the minimum finance charge.

On Balances Above That   Enter the annual interest rate Peachtree Accounting will use for balances greater than the amount in the Days Overdue, Up To field.

Minimum Finance Charge   Enter a dollar amount for the minimum finance charge. This amount will be applied to any late invoice.

Charge Interest on Finance Charges   Check this box to calculate interest on a compounded rather than a simple interest basis.

C A U T I O N : Some states have very strict rules regarding allowable interest rates and the use of compound versus simple interest. Check with your state agencies regarding these restrictions.

Finance Charge GL Account   Enter the General Ledger account used for Accounts Receivable finance charges. This must be an Income account type.

Entering Pay Methods Defaults

When you're satisfied with your entries, click the Pay Methods tab to enter finance charge information. The Pay Methods folder appears, as shown in Figure 5-5.

Enter the types of payment your company accepts. The types of payment method you set up here appear on the Sales/Invoicing and the Receipts windows.

Payment Methods   Enter up to ten payment methods in this field of up to 20 characters each. Make the payment methods descriptive, such as "Cash," "Check," "On account," or "VISA."

When you are satisfied with your entries, click OK. As usual, Peachtree Accounting will ask if you want to mark this task as completed on the Setup Checklist. If you choose Yes, Peachtree puts a check mark next to the item to indicate that you've completed this portion of the setup.

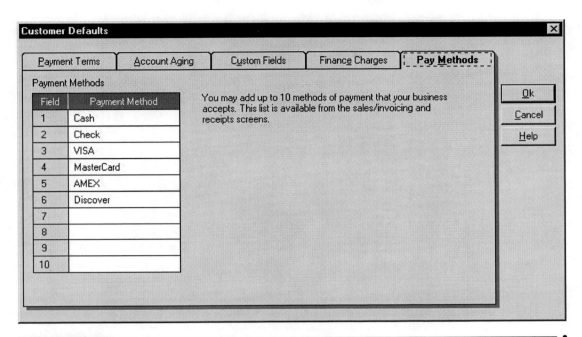

FIGURE 5-5 Customer Defaults window showing the Pay Methods folder

Setting Up Statement and Invoice Defaults

The next step in setting up Accounts Receivable is to set up the statement and invoice defaults. These defaults determine how statements and invoices are printed and when dunning messages are triggered.

From the Setup Checklist, click the Statement and Invoice Defaults item. (You can also display this window by selecting the Default Information option from the Maintain menu, then selecting the Statement/Invoices option from the submenu.) The Statement/Invoices Defaults window appears with the Print Options folder already selected (shown in Figure 5-6).

Entering Print Options

The Print Options folder lets you set the print options for the statements and invoices. You can change these defaults at any time, for instance to change the options for a given statement or invoice.

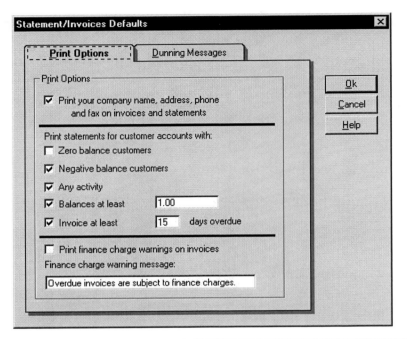

Print Your Company Name...   Check this box to print your company name, address, phone, and fax number on invoices and statements. This is useful if you're using plain invoice and statement forms rather than preprinted forms. Peachtree Accounting gets this information from the first Company Information window, shown in Chapter 3.

The next group of checkboxes tells Peachtree Accounting whether you want to print statements and invoices for certain groups of customers. If you don't check a box for a group, Peachtree Accounting will not print statements or invoices for that group. If you check several boxes, Peachtree Accounting will print statements or invoices for customers that meet any one of the criteria. For example, if you check Negative Balance Customers and Any Activity, Peachtree Accounting will print statements and invoices for customers with either a negative balance or any activity in the billing period.

Zero Balance Customers   Check this box to print statements for customers with a zero balance. Some customers use these statements to verify payment on their account.

Negative Balance Customers   Check this box to print statements for customers with a negative balance. This can also be used to track prepayment or credit adjustments.

Any Activity   Check this box to print statements for customers who have shown activity during the billing period.

Balances at Least   Check this box to print statements for customers with a minimum balance entered in the amount field next to the checkbox. The default is for this box to be checked with a one dollar (1.00) amount in the field. This default will cause Peachtree Accounting to print statements for all customers regardless of activity, except for those with a negative balance.

You can even enter a negative amount in this field if you want. This would print statements for all customers, including those with a negative balance of up to a certain amount. You could use this to force statements for every customer.

Invoice at Least   Check this box to print statements for customers with invoices overdue by a number of days (specified in the box to the right of the checkbox).

Print Finance Charge Warnings on Invoices   Check this box to print a finance charge warning on invoices. You enter the text for this warning in the Finance Charge Warning Message field at the bottom of the window.

Finance Charge Warning Message   Enter a warning message of up to 79 characters. Peachtree Accounting prints this message on invoices if you have checked the Print Finance Charge Warnings On Invoices field.

Entering Dunning Messages

When you're satisfied with your entries, click the Dunning Messages tab to enter defaults for dunning messages to customers. The Dunning Messages folder appears, as shown in Figure 5-7.

Invoices < ... Days Overdue   Enter a number of days in the field. If the invoice is overdue by fewer than or exactly the number of days in this field, Peachtree Accounting prints the associated message. You can enter a message of up to 47 characters in the message field. You probably want these periods to match the

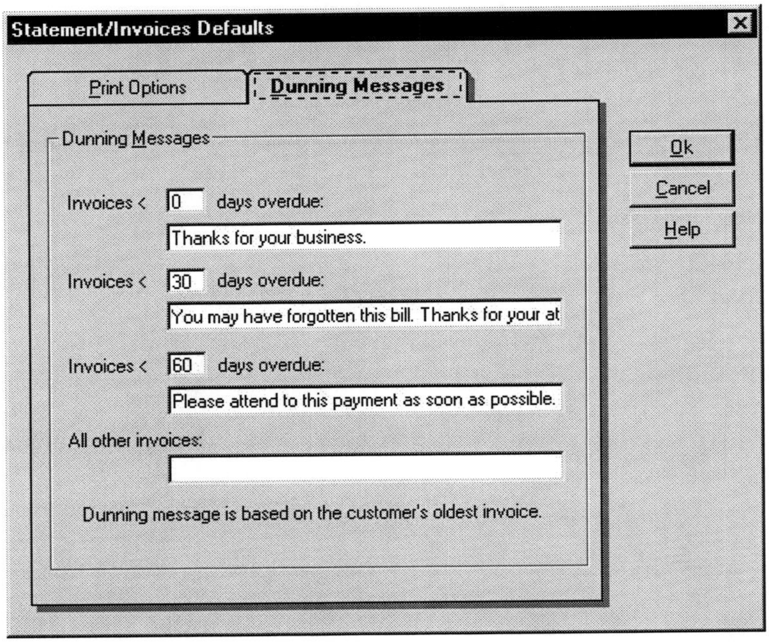

FIGURE 5-7 Statement/Invoices Defaults window showing the Dunning Messages folder

periods in the account aging defaults. (These are set in the Account Aging folder of the Customer Defaults window—see Figure 5-2.)

All Other Invoices   Enter a message of up to 47 characters in the field. If the invoice is overdue by more than the number in the previous Invoices < ... Days Overdue fields, Peachtree Accounting prints this message on the invoices.

When you are satisfied with your entries, click OK to return to the Setup Checklist as usual.

Entering Sales Tax Information

The next step in setting up Accounts Receivable involves setting up sales tax information.

Putting It to Work

Although the Dunning Messages folder is designed for printing dunning messages on a customer's invoice, you can also use it for goodwill and marketing messages. For example, you can let people know about an upcoming sale, a special price on a specific item, or an announcement about your business such as a name change or new Web site. Here's how to do this:

1. In the first Invoices < ... Days Overdue field, enter **0** (for 0 days overdue).

2. Enter an appropriate message in the corresponding message field, such as "Thank you for your business" or "Don't forget the upcoming 3-day sale!"

3. Print the invoices as usual.

The message will be printed on all current invoices. You may want to change the message after you print the invoices. If you find that you're not using the dunning message generally, or you want to dedicate the first slot to messages, you can add messages about sales and company information on a regular basis.

 C A U T I O N : The defaults for entering numbers apply to this field. If you have set the default decimal places to 2, entering 4 in this field would be treated as .04, resulting in a percentage of .04%. Add a decimal point after the percentage (4.) to make sure that you've specified a tax rate of 4%.

Peachtree Accounting has *sales tax authorities* and *sales tax* codes. Sales tax authorities are the taxing agencies who are able to levy taxes, such as federal, state, county, and city agencies. Sales tax codes are comprised of from one to five sales tax authorities. For example, you might have a 4.5 percent state sales tax, a 1 percent county tax, and a 0.75 percent city tax. Each of these separate taxes is entered as a sales tax authority. The sum of the taxes is a single sales tax code. The sales tax codes are assigned to the customers when you set up customer records. Unless you do business in a number of different locations, you'll probably only have one or two sales tax codes.

Entering Sales Tax Authorities

You need to set up sales tax authorities before you can set up sales tax codes. To set up sales tax information, first select the Sales Taxes option from the Maintain menu, then select Sales Tax Authorities from the submenu. The Maintain Sales Tax Authorities window appears, as shown in Figure 5-8.

ID   Enter an ID of up to eight characters for the tax authority. If you are doing business in only one or two locations and have only a few tax authorities, you can probably use IDs like STATE, COUNTY, and CITY.

Description   Enter a description of up to 30 characters, such as "State Dept. of Revenue - 4%" or "City Sales Tax."

Tax Rate   Enter the tax percentage.

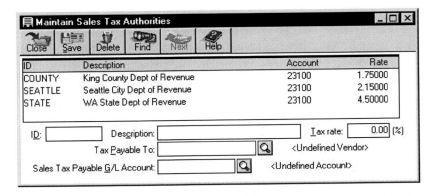

FIGURE 5-8   Maintain Sales Tax Authorities window

Tax Payable To   Enter the authority that receives the sales tax. This is frequently the state agency (which distributes the taxes to the local and regional authorities), but local and regional authorities in some states collect taxes directly.

As you enter tax authorities, keep in mind that Peachtree Accounting treats tax authorities as vendors—people and companies you pay money to—within Accounts Payable. If you are setting up Peachtree Accounting for the first time, you will need to enter the vendor IDs associated with the tax authorities. You can do this through Accounts Payable before you set up tax authorities and tax codes, or you can right-click in Tax Payable To and then click New at the bottom of the drop-down list to display the Maintain Vendors window. You can enter the vendor information through this window, save the vendor record, then continue entering the tax authority. For more information on adding vendors, see Chapter 6.

Sales Tax Payable G/L Account   Enter the General Ledger account number for sales tax. This will always be an Other Current Liabilities account type.

When you're satisfied with the information you've entered, click OK. You can continue entering sales tax authorities, clicking Save after each one. When you're done, click Close.

Entering Sales Tax Codes

Once you've set up sales tax authorities, you can set up sales tax codes. Select the Sales Tax option from the Maintain menu, then select Sales Tax Codes from the submenu. The Maintain Sales Tax Codes window appears, shown in Figure 5-9 with a sample tax code entered.

You set up a sales tax code by entering a code, a description, and from one to five tax authorities.

Sales Tax Code   Enter a sales tax code of up to eight characters. If you're going to have just a few sales codes, you don't need long names—1, 2, 3, or A, B, C may be adequate.

Description   Enter a description of up to 30 characters, such as "Seattle City Sales" or "Bellevue Retail Sales."

Tax Freight   Check this box if you are required to add sales tax to any freight charges your customers pay for shipping services.

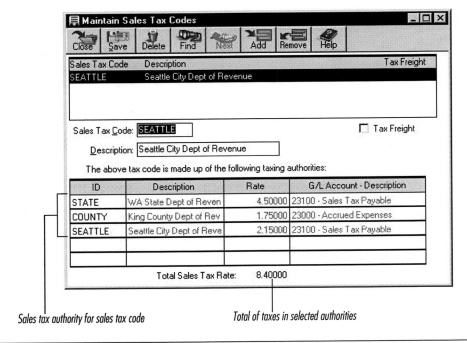

Sales tax authority for sales tax code   Total of taxes in selected authorities

FIGURE 5-9   Maintain Sales Tax Codes window

 N O T E : Check with your local sales tax authority, as this requirement varies from state to state.

ID   Enter the ID of the sales tax authority. You can right-click this field to select a sales tax authority ID from the list. Enter a + or double-click in the field to add a new sales tax authority.

Once you've selected an ID, Peachtree Accounting fills in the remaining fields in the lower portion of the window. As you add sales tax authorities, the total tax rate appears at the bottom of the window. Click Save to save the sales tax code.

If you are selling to both wholesale and retail customers, you may have cases where one customer transaction is taxable and the next is exempt. For this situation, you should establish a sales tax code that is exempt, but also has all the appropriate sales tax information. When you enter a transaction for a wholesale customer (usually untaxed), you can leave the sales tax code as exempt. When you enter a transaction for a retail customer, you can change the status to taxable. You can also set up the sales tax code in maintain customers as exempt or taxable.

When you have entered the sales tax codes, you can print a Sales Tax Codes report that lists the sales tax codes, the authorities that comprise them, and the tax rates, account IDs, and vendor IDs.

To print a Sales Tax Codes report, select the Accounts Receivable option from the Reports menu. Then select Sales Tax Codes from the Reports List window, select Options, then select the Type column to enter the desired range of sales tax IDs to print (or All to print all of them), and click OK.

Setting Up and Maintaining Customer Records

Once you've set up your Accounts Receivable defaults and the sales tax codes, you're ready to start entering customer records. Each customer will have a file of information. Once you have entered customer information, you can enter customer beginning balances.

Entering a Customer Record

There are four types of information you enter to set up customer records: general customer information, customer invoice defaults, custom fields, and customer history. You also need to enter a beginning balance for the customer if necessary. This section shows you how to enter all this information.

Entering General Customer Information

From the Setup Checklist, click the Customer Records item. (You can also display this window by selecting the Customers/Prospects option from the Maintain menu.) The Maintain Customers/Prospects window appears with the General folder already selected (shown in Figure 5-10).

Enter information for a customer as follows:

Customer ID   Enter the customer ID. Customer IDs can be up to 20 characters long, and they can contain any characters except the asterisk (*), question mark (?), or plus sign (+).

Although you have up to 20 characters to work with, you should keep your customer IDs simple, perhaps 6 or 8 characters long. A common way to create a customer ID is to begin the ID with the first few letters of the customer's name and follow that with a number. For example, if the customer's name was Oberon Computers, the customer ID would be something like OBE001. If there were another company with the same first three letters, such as Oberto & Calamari, their customer ID would be OBE002. Using the first few letters of

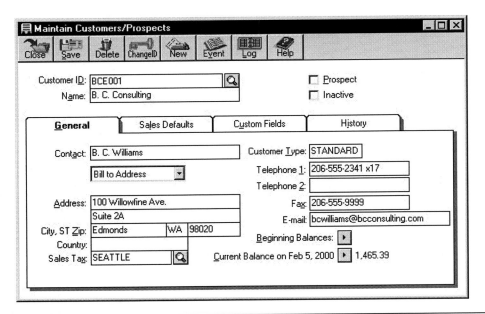

FIGURE 5-10 Maintain Customers/Prospects window showing the General folder

the customer's name gives you a reasonably intuitive way of looking up the customer in the file without requiring a lot of typing. As with General Ledger account IDs, customer IDs are case sensitive, so Peachtree Accounting treats the customer IDs OBE001 and obe001 differently. You may want to set a policy that all letters in customer IDs be entered as capital letters.

T I P : If you need to change a customer ID from the Maintain menu, select Customers/Prospects. To display a list of existing customers, type **?** in the Customer ID field, or select the Lookup button. Select the Change ID button on the window toolbar. Type the new ID you want to use instead of the current ID. Select OK to change the ID. If you change a customer ID, all current and past data records and transactions will be changed.

Name   Enter the customer's name. You can enter up to 30 characters in this field. Accounts Receivable will list the customer name as you have entered it on customer invoices and statements and on the Aged Receivables report and the Invoice Register. (Information on printing these reports appears at the end of this chapter in the "Printing Accounts Receivable Reports" section.)

Prospect   Check this box to identify this company as a prospect rather than an actual customer. Prospects are not included on customer reports, although you can print a specific Prospect List, described at the end of this chapter. Clearing the checkbox or creating an invoice will cause Peachtree Accounting to treat this record as a customer.

Inactive   Check this box to set the customer to inactive status. Although you can update the name and address information, Peachtree Accounting will warn you if you try to post a sale to an inactive customer. Peachtree Accounting will also display <Inactive Customer> in the drop-down lists of customers. Setting a customer to inactive is easier than deleting the customer. If the customer should become active again after you deleted them, you would have to reenter the customer information.

Contact   Enter the contact name for the customer. This field can be up to 20 characters. Accounts Receivable includes the customer contact name on the Customer List (described later in this chapter).

Customer Type   This is a custom field in which you can enter up to eight characters to identify the type of customer or prospect. This field allows you to group customers in order to print statements or a report for one class of customers. For example, you might set up a coding system to group customers by salesperson, geographic region, sales territory, type of business, type of purchase, or amount of money the customer is likely to spend in the future. For example, all customers or prospects stemming from a convention in Dallas might be typed as DALLAS95. This field is case sensitive.

Bill to/Ship to Addresses   Select one of the Bill To or Ship To options from the drop-down list. You can enter one Bill To and up to nine Ship To addresses for each customer. You select the address you want to use when entering sales and invoice information (you'll see how to do this later in this chapter).

Address   Enter the address (not including the city, state, and ZIP code). If you only have one line of address information, enter it on the first line and leave the second line blank. This information will be stored under the appropriate Bill To or Ship To address option selected in the previous field.

City, ST Zip   Enter the city, state, and ZIP code for this address. This information will be stored under the appropriate Bill To or Ship To address option selected in the previous field.

Country   Enter the country for this address. This information will be stored under the appropriate Bill To or Ship To address option selected in the previous field.

Sales Tax   Enter the sales tax code for this customer. (Sales tax codes are set up as part of the Accounts Receivable setup process. Refer to "Entering Sales Tax Information" earlier in this chapter for more information.) The default sales tax code you set up for a customer is automatically applied to customer sales.

Telephone 1   Enter the primary telephone number for the customer.

Telephone 2   Enter any other important telephone number for the customer.

Fax   Enter the fax number for the customer.

E-mail   Enter the e-mail address for the customer.

Beginning Balances   Click on the button to view the current customer's beginning balances. (You'll see how to enter a beginning balance for customers later.)

Entering Customer Invoice Defaults

After you have entered the general customer information, click the Sales Defaults tab. The Sales Defaults folder appears, as shown in Figure 5-11.

You set sales defaults for such things as the customer's sales rep, shipping options, pricing level, and terms of sale.

As you can see, the information in the top part of the Sales Defaults folder is carried forward from the information you entered in the General folder. You can work with this customer or select another one by clicking on the magnifying glass or right-clicking in the Customer ID field. You can also change the name, prospect, and inactive information for the customer from this folder.

Enter the invoice defaults as follows:

Sales Rep   Enter the ID of the sales representative for this customer, if any.

TIP: If you are setting up Peachtree Accounting for the first time, you may want to leave this field blank until you've entered the employee information. Alternately, you can right-click in Sales Rep and then click New Record at the bottom of the drop-down list to display the Maintain Employees/Sales Reps window. You can enter the sales rep information through this window, save the sales rep record, then continue entering the Invoice defaults. See Chapter 7 for information on setting up sales reps.

Information from General folder

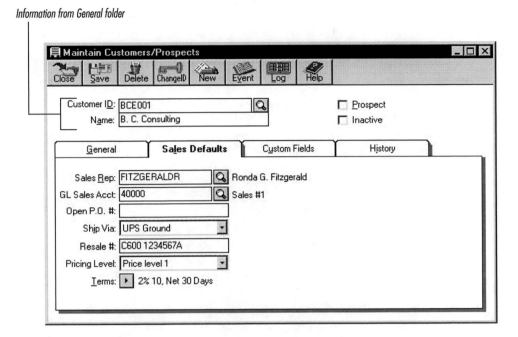

| FIGURE 5-11 | Maintain Customers/Prospects window showing the Sales Defaults folder |

GL Sales Acct Enter the default sales account for this customer (this will almost always be an Income account).

Open P.O. # Enter the open purchase order number for the customer. This default purchase order number will be a recurring "open purchase order" on the Quotes, Sales Orders, and Sales/Invoicing windows. You can override it during invoicing or leave this blank if there is no purchase order for this customer.

Ship Via Enter the default shipper for this customer. This information is the default used for this customer's invoices (set up in Inventory). Shipping methods are entered as part of the default information for Inventory. If you are setting up Peachtree Accounting for the first time here, you may want to enter shipping methods as necessary so you don't have to edit the customer records later. See Chapter 8 for more information.

Resale #   Enter the customer's resale or seller's permit number. Resale or seller's permit numbers are required in many states for a customer to legally buy wholesale and to avoid paying sales tax on items purchased for resale. This field is display-only. It does not affect the sales tax calculation. Set up and use an exempt tax authority and sales tax table for these customers. (For more information, see "Entering Sales Tax Information" earlier in this chapter.)

Pricing Level   Select the pricing level from one of five pricing levels. Pricing levels are usually based on customer purchasing patterns or group discounts, with price breaks for quantity or payment record. They are entered as part of the default information for Inventory. You can select pricing levels even though they have not been set up in Inventory yet. See Chapter 8 for more information.

Terms   The default value for payment terms (based on the customer defaults you entered earlier) appears to the right of the Terms button. Click Terms to select the terms. The Customer Terms window appears (shown in Figure 5-12).

The default for any customer is to use the standard terms. When the Customer Terms window first appears, the Use Standard Terms checkbox is checked and all other options are grayed out. You must clear the Use Standard Terms checkbox to select another option in the window.

Select the terms you want to use for this customer. The options and fields are the same as those you set for the customer defaults on the Payment Terms folder (shown earlier in Figure 5-1). If you want to use the customer defaults, leave the Use Standard Terms box checked. Click OK to accept the changes you've made, or Cancel to exit the screen without changing the payment options.

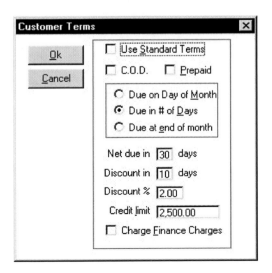

FIGURE 5-12   Customer Terms window

Entering Custom Fields

When you are satisfied with the invoice default information, click the Custom Fields tab. The Custom Fields folder appears, as shown in Figure 5-13.

As in the Statement/Invoices Defaults folder, the customer information in the top part of the folder is carried forward from the information you entered in the General folder. You can work with this customer, select another one, or change the name, prospect, and inactive information for the customer from this folder.

In the window shown in Figure 5-13, three of the custom fields are labeled with information entered through the Custom Fields folder of the Customer Defaults window (shown earlier in Figure 5-3).

Custom field information is primarily for ready reference and "tickler file" types of information. You can print custom field information on reports, but you cannot sort or select customers based on this information. For example, in the first custom field labeled "Win 98/Win NT" in Figure 5-13, you might enter "Win 98." You can print this information later on a report, but you couldn't select all customers with "Win 98" in that field.

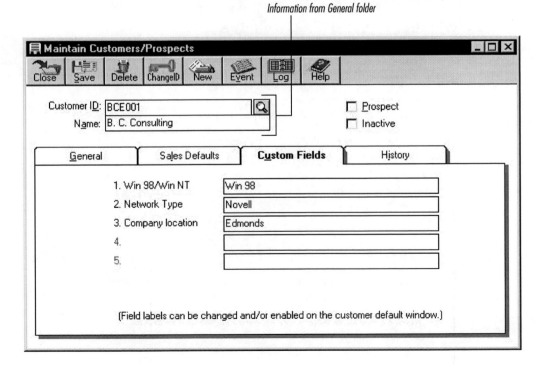

FIGURE 5-13   Maintain Customers/Prospects window showing the Custom Fields folder

Entering Customer History

When you are satisfied with the custom field information for this customer, click the History tab. Figure 5-14 shows the History folder.

As in the previous customer folders, the customer information in the top part of the folder is carried forward from the information you entered in the General folder. You can work with this customer, select another one, or change the name, prospect, and inactive information for the customer from this folder.

If you're using Peachtree Accounting for Windows, the History folder of the Maintain Customers/Prospects window is slightly different, as shown in Figure 5-15 with sample data entered.

When you're setting up the customer, you can enter information in this folder. Once you save this customer, Peachtree Accounting locks this folder so that it is read-only—you'll be able to see the customer's history on the folder,

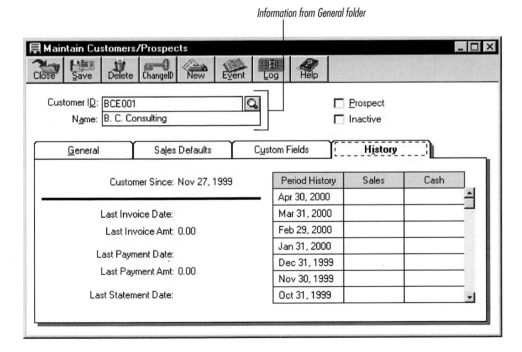

FIGURE 5-14 Maintain Customers/Prospects window showing the History folder

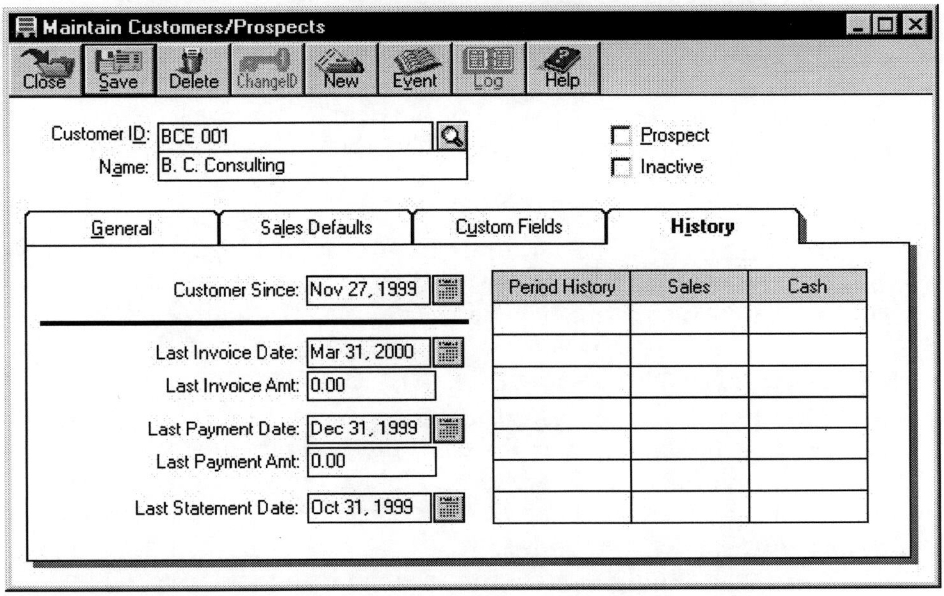

FIGURE 5-15 Maintain Customers/Prospects window showing the History folder in Peachtree Accounting for Windows

but you won't be able to make any changes to it. The Period History information is the summary of the customer activity during each period in the fiscal year.

Customer Since   Enter the date of the first sale to the customer.

Last Invoice Date   Enter the date of the customer's most recent invoice.

Last Invoice Amt   Enter the amount of the customer's most recent invoice.

Last Payment Date   Enter the date of the customer's most recent payment.

Last Payment Amt   Enter the amount of the customer's most recent payment.

Last Statement Date   Enter the date of the customer's most recent statement.

When you're satisfied with the customer history information, you can save the customer record. Click Save at the top of the window. Peachtree Accounting saves the customer information.

N O T E : If you are converting to a new version of Peachtree Accounting and you want your customers' historic information to be included as part of the conversion, you must be sure to enter the customer information before saving the customers' records. Once a customer record is saved, you can no longer make or change entries in the fields in this folder.

You can enter additional customer records by clicking New at the top of the window (this will clear the entries in all four folders of the Maintain Customers window) and then entering new information in each folder.

Entering Customer Beginning Balances

As the last step to setting up a customer, you enter the customer's beginning balance. You could have entered the customer's beginning balance when you entered the information on the General folder, but you would have had to save the record first, and this would have prevented you from entering information in the History folder.

To enter a beginning balance for a customer, go to the General folder in the Maintain Customer window and click Beginning Balances. The Customer Beginning Balances window appears with the Invoices folder displayed. Figure 5-16 shows this window with sample invoices already entered.

You enter beginning balances for the customer from the previous window. The customer ID and name appear on the folder tab. The beginning balance is based on the customer's outstanding invoices. (If this is a new customer with no prior activity, you won't need to enter a beginning balance.)

This information is *not* posted to the General Ledger, as later invoices will be during invoice processing. These balances should add up to what you posted as your beginning balance in the General Ledger.

Invoice Number   Enter the outstanding invoice number. (This is a required entry to enter beginning balances for a customer.)

Date   Enter the date of the outstanding invoice. Click the Calendar button or right-click in this field to display the Peachtree Accounting date-selection calendar.

Purchase Order Number   Enter the purchase order number. (If there is no purchase order number, leave this field blank.)

Amount   Enter the invoice amount.

Customer ID   Customer name

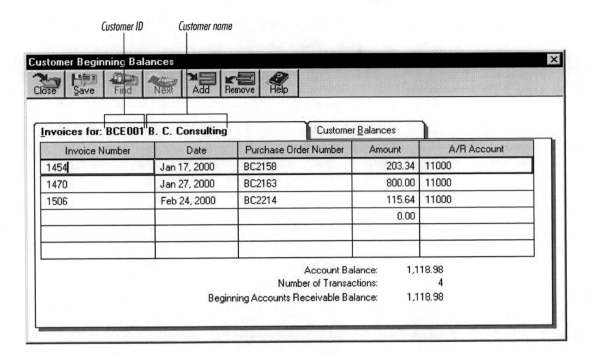

FIGURE 5-16 Customer Beginning Balances window showing the Invoices folder with sample invoices

A/R Account   If you are using accrual accounting, enter the Accounts Receivable account for this customer. You can right-click in the field for a drop-down list of accounts. If you are using cash accounting, you won't be able to enter an account number in this field. Instead, the field will be grayed out and will read "<cash basis>."

Press ENTER to move to the next invoice line. As you enter new invoices, the balance for the customer appears in the Beginning Accounts Receivable Balance total at the bottom of the window. When you're satisfied with the invoice information you've entered, click Save at the top of the window.

The Customer Balances folder shows you the current balances for customers and the total of the beginning accounts receivable balances. Figure 5-17 shows the Customer Balances folder in the Customer Beginning Balances window after entering the first three customer records. Remember that the balance at the bottom of the window must match the beginning balance you entered in the General Ledger for the Accounts Receivable account.

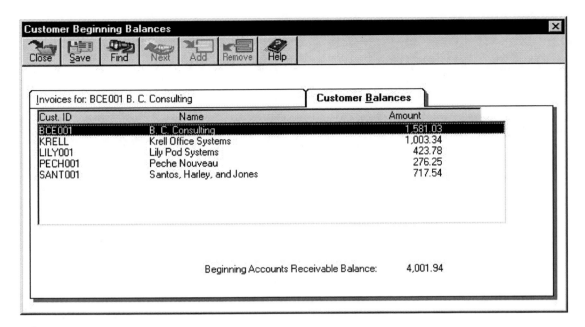

FIGURE 5-17 Customer Beginning Balances window showing the Customer
Balances folder

This folder is only for viewing balances. You cannot enter information here,
but you can double-click a customer line and display the invoice information
for the customer. To correct or change beginning balances for a customer, you
can switch to Period 1, unpost all the journals, edit the customer's beginning
balance information, and then repost the journals. (The Unpost window is
identical to the Post window.)

To close the Customer Beginning Balances window and return to the
Maintain Customers window, click Close at the top of the window. As shown
in Figure 5-18, this window now shows a current balance as of the current date.

You can see an onscreen printout of the customer's balance by clicking
Current Balance at the bottom of the window. A sample customer balance
appears in Figure 5-19.

If you want to print customer ledgers for detailed transaction information
(instead of simply viewing them on screen), you need to select the Customer
Ledgers report from the list of Accounts Receivable reports available through
the Reports menu, as shown in the next section. To print this individual
customer ledger, you can select the Print option from the File menu.

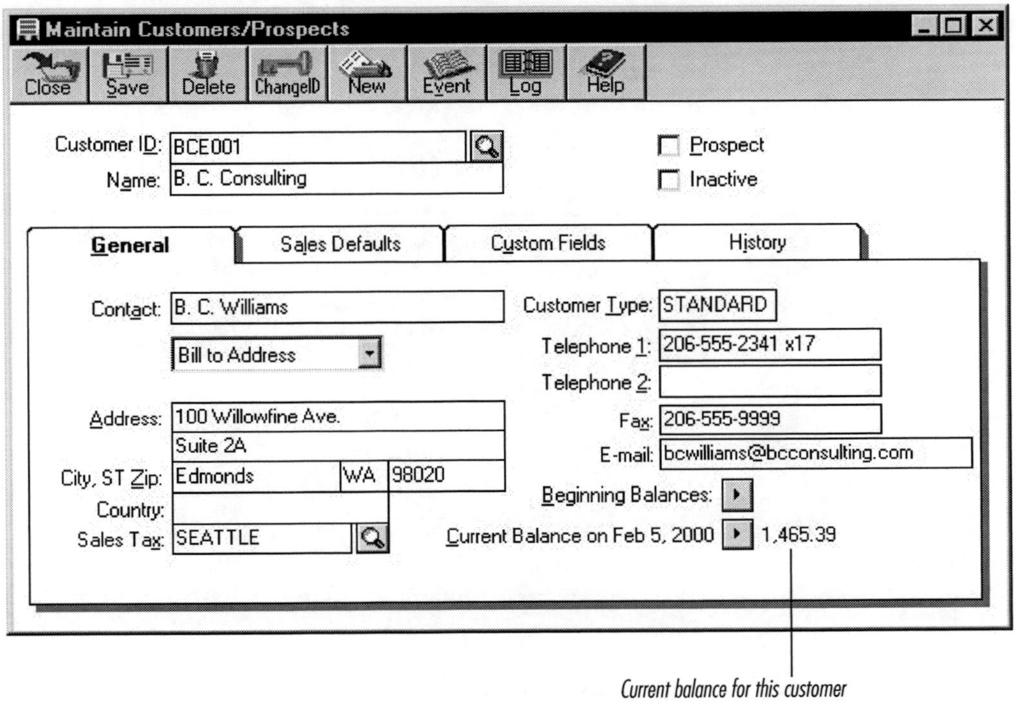

Current balance for this customer

FIGURE 5-18 General folder with a current balance for the customer

FIGURE 5-19 Sample customer ledger

Deleting Customer Records

You can delete a customer record by selecting a customer record and then clicking Delete at the top of the screen. Peachtree Accounting asks you if you're sure you want to delete this record. Click Yes to delete the customer record.

 CAUTION: You cannot delete a customer record that is associated with a journal entry. In such a case, you can delete the entries and then delete the customer. Alternately, you may want to flag the customer as inactive so that activity is not entered for the customer without Peachtree Accounting warning you that the customer is inactive and asking you if you want to post activity to the customer.

Printing Customer Reports

Now that you've entered the customer information, you can print a report of the customers to verify the information you've entered. There are three reports for customer information:

- **Customer List**   Lists each customer along with their contact name, telephone numbers, and resale number.
- **Customer Master File List**   Lists the detail information entered in the Maintain Customers window.
- **Customer Ledgers**   Lists the detailed transaction information and outstanding balance for each customer.

To print each of the reports, select the Accounts Receivable option from the Reports menu. The Report List window appears with the Accounts Receivable option selected. Next, select the appropriate report from the list by double-clicking or by highlighting the report and click Screen or Print at the top of the screen. Enter the report selection information in the report selection windows and click OK. The report appears on the screen or is sent to the printer. Figures 5-20, 5-21, and 5-22 show these three reports for selected customer information.

Big Business, Inc.
Customer List

Filter Criteria includes: 1) Customers only. Report order is by ID.

Customer ID	Customer	Contact	Telephone 1	Resale No
BCE001	B. C. Consulting	B. C. Williams	206-555-2341 x1	C600 1234567A
KRELL	Krell Office Systems	Missy Krell	206-555-1433	C600 9876543Q
LILY001	Lily Pod Systems	Mr. Wan	360-555-0203	C600 2468013M
PECH001	Peche Nouveau	Bubbles Marston	206-5554614	C600 1357924T
SANT001	Santos, Harley, and Jones	Heather Niva	206-555-7893	C600 0101010U

FIGURE 5-20   Sample Customer List report

Big Business, Inc.
Customer Master File List

Filter Criteria includes: Report order is by ID.

Customer ID Customer	Address line 1 Address line 2 City ST ZIP	Contact Telephone 1 Telephone 2 Fax Number	Tax Code Resale No Terms Cust Since
BCE001 B. C. Consulting	100 Willowfine Ave. Suite 2A Edmonds, WA 98020	B. C. Williams 206-555-2341 x17 206-555-9999	SEATTLE C600 1234567A 2% 10, Net 30 Days 11/27/99
KRELL Krell Office Systems	Rainer Tower Seattle, WA 98010-0322 USA	Missy Krell 206-555-1433	C600 9876543Q 2% 10, Net 30 Days 11/27/99
LILY001 Lily Pod Systems	1523 Carnelian Tulalip, WA 98545-0203	Mr. Wan 360-555-0203	C600 2468013M 2% 10, Net 30 Days 11/27/99
PECH001 Peche Nouveau	PO Box 240921 Seattle, WA 98133-0921 USA	Bubbles Marston 206-5554614	C600 1357924T 2% 10, Net 30 Days 11/27/99

FIGURE 5-21   Sample Customer Master File List report

Big Business, Inc.

Customer Ledgers

For the Period From Apr 1, 2000 to Apr 30, 2000

Filter Criteria includes: Report order is by ID. Report is printed in Detail Format.

Customer ID Customer	Date	Trans No	Typ	Debit Amt	Credit Amt	Balance
BCE001 B. C. Consulting	4/1/00	Balance Fwd				1,581.03
KRELL Krell Office Systems	4/1/00	Balance Fwd				1,003.34
LILY001 Lily Pod Systems	4/1/00	Balance Fwd				423.78
PECH001 Peche Nouveau	4/1/00	Balance Fwd				276.25
SANT001 Santos, Harley, and Jones	4/1/00	Balance Fwd				717.54

FIGURE 5-22   Sample Customer Ledgers report

You can also select a Prospect List from the list. This report is similar to the Customer List, but shows sales prospects rather than customers. (You saw how to enter someone as a prospect in the "Entering a Customer Record" section earlier.) You can print the Prospect List out by customer ID or customer type and give it to the salespeople.

When you display the Customer Ledgers report on the screen, you can double-click a line to display the transaction and optionally edit the information through the Sales/Invoicing window described later in this chapter.

The customer information is now complete. In the future, you will simply add, update, and delete customer and sales tax information as necessary.

TIP: When all customers are entered, print a Customer Ledgers report to tie back to Accounts Receivable beginning balances in the General Ledger. Retain this report as part of your transitional records. This is crucial as it is only on this report that this information is available.

Entering Sales

Now that you've set up customer information and defaults, you can start entering sales information for your customers. Peachtree Accounting has two types of sales. Invoiced sales require an invoice, and you enter them through the Sales/Invoicing window. Cash sales don't require an invoice, and you enter them through the Receipts window (discussed under "Entering Cash Sales and Payments" later in this chapter).

Entering Invoiced Sales

You enter invoiced sales for any sales transaction that involves future funds. Usually these are transactions that bring in money as the result of a bill sent to a customer. Entries made through the Sales/Invoicing window are posted to the General Ledger, the customer records, and optionally to the related inventory and job records. You also use the Sales/Invoicing window to enter and print invoices and to set up recurring invoices for a customer.

To enter invoiced sales for a customer, select the Sales/Invoicing option from the Tasks menu. The Sales/Invoicing window appears, as shown in Figure 5-23. (If you selected the option for one-line item entry display rather than two lines on the Maintain Global Options window, the line item entry area will look slightly different, but the way it works will be the same. See the "Setting Global Options" section in Chapter 3 for more information.)

The Sales/Invoicing window's toolbar is more complicated than the toolbars you've been seeing in the maintenance windows. Table 5-1 shows you a list of the buttons and what they're used for.

Customer ID   Enter the customer ID in the field.

NOTE: If this is a cash sale, you don't need a customer ID. Cash sales are handled through the Receipts window. See the "Entering Cash Sales and Payments" section later in this chapter.

When you select the customer ID, Peachtree Accounting enters the customer name, Bill To, and Ship To addresses in the appropriate fields. Peachtree Accounting will also enter customer defaults such as the Customer PO, Ship Via information, Ship Date, Terms, Sales Rep ID, GL Account, A/R Account, and the Sales Tax Code in the appropriate fields.

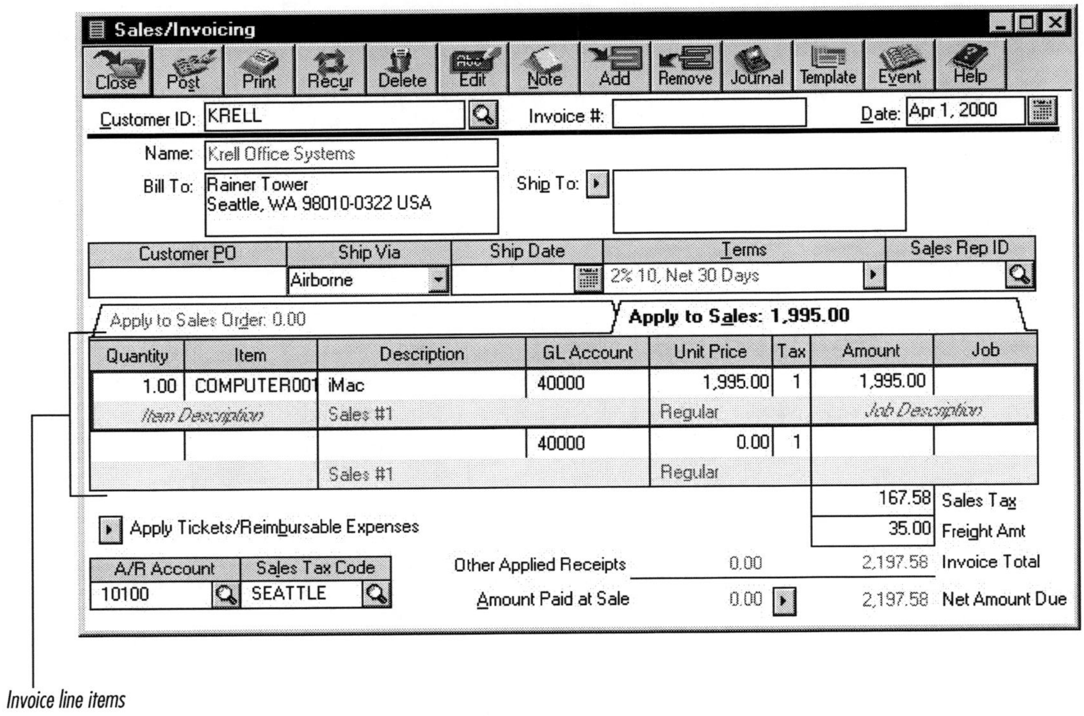

Invoice line items

FIGURE 5-23 Sales/Invoicing window

Invoice # If you are entering this invoice to record a manual invoice or an invoice that's already printed, or you don't plan to print this invoice, enter the invoice number (or other reference information) for the invoice in the field. This can be up to 20 alphanumeric characters. If you leave this field blank, Peachtree Accounting will print the invoice and automatically increment the invoice number.

If you enter a number or other reference information in this field and then print the invoice, Peachtree Accounting prints the word "Duplicate" on the invoice.

BUTTON	NAME	DESCRIPTION
Close	Close	Closes the window and the current invoice without saving the information.
Post	Post	Posts the information in the fields.
Print	Print	Prints and posts an invoice.
Recur	Recur	Creates a recurring invoice.
Delete	Delete	Deletes the current transaction.
Edit	Edit	Edits the records for a customer.
Note	Note	Creates notes to print on an invoice before or after the invoice's line items.
Add	Add	Adds a line item to the invoice or quote.
Remove	Remove	Removes a line item from the invoice or quote.
Journal	Journal	Displays the Accounting Behind the Screens window.
Template	Template	Displays a list of available templates for the displayed task window.
Event	Event	Shows or creates daily events related to the displayed customer.
Help	Help	Gets help on the Sales/Invoicing window.

TABLE 5-1 Toolbar Buttons in the Sales/Invoicing Window

Date Enter the date for the invoice. Peachtree Accounting will automatically fill in the first day of the current accounting period in this field, or the system date if you are working in the same month. Click the Calendar button for the standard calendar display. Each time you save, post, or print the invoice, Peachtree Accounting resets the date in this field to the first day of the current accounting period or to the system date.

Name This field is for display purposes only. The information comes from the information in the customer record.

Bill To This field is for display purposes only. The information comes from the information in the customer record.

Good Thru (Quotes window only.) Enter the date the quote is good through. Peachtree Accounting automatically displays a date one month after the date in the Date field. Click the Calendar button for the standard calendar display.

Ship To Peachtree Accounting displays the default shipping address in the customer record in this field. You can select an alternate Ship To address by clicking the button and selecting from the Ship To Address window that appears (shown in Figure 5-24). The customer record you entered earlier can have up to nine Ship To addresses you can select from. Click the Drop Ship box in the Ship To Address window if you want this to be a drop shipment, that is, if you want your vendor to ship the order directly to your customer.

When you enter or modify information for one of the Ship To addresses, Peachtree Accounting updates the customer record appropriately.

Customer PO Peachtree Accounting displays the default open purchase order number in the customer record (if you set one up). If there is no default open PO, enter a PO number (or other reference number) of up to 20 alphanumeric characters. The information you enter here will be printed on the customer invoice.

Ship Via Peachtree Accounting displays the default shipping method for the customer (if you set one up in the customer record). You can select an alternate shipping method by clicking the button to the right of the field and selecting a shipping method from the drop-down list.

Ship Date Enter the ship date in this field. Click the Calendar button for the standard calendar display. This information is printed on the invoice, but is not used anywhere within Peachtree Accounting.

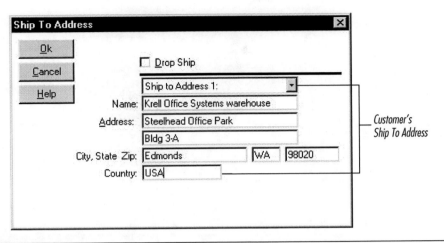

FIGURE 5-24 Ship To Address window

Terms Peachtree Accounting displays the default terms in the customer record (if you set terms up). You can change the terms by clicking on the button to the right of the field. The Terms Information window appears (as shown in Figure 5-25).

- **Date Due** Enter the date the amount is due.
- **Discount Amount** Enter the actual discount amount for early payment.
- **Discount Date** Enter the discount date (the date by which the customer must pay in order to qualify for the discount).
- **Displayed Terms** Enter a name for the terms, such as "2%-10, Net 30" or "1%-5, Net 15." This will appear on the invoice.

Sales Rep ID Back in the Sales/Invoicing window (Figure 5-23), Peachtree Accounting displays the default sales rep ID you entered for the customer (if you set one up). For more information on adding a new sales rep ID through the Maintain Employee/Sales Reps window, see Chapter 7.

Once you've added the heading information for the invoice, you're ready to add line items. You can add up to 154 line items per invoice. The invoice information you enter depends on the items and prices set up in the Inventory section. If you haven't set up items yet for your business, you may have to enter items before you can create the invoice. See Chapter 8 for more information.

Quantity Enter the quantity of the item purchased.

Terms Information   ✕

Ok	Date Due	
Cancel	Discount Amount:	43.95
	Discount Date:	
	Displayed Terms:	2% 10, Net 30

FIGURE 5-25   Terms Information window

 C A U T I O N : The defaults for entering numbers apply to this field. If you have set the default decimal places to 2, entering 4 in this field would be treated as .04, resulting in a percentage of .04%. Add a decimal point after the number (4.) to make sure that you've specified 4 items. See Chapter 3 for more information on setting up this global option.

Item   Enter the item ID in this field. You can enter a new item ID or pick from the list by clicking on the magnifying glass.

When you are first setting up Peachtree Accounting for your business, you will not have any items set up. Enter a + or double-click in the field to add a new item. For more information on setting up items, see Chapter 8.

Description   The default description is the description for the item. You can enter up to 160 alphanumeric characters in this field.

GL Account   The default General Ledger account number is the General Ledger account number for the item. You can enter a different General Ledger account number for this item if you want. This will be one of your Sales accounts.

Unit Price   The default unit price is the unit price for the item. If you have set up multiple price levels for an item in Inventory, you can click the button for a drop-down list of unit prices. You can skip this field by pressing ENTER and just entering a total for the transaction in the Amount column, if you prefer. See Chapter 8 for more information on pricing levels.

Tax   The default sales tax type is the sales tax type for the item. You can right-click in the field for a drop-down list of tax types. These sales tax types are set up in Inventory. See Chapter 8 for more information on sales tax types.

Amount   Peachtree Accounting computes the amount from the unit price and the quantity. You can accept the computed amount or enter a different amount.

Job The Job column appears only if you have set up a job through the Maintain Jobs window (described in Chapter 9). Enter the job ID that this invoice should be applied to.

Once you enter the item information for a single line item, Peachtree Accounting moves you to the next line in the line item section. You can enter up to 154 line items on any single invoice. The Add and Remove buttons let you add and remove line items from the invoice.

Apply Tickets/Reimbursable Expenses Click this button if you want to apply reimbursable expenses. (See the section "Applying Time Tickets, Expense Tickets, and Reimbursable Expenses," later in this chapter for information on how to fill out this window.)

A/R Account Enter the General Ledger account to which the invoice will be applied. The default entry for this field is the last account entered in the field. This will be an Asset or Accounts Receivable account type. Group these accounts as you do your departments, units, and so on, or just summarize the whole company into one account. You will be able to get aging and payment reports from Accounts Receivable to use as an analysis tool.

Sales Tax Code The default entry for this field is the default sales tax code for the customer.

Sales Tax Peachtree Accounting computes the sales tax based on the tax rate specified by the sales tax code and the total amount of the invoice. You can accept the computed amount or enter a different amount if you want.

Freight Amt Enter the freight charges (if any) for this sales transaction.

Invoice Total Peachtree Accounting computes the invoice total as the sum of the sales tax, the freight amount, and the invoice amount. This field is display-only.

Net Amount Due Peachtree Accounting computes the outstanding balance on the invoice. This field is display-only.

When you are satisfied with your entries, you can save the invoice by clicking Post on the toolbar. You can also post the invoice and print it by clicking Print on the toolbar. You will need to go to the Reports menu if you want to print a batch of invoices. (Printing customer invoices is discussed near the end of this chapter in the "Printing Invoices, Sales Orders, Credit Memos, and Quotes" section.)

Peachtree Accounting will automatically print the invoice when you print reports if you save or post an invoice without an invoice number in the Invoice # field.

Applying Payments

The Amount Paid At Sale field at the bottom of the Sales/Invoicing window shown earlier in Figure 5-23 shows the payments applied against this invoice. If you have received full or partial payment on this invoice, click the Amount Paid at Sale button to display the Receive Payment window (shown in Figure 5-26 with a sample sales order entered).

Deposit Ticket ID   The default entry in this field is the current system date. Although you can change it to another reference number if you want, it's a good idea to use a date reference for purposes of account reconciliation.

Reference   Enter a payment reference of up to 20 alphanumeric characters in this required field, such as "CASH," a customer check number, a credit card number, or other identification.

Customer ID   This display-only field shows the customer ID from the invoice you're applying the payment to.

Date   This display-only field shows the invoice date.

Name   This display-only field shows the customer's name and billing address. Any changes made to this information as it appears on the related invoice are reflected in this field.

Receipt Amount   Enter the amount being paid.

Payment Method   Select the payment method from the list. (You can add, change, or delete payment methods through the Maintain Customer Defaults window in the Pay Methods folder as described earlier in this chapter.)

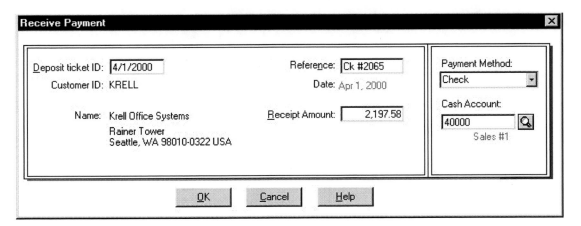

FIGURE 5-26   Receive Payment window

Cash Account The default account number is the last account number you used when you entered a payment through the Receive Payment window. You can enter a different General Ledger account number for this item if you want. (You will probably want to use your Cash account.)

When you are satisfied with your entries, click OK. You return to the Sales/Invoicing window, which will show the new total for the amount paid in the Amount Paid field, as shown in Figure 5-27. The Amount Due field will be reduced accordingly.

Applying Time Tickets, Expense Tickets, and Reimbursable Expenses

If you are tracking time, expense, or job costs, you will want to apply expenses to the customer's invoice. The process of applying time tickets, expense tickets, and reimbursable expenses is to display the possible expenses, select the expenses you want to bill the customer for on the invoice you are creating, and mark up the costs appropriately. Peachtree Accounting then adds the expenses as line items on the invoice.

Peachtree invoice number   Customer's Ship To address

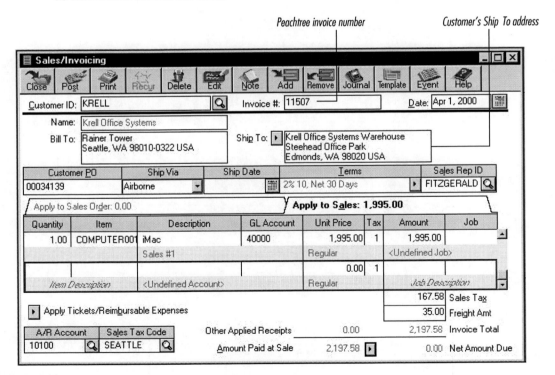

FIGURE 5-27 Completed Receive Payment window

To apply expenses for a customer, enter the Customer ID in the Customer ID field, then click Apply Tickets/Reimbursable Expenses on the Sales/Invoice window. The Apply Tickets/Reimbursable Expenses window displays the time and expense tickets entered through Peachtree Accounting's Time & Billing as well as any reimbursable expenses that have been previously entered through the Purchases, Payments, Payroll, or General Journal Entry windows. Time tickets and expense tickets are discussed in detail in Chapter 10.

Figure 5-28 shows the Apply Tickets/Reimbursable Expenses window with sample time tickets ready to apply to the customer.

Time tickets record any activity measured in units of time (usually hours). Time-based activities can be any kind of labor or service, consultation, design, planning, or phone calls with clients. (Time tickets are entered through the Time Tickets window, described in Chapter 10.)

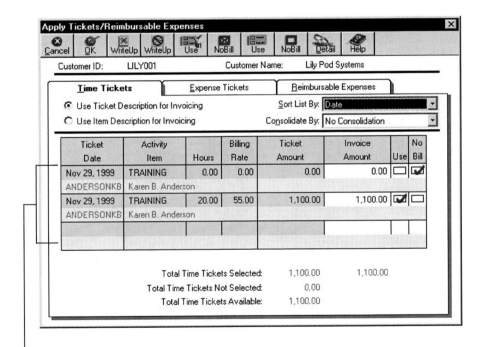

Time ticket line items

FIGURE 5-28   Time Tickets folder in the Apply Tickets/Reimbursable Expenses window

The Time Tickets folder of the Apply Tickets/Reimbursable Expenses window contains a number of new buttons, which are described in Table 5-2.

Enter information on the Time Tickets folder of the Apply Tickets/ Reimbursable Expenses window as follows. (Most of the information on the three folders of the Apply Tickets/Reimbursable Expenses window comes from the original transaction and is display-only.)

Customer ID   This display-only field shows the customer ID.

Customer Name   This display-only field shows the customer name.

Sort List By   Select a sort option from the drop-down list. You can sort by the following fields: date, activity item/date, activity item/employee-vendor, job/date, job/activity item, job/employee-vendor ID, employee-vendor ID/date, employee-vendor ID/activity date, employee-vendor ID/job, or ticket ID.

BUTTON	NAME	DESCRIPTION
WriteUp	WriteUp	Selects items to write the amount passed on to the customer up or down.
WriteUp	Remove WriteUp	Removes the amount written up or down and uses the original billing amount.
Use	Select Tickets to Use	Selects the tickets you want to use.
NoBill	Select Tickets to No Bill	Selects the tickets you want not to bill.
Use	Clear Use	Clears tickets previously selected for use.
NoBill	Clear No Bill	Clears tickets previously selected for no billing.
Detail	Detail	Displays additional information and descriptions for the selected item.

TABLE 5-2   Toolbar Buttons in the Time Tickets Folder of the Apply Tickets/Reimbursements Expense Window

Consolidate By   Select a consolidation option from the drop-down list. Peachtree Accounting will consolidate detail information from the selected tickets depending on the consolidation option you select, as follows:

- **No Consolidation**   Each time ticket will appear on the customer invoice as a separate line item.
- **By Activity Item**   The selected time tickets are consolidated on the customer invoice as a single line item for each activity item.
- **Employee/Vendor ID**   The selected time tickets are consolidated on the customer invoice as a single line item for each employee/vendor ID.
- **By Job**   The selected time tickets are consolidated on the customer invoice as a single line item for each job.
- **By Job and Phase**   The selected time tickets are consolidated on the customer invoice as a single line item for each job and phase.
- **By Job, Phase, and Cost Code**   The selected time tickets are consolidated on the customer invoice as a single line item for each job, phase, and cost code.
- **Consolidate All**   The selected time tickets are consolidated on the customer invoice as a single line item.

Use Ticket Description for Invoicing   Use the time ticket description on the invoice for the line item description. (You can select this option only if you have already selected No Consolidation in the Consolidate By field.) You enter the time ticket description through the Time Ticket window, discussed in Chapter 10.

Use Item Description for Invoicing   Use the ticket's activity item description on the invoice for the line item description. (You can select this option only if you have already selected No Consolidation in the Consolidate By field.) You enter the activity item's description through the Maintain Inventory Items window, discussed in Chapter 8.

Ticket Date   This display-only field shows the date the time ticket was originally entered.

Activity Item   This display-only field shows the activity item associated with the time ticket. For more information on setting up activity items, see Chapter 8.

Hours   This display-only field shows the total duration (in decimal format) on the time ticket.

Billing Rate   This display-only field shows the time ticket's billing rate. Peachtree Accounting uses the billing rate to calculate the ticket amount.

Ticket Amount   This display-only field shows the billable amount for the time ticket. Peachtree Accounting calculates this as the hours multiplied by the billing rate.

Invoice Amount   Peachtree Accounting applies the amount in this field to the customer invoice. The default value is the ticket amount. You can use the default, enter a different amount, or write the amount up or down by clicking WriteUp at the top of the window. Peachtree Accounting displays the Select Tickets To Write Up/Down window (shown in Figure 5-29).

Enter the information on this window as follows:

All   Write all tickets up or down by the amount or percentage entered.

Job   Write all tickets for the job specified in the Job field up or down by the amount or percentage entered.

Item   Write all tickets for the item specified in the Item field up or down by the amount or percentage entered.

Date Range   Write all tickets within the date range specified in the From and To fields up or down by the amount or percentage entered.

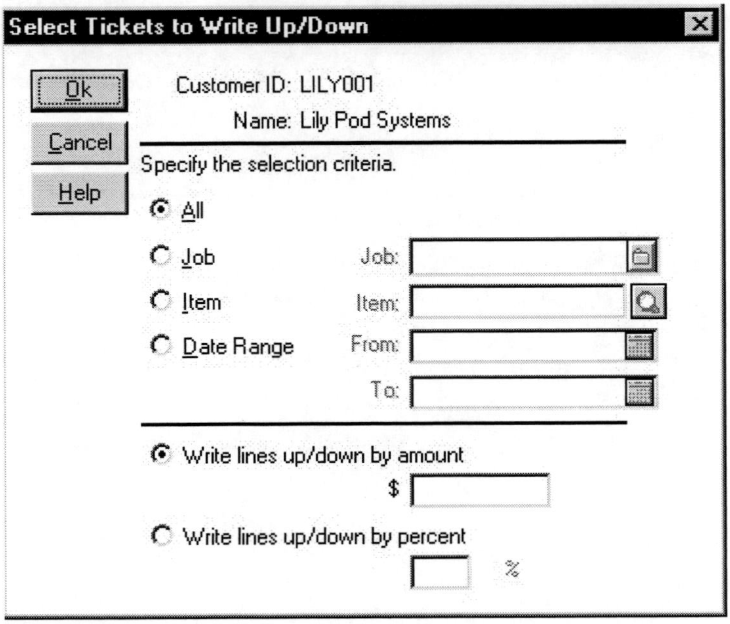

FIGURE 5-29   Select Tickets To Write Up/Down window

Write Lines Up/Down by Amount   Enter the amount to write the selected tickets up or down by. (Use a negative number to identify an amount to write down.)

Write Lines Up/Down by Percent   Enter the percent to write the selected tickets up or down by. (Use a negative number to identify a percent to write down.)

When you are satisfied with your entries, click OK to return to the Time Tickets folder.

You can clear the write up/write down information by clicking Remove WriteUp at the top of the window. Peachtree Accounting clears the amount or percentage you entered on the Select Tickets to Write Up/Down window and resets the affected line items to their original billing amounts.

You can adjust the billing amounts for individual time tickets by making an entry in the Invoice Amount field even if you have already adjusted the billing amounts for tickets using the Select Tickets to WriteUp/Down window.

Use   Click this box to select the ticket on this line. Peachtree Accounting will apply this ticket to the customer invoice. You can also select tickets by clicking Select Tickets To Use at the top of the window. Peachtree Accounting displays the Select Tickets To Use window (shown in Figure 5-30).

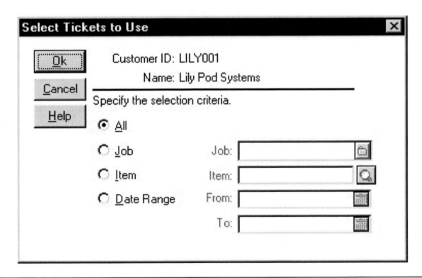

FIGURE 5-30   Select Tickets To Use window

Enter the information on this window as follows:

All   Select all tickets.

Job   Select all tickets for the job specified in the Job field.

Item   Select all tickets for the item specified in the Item field.

Date Range   Select all tickets within the date range specified in the From and To fields.

When you are satisfied with your entries, click OK to return to the Time Tickets folder.

You can select individual time tickets by checking Use even if you have already selected time tickets with the Select Tickets to Use window. You can deselect the tickets by clicking Clear Use at the top of the window. Peachtree Accounting deselects the tickets you entered on the Select Tickets to Use window.

No Bill   Click this box to identify that the ticket on this line should not be billed. Peachtree Accounting will not apply this ticket to the customer invoice nor will this ticket be available for future customer invoices. (If you need to change the billing status back to billable, you must do so through the Time Tickets window. For more information, see Chapter 10.) You can also select tickets by clicking Select Tickets To No Bill at the top of the window. Peachtree Accounting displays the Select Tickets To Mark "No Bill" window (shown in Figure 5-31).

Enter the information on this window as follows:

All   Mark all tickets "no bill."

Job   Mark all tickets "no bill" for the job specified in the Job field.

Item   Mark all tickets "no bill" for the item specified in the Item field.

Date Range   Mark all tickets "no bill" within the date range specified in the From and To fields.

When you are satisfied with your entries, click OK to return to the Time Tickets folder.

You can select individual time tickets by checking Select Tickets to No Bill even if you have already selected time tickets with the Select Tickets to Mark "No Bill" window. You can deselect the marked tickets by clicking Clear No Bill at the top of the window. Peachtree Accounting deselects the tickets you entered on the Select Tickets to Mark "No Bill" window.

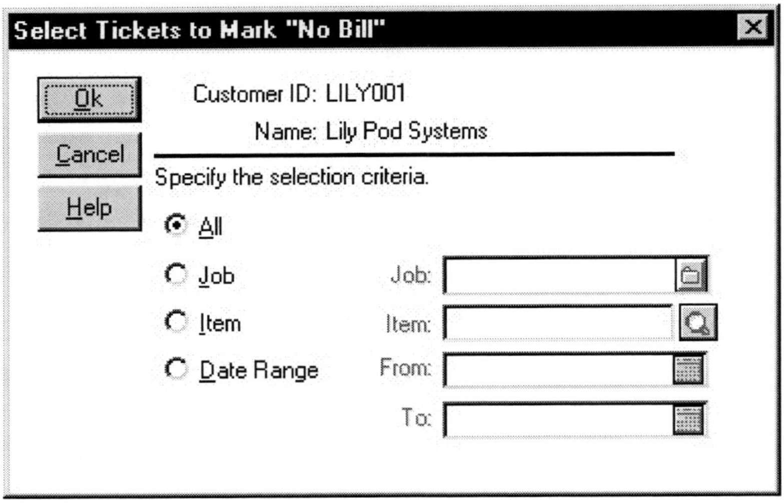

FIGURE 5-31 Select Tickets To Mark "No Bill" window

Customer ID This display-only field identifies the employee or vendor ID this time ticket is for.

Name This display-only field identifies the name of the employee or vendor this time ticket is for.

Job, Phase, Cost Code This display-only field identifies the job ID, phase, or cost code associated with the time ticket (if any).

Total Time Tickets Selected This display-only field shows the total invoice amount and adjusted amount for the selected tickets.

Total Time Tickets Not Selected This display-only field shows the total invoice amount for the tickets that are not selected.

Total Time Tickets Available This display-only field shows the total invoice amount for all tickets that could be applied to this customer invoice.

When you are satisfied with your entries in this folder, click the Expense Tickets tab. The Expense Tickets folder (shown in Figure 5-32) appears.

Expense tickets record how company resources are used. Typical expensed items include photocopies, long-distance calls, other office supplies, mileage, filing and recording fees, postage, faxes, charges for online services, and floppy

Expense ticket line items

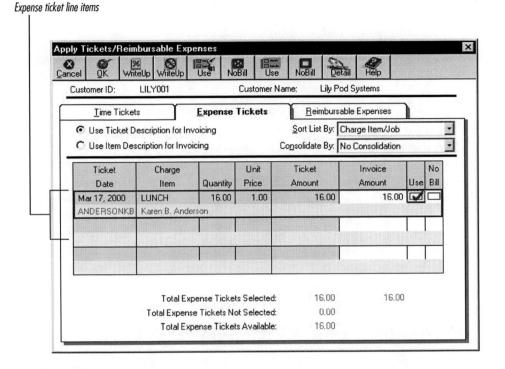

FIGURE 5-32 Expense Tickets folder in the Apply Tickets/Reimbursable Expenses window

disks, toner cartridges, and other computer supplies. (Expense tickets are entered through the Expense Tickets window, described in Chapter 10.)

Enter information on the Expense Tickets folder of the Apply Tickets/Reimbursable Expenses window as follows:

Customer ID   This display-only field shows the customer ID.

Customer Name   This display-only field shows the customer name.

Sort List By   Select a sort option from the drop-down list. You can sort by the following fields: date, charge item/date, charge item/employee, charge item/job, job/date, job/charge item, job/employee-vendor ID, employee-vendor ID/date, employee-vendor ID/charge, employee-vendor ID/job, or ticket ID.

Consolidate By   Select a consolidation option from the drop-down list. Peachtree Accounting will consolidate detail information from the selected tickets depending on the consolidation option you select, as follows:

- **No Consolidation**   Each expense ticket will appear on the customer invoice as a separate line item.
- **By Charge Item**   The selected expense tickets are consolidated on the customer invoice as a single line item for each charge item.
- **By Employee Vendor ID**   The selected expense tickets are consolidated on the customer invoice as a single line item for each charge item.
- **By Job**   The selected expense tickets are consolidated on the customer invoice as a single line item for each job.
- **By Job and Phase**   The selected expense tickets are consolidated on the customer invoice as a single line item for each job and phase.
- **By Job, Phase, and Cost Code**   The selected expense tickets are consolidated on the customer invoice as a single line item for each job, phase, and cost code.
- **Consolidate All**   The selected expense tickets are consolidated on the customer invoice as a single line item.

Use Ticket Description for Invoicing   Use the time ticket description on the invoice for the line item description. (You can select this option only if you have already selected No Consolidation in the Consolidate By field.) You enter the time ticket description through the Time Ticket window, discussed in Chapter 10.

Use Item Description for Invoicing   Use the ticket's activity item description on the invoice for the line item description. (You can select this option only if you have already selected No Consolidation in the Consolidate By field.) You enter the activity item's description through the Maintain Inventory Items window, discussed in Chapter 8.

Ticket Date   This display-only field shows the date the expense ticket was originally entered.

Charge Item   This display-only field shows the charge item associated with the expense ticket. For more information on setting up charge items, see Chapter 8.

Quantity   This display-only field shows the total duration (in decimal format) on the expense ticket.

Unit Price   This display-only field shows the time ticket's billing rate. Peachtree Accounting uses the billing rate to calculate the ticket amount.

Ticket Amount   This display-only field shows the billable amount for the time ticket. Peachtree Accounting calculates this as the hours multiplied by the billing rate.

Invoice Amount   Peachtree Accounting applies the amount in this field to the customer invoice. The default value is the ticket amount. You can use the default, enter a different amount, or write the amount up or down by clicking WriteUp at the top of the window. Peachtree Accounting displays the Select Tickets to Write Up/Down window (as shown earlier in Figure 5-29). Make your selections on this window as described earlier and then click OK to return to the Expense Tickets folder.

You can adjust the invoice amount for individual expense tickets by making an entry in the Invoice Amount field even if you have already adjusted the expense amounts for tickets using the Select Tickets to WriteUp/Down window.

Use   Click this box to select the ticket on this line. Peachtree Accounting will apply this ticket to the customer invoice. You can also select tickets by clicking Select Tickets to Use at the top of the window. Peachtree Accounting displays the Select Tickets to Use window (shown earlier in Figure 5-30). Make your selections on this window as described earlier and then click OK to return to the Expense Tickets folder.

You can select individual expense tickets by checking Use even if you have already selected expense tickets with the Select Tickets to Use window.

No Bill   Click this box to identify that the ticket on this line should not be billed. Peachtree Accounting will not apply this ticket to the customer invoice nor will this ticket be available for future customer invoices. (If you need to change the billing status back to billable, you must do so through the Expense Tickets window. For more information, see Chapter 10.) You can also select tickets by clicking Select Tickets to No Bill at the top of the window. Peachtree Accounting displays the Select Tickets to Mark "No Bill" window (shown earlier in Figure 5-31). Make your selections on this window as described earlier and then click OK to return to the Expense Tickets folder.

You can select individual expense tickets by checking Select Tickets to No Bill even if you have already selected expense tickets with the Select Tickets to Mark "No Bill" window.

Employee/Vendor ID   This display-only field identifies the employee or vendor ID this expense ticket is for.

Employee/Vendor Name   This display-only field identifies the name of the employee or vendor this expense ticket is for.

Job, Phase, Cost Code   This display-only field identifies the job ID, phase, or cost code associated with the expense ticket (if any).

Total Expense Tickets Selected   This display-only field shows the total invoice amount and adjusted amount for the selected tickets.

Total Expense Tickets Not Selected   This display-only field shows the total invoice amount for the tickets that are not selected.

Total Expense Tickets Available   This display-only field shows the total invoice amount for all tickets that could be applied to this customer invoice.

When you are satisfied with your entries in this folder, click the Reimbursable Expenses tab. The Reimbursable Expenses folder (shown in Figure 5-33) appears.

Reimbursable expense line items

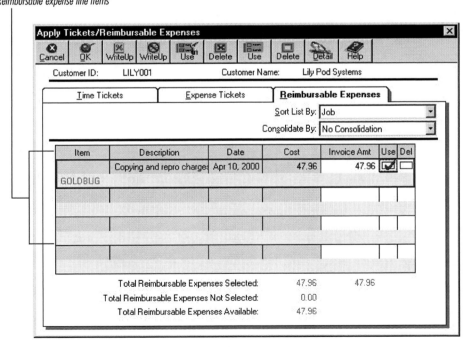

FIGURE 5-33   Reimbursable Expenses folder in the Apply Tickets/Reimbursable Expenses window

Reimbursable expenses include such things as services passed directly to the customer (for example, shipping charges, filing fees, or professional service fees) and expenses generated by a subcontractor. To enter a transaction that will later be applied as a reimbursable expense, you must enter a job ID in the appropriate field on the Purchases/Receive Inventory window (described in Chapter 6 as part of the normal purchase entry process. Jobs are normally set up for a specific customer. Peachtree Accounting uses the job ID to track the expenses. (Setting up and maintaining jobs is discussed in Chapter 9) You can also enter reimbursable expenses as part of Payroll entry. You would assign the job ID as part of the payroll entry process, as described in Chapter 7. When you subsequently display the Reimbursable Expenses folder after entering reimbursable expenses, Peachtree Accounting displays any vendor purchases or payroll expenses that are related to this customer by the job code you assigned.

You cannot apply expenses for items that are listed as inventory items.

TIP: Your company may not need the level of detail tracking that Peachtree Accounting's Time & Billing features offer. If you don't choose to use time tickets and expense tickets, you can use the reimbursable expenses feature to enter faxes and long-distance phone charges, copying, mailing, and non-inventory items.

The Apply Tickets/Reimbursable Expenses window contains four new buttons, which are described in Table 5-3.

BUTTON	NAME	DESCRIPTION
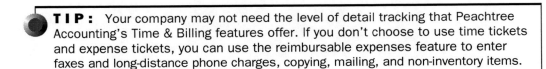 Use	Select Expenses to Use	Selects the expenses you want to use.
Delete	Select Expenses to Delete	Selects the expenses you want to delete.
Use	Clear Use	Clears the expenses previously selected for use.
Delete	Clear Delete	Clears the expenses previously selected for deletion.

TABLE 5-3 Toolbar Buttons in the Apply Tickets/Reimbursable Expenses window

Sort List By   Select a sort option from the drop-down list. You can sort by date or job.

Consolidate by   Select a consolidation option from the drop-down list. Peachtree Accounting will consolidate detail information from the selected expenses depending on the consolidation option you select, as follows:

- **No Consolidation**   Each expense will appear on the customer invoice as a separate line item.
- **By Job**   The selected expenses are consolidated on the customer invoice as a single line item for each job.
- **By Job and Phase**   The selected expenses are consolidated on the customer invoice as a single line item for each job and phase.
- **By Job, Phase, and Cost Code**   The selected expenses are consolidated on the customer invoice as a single line item for each job, phase, and cost code.
- **Consolidate All**   The selected expenses are consolidated on the customer invoice as a single line item.

Item   This display-only field shows the item (if any).

Description   This display-only field shows the description for the item or service.

Date   This display-only field shows the date of the original transaction.

Cost   This display-only field shows the cost (amount). This field is the cost to you before any write ups or write downs are applied.

Invoice Amt   Enter the amount to be charged to the customer. If you are using the write up feature (described earlier in this section), Peachtree Accounting will enter an amount for you. You can override this by entering a different amount if you prefer.

Use   Check the Use box to apply this line item as part of the customer invoice. You can also select expenses by clicking Select Expenses to Use at the top of the window. Peachtree Accounting displays the Select Expenses to Use window (the fields are the same as the Select Tickets to Use window shown earlier in Figure 5-30). Make your selections on this window and then click OK to return to the Reimbursable Expenses folder.

You can select individual expenses by checking Use even if you have already selected expenses with the Select Expenses to Use window.

Del   Check the Del box to delete this line item so that it cannot be applied to this customer.

You can also delete expenses by clicking Select Expenses to Delete at the top of the window. Peachtree Accounting displays the Select Expenses to Delete window (the fields are the same as the Select Tickets to Use window shown in Figure 5-30). Make your selections on this window and then click OK to return to the Reimbursable Expenses folder.

You can delete individual expenses by checking Del even if you have already deleted expenses with the Select Expenses to Delete window.

Job   This display-only field shows the job ID (in this figure, the job ID is "GOLDBUG").

Total Reimbursable Expenses Selected   This display-only field shows the total invoice amount and adjusted amount for the selected reimbursable expenses.

Total Reimbursable Expenses Not Selected   This display-only field shows the total invoice amount for the reimbursable expenses that are not selected.

Total Reimbursable Expenses Available   This display-only field shows the total invoice amount for all reimbursable expenses that could be applied to this customer invoice.

When you are satisfied with your entries on the Reimbursable Expenses window, click OK to return to the Sales/Invoicing window. The line items you selected appear as line items on the invoice with the marked-up amounts appearing in the Amount field.

Although most reimbursable expenses will be charges passed through to the customer, you may generate expenses on your own (such as copies, deliveries, faxes, and telephone charges) for which the entry will be made in the General Journal. A handy way to create a line item for such reimbursable expenses is to make a General Journal entry for the expense as a cost of sales account, with debits and credits to the same account. Figure 5-34 shows a General Journal entry for faxes and long distance.

Enter a dummy amount for the expense. Save or post the General Journal entry as normal. The expense will then appear as a line item on the Reimbursable Expense window. You can override any default and mark up the amount as appropriate. (Figure 5-33 showed an entry for faxes and long-distance charges that was entered this way and then changed manually.)

Adding a Note to an Invoice

If you need to add a note to the invoice, click Note. The Note window appears (as shown in Figure 5-35).

Journal entry line items

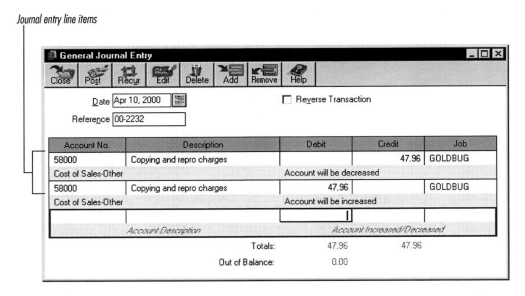

FIGURE 5-34 General Journal Entry window showing entry for a reimbursable expense

FIGURE 5-35 Note window

You can enter a note of up to 250 characters. The text you enter will print before or after the line items, depending on which Print Note option button you select. Use this option to enter a personal note to a customer about an invoice.

Entering Service Invoices

The preceding section showed you how to enter a standard invoice for goods. Depending on the nature of your business, you may need to create service invoices as well. Service invoices will bill a customer for things such as consultations, reports, work done on an hourly or contract basis, and miscellaneous office expenses, such as faxes and copying.

Click Template on the toolbar, and select Service to tell Peachtree Accounting that you want to enter a service, rather than a standard, invoice. Figure 5-36 shows the Sales/Invoicing window for service invoices.

Creating a service invoice is much like the process you just saw for creating an invoice for goods. The most notable difference is that you must enter the

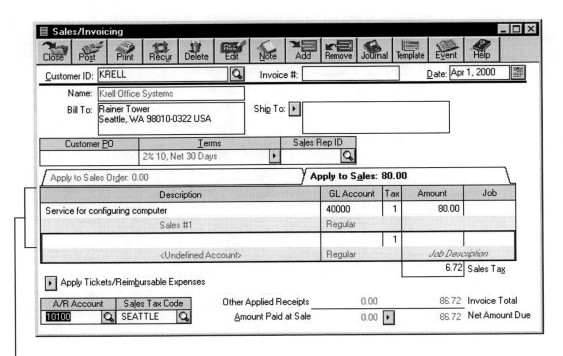

Service line items

FIGURE 5-36 Sales/Invoicing window for creating a service invoice

description of services and the amount for each line item, rather than depending on the predefined descriptions and amounts stored with inventory items. Costs can be charged to service invoices also, and should be taxed according to rules as required by the state. Some states tax costs only.

C A U T I O N : Don't print a batch of service and standard invoices together. Service and standard invoices usually use different forms when printing.

Entering Recurring Invoices

Recurring invoices are invoices that Accounts Receivable posts to a customer's account on a regular basis. If any of your customers pays you rents or leases, a fixed royalty amount for a given period, or a credit balance on a fixed contract, you can set up an automatic transaction.

When you set up a recurring invoice, you tell Accounts Receivable to bill a customer a fixed amount weekly, biweekly, monthly, per period, quarterly, or annually. At the predetermined time, Accounts Receivable automatically generates these transactions. Setting up automatic transactions can free you from a considerable amount of repetitious work.

Start by entering a transaction in the Sales/Invoicing window, as described in the preceding sections. Instead of clicking Post to enter the information, click Recur on the toolbar. The Create Recurring Journal Entries window appears. (The Create Recurring Journal Entries window is the same as the Create Recurring Journal Entries window shown in Figure 4-17 of Chapter 4.)

You can set up the invoice to recur up to 52 times (but not past the end of the next year). Invoices can recur weekly, biweekly, monthly, per period, quarterly, or annually.

Entering Sales Orders

A sales order differs from a sales invoice in that a sales order lets you make a partial shipment on an order. You can enter an order from a customer, and as items become available, you can invoice and ship them. This is useful for tracking back orders if an item is currently out of stock or if you are shipping a non-inventory item that is a special order. (In contrast, a sales invoice is used for processing the entire order.)

To enter a sales order for a customer, select the Quotes/Sales Orders option from the Tasks menu, then select Sales Order from the submenu. The Sales Order window appears, as shown in Figure 5-37.

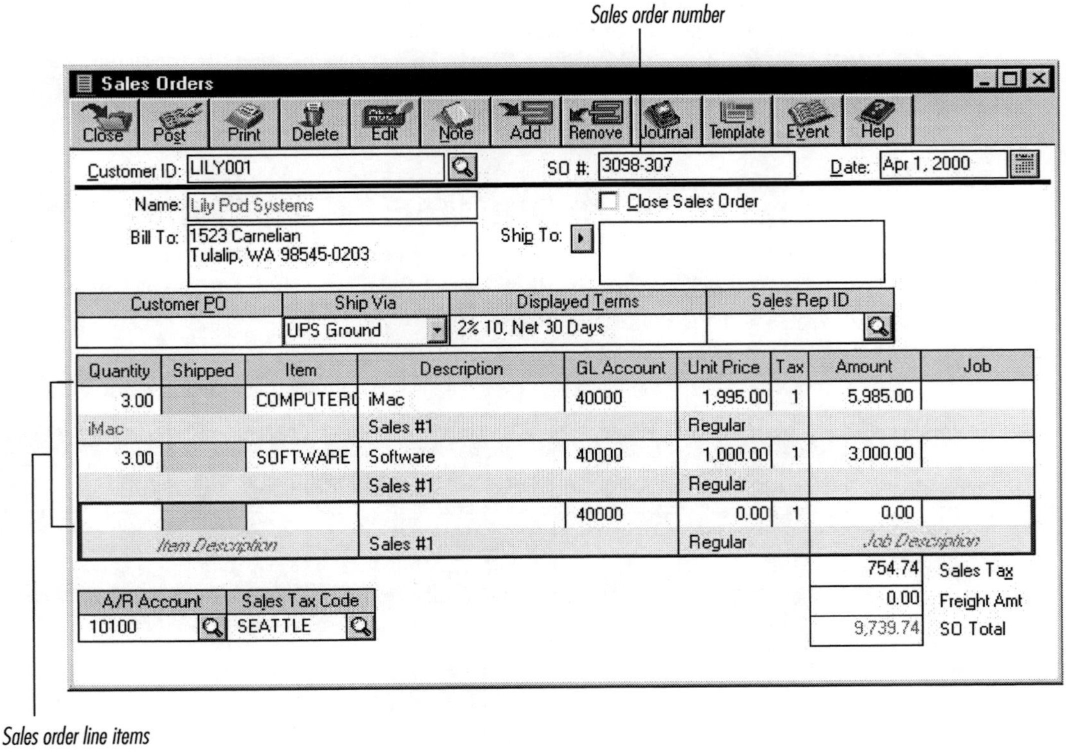

Sales order number

Sales order line items

FIGURE 5-37 Sales Order window

The Sales Order window is almost identical to the Sales/Invoicing window shown earlier in Figure 5-23 except that the total amount is a sales order total (shown in the figure as SO Total) rather than an amount due. In addition, Peachtree Accounting automatically numbers the sales orders.

Entering Credit Memos

You enter credit memos (also known as credit invoices) in much the same way as you enter a standard or service invoice. If you charged inventory items on an invoice, be sure to enter negative quantities for those items (for example, –4.00) when you enter a credit memo so that the amount is calculated as a negative amount. If you are issuing a credit memo for an item not in inventory, such as a service, enter the amount as a negative with a leading minus sign (for example, –286.50). Returns will increase the quantity of items available in inventory.

To apply the credit memo, select Receipts from the Tasks menu. The credit memo will appear in the line item list for the customer. Highlight the credit memo and click the Pay checkbox. You cannot apply a credit memo if the customer has no outstanding invoices. Be aware that if you are using batch posting, you need to post the credit memo before you can apply the credit.

Editing Invoices, Credit Memos, and Sales Orders

To edit an invoice, you need to select the invoice you want to change. Start by clicking Edit Records on the toolbar in the Sales/Invoicing window. The Select Invoice window appears, as shown in Figure 5-38.

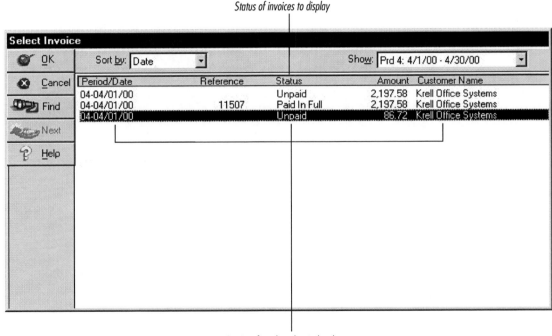

FIGURE 5-38   Select Invoice window

The Select Invoice window shows the invoices. You can sort records by date, reference, or ID. If you're in batch mode, you can also display unposted, posted, or all transactions. (If you're in real-time mode, this doesn't apply, as all transactions are posted automatically and will appear in the window.) You can also select transactions from a specific period or all transactions by clicking in the Show field for a drop-down list of periods. The period and date, reference number (if any), amount, and customer or prospect name appear in the window. You can edit real-time transactions even if they've already been posted. Peachtree Accounting edits the General Ledger and other ledgers the invoice may affect. Recurring entries post at the date of the invoice, so any changes you make need only be done in the Sales/Invoicing window.

Double-click the invoice you want to edit. Peachtree Accounting displays the information in the Sales/Invoicing window. Make the changes to the invoice. When you are satisfied, click Post on the toolbar to save your changes.

If you're editing a recurring entry, a note will appear below the line item area on the Sales/Invoicing window that identifies the invoice as a recurring entry and shows the number of remaining additional entries, as shown here:

> *** The selected entry is a recurring entry.
> There are 2 additional entries. ***

You can choose to make changes to the entry you are working on, or to all subsequent recurring entries as well.

Deleting Invoices, Credit Memos, and Sales Orders

You can delete invoices and credit memos, even ones you've posted. To delete an invoice or credit memo, start by clicking Edit Records to display the Select Invoice window (shown earlier in Figure 5-38). Double-click the invoice or credit memo you want to delete. Peachtree Accounting displays the information in the Sales/Invoicing window. Click Delete on the toolbar.

You've seen how to edit transactions using the various Accounts Receivable windows. Peachtree Accounting's new Accounting Behind the Screens feature lets you fine-tune the information you are entering by letting you edit the journal entries associated with the transaction.

For Accounts Receivable, you can use Accounting Behind the Screens on the Quotes, Sales Orders, Sales/Invoicing, and Receipts windows. You can use the Accounting Behind the Screens feature to change the Cost of Sales or Inventory posting accounts. (The Sales and Accounts Receivable account information can be edited on the task window.)

To edit a transaction using Accounting Behind the Screens, do the following:

1. Open the Quotes/Sales Orders, Sales/Invoicing, or Receipts window from the Tasks menu.

2. Enter a transaction in the window or select a transaction from the Edit Records window.

3. Click Journal in the window's toolbar. The Accounting Behind the Screens window appears. Depending on the task, Peachtree Accounting will display information in one or more journal folders. For example, for a sales invoice, you will see the Sales Journal and the Cash Receipts Journal (as shown in Figure 5-39).

4. Select the folder tab of the journal you want to edit.

5. Select the line item you want to edit and enter a different account ID.

6. When you are satisfied with your entries, click OK to return to the task window you started from.

7. Click Post to save your changes. (Clicking Print will save and print the transaction.)

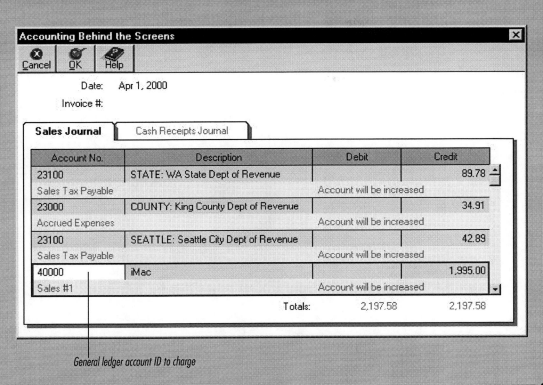

General ledger account ID to charge

FIGURE 5-39 Accounting Behind the Screens display for a sales invoice

Peachtree Accounting asks if you are sure you want to delete the record. Click Yes to delete the record. If receipts or credit memos have been applied to an invoice you want to delete, you must delete the receipts and credit memos before you can delete the invoice.

Entering and Converting Quotes

Quotes are an offer to a customer. They have most or all of the same information as an invoiced sale, but they are not entered into Accounts Receivable because they are not completed. However, you will frequently want to change quotes to sales orders or sales invoices when a customer accepts the offer.

Entering a Quote

To enter a quote for a customer, select the Quotes/Sales Orders option from the Tasks menu, then select Quotes from the submenu. The Quotes window appears, as shown in Figure 5-40.

The Quotes window is almost identical to the Sales Order and Sales/Invoicing windows shown earlier in this chapter except that the only total amount is a quote total rather than an amount due or a sales order total. You can enter

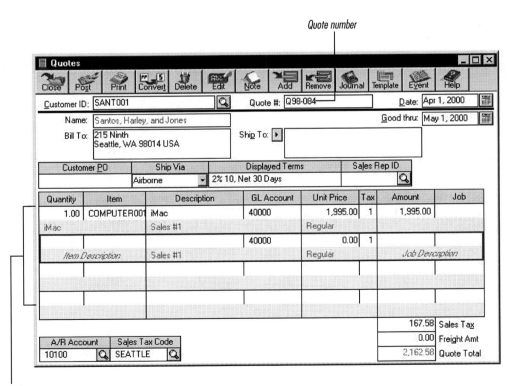

FIGURE 5-40 Quotes window

quotes for service just like entering a service invoice by clicking Template on the toolbar, then Service. An example of the Quotes window for service quotes appears in Figure 5-41.

The information you enter here is not entered into your Accounts Receivable. To enter information in Accounts Receivable from a quote, you must convert the quote, as shown in the next section.

Converting Quotes to Sales Orders or Sales Invoices

When a customer has accepted a quote, you can convert the quote to a sales order (for partial shipment) or a sales invoice (for full shipment). This enters the quote information into your Accounts Receivable.

To convert a quote to a sales order or sales invoice, click Edit Records on the toolbar. The Select Quote window, which is identical in appearance to the Select Invoice windows shown earlier in Figure 5-38, appears. Select the quote you want to convert from this window. With the quote displayed in the Quote window, click Convert. The Convert Quote window, shown in Figure 5-42, appears.

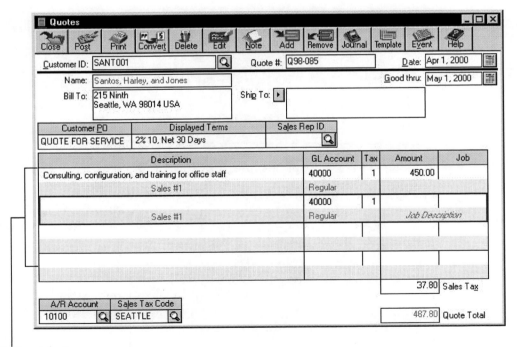

Service quote line items

FIGURE 5-41 Quotes window for service quotes

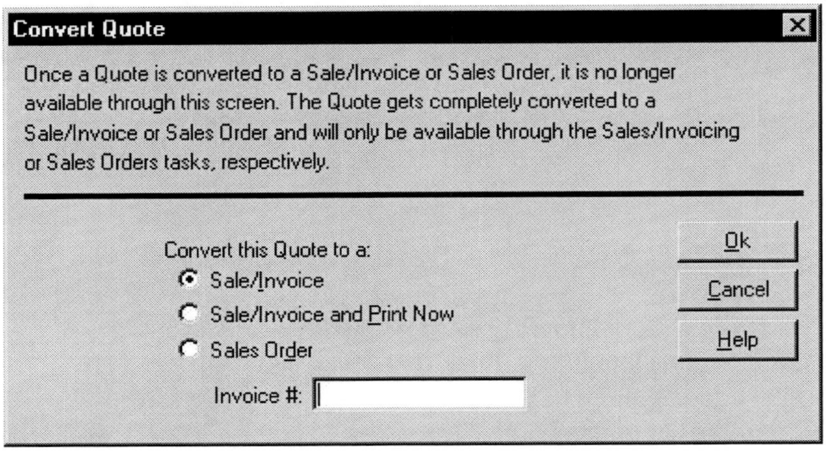

Convert Quote

Once a Quote is converted to a Sale/Invoice or Sales Order, it is no longer available through this screen. The Quote gets completely converted to a Sale/Invoice or Sales Order and will only be available through the Sales/Invoicing or Sales Orders tasks, respectively.

Convert this Quote to a:
- Sale/Invoice
- Sale/Invoice and Print Now
- Sales Order

Invoice #:

Ok
Cancel
Help

FIGURE 5-42   Convert Quote window

The toolbar for the Quotes window is similar to the one in the Sales/Invoices window, but there is a new button, as shown here:

BUTTON	NAME	DESCRIPTION
 Convert	Convert	Converts a quote to a sales order or a sales invoice.

Select one of the three options for converting the quote:

- **Sale/Invoice**   This converts the quote to a sales invoice. You can enter an invoice number for this sales invoice in the Invoice # field at the bottom of the window. If you prefer to have Peachtree Accounting assign a number when you print the invoice, leave this field blank.
- **Sale/Invoice and Print Now**   This converts the quote to a sales invoice and also prints the invoice immediately. If you select this option, Peachtree Accounting will display the Print Forms: Invoices/Credit Memo window (shown in Figure 5-43) so you can select the appropriate form on which to print the invoice. (Information on printing invoices and credit memos appears at the end of this chapter.)

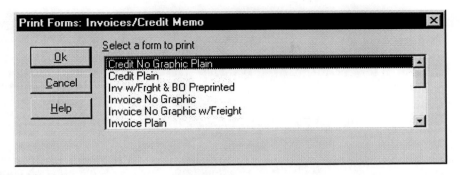

FIGURE 5-43 Invoices/Credit Memo window

- **Sales Order** This converts the quote to a sales order. Use this option if some of the items on the quote are not currently in stock. As with the Sale/Invoice option, you can enter a sales order number for this sales order in the SO# field at the bottom of the window. Once you've entered a sales order, Peachtree Accounting will automatically enter the next available sales order number in the SO# field. You can accept the default entry or enter a new sales order number.

Click OK to convert the quote and enter the information for the sales order or sales invoice in your Accounts Receivable.

C A U T I O N : Once you have converted a quote, you cannot edit the quote further through the Quotes window. To change the information, you must edit the transaction through either the Sales Order or Sales/Invoices window.

Entering Cash Sales and Payments

You enter cash sales for any sales transaction that involves real money (such as cash, checks, and credit card vouchers). You also need to enter payments from customers and apply the cash receipts either to open invoices or directly to income. Record and distribute cash received from customers in the Receipts window.

Entering Cash Sales

To enter cash sales for a customer, select the Receipts option from the Tasks menu. The Receipts window appears, as shown in Figure 5-44. If you selected the option for one-line item entry display rather than two lines in the Maintain Global Options window, the line item entry area will look slightly different, but the way it works will be the same. See the "Setting Global Options" section in Chapter 3 for more information.

 N O T E : If you are using batch posting rather than real-time entry, Peachtree Accounting may prompt you to post several journals before displaying the Receipts window.

Open invoices for customer

Revenue and prepayment information for customer

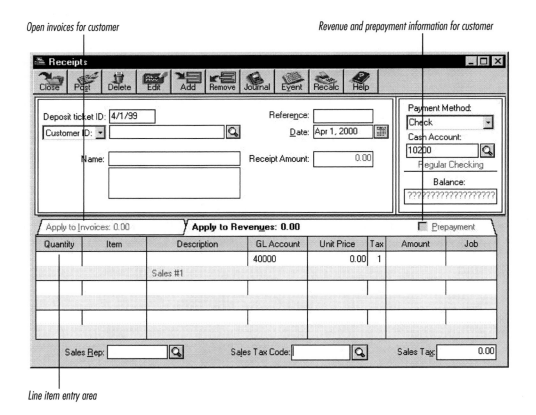

Line item entry area

FIGURE 5-44   Receipts window

The toolbar for the Receipts window is similar to the one in the Sales/Invoices window, but there is a new button, which looks like this:

BUTTON	NAME	DESCRIPTION
Recalc	Recalc	Recalculates the balance for the cash balances (if you have not selected the Automatic Recalculation of Cash option in the Maintain Global Options window).

Enter information in this window as follows:

Deposit Ticket ID   Enter an ID of up to eight alphanumeric characters for the deposit ticket. Peachtree Accounting enters the current date as the default for this field. The deposit ticket ID ties the receipts to the deposit total, making it easy to reconcile the deposits for a deposit ticket. If you deposit less frequently than every day, type in the desired deposit date. Because Peachtree Accounting groups all deposits with the same deposit ticket ID into a single transaction in Accounts Receivable, you should use the date followed by a letter or other unique entry, such as "112099aa" or "11209901."

Customer ID/Vendor ID   Select either Customer ID (if you are entering a customer receipt) or Vendor ID (if you are entering a vendor receipt). When you click the magnifying glass in the ID field (described below), Peachtree Accounting will display customer IDs or vendor IDs depending on what you selected in this field. (Vendor receipts are discussed in Chapter 6.)

ID   Enter the customer ID in the field. When you select the customer ID, Peachtree Accounting enters the customer name.

If you leave the Customer field blank, Peachtree Accounting assumes that you are recording a cash transaction from a person you don't want to set up as a customer, and it will update the General Ledger without affecting any customer records. Figure 5-45 shows the Receipts window after selecting a customer from the drop-down list. Note the invoice information in the lower half of the window.

Name   If you entered a customer ID in the previous field, Peachtree Accounting fills the customer name in automatically. If this is a direct sale with no customer record, type the customer name in this field. If you are dealing with a large quantity of direct sales with no corresponding customer names, you may want to just enter a generic name such as DIRECT in this field.

Reference   Enter a reference entry of up to 20 alphanumeric characters, such as the word CASH, the customer's check number, or the authorization code for the credit card transaction. Whatever you use should fit with your style of record keeping.

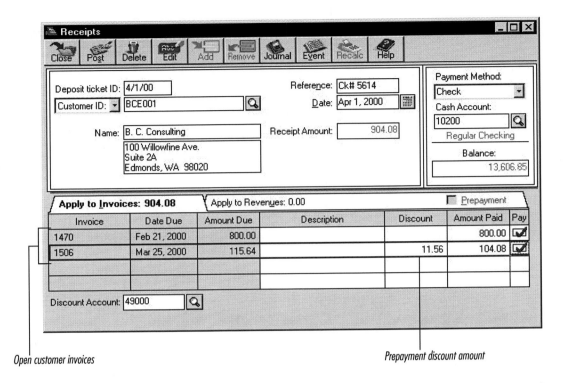

Open customer invoices   Prepayment discount amount

FIGURE 5-45 | Receipts window with customer information and open invoices

Date   Enter the deposit date for the receipt. Click the Calendar button or right-click in this field to display the Peachtree Accounting date-selection calendar.

Receipt Amount   Peachtree Accounting calculates this field for you based on the amounts you enter in the lower half of the screen. This field is display-only.

Payment Method   Select one of the payment methods in this list. The options you can select from are the payment methods you set up earlier in the Pay Methods folder of the Customer Defaults window.

Cash Account   Enter the General Ledger account to apply the deposit to.

Balance   The balance in this display-only field is the cash balance as of this accounting period.

When you first display the Receipts window, you may see question marks in the Balance field. Click Recalc in the toolbar to recalculate the balance and display it in this field. You can tell Peachtree Accounting to automatically recalculate the balance by checking the checkbox in the Global Options window called Recalculate Cash Balance Automatically in Receipts and Payments.

Having entered the header information for this receipt, you now need to tell Peachtree Accounting how to distribute the receipt. The default is for Peachtree Accounting to apply receipts to the customer's open invoices (if any)— otherwise, Peachtree Accounting applies the receipt to revenue. You can apply a receipt to both invoices and revenue by clicking on each tab and entering the appropriate distributions in each section.

Entering Credit Card Sales

Treat credit card sales just as if they were cash sales. Enter the amount of the charge in the Amount Paid field and select the appropriate credit card listing in the Payment Method field.

NOTE: You will have to enter the discount percentage for your credit card sales as an entry in the General Journal. See Chapter 4 for more information. The credit card discount account in the General Ledger will be an expense account.

Applying Receipts to Open Invoices

The most agreeable part of Accounts Receivable is receiving payments from your customers. You should post payments to customer accounts as soon as you receive them.

To apply some or all of a receipt to a customer's open invoices, first click on the Apply to Invoices tab in the lower half of the window to display the customer's open invoices (as shown in Figure 5-45). The invoice ID, date due, and amount due are taken from the invoice information you entered in the Sales/Invoices window.

Description   Enter a description of the transaction in this field. This description appears on selected Accounts Receivable reports.

Discount   The default for this field is the early payment discount set up for this customer. Peachtree Accounting displays this if the invoice is still within the discount time. You can enter a different discount amount if you want.

Amount Paid   Enter the amount you want to pay on this invoice. For a partial payment, enter an amount in the Amount Paid column. Peachtree Accounting keeps a running total in the Receipt Amount field. Make sure that you don't enter more money than you've received. A customer may include a credit invoice with a payment. Be sure to indicate this as paid when cash is applied. (If the customer is paying off the entire invoice, you can simply click the Pay checkbox for this item. Peachtree Accounting fills in the receipt total in this field.)

Pay   Peachtree Accounting automatically checks this box when you make an entry in the associated Amount Paid field. If you uncheck the Pay checkbox, any entry in the Amount Paid field is erased.

When you're satisfied with your entries, you can click Post to complete the receipt, or click the Apply to Revenues tab to apply the remainder of the receipt to revenues.

Applying Receipts to Revenues

You apply receipts to revenues if the receipt is for a cash sale for which there is no invoice, or if the receipt is for an invoice not yet entered in Peachtree Accounting. Click the Apply to Revenues tab to display the revenue information in the lower half of the Receipts window (as shown earlier in Figure 5-45).

Check the Prepayment box if the receipt is for an invoice not yet entered in Peachtree Accounting. You can also check the Prepayment box if you've received a down payment. (You must have specified a customer ID to check the Prepayment box. You cannot apply a prepayment to an invoice. You also cannot split a prepayment.)

Enter information in the Quantity, Item, Description, GL Account, Unit Price, Tax, Amount, Job, Sales Rep, Sales Tax Code, and Sales Tax fields as you did on the Sales/Invoicing windows earlier.

When you're satisfied with your entries, you can click Post to complete the receipt.

Invoice Payment Status

You can now view the current payment status of invoice transactions in the Purchase/Receive, Sales/Invoicing, and Inventory task windows. After you post the invoice or apply a payment to it, the payment status is displayed. The payment status can be Unpaid, Partially Paid, or Paid in Full. If you make a payment on an invoice, Peachtree Accounting displays the net amount due in the invoice task window. Figure 5-46 shows a sales invoice Paid in Full.

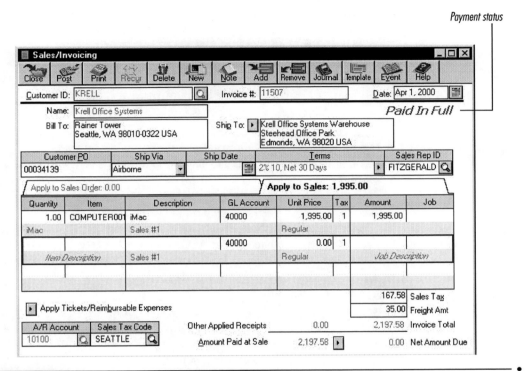

FIGURE 5-46   Paid in Full Sales/Invoicing window

Posting Accounts Receivable Transactions

In Chapter 3, you saw how to set up your business for either batch or real-time posting. In real-time posting, Peachtree Accounting immediately updates the company's financial information (when you click Post on the task window), while batch posting saves the entries in a temporary file (when you click Save on the task window) that you can review before you post them.

If you're using real-time rather than batch processing, you don't need to post entries as a separate step. Peachtree Accounting does it for you automatically. But if you are using batch posting, you need to post transactions to the customers' accounts. The posting process clears the Invoice Register of outstanding unposted invoices, updates the inventory information based on the sales and returns, and updates customer account and invoice balances. To post invoices, select the System option from the Tasks menu, then select Post from the submenu. The Post window appears, as shown in Figure 5-47.

Click the checkbox for All Journals (the default) to post all transactions, or click the checkboxes for the various journals, such as the Cash Receipts Journal and the General Journal, to post to just those journals.

C A U T I O N : If you aren't posting to all journals at once and you're using inventory, be sure to post purchases and payments before posting sales and receipts.

Click OK to post the transactions. Peachtree Accounting displays the progress for posting to each journal on the screen. If you have a transaction that would post to a journal you haven't selected for posting—for example, if you have a payroll transaction, but haven't selected the payroll journal—Peachtree Accounting doesn't post that transaction.

You can also unpost transactions from selected journals or all journals. Unposting removes posted transactions from the General Ledger for the current period and periods forward. You can then edit or delete these transactions and then repost them. To unpost transactions, select the System option from the

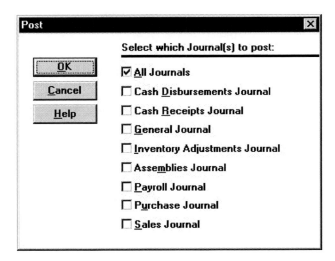

FIGURE 5-47 Post window

Tasks menu, then select Unpost from the submenu. The Unpost window appears. Choose the journals you want to unpost transactions from and click OK to begin unposting.

 NOTE: You can only post and unpost if you are using batch processing.

Applying Finance Charges

Peachtree Accounting makes computing finance charges very easy. Select the Finance Charge option from the Tasks menu. The Calculate Finance Charges window appears, as shown in Figure 5-48.

Starting Customer   Enter the starting customer ID in the range to compute finance charges for. To apply finance charges for a single customer, enter the customer ID in this field and click Starting Customer Only at the bottom of the window. If you leave the starting and ending fields blank, Peachtree Accounting will apply finance charges for all customers.

Ending Customer   Enter the ending customer ID in the range to compute finance charges for.

Type Mask   Enter an optional customer type to select a specific group of customers. For more information, see the discussion of masking in the "Account Types" section of Chapter 4.

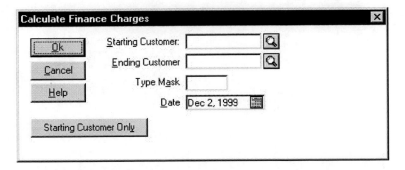

FIGURE 5-48   Calculate Finance Charges window

Date Enter the date you want to calculate the finance charges for. The default for this field is the current date.

When you are satisfied with your entries, click OK. The Apply Finance Charges window appears, as shown in Figure 5-49.

From the Apply Finance Charges window, you set options for applying or not applying finance charges and printing reports. You can print a report of the finance charges without actually applying them (select the Yes option button under Print Calculation Sheet). When you print a report, the Finance Charge Report Selection window appears, from which you choose a summary or detail report sorted by ID or name.

Writing Off Bad Debts

You will occasionally have to write off some invoices as unrecoverable bad debts. Peachtree Accounting lets you write off bad debts in one of two ways: direct and allowance.

To write off a bad debt using the direct method, you would post the bad debt directly to the Bad Debt expense account at the time of the write-off. To write off a bad debt using the allowance method, you assume that a certain percentage of your receivables are going to be unrecoverable, and then just write off that percentage each year.

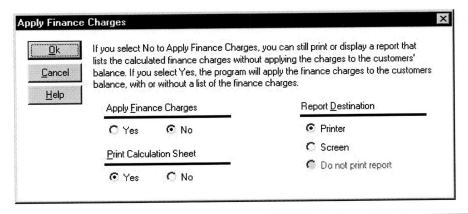

FIGURE 5-49 Apply Finance Charges window

C A U T I O N : Unless you are dealing with a high volume of bad debts, or there are specific tax reasons why you should do so, you should not use the allowance method of expensing bad debts. Consult with your tax accountant for further information.

To write off a bad debt using the direct method, you enter a payment on the invoice exactly as if you had received a payment from the customer, except that you change the Cash Account field to the General Ledger account for Bad Debt expense.

Enter the appropriate amount you are writing off (you may want to write off only part of an invoice, for example). Peachtree Accounting will apply the money on the invoice to the Bad Debt expense account rather than the cash account.

Printing Accounts Receivable Reports

You should print invoices and credit memos as soon as possible after you have entered them so you can distribute them to your customers quickly. The due dates for invoices and credit memos are based on the date you enter the information rather than when the invoices and credit memos are printed. This section shows you how to print invoices and credit memos, as well as a variety of other Accounts Receivable reports.

You've already seen how to select some of the Accounts Receivable reports when you printed the customer reports. Peachtree Accounting has an extensive collection of Accounts Receivable reports, statements, and invoices, as shown in Table 5-4.

In addition to these specific reports, there are six folders of forms:

- Invoices/Credit Memos/Packing Slips
- Customer Statements
- Labels - Customer
- Customer Quotes
- Sales Orders
- Collection Letters

Each of the folders contains a selection of forms. Forms are reports that are print-only—you can print them, but you can't see them on the screen.

Customer List	Prospect List
Customer Master File List	Invoice Register
Quote Register	Sales Journal
Cash Receipts Journal	Sales Rep Reports
Customer Ledgers	Sales Tax Codes
Aged Receivables	Taxable/Exempt Sales
Sales Order Register	Sales Order Journal
Sales Order Report	Sales Backorder Report
Picklist Report	Customer Sales History
Items Sold to Customers	

TABLE 5-4   Accounts Receivable Reports

To print a report or a form, select the appropriate report or form from the Accounts Receivable option from the Reports menu, enter the report options, and click OK. You can customize all the Accounts Receivable reports and forms or create new ones using Peachtree Accounting's Forms Designer. See Chapter 12 for more information on how to do this.

Space considerations make it impractical to show samples of all the reports and forms that Peachtree Accounting has to offer, but there are a few reports and forms you will be using regularly that you should know about.

Printing an Aged Receivables Report

The most important Accounts Receivable summary report is the Aged Receivables report. The Aged Receivables report lets you check your anticipated income quickly and easily.

To print an Aged Receivables report, select the Accounts Receivable option from the Reports menu. Then select the Aged Receivables report from the Select a Report window, enter the range of customer IDs and customer types, and click OK. Figure 5-50 shows a typical Aged Receivables report as displayed on the screen. The beginning balances for the customers appear in the current column. As with many other reports, you can double-click on the highlighted area and drill down to get more detail on a specific Accounts Receivable item.

Many accounting systems require you to actively "age" the accounts before printing an Aged Receivables report. Peachtree Accounting automatically calculates the aging for each balance based on the current date. You can perform more sophisticated aging analysis with the Collection Manager, described in Chapter 13.

Big Business, Inc.
Aged Receivables
As of Apr 30, 2000
Filter Criteria includes: Report order is by ID. Report is printed in Detail Format.

Customer ID Customer Contact Telephone 1	Invoice No	0-30	31-60	61-90	Over 90 days	Amount Due
BCE001 B. C. Consulting B. C. Williams 206-555-2341 x17	1470 1506		115.64	800.00		800.00 115.64
BCE001 **B. C. Consulting**			**115.64**	**800.00**		**915.64**
KRELL Krell Office Systems Missy Krell 206-555-1433	KRE001	2,197.58 86.72			1,003.34	1,003.34 2,197.58 86.72
KRELL **Krell Office Systems**		**2,284.30**			**1,003.34**	**3,287.64**

FIGURE 5-50	Sample Aged Receivables report

Printing Invoices, Sales Orders, Credit Memos, and Quotes

There are reports and forms for invoices, credit memos, sales orders, and quotes. The three corresponding reports are the Invoice Register, the Sales Order Register, and the Quote Register, which list an overview of the invoice, sales order, and quote activity for a period, respectively. Forms include invoices, credit memos, packing slips, customer statements, customer labels, customer quotes, sales orders, and collections letters.

Printing Registers

The most important invoice report is the Invoice Register, a summary report of invoices. You use the Invoice Register to check your entries for the invoices and credit memos you've entered before posting them, as well as for a record of the invoices and credit memos posted in a given period.

To print an Invoice Register, select the Accounts Receivable option from the Reports menu. Then select the Invoice Register from the Select a Report window and enter the range of invoice numbers, customer IDs, customer types, and the printed status (whether or not the invoice has been printed yet), and click OK. Figure 5-51 shows a typical Invoice Register as displayed on the screen.

As with the Aged Receivables report, when you display the Invoice Register on the screen, you can double-click any line item on the Invoice Register to display the actual invoice information in the Sales/Invoicing window.

There are matching reports for sales orders and quotes called the Sales Order Register and the Quote Register. The Sales Order Register lists all sales orders, open or closed. The Quote Register lists the outstanding quotes for customers. Like the Invoice Register, if you display these reports on the screen, you can double-click any line item on the report to display the actual information in the appropriate window.

Printing Forms

Peachtree Accounting offers you a wide variety of invoices, packing slips, customer statements, and customer quotes. All of these are for printing only—you cannot display forms on the screen.

For all forms, you can print an alignment form by clicking Align in the Report Options window rather than OK. This lets you align the forms on your printer before printing. Peachtree Accounting lets you specify vertical and horizontal offsets through the program rather than having to manually adjust the forms in the printer. (This is required for laser printers, which can't be

Big Business, Inc.
Invoice Register
For the Period From Apr 1, 2000 to Apr 30, 2000
Filter Criteria includes: Report order is by Invoice Number.

Invoice No	Date	Quote No	Name	Amount
	4/1/00		Krell Office Systems	2,197.58
	4/1/00		Krell Office Systems	86.72
	4/1/00		Lily Pod Systems	
11507	4/1/00		Krell Office Systems	2,197.58
Total				**4,481.88**

FIGURE 5-51 Sample Invoice Register

adjusted like a dot matrix or daisy wheel printer.) You can also print a practice form (one with Xs in the fields) by clicking Practice.

You'll want to print customer invoices whenever there is customer invoice or credit memo activity. At the beginning of every accounting period, you may also want to send statements to all customers with active accounts. These statements show the customers a summary of their account activity along with their current account balance. You can create customer statements at any time in the accounting period and print them as often as you like. Like invoices, you print quotes whenever you create a quote for a customer, but you can also print them at any other time in the period.

To print a customer form, select the Accounts Receivable option from the Reports menu. Then select the appropriate folder of reports from the report list, and double-click the specific form within the folder. Enter the selection options and click OK to start printing.

 TIP: Peachtree Accounting comes with a wide range of forms. You may want to spend some time printing samples of each of the types of form you are likely to use for a more detailed examination.

Printing Journal Reports

There are three Accounts Receivable journal reports: the Sales Journal report, the Cash Receipts Journal report, and the Sales Order Journal report. The Sales Journal report lists the sales transactions in a journal format. The Cash Receipts Journal report lists the receipts in a journal format. The Sales Order Journal lists the sales orders in a journal entry format. You use all three reports to verify the General Ledger postings.

Printing a Sales Rep Report

The Sales Rep report lists the total sales for each salesperson and shows the appropriate commissionable sales for each sale. You can print this report as often as you like. You must assign sales rep IDs to invoices and receipts to use this report. For more information on entering sales reps, see Chapter 7.

Printing Other Sales Order Reports

In addition to the Sales Order Register and the Sales Order Journal reports described earlier, Peachtree Accounting comes with three other Sales Order reports:

- **Sales Order Report** This report shows detailed information about open sales orders.
- **Sales Backorder Report** This detailed report lists each item that appears on the outstanding sales orders, the stock on hand, and the number you have ordered on outstanding purchase orders. (Run this report after applying your sales orders to outstanding invoices to get an accurate picture of your inventory versus your sales orders.)
- **Picklist Report** This report lists the items for each open sales order in a worksheet format. It will be used primarily by your company's order fulfillment department to assemble sales orders in the warehouse.

Printing Taxable/Exempt Sales Report

The Taxable/Exempt Sales report lists the totals accumulated for the tax codes you have set up. You can use this information to send payments to the various state, county, and city tax agencies.

Printing Collection Letters

You may occasionally have to send collection letters to customers whose balances are overdue. Most customers will respond to a friendly reminder letter, but some will need a firmer reminder.

Peachtree Accounting comes with a variety of predefined collection letters. To print collection letters, select the Accounts Receivable option from the Reports menu. Then select the Collection Letters folder from the Select a Report window and choose the letter you want. Enter the range of customer IDs, customer types, the age of the oldest outstanding invoice, and the sales rep ID, and click OK to start printing.

As with other forms, you can print an alignment form by clicking Align rather than OK, and a sample by clicking Practice.

Printing Customer Labels

Peachtree Accounting lets you print shipping and mailing labels for customers. These make it easy both to ship product to customers and to send your customers invoices, advertisements, or other mailings. Select the Labels - Customer folder from the list of Accounts Receivable reports, then select the labels you want to print.

Printing Other Accounts Receivable Reports

In addition to the reports and forms listed earlier in this chapter, there are several other Accounts Receivable reports:

- **Prospect List**   This report lists the names and telephone numbers of prospects.
- **Customer Ledgers**   This report lists detailed transaction information on outstanding Accounts Receivable balances for customers.
- **Sales Tax Codes**   This report lists sales tax codes, sales tax authorities, tax rates, and associated vendor information.

Using Management Tools

In addition to the Accounts Receivable reports and forms, Peachtree Accounting has a selection of management tools to help you manage your business (including your receivables).

- The Action Items window lets you log business events for customers, create to-do lists, and set alerts (for events such as inventory or cash on hand falling below a minimum level, or customers exceeding a credit limit or sales volume). The Action Items window is a simple personal information manager (PIM) that is integrated into Peachtree Accounting.
- The Cash Manager helps you project income and cash flow. You can use the Cash Manager to display transactions in Accounts Receivable, Accounts Payable, and Payroll. You can also use the Cash Manager to enter forecasted income and expenses.

- The Collection Manager focuses specifically on Accounts Receivable. You can analyze your Accounts Receivable information, do detailed aging of receivables, and graph income.

The Action Items and the tools in the Manager Series are discussed in detail in Chapter 13.

Summary

Setting up Accounts Receivable is one of the most lengthy tasks in setting up your business in Peachtree Accounting, but it is also one of the most pleasant: you are now ready to receive money from your customers. In this chapter, you've seen how to set up Accounts Receivable defaults for customers, statements, invoices, and sales tax codes. You've also seen how to create and maintain customer records, enter sales and receipts, print a variety of Accounts Receivable reports, and post transactions. In the next chapter, you'll see how to set up Accounts Payable, add vendors, enter invoices and credits, issue payments, and print checks.

Accounts Payable and Purchase Orders

B A S I C S
- How to set up vendor defaults
- How to enter vendor records
- How to enter purchase orders
- How to make payments
- How to print Accounts Payable reports and checks

B E Y O N D
- How to post Accounts Payable transactions
- How to receive inventory
- How to enter credit memos
- How to void checks

In this chapter, you'll learn how to set up Accounts Payable defaults, enter vendor records, create purchase orders and one-time purchases, receive inventory, and print checks. You'll also see how to generate credit memos, void checks, and print a wide variety of Accounts Payable reports and statements.

In Chapter 5, you saw how to set up Accounts Receivable defaults for customers, statements, and invoices; create sales tax codes and customer records; enter sales and receipts; print a variety of Accounts Receivable reports; and post transactions. In this chapter, you'll see how to set up and use these Accounts Payable functions: add and edit vendor information, print vendor reports, enter vendor invoices and purchase orders, select bills for payment, print checks and assorted Accounts Payable reports, and post Accounts Payable transactions.

Accounts Payable is the third and final component, along with General Ledger and Accounts Receivable, of the basic accounting cycle. Accounts Payable is simply the money you owe to vendors. Each time you purchase a product or service from a vendor on credit, the amount you owe the vendor is charged to the Accounts Payable account in the General Ledger. Where Accounts Receivable increases your company's assets, Accounts Payable increases your company's liabilities. The steps for setting up and using Accounts Payable are as follows:

1. Set up Accounts Payable and vendor defaults.
2. Add, modify, and delete vendors.
3. Add, modify, and delete vendor invoices.
4. Select invoices for payment.
5. Print checks.

The process for setting up Accounts Payable is very much like the process for setting up Accounts Receivable. If you have not already set up Accounts Receivable, review Chapter 5 for more information.

Setting Up Accounts Payable Defaults

Accounts Payable does not require nearly as much information as Accounts Receivable before you are ready to enter transactions and generate payments. However, extra time spent planning how you will use Accounts Payable will save you a great deal of time later on.

 N O T E : If you haven't done so already, you should set up the business and the General Ledger (see Chapters 2, 3, and 4). You use Accounts Payable to post information about payables to the General Ledger automatically. You should also familiarize yourself with the procedures described in Chapter 5, which are very similar to the procedures in this chapter.

The first step in setting up Accounts Payable is to set up your vendor defaults. Vendor defaults determine such things as standard payment terms for your company, account aging for invoices, and custom fields with which you can track specific vendor information.

You've seen how to select an option from the Setup Checklist in previous chapters when you entered the General Ledger and Accounts Receivable defaults. If the Setup Checklist is not already displayed, select the Setup Checklist option from the Maintain menu. From the Setup Checklist, click the Vendor Defaults item. The Vendor Defaults window appears with the Payment Terms folder already selected, as shown in Figure 6-1. (You can also display this window by selecting the Default Information option from the Maintain menu, then selecting the Vendors option from the submenu.)

The Payment Terms folder lets you set the default payment terms. (Vendor defaults can be overridden for any one vendor in the vendor record or for a specific purchase.)

Standard Terms   Select the default payment terms used by vendors. You can select C.O.D., Prepaid, Due in number of days, Due on day of next month, or Due at end of month. If you select C.O.D. or Prepaid, you won't need to set up defaults for most of the other fields in the Payment Terms folder.

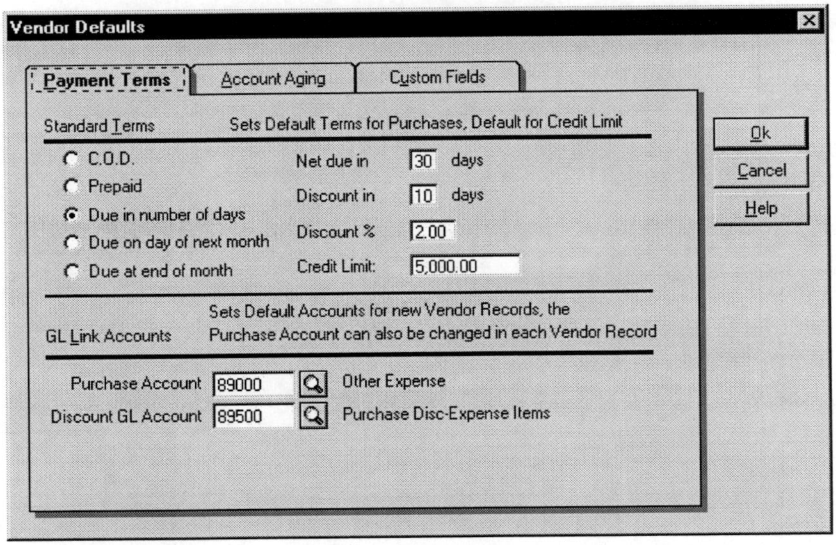

| FIGURE 6-1 | Vendor Defaults window showing the Payment Terms folder |

Net Due in ... Days   Enter the number of days after the date of the invoice before the invoice comes due. Typically, you will enter 0 (due immediately) or a number from 10 to 30 days.

Discount in ... Days   Enter the limit on discounts. This would typically be from 0 to 15 days.

Discount %   Enter the percentage most of your vendors allow for an early payment.

Credit Limit   Enter the default credit limit for your vendors. For example, you may want to set up a credit limit of $500.00. If you don't use or don't want to assign a credit limit, leave the default at $0.00.

Purchase Account   Enter the default General Ledger account used for purchases. Use a Cost of Goods Sold account type to accurately track the cost of your products or services.

Discount GL Account   Enter the General Ledger account used for Accounts Payable discounts. Use a Cost of Goods Sold account type to accurately track the cost of your products or services.

When you're satisfied with your entries, click the Account Aging tab to enter account aging defaults. The Account Aging folder appears, as shown in Figure 6-2.

The Account Aging folder lets you set the aging options for payables.

Age Invoices By   Select either Invoice Date or Due Date as your means of determining aging. You may want to set your vendor aging by due date, and your Accounts Receivable customer aging (discussed in Chapter 5) by invoice date. This will help extend your payables to the limit while getting your receivables as quickly as possible.

Aging Categories   Set the number of days for each aging category and the appropriate heading for the column on the aging report. Aging categories are typically set for 30, 60, and 90 days, but you can also enter other values; for example, entering 0 for the first field will show all current invoices. The fourth aging category is whatever is older than the final aging category.

The Aged Payables report is a standard analysis tool used to monitor cash flow and set up timed and future payments. How you use this report will depend on your cash receipts pattern in Accounts Receivable as compared to recurring payments that must be made (such as rent and payroll taxes). When you're satisfied with your entries, click the Custom Fields tab to enter custom tracking information. The Custom Fields folder appears, as shown in Figure 6-3.

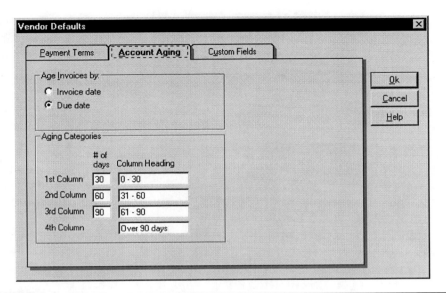

FIGURE 6-2 Vendor Defaults window showing the Account Aging folder

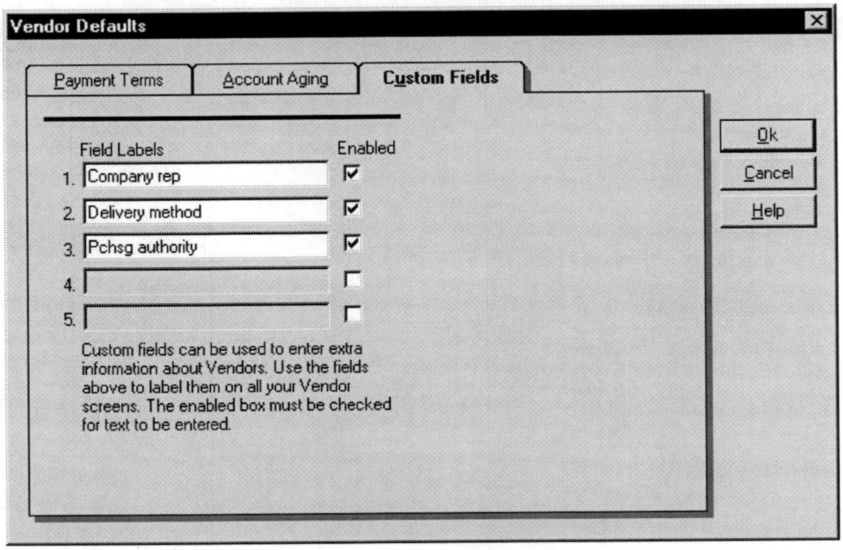

FIGURE 6-3 Vendor Defaults window showing the Custom Fields folder

The Custom Fields folder lets you set default labels for tracking specific vendor information that you enter in the Maintain Vendors window for each vendor. (The Maintain Vendors window is discussed later in this chapter.) For example, you may want to set up custom fields for the company services, sales rep or secondary contact, or anticipated annual purchases.

Field Labels   Enter up to five categories in the fields here. The information in these fields is used for headings in the Maintain Vendor window, as well as on some of the Accounts Payable reports.

Enabled   Click the box to enable or disable the field label. If the Enabled box is not checked, the field label will not appear in the Custom Fields folder in the Maintain Vendor window. The Enabled box must be checked for you to enter text in the associated Field Labels field.

When you are satisfied with your entries, click OK. As usual, Peachtree Accounting will ask if you want to mark this task as completed on the Setup Checklist. If you choose Yes, Peachtree puts a checkmark next to the item to indicate that you've completed this portion of the setup.

Setting Up and Maintaining Vendor Records

Once you've set up your Accounts Payable and vendor defaults, you're ready to start entering vendor information. A vendor is anyone from whom the company buys goods or services. You enter vendor information for each of your company's suppliers. Each vendor will have a record similar to the customer records you entered earlier in Accounts Receivable. Once you have entered vendor information, you can enter vendor beginning balances. (Chapter 5 introduced you to one type of vendor: sales tax authorities.)

Entering a Vendor Record

There are four types of information you enter to set up a vendor record: general vendor information, purchase defaults, custom fields, and vendor history. You also need to enter a beginning balance for the vendor if you have any outstanding invoices for them. This section shows you how to enter all this information.

Entering General Vendor Information

From the Setup Checklist, click the Vendor Records item. The Maintain Vendors window appears with the General folder already selected (shown in Figure 6-4). (You can also display this window by selecting the Vendors option from the Maintain menu.)

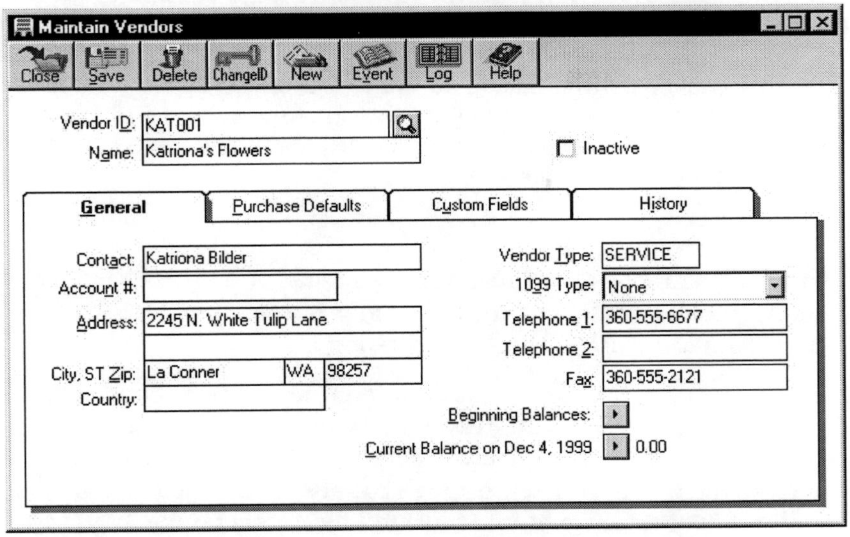

FIGURE 6-4 Maintain Vendors window showing the General folder

Enter information for a vendor as follows:

Vendor ID   Enter the vendor ID. Vendor IDs can be up to 20 characters long and can contain any characters except the asterisk (*), question mark (?), or plus sign (+). Click the magnifying glass to the right of the field to show a drop-down list of the existing vendor IDs.

If you are setting up the accounting system for an established business, you may be able to use their existing vendor IDs. If you are just starting out on your own, you may need to set up a vendor ID system of your own. A common vendor ID is the first few letters of the vendor's name followed by a number. For example, if the vendor's name were "Consolidated Amalgamations," the vendor ID would be something like CON001. If there were another company with the same first three letters, such as "Construction Suppliers," their vendor ID would be CON002. Using the first few letters of the company's name gives you a reasonably intuitive way of looking up the company in the vendor file.

Although you have up to 20 characters to work with, you should keep your vendor IDs simple, perhaps 6 or 8 characters long. As with General Ledger account IDs and customer IDs, vendor IDs are case sensitive, so Peachtree Accounting treats the vendor IDs CON001 and con001 differently. You may want to set a policy that all letters in vendor IDs be entered as capital letters.

TIP: If you need to change a vendor ID from the Maintain menu, select Vendors. To display a list of existing vendors, type **?** in the Vendor ID field, or select the Lookup button. Select the Change ID button on the window toolbar. Type the new ID that you want to use instead of the current ID. Select OK to change the ID. If you change a vendor ID, all current and past data records and transactions will be changed.

Name   Enter the vendor's name. You can enter up to 30 characters in this field. Accounts Payable will list the vendor name as you have entered it on vendor purchase orders, checks, and reports.

Inactive   Check this box to set the vendor to inactive status. Although you can update the name and address information, Peachtree Accounting will warn you if you try to post a purchase order or payment to an inactive vendor. When you close the fiscal year, Peachtree Accounting will delete the vendor records for all inactive vendors with no outstanding transactions.

To delete inactive vendors, you must purge them. This is usually done at the end of the fiscal period or the fiscal year. Purging vendors is discussed in Chapter 13. You may want to set a vendor to inactive instead of deleting the vendor because you need to run 1099s or other reports at year-end processing. This lets you maintain a record of the vendor information until you close the fiscal year.

Contact   Enter the contact name for the vendor. This field may be up to 20 characters. Accounts Payable includes the vendor contact name on the Vendor List report. (The Vendor List is discussed later in the "Printing Vendor Reports" section.)

The contact information will not print on the check. If you need the check to go to a specific person, consider putting the name in the address data fields.

Address   Enter the address (not including the city, state, and ZIP code). If you have only one line of address information, enter it on the first line and leave the second line blank.

City, ST Zip   Enter the city, state, and zip code for this address.

Country   Enter the country for this address. If you prefer, you can use this line for reference information, such as "ATTN: AP."

Vendor Type   This is a custom field in which you can enter up to eight characters to identify the type of vendor. You might set up a coding system to group vendors by salesperson, geographic region, sales territory, type of business, or type of purchase. For example, all vendors dealing in office supplies might have a vendor type of "SUPPLIES." This field is case sensitive.

1099 Type   There are three types of 1099 classification: None, Interest, and Independent Contractor. Select Independent Contractor if the vendor has received more than $600 in a given year as an outside contractor. Select Interest if the vendor has received more than $10 from you on a loan. Select None for all other vendors. 1099s are discussed later in this chapter in the "Printing 1099s" section.

Telephone 1   Enter the primary telephone number for the vendor.

Telephone 2   Enter the secondary telephone number for the vendor.

Fax   Enter the fax number for the vendor.

Entering Purchase Defaults

After you have entered the general vendor information, click on the Purchase Defaults tab. The Purchase Defaults folder appears, as shown in Figure 6-5. (You'll see how to enter a beginning balance for vendors later.)

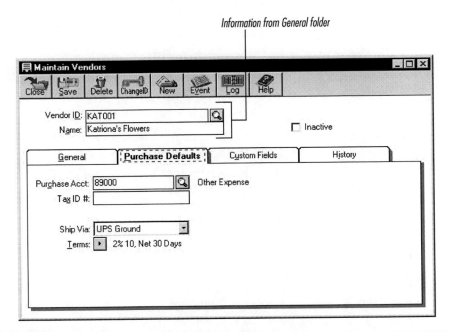

You set purchase defaults for such things as the vendor's tax ID, shipping options, and terms of sale. As you can see, the information in the top part of the Purchase Defaults folder is carried forward from the information you entered in the General folder. You can work with this vendor or select another one by clicking on the magnifying glass or right-clicking in the Vendor ID field. You can also change the name and inactive information for the vendor from this folder.

Enter the purchase defaults as follows:

Purchase Acct   Enter the General Ledger sales account for this vendor's purchase account. (You will normally want to use an Expense account.) Select the General Ledger account that describes the most common expense item for this vendor (for example, use the Rent Expense account for payments to your landlord). Choose the Inventory account for adding items to stock.

If the vendor is likely to supply items or services that are reimbursable expenses or can otherwise be passed through to the customer (such as filing fees, copies, faxes, or professional services), you may want to set up an expense and income set of General Ledger accounts with an account type of Cost of Sales in order to record the amounts paid and the amounts received. This will let you track the net profit of your cost of sales easily.

Tax ID #   Enter the vendor's federal tax ID number. This information will appear on 1099 forms. (You only need to do this if you send the vendor a 1099 form.) The best source for this information is the vendor's W-9 form.

Ship Via   Enter the default shipper the vendor uses. Carriers are entered as part of the default information for Inventory, discussed in Chapter 8. If you are setting up Peachtree Accounting for the first time here, you will have to leave this field blank until you've entered the inventory information.

Terms   The default value for payment terms (based on the vendor defaults you entered earlier) appears to the right of Terms. Click Terms to select the terms for the current vendor record. The Vendor Terms window appears (shown in Figure 6-6).

Select the terms you want to use for this vendor. The options and fields are the same as those you set in the Payment Terms folder of the Vendor Defaults window (shown earlier in Figure 6-1).

The default for any vendor is to use the standard payment terms, which you set up in the Vendor Defaults window. When the Vendor Terms window first appears, the Use Standard Terms checkbox is checked and all other options are grayed out. You must clear the Use Standard Terms checkbox to select another option in the window. If you want to use the vendor defaults, leave the Use Standard Terms box checked. Click OK to accept the changes you've made, or Cancel to exit the window without changing the payment options.

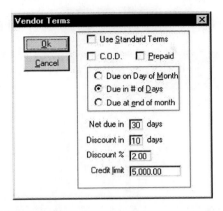

FIGURE 6-6 Vendor Terms window

Entering Custom Fields

When you are satisfied with the purchase default information, click on the Custom Fields folder. The Custom Fields folder appears, as shown in Figure 6-7. As you saw earlier in the Purchase Defaults folder, the vendor information in the top part of the folder is carried forward from the information you entered in the General folder. You can work with this vendor, select another one, or change the name and inactive information for the vendor from this folder.

In the window shown in Figure 6-7, three of the custom fields are labeled with information entered through the Custom Fields folder of the Vendor Defaults window (shown earlier in Figure 6-3).

As with the custom fields in customer records shown in Chapter 5, custom field information is primarily for ready reference and "tickler file" types of information. You can print custom field information on reports, but you cannot sort or select vendors based on this.

Entering Vendor History

When you are satisfied with the custom field information for this vendor, click the History tab. The History folder appears, as shown in Figure 6-8. As you saw in the previous vendor folders, the vendor information in the top part of the folder is carried forward from the information you entered in the General folder. You can work with this vendor, select another one, or change the name and inactive information for the vendor from this folder.

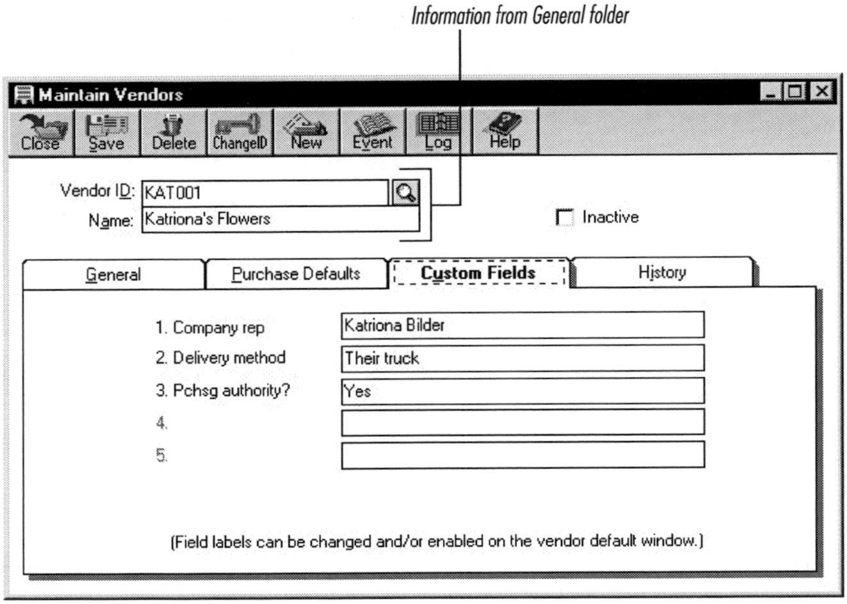

Information from General folder

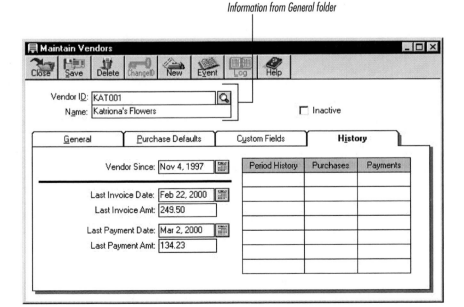

FIGURE 6-7   Maintain Vendors window showing the Custom Fields folder

Information from General folder

FIGURE 6-8   Maintain Vendors window showing the History folder

When you're setting up the vendor, you can enter information in this folder. Once you save the vendor record, Peachtree Accounting locks this folder so that it is read-only—you'll be able to see the vendor's history in the folder, but you won't be able to make any changes to it.

Vendor Since Enter the date of the first purchase from the vendor.

Last Invoice Date Enter the date of the vendor's most recent invoice.

Last Invoice Amt Enter the amount of the vendor's most recent invoice.

Last Payment Date Enter the date of the vendor's most recent payment.

Last Payment Amt Enter the amount of the vendor's most recent payment.

When you're satisfied with the vendor history information, you can save the vendor record. Click Save at the top of the window. Peachtree Accounting saves the vendor information.

You can enter additional vendor records by clicking New at the top of the window (this will clear the entries in all four folders of the Maintain Vendors window) and then entering new information in each folder.

Entering Vendor Beginning Balances

As the last step to setting up a vendor, you enter the vendor's beginning balance. You could have entered the vendor's beginning balance when you entered the information in the General folder, but you would have had to save the record first, and this would have prevented you from entering information in the History folder.

To enter a beginning balance for a vendor, go to the General folder in the Maintain Vendors window and select the vendor by entering an ID in the Vendor ID field, then click Beginning Balances. The Vendor Beginning Balances window appears with the Purchases From folder displayed. Figure 6-9 shows this window with sample invoices already entered.

You enter beginning balances for the vendor from the previous window. The vendor ID and name appear on the folder tab. The beginning balance is based on the vendor's outstanding invoices. (If this is a new vendor with no prior activity, you won't need to enter a beginning balance.)

This information is *not* posted to the General Ledger, as later invoices will be during invoice processing. These balances must add up to what you posted as your beginning balance in the General Ledger. You can change the beginning balance as long as a payment is not applied to the vendor. Once you have applied a payment to this vendor, you must first delete the payment before you can edit the beginning balance.

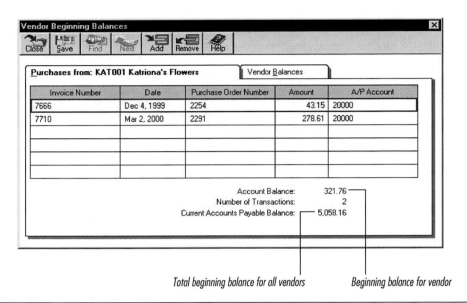

Total beginning balance for all vendors   Beginning balance for vendor

FIGURE 6-9 Vendor Beginning Balances window with sample invoices

Invoice Number Enter the outstanding invoice number. (This is a required entry to enter beginning balances for a vendor.) If a vendor only issues statements, it's a common accounting practice to use the date of the statement as the invoice number.

Date Enter the invoice date. Right-click in this field to display the Peachtree Accounting date-selection calendar.

Purchase Order Number Enter the purchase order number. (If there is no purchase order number, leave this field blank.)

Amount Enter the invoice amount.

A/P Account If you are using accrual accounting, enter the Accounts Payable account for this customer. You can right-click in the field or click on the magnifying glass icon for a drop-down list of accounts. If you are using cash accounting, you won't be able to enter an account number in this field. Instead, the field will be grayed out and will read "<Cash Basis>."

Press ENTER to move to the next invoice line. As you enter new invoices, the balance for the vendor appears in the Account Balance total at the bottom of the window. When you're satisfied with the invoice information you've entered, click Save at the top of the window.

The Vendor Balances folder shows you the current balances for vendors and the total of the beginning Accounts Payable balances. Figure 6-10 shows the Vendor Balances folder in the Vendor Beginning Balances window after entering the first few vendor records. Keep in mind that the balance at the bottom of the window must match the beginning balance you entered in the General Ledger for the Accounts Payable account.

This folder is only for viewing balances. You cannot enter information here, but you can double-click on a vendor line and display the invoice information for the vendor. To close the Vendor Beginning Balances window and return to the Maintain Vendors window, click Close at the top of the window. As shown in Figure 6-11, this window now shows a current balance as of the current date.

You can see an onscreen printout of the vendor's ledger by clicking Current Balance at the bottom of the window. A sample vendor ledger appears as in Figure 6-12. (If you want to print vendor ledgers for detailed transaction information, you need to select the Vendor Ledgers report from the list of Accounts Payable reports available through the Reports menu, as shown later in this chapter.)

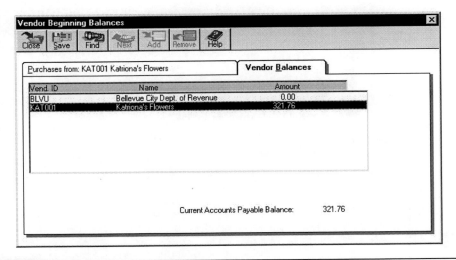

FIGURE 6-10 Vendor Beginning Balances window showing the Vendor Balances folder

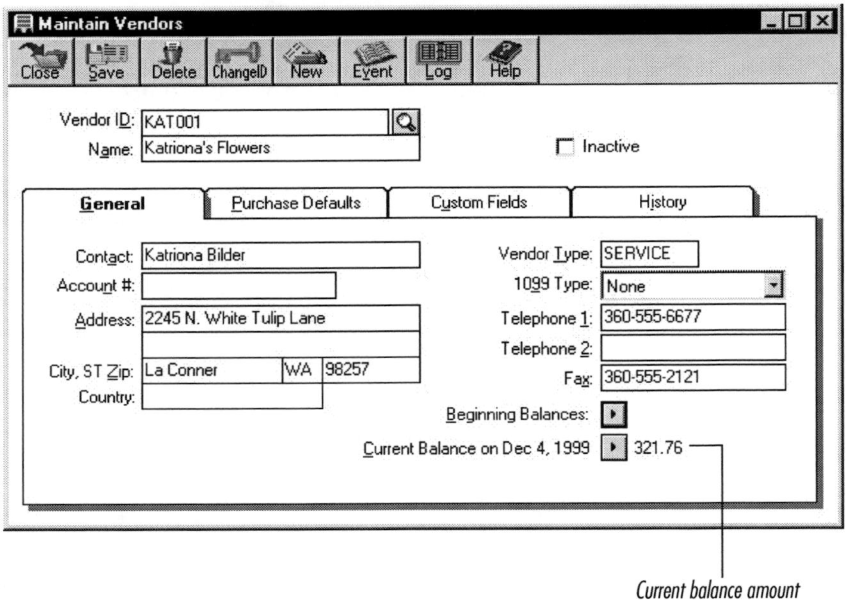

Current balance amount

FIGURE 6-11 | Maintain Vendors window with a current balance for the vendor

Modifying Vendor Records

Once you've entered a vendor record, you can modify it. Modifying a vendor record is easy. First, display the vendor record in the Maintain Vendors window by entering the vendor ID in the Vendor ID field. You can then change any of

FIGURE 6-12 | Sample vendor ledger

the vendor information except for the vendor ID itself. If you want to change a vendor ID from the Maintain menu, select the Change ID button on the window toolbar. Type the new ID you want to use instead of the current ID. Select OK to change the ID. If you change a vendor ID, all current and past data records and transactions will be changed.

Deleting Vendor Records

You can delete a vendor record by selecting a vendor record and then clicking Delete at the top of the window. Peachtree Accounting asks if you're sure you want to delete this record. Click Yes to delete the vendor record.

C A U T I O N : You cannot delete a vendor record if there are any transactions against the vendor. In such a case, you may want to flag the vendor as inactive so activity is not entered for the vendor without Peachtree Accounting warning you that the vendor is inactive and asking you if you want to post activity to the vendor.

Printing Vendor Reports

Now that you've entered the vendor information, you can print a report of the vendors to verify the information you've entered. There are three reports for vendor information:

- **Vendor List**   Lists each vendor along with their contact name, telephone numbers, and resale number.
- **Vendor Master File List**   Lists the detailed information entered in the Maintain Vendor window.
- **Vendor Ledgers**   Lists the detailed transaction information and outstanding balance for each vendor.

   To print each of the reports, select Accounts Payable from the Reports menu. The Select a Report window appears with the Accounts Payable option selected. Next, select the appropriate report from the list by double-clicking or by highlighting the report and selecting Screen or Print at the top of the screen. Enter the report selection information on the report selection screens and click OK. The report appears on the screen or is sent to the printer. Figures 6-13, 6-14, and 6-15 show these three reports for selected vendor information.

Big Business, Inc.
Vendor List

Filter Criteria includes: Report order is by ID.

Vendor ID	Vendor	Contact	Telephone 1	Tax Id No
ABR001	ABR Microcomputer Supply	Fred Carlson	425-555-8533	C600 000 0540
BLVU	Bellevue City Dept. of Revenue	Gerry Smith	425-555-6415	
FUZ002	Fuzzy Llama Software	O. Guanaco	206-555-1642	C600 000 0101
KAT001	Katriona's Flowers	Katriona Bilder	360-555-6677	C600 000 0009
KING	King County Dept. of Revenue	Bill Luttner	360-555-6677	
KIRKLAND	Kirkland City Dept. of Revenue	James K. Habbakuk	425-555-0931	
SEATTLE	Seattle City Dept. of Revenue	Bill Wooten	206-555-1726	
VSC001	Visual Senses Computing	J. Stewart	253-555-2341	C600 999 9876
WAREV	WA State Dept. of Revenue	Margaret Sutton	206-555-4205	

FIGURE 6-13 Sample Vendor List report

Big Business, Inc.
Vendor Master File List

Filter Criteria includes: Report order is by ID.

Vendor ID Vendor	Address line 1 Address line 2 City ST ZIP	Contact Telephone 1 Telephone 2 Fax Number	1099 Type Tax Id No Terms Vend Since
ABR001 ABR Microcomputer Supply	12401 Northup Way Suite 44 Bellevue, WA 98007	Fred Carlson 425-555-8533	None C600 000 0540 2% 10, Net 30 Days 12/5/99
BLVU Bellevue City Dept. of Revenue	Bellevue City Hall Room 224A Bellevue, WA 98004	Gerry Smith 425-555-6415	None 2% 10, Net 30 Days 11/21/99
FUZ002 Fuzzy Llama Software	5656 Aurora Seattle, WA 98103	O. Guanaco 206-555-1642	None C600 000 0101 2% 10, Net 30 Days 12/5/99
KAT001 Katriona's Flowers	2245 N. White Tulip Lane La Conner, WA 98257	Katriona Bilder 360-555-6677 360-555-2121	None C600 000 0009 2% 10, Net 30 Days 11/4/97

FIGURE 6-14 Sample Vendor Master File List report

Big Business, Inc.
Vendor Ledgers
For the Period From Apr 1, 2000 to Apr 30, 2000

Filter Criteria includes: Report order is by ID.

Vendor ID Vendor	Date	Trans No	Type	Paid	Debit Amt	Credit Amt	Balance
ABR001 ABR Microcomputer Supply	4/1/00	Balance Fwd					4,215.00
BLVU Bellevue City Dept. of Reven	4/1/00	Q4-99 Taxes	PJ			412.38	412.38
FUZ002 Fuzzy Llama Software	4/1/00	5234A	PJ			22.00	22.00
KAT001 Katriona's Flowers	4/1/00	Balance Fwd					922.13
KING King County Dept. of Revenu	4/1/00	1999 County B&	PJ			984.01	984.01
KIRKLAND Kirkland City Dept. of Reven	4/1/00	Balance Fwd					96.52
SEATTLE Seattle City Dept. of Revenue	4/1/00	Balance Fwd					278.61

FIGURE 6-15	Sample Vendor Ledgers report

As with many other reports, when you display the Vendor Ledgers report on the screen, you can double-click on a line to display and optionally edit the actual transaction through the Purchases window, described later in this chapter.

The vendor information is now complete. In the future, you will simply add, update, and delete vendor records as necessary. You are now ready to start entering purchase orders and vendor invoices.

Entering Purchases

Now that you've set up vendor defaults and vendor records, you can start entering purchase orders and vendor invoices. Entering purchase orders and vendor invoices is very similar to the process for entering customer sales orders, sales invoices, and quotes as described in Chapter 5.

Purchase orders are similar to quotes, in that the accounting information you enter is not entered into Accounts Payable, because you have not yet received the merchandise. You create and print a purchase order to send to a vendor.

Entering Purchase Orders

A purchase order is an authorization to a vendor for a specified list of items. Purchase orders are not entered into the vendor totals or the General Ledger until you receive the items listed on the purchase order or, if your company uses cash rather than accrual accounting, when you enter a payment for the vendor. Peachtree Accounting lets you enter vendor invoices for which there are no preceding purchase orders through the Purchases/Receive Inventory window—for example, when you receive an invoice from your vendor.

To enter a purchase order, select the Purchase Orders option from the Tasks menu. The Purchase Orders window appears, as shown in Figure 6-16. If you selected the option for one-line item entry display rather than two lines in the Maintain Global Options window (described in Chapter 3), the line item entry area will look slightly different, but the way it works will be the same.

The Purchase Orders window has the same features as the Sales/Invoicing window discussed in Chapter 5. Table 6-1 shows you a list of the buttons and what they're used for.

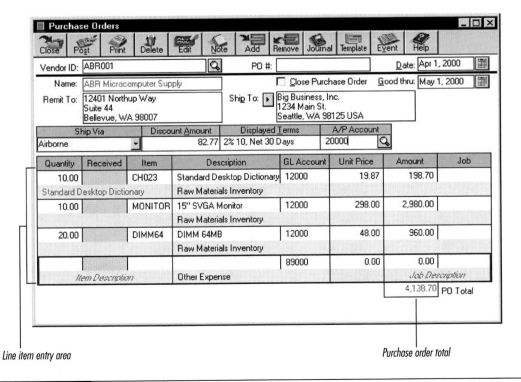

Line item entry area

Purchase order total

FIGURE 6-16   Purchase Orders window

BUTTON	NAME	DESCRIPTION
	Close	Close the window and the current purchase order without saving the information.
	Post	Post the information in the fields.
	Print	Print and post a purchase order.
	Delete	Delete the current transaction.
	Edit	Edit the records for a vendor.
	Note	Create notes to print on a purchase order before or after the purchase order's line items.
	Add	Add a line item to the purchase order.
	Remove	Remove a line item from the purchase order.
	Journal	Displays the Accounting Behind the Screens window.
	Template	Displays a list of available templates for the displayed task window.
	Event	Show or create daily events related to the displayed vendor.
	Help	Get help in the Purchase Orders window.

TABLE 6-1　Toolbar Buttons in the Purchase Orders Window

To enter a purchase order, fill in the fields in the Purchase Orders window.

 N O T E :　The Purchase Orders window is used for entering purchase orders only. To enter a purchase invoice (for material purchased directly) or to receive inventory ordered with a purchase order, you must use the Purchases/Receive Inventory window, discussed later in this chapter.

Vendor ID　Enter the vendor ID in the field. The vendor must already be set up through the Maintain Vendors window. If you are entering a one-time purchase from a vendor you don't want to add to the vendor list, use the Payments window (described later in this chapter) instead of this window.

When you select the vendor ID, Peachtree Accounting enters the vendor name and the Remit To address in the appropriate fields. Peachtree Accounting will also enter vendor defaults such as the Ship To information, Ship Via information, Discount Amount, Displayed Terms, and A/P Account.

PO #   Enter the purchase order number (or other reference number) in the field. This can be up to 20 alphanumeric characters. If you are planning to print the purchase order, leave this field blank. Peachtree Accounting will automatically assign the next available purchase order number. You can also assign a number when you print the purchase order.

Date   Enter the date from the vendor's invoice. If your system date falls within your current accounting period (such as October 25 within the 10th accounting period), Peachtree Accounting uses the system date as the default date. Otherwise, Peachtree Accounting defaults to the first day of the accounting period. Click the Calendar button or right-click in the field to display the date-selection calendar.

Name   This field is for display purposes only. The information comes from the vendor record.

Close Purchase Order   Mark the checkbox to close the purchase order. Peachtree Accounting automatically closes the purchase order when you have logged all the items as being received in Inventory, at which time you can then purge the purchase order. (You may also want to close a purchase order if you know that the vendor will never ship all the items on the purchase order to you.)

Good Thru   Enter a date that the purchase order will be good through. This date appears on the printed purchase orders. Click the Calendar button or right-click in the field to display the date-selection calendar.

Remit To   The default for this field is the vendor's address. This field is display-only. You can change this information through the Maintain Vendors window.

Ship To   Peachtree Accounting displays the primary address for your company as it appears in the Maintain Company Information window described in Chapter 3. You can change the ship-to address by clicking the button to the left of the field. The Ship To Address window (shown in Figure 6-17) appears, in which you can change the shipping address for this invoice. You can also use this address for drop shipments.

Ship Via   Peachtree Accounting displays the default shipping method for the vendor (if you set one up in the vendor record). You can select an alternate shipping method by clicking the button to the right of the field and selecting a shipping method from the drop-down list.

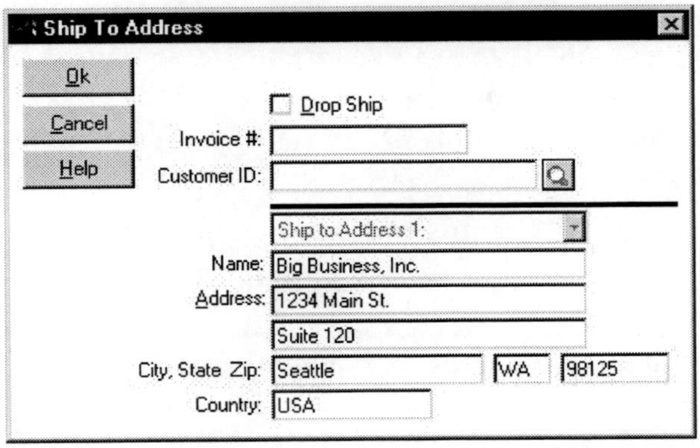

FIGURE 6-17 Ship To Address window

Discount Amount Peachtree Accounting calculates the default discount amount based on the discount terms in the vendor record and the amount of the line items in the invoice. You can override the default discount amount by entering the discount amount for early payment. Enter volume or other large discounts that aren't date-dependent as a credit line item on the invoice.

Peachtree Accounting recalculates the discount amount each time you enter a new line item. If you want to make changes to the discount amount, wait until you have entered all the line items on the invoice.

Displayed Terms Peachtree Accounting displays the default terms in the vendor record (if you set terms up). You can type a different entry in this field if you want.

N O T E : Changing the displayed terms will not automatically recalculate any discounts for you. They will have to be manually changed in the discount amount field.

A/P Account Enter the General Ledger account to apply the invoice to. The default entry for this field is the last account entered in the field. If you are entering a purchase for a cash-basis company, Peachtree Accounting grays out this field and enters the phrase "<Cash Basis>." Enter the discount amount in the Discount Amount field. You can distribute this to specific General Ledger accounts from the Payments window, discussed later in this chapter.

Once you've added the heading information for the purchase order, you're ready to add line items. You can add up to 155 line items per purchase order. The purchase order information you enter depends on the items and prices set up in the Inventory section. If you haven't set up items yet for your business, you'll need to add items as described in Chapter 8.

Quantity   Enter the quantity of the item purchased.

C A U T I O N :   The defaults for entering numbers apply to this field. If you have set the global options to automatic decimal point entry, entering 4 in this field would be treated as .04, resulting in a quantity of .04 units. Add a decimal point after the quantity (4.) to make sure that you've specified a quantity of 4. See Chapter 3 for more information on setting this global option.

Received   This field is grayed out when you enter the purchase order information. When you apply inventory received against this purchase order, Peachtree Accounting updates the Received field to show the quantity received. You can enter this in the Purchases/Receive Inventory window.

Item   Enter the item ID in this field. This is not a required field; if you are entering an item that is not set up in Inventory, or you do not use Peachtree Accounting's Inventory features, press TAB to skip this field. Be aware that when you are first setting up Peachtree Accounting for your business, you will not have any items set up. For more information on setting up items, see Chapter 8.

Description   The default description is the description for the item. You can enter up to 160 alphanumeric characters in this field.

GL Account   The default General Ledger account number is the General Ledger account number for the item if you set one up in Inventory. If you did not enter an item in the Item field, Peachtree Accounting uses the General Ledger account you set up for this vendor in the vendor record. You can enter a different General Ledger account number for this item if you want.

Unit Price   The default unit price is the unit price for the item if you set one up in Inventory. You can skip this field by pressing ENTER and just enter a total for the transaction in the Amount column if you prefer.

Amount   Peachtree Accounting computes the amount from the unit price and the quantity. You can accept the computed amount or enter a different amount.

Job   Enter the job ID this purchase order should be applied to. If there is no job that applies to this expense, leave the field blank. (For more information on setting up jobs, see Chapter 9.) If this purchase is to be passed through to a customer as a reimbursable expense, you cannot enter an item in the Item field. See the "Applying Reimbursable Expenses" section in Chapter 5 for more information.

Once you enter the item information for a single line item, Peachtree Accounting moves you to the next line in the line item section. You can enter up to 155 line items on any single purchase order. The Add and Remove buttons let you add and remove line items from the purchase order.

PO Total   Peachtree Accounting computes the purchase order total as the sum of the individual line item amounts.

When you are satisfied with your entries, you can post the purchase order by clicking Post on the toolbar.

Adding a Note to a Purchase Order

If you need to add a note to a purchase order, click Note. The Note window appears (as shown in Figure 6-18).

You can enter a note of up to 250 characters. The text you enter will print before or after the line items, depending on which Print Note option you select. Use this to enter a personal note to a vendor about the purchase order.

FIGURE 6-18   Note window

Editing Purchase Orders

To edit a purchase order, you need to select the purchase order you want to change. Start by clicking Edit on the toolbar in the Purchase Orders window. The standard selection window appears. Double-click the purchase order you want to edit. Peachtree Accounting displays the information in the Purchase Orders window. Make the changes to the record. When you are satisfied, click Post on the toolbar to save your changes.

Printing Purchase Orders

Once you have entered your purchase orders, you'll need to print them to send them to your vendors. To print a purchase order, click Print on the toolbar. The Print Forms: Purchase Orders window appears:

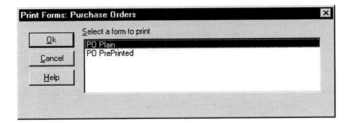

Peachtree Accounting has two predefined purchase order print options in the Purchase Orders folder within the Accounts Payable report list. The first, PO Plain, prints purchase orders on plain paper. The second, PO PrePrinted, prints purchase orders on a standard preprinted purchase order form. The preprinted purchase orders (and other preprinted checks and forms shown in this chapter) can be obtained from Peachtree. A catalog of preprinted stock is included in the Peachtree Accounting package, or you can phone Peachtree directly at (800) 61-PEACH for information.

Select the purchase order form you want to print and click OK. The Print Forms window for that purchase order form appears:

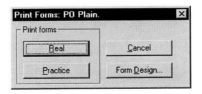

As with forms described in other chapters, you can print a practice form (one with Xs in the fields) by clicking Practice. This lets you see what the form looks like before you print a real one and shows how to align the forms on your printer before printing. Peachtree Accounting lets you specify vertical and horizontal offsets through the program rather than having to manually adjust the forms in the printer. (This is required for laser printers, which can't be adjusted like a dot matrix or daisy wheel printer.) Remember, the purchase order forms only print on the printer; they don't appear on the screen.

When you print the real purchase order (by clicking Real), Peachtree Accounting displays the About to Print Purchase Order window (shown here) and asks you to specify the starting number for the purchase order.

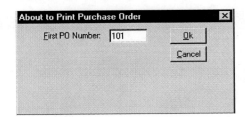

Peachtree Accounting enters a default purchase order number of 101, but you can change this if you like. When you click OK, Peachtree Accounting starts printing the purchase order. When you look at the purchase order again in the Purchase Orders window, you will see that Peachtree Accounting has assigned the purchase order number to the purchase order.

To print all the purchase orders you have entered (or a range of purchase orders), select Accounts Payable from the Reports menu. The Select a Report window appears with the Accounts Payable option selected. Next, select the Purchase Orders folder from the list, then select the purchase order report you want. Enter the information in the report selection windows and click OK. (Remember, purchase orders only print if you haven't entered a purchase order number.)

Although the standard reports and forms in Peachtree Accounting will do for a wide range of business situations, you can customize all the reports and forms or create new ones using Peachtree Accounting's Forms Designer. See Chapter 12 for more information on how to do this.

Entering a Vendor Invoice

Depending on how your business operates, you may not use a formal purchase order process all the time. For example, you may phone a vendor and ask them to send you merchandise. When the merchandise comes, you will receive a vendor invoice with the shipment. You need to enter this information directly into Accounts Payable.

To enter a vendor invoice, select the Purchases/Receive Inventory option from the Tasks menu. The Purchases/Receive Inventory window appears, shown in Figure 6-19 with a typical purchase entered.

The Purchases/Receive Inventory window has roughly the same features as the Sales Orders window discussed in Chapter 5. There is one additional button that appears in the Purchases/Receive Inventory window that does not appear in the Purchase Orders window, as shown here:

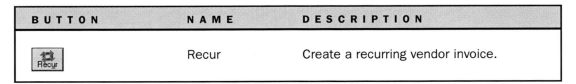

BUTTON	NAME	DESCRIPTION
Recur	Recur	Create a recurring vendor invoice.

To enter a vendor invoice, fill in the fields in the Purchases/Receive Inventory window.

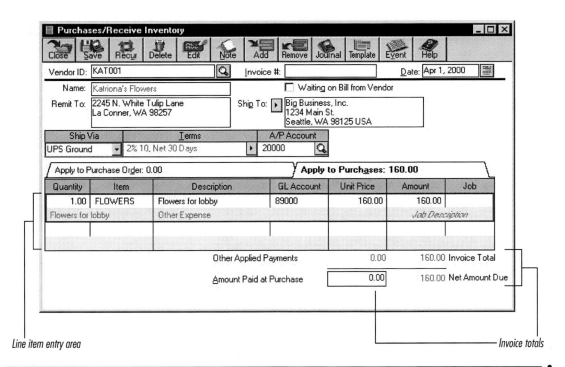

Line item entry area

Invoice totals

FIGURE 6-19 Purchases/Receive Inventory window

Vendor ID   Enter the vendor ID in the field. If the vendor has not already been set up through the Maintain Vendors window, you can enter the vendor on the fly by clicking the New Record button at the bottom of the drop-down list. If you are entering a one-time purchase from a vendor you don't want to add to the vendor list, use the Payments window (described later in this chapter) instead of this window.

When you select the vendor ID, Peachtree Accounting enters the vendor name and the Remit To address in the appropriate fields. Peachtree Accounting will also enter vendor defaults such as the Ship To information, Ship Via information, Terms, and A/P Account.

Invoice #   Enter the vendor's invoice number (or other reference number) for the vendor's invoice in the field. This can be up to 20 alphanumeric characters. It's a common accounting practice to use the date of the statement as the invoice number for vendors that only issue statements.

Date   Enter the date from the vendor's invoice. If your system date falls within your current accounting period (such as October 25 within the 10th accounting period), Peachtree Accounting uses the system date as the default date. Otherwise, Peachtree Accounting defaults to the first day of the accounting period. Click the Calendar button or right-click in the field to display the date-selection calendar.

Name   This field is for display purposes only. The information comes from the vendor record.

Waiting on Bill from Vendor   Check this field only when you have not yet received a bill from the vendor, such as when you are entering inventory receipts. (This process is discussed later in the section "Receiving Inventory.") Otherwise, leave this checkbox blank when you are entering a vendor invoice.

Remit To   The default for this field is the vendor's address. This field is display-only. You can change this information through the Maintain Vendors window.

Ship To   Peachtree Accounting displays the primary address for your company as it appears in the Maintain Company Information window described in Chapter 3. You can change the ship-to address by clicking the button to the left of the field. The Ship To Address window (shown earlier in Figure 6-17) appears, in which you can change the shipping address for this invoice.

Ship Via   Peachtree Accounting displays the default shipping method for the vendor (if you set one up in the vendor record). You can select an alternate shipping method by clicking the button to the right of the field and selecting a shipping method from the drop-down list.

Terms   The default terms for this vendor appear in this field. These are the terms as entered for the vendor in the Maintain Vendors window. You can click on the arrow to the right of this field to display the Terms Information window where you can enter new or different payment terms.

A/P Account   Enter the General Ledger account to apply the invoice to. The default entry for this field is the last account entered in the field. If you are entering a purchase in a cash-basis company, Peachtree Accounting grays out this field and enters the phrase "<Cash Basis>." You can distribute this to specific General Ledger accounts from the Payments window, discussed later in this chapter.

Once you've added the heading information for the vendor invoice, you're ready to add line items. You can add up to 155 line items per purchase invoice. The vendor invoice information you enter depends on the items and prices set up in the Inventory section. If you haven't set up items yet for your business, you'll need to add items as described in Chapter 8.

Quantity   Enter the quantity of the item purchased.

C A U T I O N :   The defaults for entering numbers apply to this field. If you have set the global options to automatic decimal point entry, entering 4 in this field would be treated as .04, resulting in a quantity of .04 units. Add a decimal point after the quantity (4.) to make sure that you've specified a quantity of 4.

Item   Enter the item ID in this field. This is not a required field; if you are entering an item that is not set up in Inventory, or you do not use Peachtree Accounting's Inventory features, press TAB to skip this field. (When you are first setting up Peachtree Accounting for your business, you will not have any items set up. For more information on setting up items, see Chapter 8.)

Description   The default description is the description for the item. You can enter up to 160 alphanumeric characters in this field.

GL Account The default General Ledger account number is the General Ledger account number for the item if you set one up in Inventory. If you did not enter an item in the Item field, Peachtree Accounting uses the General Ledger account you set up for this vendor in the vendor record. You can enter a different General Ledger account number for this item if you want.

Unit Price The default unit price is the unit price for the item if you set one up in Inventory. You can skip this field by pressing ENTER and just enter a total for the transaction in the Amount column if you prefer.

Amount Peachtree Accounting computes the amount from the unit price and the quantity. You can accept the computed amount or enter a different amount.

Job Enter the job ID that this invoice should be applied to. If there is no job that applies to this expense, leave the field blank. For more information on setting up jobs, see Chapter 9. If this purchase is to be passed through to a customer as a reimbursable expense, you cannot enter an item in the Item field. See the "Applying Reimbursable Expenses" section in Chapter 5 for more information.

Once you enter the item information for a single line item, Peachtree Accounting moves you to the next line in the line item section. You can enter up to 155 line items on any single purchase invoice. The Add and Remove buttons let you add and remove line items from the purchase invoice.

Invoice Total Peachtree Accounting computes the invoice total as the sum of the individual line item amounts.

Amount Paid at Purchase Enter any payment you've made on this vendor invoice.

Net Amount Due Peachtree Accounting calculates the amount due as the difference between the Invoice Total less the Amount Paid (if any). This field is display-only.

When you are satisfied with your entries, you can post the vendor invoice by clicking Post on the toolbar. You can then print the purchase orders you've just entered using the procedure for printing purchase orders described earlier in this chapter.

Receiving Inventory

After you have printed a purchase order for your vendor, the next step is to receive the inventory for that purchase order as it arrives.

To receive inventory, select the Purchases/Receive Inventory option from the Tasks menu. The Purchases/Receive Inventory window appears, as shown in Figure 6-20. You can see in this figure that the Note icon looks slightly different. The squiggly red line shows that there is a note currently entered. In addition, as in other windows, if you selected the option for one-line item entry display rather than two lines in the Maintain Global Options window (described in Chapter 3), the line item entry area will look slightly different, but the way it works will be the same.

To receive inventory against a purchase order, enter the vendor number in the Vendor ID field. If there are open purchase orders against this vendor, the Apply to Purchase Order # folder (the left tab) will be displayed. Click the unlabeled drop-down field in the folder tab. All the open purchase orders for that vendor appear in the list. When you click on the purchase order against which you want to receive inventory, the purchase order information appears in the window, as shown in Figure 6-21.

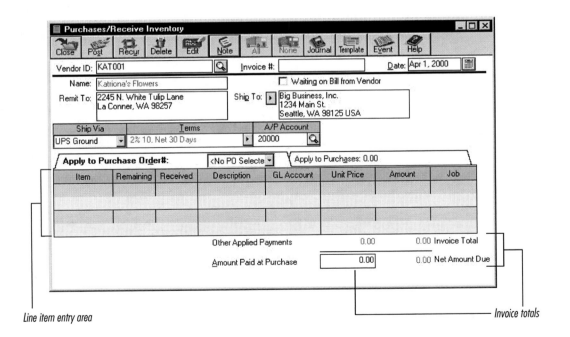

Line item entry area

Invoice totals

FIGURE 6-20 Purchases/Receive Inventory window

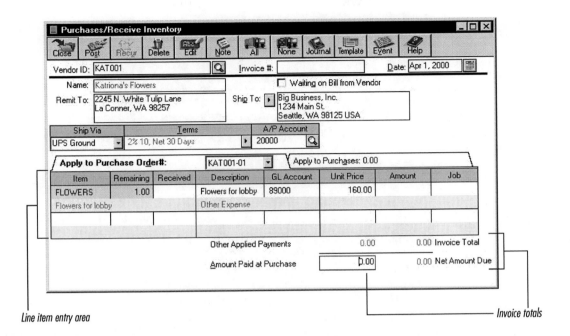

Line item entry area

Invoice totals

FIGURE 6-21   Purchases/Receive Inventory window with open purchase order displayed

The fields in the Purchases/Receive Inventory window are almost identical to those in the Purchase Orders window shown earlier.

To log receipt of inventory, enter the number of items received in the Received field for each line item for which you have received inventory. If you received a bill from the vendor (many vendors will include the invoice with the shipment), enter the number for the vendor's invoice in the Invoice # field. If you have not received a bill from the vendor for this purchase order, check the Waiting on Bill from Vendor box. When you subsequently receive the bill from the vendor, edit the vendor invoice and uncheck the Waiting on Bill from Vendor box and enter the vendor's invoice number. You will then be able to select the invoice for payment. You can't enter a payment for an invoice you have not received, although it will appear in the Payments window. If you have already entered a vendor invoice for inventory, such as from a phone order for which there was no purchase order, and have entered this purchase using the Waiting on Bill option, you will see a warning when you select the vendor so you don't accidentally enter the information twice.

When you are satisfied with your entries, you can post the inventory receipt by clicking Post on the toolbar.

> **N O T E :** From this point forward, transactions that you enter in the Purchases journal will post to the General Ledger and increase and decrease your Accounts Payable accounts automatically.

Entering Recurring Vendor Invoices

Recurring vendor invoices are invoices that Accounts Payable posts to a vendor's account on a regular basis. You may want to set up a recurring vendor invoice if you purchase supplies or materials from a vendor at fixed intervals. You can also use recurring vendor invoices for mortgages or leases, auto, health, and business insurance, loans and notes, and licenses. When you set up a recurring vendor invoice, you tell Peachtree Accounting to pay a fixed amount to a vendor weekly, biweekly, monthly, per period, quarterly, or yearly. At the predetermined time, Peachtree Accounting automatically generates invoices for each of the recurring invoice amounts. You can then select the invoices for payment as you normally would. (Adding recurring entries is discussed in more detail in Chapter 4.)

Setting up automatic transactions can free you from a considerable amount of repetitive work. The following example shows how to set up an automatic transaction for one of Big Business, Inc.'s vendors, who supplies parts to Big Business, Inc., on a monthly basis.

Start by entering a transaction in the Purchases window, as shown in the preceding sections, leaving the invoice number blank. Instead of clicking Post to enter the information, click Recur on the toolbar. The Create Recurring Journal Entries window appears. (The Create Recurring Journal Entries window is the same as the other recurring entries windows described in Chapters 4 and 5.)

You can set up the vendor invoice to recur up to 99 times (but not past the end of the next year). Invoices can recur weekly, biweekly, monthly, per period, quarterly, or yearly. You must have Peachtree Accounting assign invoice numbers automatically.

As usual, if you're editing a recurring entry, a note will appear below the line item area in the Purchases window that identifies the invoice as a recurring entry and shows the number of remaining additional entries.

Putting It to Work

Using Accounting Behind the Screens

You've seen how to edit transactions using the various Accounts Payable windows. Peachtree Accounting's new Accounting Behind the Screens feature lets you fine-tune the information you are entering by letting you edit the journal entries associated with the transaction.

For Accounts Payable, you can use Accounting Behind the Screens in the Purchase Orders, Purchases/Receive Inventory, and Payments windows.

To edit a transaction using Accounting Behind the Screens, do the following:

1. Open the Purchase Orders, Purchases/Receive Inventory, or Payments window from the Task menu.
2. Enter a transaction in the window or select a transaction from the Edit Records window.
3. Click Journal in the window's toolbar. The Accounting Behind the Screens window appears. Depending on the task, Peachtree Accounting will display information in one or more journal folders. Figure 6-22 shows a sample Accounting Behind the Screens window for a transaction from the Purchases/Receive Inventory window.
4. Select the folder tab of the journal you want to edit.
5. Select the line item you want to edit and enter a different account ID.
6. When you are satisfied with your entries, click OK to return to the task window you started from.
7. Click Post to save your changes. (Clicking Print will save and print the transaction.)

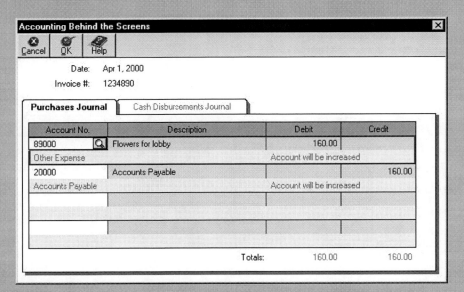

FIGURE 6-22   Accounting Behind the Screens display for a purchase

You can edit all transactions even if they've already been posted. Peachtree Accounting edits the General Ledger and other ledgers the invoice may affect. You can't edit an invoice that's already been paid unless you delete the payment first. See the "Voiding Checks" section later in this chapter for more information.

Deleting Purchase Orders

To delete a purchase order, start by clicking Edit Records in the Purchase Orders window to display the standard selection window. Double-click the purchase order you want to delete. Peachtree Accounting displays the information in the Purchase Order window. Click Delete on the toolbar. Peachtree Accounting asks if you are sure you want to delete the record. Click Yes to delete the record. If receipts have already been applied to the purchase order, Delete will be grayed out. In this case, click the Close Purchase Order box.

Printing Purchase Reports

The final step in the purchase order and vendor invoice process is to print reports. The Accounts Payable reports listed in Table 6-2 are useful for tracking purchase orders and purchases.

 TIP: You can use the Purchase Order Register as a shipping receipt report as well as a tool for purchasing agents to track outstanding purchase orders.

REPORT	DESCRIPTION
Purchase Order Register	Lists the purchase orders and related amounts.
Purchase Journal	Lists the purchases in journal entry format.
Purchase Order Journal	Lists the purchase orders in journal entry format.
Purchase Order Report	Lists the purchase orders in detail format showing what's been ordered and received.

TABLE 6-2   Selected Accounts Payable Reports

To print any of these reports, select Accounts Payable from the Reports menu. The Select a Report window appears with the Accounts Payable option selected. Next, select the Purchase Order Register or the Purchase Journal from the list by double-clicking or by highlighting the report and selecting Screen or Print at the top of the screen. Enter the report selection information in the report selection windows and click OK. The report appears on the screen or prints on the printer. Figures 6-23 through 6-26 show examples of each of these reports.

Big Business, Inc.
Purchase Order Register
For the Period From Apr 1, 2000 to Apr 30, 2000
Filter Criteria includes: Report order is by Date.

PO No	Date	Good Thru	Vendor ID	Amount
KAT001-01	4/1/00	5/1/00	KAT001	160.00
KAT001-02	4/10/00	5/10/00	KAT001	160.00
KAT001-03	4/17/00	5/17/00	KAT001	160.00
				480.00

FIGURE 6-23 Purchase Order Register

Big Business, Inc.
Purchase Journal
For the Period From Apr 1, 2000 to Apr 30, 2000
Filter Criteria includes: Report order is by Date. Report is printed in Detail Format.

Date	Account ID Account Description	Invoice #	Line Description	Debit Amount	Credit Amount
4/1/00	89000 Other Expense	1234890	Flowers for lobby	160.00	
	20000 Accounts Payable		Katriona's Flowers		160.00
4/1/00	20000 Accounts Payable	1234	Katriona's Flowers		
4/1/00	89000 Other Expense	1235	Flowers for lobby	160.00	
	20000 Accounts Payable		Katriona's Flowers		160.00

FIGURE 6-24 Purchase Journal

Big Business, Inc.
Purchase Orders Journal
For the Period From Apr 1, 2000 to Apr 30, 2000
Filter Criteria includes: Report order is by Date. Report is printed in Detail Format.

Date	Account ID Account Description	PO No	Line Description	Debit Amount	Credit Amount
4/1/00	89000 Other Expense	KAT001-01	Flowers for lobby	160.00	
	20000 Accounts Payable		Katriona's Flowers		160.00
4/10/00	89000 Other Expense	KAT001-02	Flowers for lobby	160.00	
	20000 Accounts Payable		Katriona's Flowers		160.00
4/17/00	89000 Other Expense	KAT001-03	Flowers for lobby	160.00	
	20000 Accounts Payable		Katriona's Flowers		160.00
				480.00	480.00

FIGURE 6-25 Purchase Orders Journal

Big Business, Inc.
Purchase Order Report
For the Period From Jan 1, 2000 to Dec 31, 2001
Filter Criteria includes: Report order is by Purchase Order Number. Report is printed with Truncated Descriptions.

PO No	PO Da	Vendor ID Vendor Name	PO Sta	Item ID Line Description	Qty Ordered	Qty Receive	Qty Remaini
KAT001-02	4/10/00	KAT001 Katriona's Flowers	Open	FLOWERS Flowers for lobby	1.00	0.00	1.00
KAT001-03	4/17/00	KAT001 Katriona's Flowers	Open	FLOWERS Flowers for lobby	1.00	0.00	1.00

FIGURE 6-26 Purchase Order Report

Making Payments

The previous sections in this chapter showed how to enter vendors, purchase orders, and vendor invoices. Keeping this information up to date is the main part of the work in Accounts Payable. Once you have your vendors and invoices entered in Peachtree Accounting, you are ready to enter payments and print checks.

Issuing payments involves several steps. First, you print a Cash Requirements report to see how much cash you need to pay all of your open invoices. Next, you select the invoices you want to pay using the Select for Payment or the Payments windows. You then print the checks themselves. Finally, you print the Check Register to show the payments you've made and provide a hard copy of your payments for audit purposes.

Printing the Cash Requirements Report

The Cash Requirements report shows all the outstanding invoices with the due date, discount amounts (if any), and the net-to-pay amounts. You use the Cash Requirements report to check the outstanding invoices against your total cash available for paying bills.

To print the Cash Requirements report, select Accounts Payable from the Reports menu. The Select a Report window appears with the Accounts Payable option selected. Next, select the Cash Requirements report from the list by double-clicking or by highlighting the report and clicking Screen or Print at the top of the window. Enter the information in the report selection windows and click OK. The report appears on the screen or prints on the printer. Figure 6-27 shows a typical Cash Requirements report.

Big Business, Inc.
Cash Requirements
As of Apr 30, 2000

Filter Criteria includes: Report order is by ID. Report is printed in Detail Format.

Vendor ID Vendor	Invoice No	Date	Date Due	Amount Due	Disc Amt	Age
ABR001 ABR Microcomputer Supply	123456	1/17/00	2/16/00	4,215.00		74
ABR001 **ABR Microcomputer Supply**				**4,215.00**		
KAT001 Katriona's Flowers	7666	12/4/99	1/3/00	321.76		118
	7710	3/2/00	4/1/00	278.61		29
	7711	3/9/00	4/8/00	321.76		22
KAT001 **Katriona's Flowers**				**922.13**		
KIRKLAND Kirkland City Dept. of Revenue	KC01234	1/10/00	2/9/00	96.52		81
KIRKLAND **Kirkland City Dept. of Reve**				**96.52**		

FIGURE 6-27 Cash Requirements report

If you have a lot of invoices, or you need to decide how to divide inadequate cash resources over many vendors, you may want to run an Aged Payables report before printing the Cash Requirements report. The Aged Payables report shows aged invoice information for each vendor. You can print the Aged Payables report by selecting it from the report list in the Select a Report window. A typical Aged Payables report appears in Figure 6-28.

Selecting Invoices for Payment

As you can see from Figure 6-27, Peachtree Accounting gives you a running total of the cash necessary to pay the open invoices. If you need to, you can add, change, or delete invoices, and then print another Cash Requirements report. You then need to tell Peachtree Accounting which invoices you want to pay.

The process of paying vendors is very similar to the process of logging payments from customers. You select vendor invoices for payment, make any adjustments necessary to individual disbursements, and print the checks. There are two ways to select invoices for payment. The first (and easiest) is to use the Select for Payments window, which lets you select invoices based on selection criteria you enter. The second is to use the Payments window, which lets you select individual invoices for payment, as well as to print checks for one-time vendors. You will probably want to use the Select for Payments window to select a group of invoices and then use the Payments window to modify or delete individual invoices.

Big Business, Inc.
Aged Payables
As of Apr 30, 2000

Filter Criteria includes: Report order is by ID. Report is printed in Detail Format.

Vendor ID Vendor Contact Telephone 1	Invoice No	0 - 30	31 - 60	61 - 90	Over 90 days	Amount Due
ABR001	123456			4,215.00		4,215.00
ABR Microcomputer Supply	123457	198.70				198.70
Fred Carlson	123789	4,138.70				4,138.70
425-555-8533						
ABR001		4,337.40		4,215.00		8,552.40
ABR Microcomputer Suppl						
BLVU	Q4-99 Taxes	412.38				412.38
Bellevue City Dept. of Reven						
Gerry Smith						
425-555-6415						
BLVU		412.38				412.38
Bellevue City Dept. of Rev						

FIGURE 6-28   Aged Payables report

To select invoices for payment, choose Select for Payment from the Tasks menu. The Select for Payments – Filter Selection window appears, shown in Figure 6-29 with sample dates entered for selecting invoices for payment.

Check Date Enter the date to be printed on the checks (the default is the current system date). Click the Calendar button or right-click in this field to display the date-selection calendar.

Invoices Due Before Peachtree Accounting includes all vendor invoices due before the date you enter in this field. Click the Calendar button or right-click in this field to display the date-selection calendar.

Or Discounts Lost By Peachtree Accounting includes all vendor invoices you would lose discounts for if you didn't pay them by the date you enter in this field. Click the Calendar button or right-click in this field to display the date-selection calendar. Use this option to select invoices to pay that are within the early payment discount period.

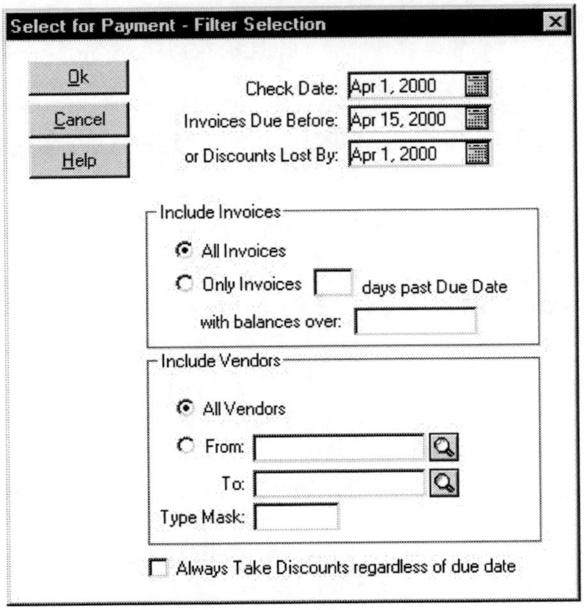

FIGURE 6-29 Select for Payments – Filter Selection window

Include Invoices   If you select All Invoices, Peachtree Accounting will select all outstanding invoices. If you select Only Invoices, you can tell Peachtree Accounting to include invoices a certain number of days past the invoice date and/or with balances over a specified amount. For example, you could specify five days past the invoice date and balances over $100. Peachtree Accounting would select all invoices that were both five or more days past the invoice date or that are over $100. Invoices that were not yet five days past the invoice date and were less than $100 would not be selected. Remember, Peachtree Accounting will include invoices that meet any one of the criteria you select. Be careful that your selections here don't include too broad a group of invoices.

Include Vendors   If you select All Vendors, Peachtree Accounting will pay all vendors or you can enter a range of vendors by specifying beginning and ending vendor IDs in the From and To fields. You can also pay all vendors of a given type by entering the vendor type in the Type Mask field. (You saw how to enter the type mask in the General folder in the Maintain Vendors window.)

Always Take Discounts Regardless of Due Date   Check this to have Peachtree Accounting calculate the discount amount for all invoices even if the due date has passed.

When you're satisfied with your entries, click OK. Peachtree Accounting selects the entries in the journal for payment and displays a detailed list of the invoices selected for payment, as shown in Figure 6-30.

The toolbar for the Select For Payment window has several new buttons, described in Table 6-3.

Check Date   This display-only field shows the check date you specified in the Select for Payment – Filter Selection window.

Cash Acct   Enter the General Ledger account ID for the cash account you will use to write the checks on.

Discount Acct   Enter the General Ledger account ID for the discount account you will use to post discounts.

Sort By   Enter the sorting method for the invoice display in the lower half of the window. The default selection is by invoice date, but you can select due date or vendor sort orders as well.

The invoice detail portion of the window lists the invoice date, due date, vendor name, invoice number, and balance. This information is display-only. You can double-click an invoice (or highlight an invoice and click Detail in the toolbar) to display the actual invoice transaction in a special display-only window (shown in Figure 6-31).

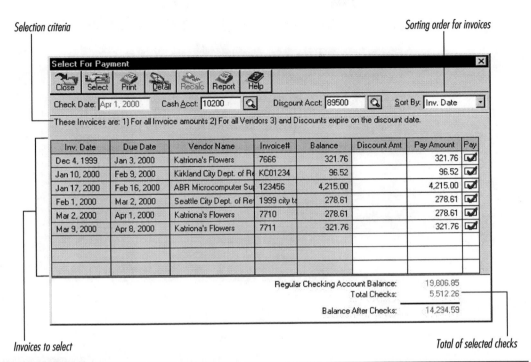

Selection criteria

Sorting order for invoices

Invoices to select

Total of selected checks

FIGURE 6-30   Select For Payment window

BUTTON	NAME	DESCRIPTION
Close	Close	Close the window without saving the information.
Select	Select	Return to the Select For Payment – Filter Selection window to change the selection criteria.
Print	Print	Print and post checks.
Detail	Detail	Show the detail for a selected invoice.
Recalc	Recalc	Recalculate the cash balance for the selected cash account.
Report	Report	Preview checks before they are posted and printed.
Help	Help	Get help in the Select For Payment window.

TABLE 6-3   Toolbar Buttons in the Select For Payment Window

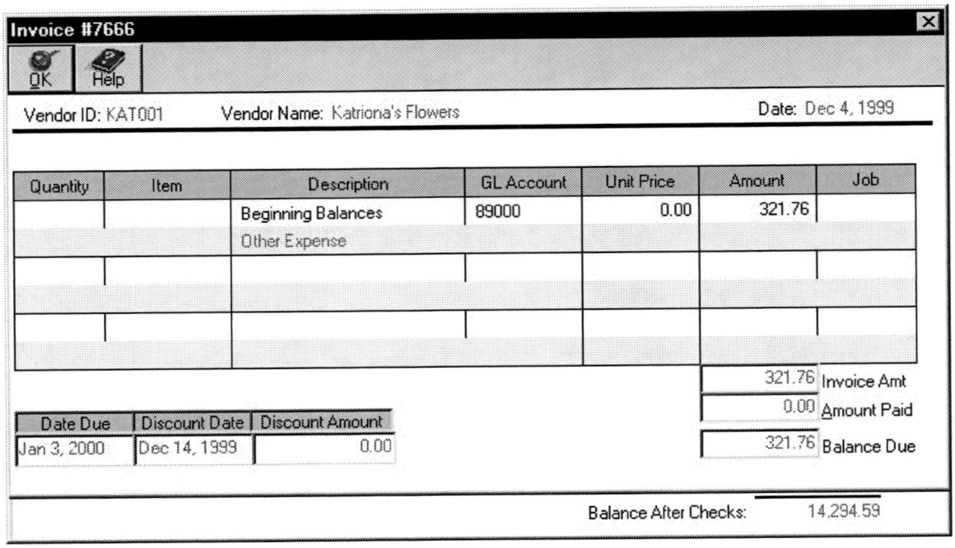

FIGURE 6-31 Invoice detail window

The invoice detail window lets you see the line items for an invoice.

Discount Amt The default for this field is the calculated discount amount. You can accept this default or enter a different amount.

Pay Amount The default for this field is the calculated payment amount. This will be the outstanding balance. You can accept this default or enter a different amount, for example, if you are making a partial payment on an invoice. You can't pay more than the outstanding balance on the invoice.

Pay This checkbox lets you select or deselect the invoice for payment. The default is for the invoices appearing on this screen to be selected for payment, but you can manually deselect an invoice by clearing the Pay checkbox on that line.

Regular Checking Account Balance The current cash in the checking account appears in this field. This field is display-only.

If the field displays question marks, click Recalc in the toolbar. Peachtree Accounting will calculate the cash in the checking account and display the amount in the field. You can set up Peachtree Accounting to always recalculate if you prefer. See the "Setting Global Options" section in Chapter 3 for more information.

Total Checks   The total of the checks selected for payment appears in this display-only field. As you select and deselect checks with the Pay checkboxes, Peachtree Accounting updates the total in this field.

Balance After Checks   Peachtree Accounting displays the balance in the checking account less the total of the checks that are selected for payment. This field is display-only. If there are question marks in the field, click Recalc to have Peachtree Accounting update the balance information. (You can select invoices for payment and print checks even if the total disbursements will leave you with a negative cash balance.)

When you are satisfied with the information you have entered, select Print to print the checks. Or if you would like to see a pre-check register click on report. (The report cannot be sent to the screen). If you select Close without printing, you lose the selections in the window. You'd then have to go back and set new selection criteria in the Select for Payment – Filter Selection window if you wanted to display the same set of invoices again.

Entering Individual Payments and Refunds

You will probably select most of your bills for payment using the Select for Payments option discussed in the previous section. However, you will occasionally want to specify individual payments, either for payments that don't have a vendor invoice or for payments to one-time vendors in the system. You will also need to enter refunds to specific customers.

Entering Individual Payments

Start by selecting Payments from the Task menu. Peachtree Accounting displays the Select a Cash Account window:

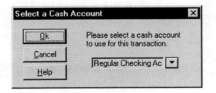

From the drop-down list, select the appropriate cash account to make payments from. (You can leave this at the default and select the cash account later from the Payments window if you prefer.) When you are satisfied with your entries, click OK. The Payments window appears, as shown in Figure 6-32 with sample information.

Check amount

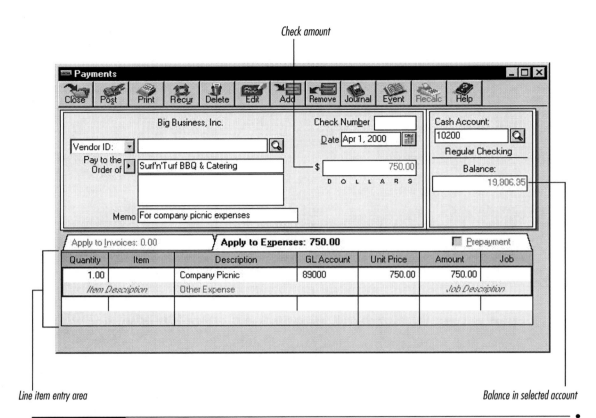

Line item entry area

Balance in selected account

FIGURE 6-32 Payments window

Vendor ID/Customer ID   Select either Vendor ID (if you are entering a vendor payment) or Customer ID (if you are entering a customer refund payment). When you click the magnifying glass in the ID field, Peachtree Accounting will display vendor IDs or customer IDs, depending on what you selected in this field.

If you leave the Vendor ID (or Customer ID) field blank, Peachtree Accounting assumes you are recording a cash transaction to a vendor that you don't want to set up with a vendor record. Peachtree Accounting will therefore only update the General Ledger cash and expense accounts without affecting any vendor records. (The sample information for Surf'n'Turf BBQ & Catering shown in Figure 6-32 is an example of a one-time expense payment.)

Enter the vendor ID in the adjacent field. When you select the vendor ID, Peachtree Accounting enters the vendor name. Peachtree Accounting will also enter vendor defaults such as the General Ledger account, vendor name, vendor address, active invoice information, and cash account balance. If there are active invoices for this vendor, Peachtree Accounting also assumes that payments will be applied to outstanding invoices rather than as an expense. Figure 6-33 shows the Payments window after selecting a vendor from the drop-down list. Note the outstanding invoice information in the lower half of the window.

Pay to the Order Of   If this is a direct payment with no vendor record, enter the vendor name manually in this field. If you are dealing with a large quantity of direct payments with no corresponding vendor names, you may want to just enter a generic name such as DIRECT in this field. (You can also use the Pay to the Order Of button to enter a different address for an existing vendor.)

Vendor Address   If this is a direct payment with no vendor record, enter the vendor address manually in this field by clicking on the button to the right of the Pay To The Order Of field. You can only make an entry in this field if you haven't entered a vendor in the Vendor ID field. If you entered a vendor ID, Peachtree Accounting fills the vendor address in automatically.

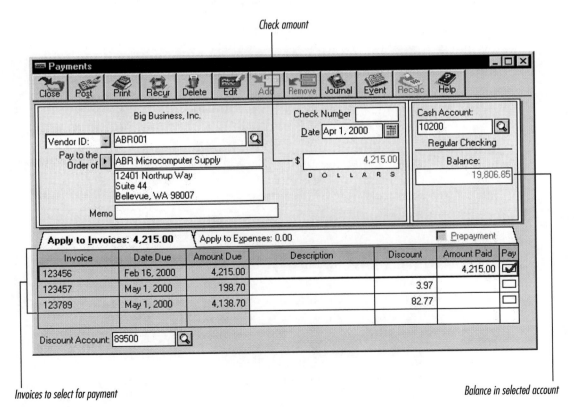

FIGURE 6-33   Payments window with vendor and active invoices

Check Number   Leave this field blank to include the check in the check run. When you prepare to run checks, Peachtree Accounting will see that this field is blank and will include the payment as part of the check run. If you are recording a payment after the check has been written (or to log a manual check), enter the check number in this field.

Date   Enter the date for the disbursement in this field. If your system date falls within your current accounting period (such as October 25 within the 10th accounting period), Peachtree Accounting uses the system date as the default date. Otherwise, Peachtree Accounting defaults to the first day of the accounting period. Click the Calendar button or right-click in this field to display the date-selection calendar.

Memo   This field is for your reference only; the information doesn't appear on the standard check forms included with Peachtree Accounting. Peachtree Accounting uses the information in the vendor's Account # field in the Maintain Vendors window as the default entry for this field. You can accept the default or enter a memo entry of up to 30 alphanumeric characters.

Check Amount   Peachtree Accounting calculates this field for you based on the amounts you enter in the lower half of the screen. This field is display-only.

Cash Account   Enter the General Ledger cash account.

Balance   The balance in this display-only field is the cash balance as of this accounting period.

N O T E : When you first display this window, you may see question marks in this field. Click Recalc in the toolbar at the top of the window to recalculate the balance and display it in this field.

Prepayment   Check this box to apply the amount to expenses only. See the following section, "Entering and Applying Prepayments," for information on entering prepayments.

Having entered the header information for this payment, you now need to tell Peachtree Accounting how to distribute the payment. To pay against a specific invoice already entered for the vendor, select the Apply to Invoices tab. Enter the amount to pay in the Amount Paid field for the line item. The description you enter in the Description field will be printed on the checks and reports. You can pay multiple invoices on a single check; in fact, you can pay all the outstanding invoices by clicking the Pay checkboxes for the line items.

If you are entering a cash purchase or a payment against a vendor invoice that hasn't been entered, select the Apply to Expenses tab. Enter the quantity, item, description, General Ledger account, unit price, amount, and job exactly as you did when entering line items in the Purchases window.

As you enter amounts in the Apply to Invoices and the Apply to Expenses sections, Peachtree Accounting keeps a running total for the vendor in the Check Amount field in the top half of the window. The total for each section also appears on the tabs. You can make payments against invoices and expenses in the same check—Peachtree Accounting will list the invoice and expense information on the check stub when it prints the check.

When you are satisfied with your entries, click Post to save the information or Print to immediately print the check.

Entering Refunds

You will occasionally need to enter a refund for a customer. Enter a credit memo to the customer (as described in Chapter 5). Then select Payments from the Task menu. When the Payments window appears (shown earlier in Figure 6-32), change the Vendor ID/Customer ID field to Customer ID and enter the refund. Finish by applying the credit memo to the payment in the Receipts window.

If you need to enter a refund from a vendor, you use a similar process. First enter a credit invoice to the vendor for inventory returned. Then display the Receipts window (this window is discussed in Chapter 5). In the Apply to Revenue folder, change the Vendor ID/Customer ID field to Vendor ID and enter the refund. This amount will appear in the Payments window as an amount owing to the vendor. Finally, you apply the credit invoice to the amount that represents the refund from the vendor to create a $0.00 refund check to the vendor. (Enter a dummy check number, such as CR REFUND, in the Check Number field when you print the check.)

Entering and Applying Prepayments

You create prepayments for down payments or to allocate funds for a bill that hasn't come in yet. (Prepayments are any disbursements for which you don't yet have a matching invoice.) You can enter prepayments by checking the Prepayment box and entering line items in the Apply to Expenses section.

N O T E : You cannot combine a prepayment with a payment to an invoice.

If you're using batch posting, you have to post the transaction using Post before you can apply the prepayment. You print checks and post disbursements for prepayments in the same way as you do for regular payments. Make sure you're using a Prepaid Expenses account for your General Ledger account number.

To apply a prepayment, display the vendor in the Payments window after posting the information. You'll see the prepayment in the Apply to Invoices section. Select the prepayment and click Pay in the toolbar. Select the vendor invoice against which to apply the prepayment and click Pay again.

Entering Credit Memos

You enter credit memos (also known as credit invoices) from your vendors in the Purchases window in much the same way as you enter a standard vendor invoice. When you enter a credit memo, be sure to enter negative quantities for items in Inventory (for example, -4.00) so the amount is calculated as a negative amount. If you are entering a credit memo for an item not in Inventory, such as a service, enter the amount as a negative amount (with a leading minus sign), for example, -286.50. Returns to a vendor will decrease the quantity of items available in Inventory.

To apply the credit memo, select Payments from the Tasks menu. The credit memo will appear in the line item list for the vendor. Select the credit memo and click Pay in the toolbar. Select the vendor invoice to which you want to apply the credit memo and click Pay again. (If you are using batch posting, you need to post the credit memo before you can apply the credit.)

Printing Checks

Once you've selected the invoices you want to pay and have made any necessary modifications, you can print checks. (You must send the checks to a printer; you cannot print checks to a file or to the screen.) Peachtree Accounting offers eight predefined check formats: two for preprinted checks (with headings), two for multipurpose checks (without headings), and four that are compatible with the Peachtree Accounting for DOS forms. The preprinted checks (and other preprinted forms shown in this chapter) can be obtained from Peachtree. A catalog of preprinted stock is included in the Peachtree Accounting package, or you can phone Peachtree directly at (800) 61-PEACH for information.

To print checks, select Accounts Payable from the Reports menu. The Select a Report window appears with the Accounts Payable option selected. Next, select Disbursements Checks from the list, then select the check format that matches your check stock. Enter the information in the report selection windows. The first time you print checks, you'll also need to tell Peachtree Accounting the starting number for the check run; after that, Peachtree Accounting keeps track of the check numbers for you.

As with any other preprinted form, it's important that you have the forms aligned correctly in the printer. Click Practice to print a check mask, a dummy block of information that Peachtree Accounting will print to help you align your check forms in the printer. Each printing position is filled with the maximum number of characters so that you can adjust the checks precisely. You can print the check mask as many times as you like. Use the Align option to align the printing position. When you're satisfied with your information, click OK.

When the checks have printed, Peachtree Accounting asks you if the checks printed correctly. If they did, select Yes. Peachtree Accounting will then post the transaction information to the appropriate journals. If not, select No; you will have to print the checks again.

If you want to make sure that the checks are going to print correctly before printing them, you can print them to plain paper and then select No, then Cancel. You can review the checks as they would be printed. This may not be practical for a large batch of checks.

Voiding Checks

You will occasionally need to void checks you have printed but for one reason or another will not be releasing to the vendor. Voiding checks reverses the entries in the journals.

Start by selecting Void Checks from the Tasks menu. The Choose A Cash Account window appears:

Account ID   Enter the ID of the General Ledger account used for creating the checks. The account name appears in the field below the Account ID field.

Putting It to Work

Blank Check Stock or Preprinted Checks?

It's hard to say which is better, blank check stock or preprinted checks. You can find people who prefer each type. What you use in your company will depend on evaluating the advantages for blank check stock and preprinted checks and seeing which makes more sense for your company.

Blank check stock has a number of advantages, including:

- Blank check stock is relatively inexpensive (perhaps $50 per 1000 checks).
- It's more flexible. If you need to change your company information, such as your phone number, address, or name, you just make a change to the information you print on the check. You can also format it to match your company's letterhead.
- It's multipurpose. You can use blank check stock for several different checking accounts without having to load new check stock in your printer.
- It's easier. You do not have to keep track of check numbers to match the checks you're printing to the number printed on the stock. Instead, you can let Peachtree Accounting track the number of the last check you printed.
- It's more secure. You don't have preprinted blank checks around the office that could be stolen and forged. For security purposes you should always keep your checks locked up.
- It's readily available. If you run out of blank check stock, you can buy more almost anywhere without having to wait for printing to be done.

On the other hand, preprinted checks have their advantages, too:

- Preprinted checks are not substantially more expensive than blank checks. A basic preprinted check can be had for as little as $70 per 1000; checks printed in two colors are less than $100 per 1000. Unless your company writes a lot of checks, the cost difference is probably negligible.
- They are faster to print. Laser printers print blank checks or preprinted checks at the same speed, but ink-jet, bubble-jet, and daisy-wheel printers print more slowly if they have to print a large block of address information as well. If you are also printing a graphic as part of the letterhead, ink-jet and bubble-jet printers may take a much longer time to print each check.

- They look more professional. The quality of printing on a preprinted check is almost certainly going to be better than anything you can do with a laser printer, more so if you have two-color printing on your checks.
- They are secure. Although preprinted checks could be stolen and forged, this may not be a problem if they're locked up securely, whereas checks printed on blank check stock could conceivably be forged by anyone with blank check stock and a scanner to duplicate your logo.

Take a look at the advantages for both types of check stock and see which works better for your company. You may even want to use both types: preprinted checks for one account with special layout requirements (such as a company payroll check) and blank check stock for the other company checking accounts.

Click OK. Peachtree Accounting displays the Void Existing Checks window:

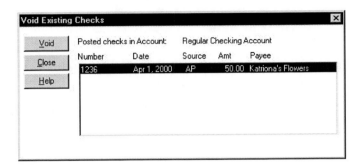

Select the check you want to void and click Void (or double-click on the line item). The second Void Existing Checks window appears:

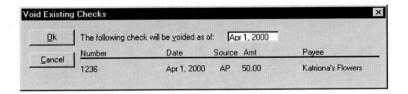

The Following Check Will Be Voided as Of   Peachtree Accounting displays a default date for voiding the check. You can enter any date in this field that is not earlier than the start of the current accounting period.

Click OK. Peachtree Accounting voids the check and creates a transaction that reverses the original transaction with a reference number made of the check number followed by a "V." For example, if you have a check number of 5027, the reversing entry will appear with a reference number of 5027V. You are then returned to the first Void Existing Check window. Peachtree Accounting updates the list of checks in the window to remove the line for the voided check. You can continue voiding checks by selecting checks and clicking Void. Click Close when you're done.

After you have printed checks, you will want to print Accounts Payable reports to provide hard copy documents for your audit trail, such as a Check Register and a Cash Disbursements Journal. The following section shows you how to print these two reports.

Printing the Check Register and Cash Disbursements Journal

The final two reports in the Accounts Payable process are the Check Register and the Cash Disbursements Journal. The Check Register is a list of all the checks you have written in the current period. It includes the check numbers, the payee, and the check amount. The Check Register is very useful for reconciling your checking account with the statements from the bank. The Cash Disbursements Journal lists payments in journal entry format. You can use it to verify General Ledger posting accounts for payment transactions.

Both the Check Register and the Cash Disbursements Journal are important documents for providing a hard copy audit trail for your transactions. It is good accounting practice to print both reports each time you print checks and save them along with your other printed reports.

To print the Check Register and the Cash Disbursements Journal, select Accounts Payable from the Reports menu. The Select a Report window appears with the Accounts Payable option selected. Next, select the Check Register or the Cash Disbursements Journal from the list by double-clicking or by highlighting the report and clicking Screen or Print at the top of the screen. Enter the information in the report selection windows and click OK. The report appears on the screen or is sent to the printer. Figure 6-34 shows a typical Check Register, and Figure 6-35 shows a typical Cash Disbursements Journal.

Big Business, Inc.
Check Register
For the Period From Apr 1, 2000 to Apr 30, 2000

Filter Criteria includes: Report order is by Date.

Check #	Date	Payee	Cash Account	Amount
1236	4/1/00	Katriona's Flowers	10200	50.00
1237	4/1/00	ABR Microcomputer Sup	10200	4,215.00
1238	4/1/00	ABR Microcomputer Sup	10200	1,035.00
1239	4/1/00	ABR Microcomputer Sup	10200	1,000.00
1236V	4/1/00	Katriona's Flowers	10200	-50.00
Total				**6,250.00**

FIGURE 6-34 Check Register

Big Business, Inc.
Cash Disbursements Journal
For the Period From Apr 1, 2000 to Apr 30, 2000
Filter Criteria includes: Report order is by Date. Report is printed in Detail Format.

Date	Check #	Account ID	Line Description	Debit Amou	Credit Amo
		10200	ABR Microcomputer Supply		1,035.00
4/1/00	1239	20000	Invoice: 123789	1,000.00	
		10200	ABR Microcomputer Supply		1,000.00
4/1/00	1236V	20000	Invoice: 1236		50.00
		10200	Katriona's Flowers	50.00	
	Total			6,350.00	6,350.00

FIGURE 6-35   Cash Disbursements Journal

Posting Accounts Payable Transactions

In Chapter 3, you saw how to set up your business for either batch or real-time posting. In real-time posting, Peachtree Accounting immediately updates the company's financial information, while batch posting holds the entries in a temporary file you can review before you post them. If you are using batch posting, you need to post transactions to the vendors' accounts.

The posting process debits Accounts Payable, credits the Cash account for the net amount of the check, and credits the Discounts Taken account if there's a discount. Peachtree Accounting also updates the inventory information based on the purchases and returns, and updates vendor account and invoice balances.

To post invoices, select System from the Tasks menu, then select Post from the submenu. The Post window appears. Click the checkbox for All Journals (the default) to post all transactions, or click the checkboxes for the various journals—such as the Cash Receipts Journal and the General Journal—to post to just those journals. Click OK to post the transactions. Peachtree Accounting displays the progress for posting to each journal on the screen.

 CAUTION: If you are using the Inventory features in Peachtree Accounting and you are posting journals separately, you should always post purchases before sales. If your sales exceeded the stock on hand before adding the inventory represented by purchases, you may end up with negative inventory. Peachtree Accounting will then post cost of goods sold for negative inventory, particularly if you purchased the items in different accounting periods.

If you have a transaction that would post to a journal you haven't selected for posting, Peachtree Accounting doesn't post that transaction.

You can also unpost transactions from selected journals or all journals. Unposting removes posted transactions from the General Ledger for the current period and periods forward. You can then edit or delete these transactions and then repost them. To unpost transactions, select System from the Tasks menu, then select Unpost from the submenu. (The Unpost window is identical to the Post window.) Choose the journals you want to unpost transactions from and click OK to begin unposting.

Printing Accounts Payable Reports

You've already seen how to select most of the Accounts Payable reports in this chapter. Peachtree Accounting has an extensive collection of Accounts Payable reports, checks, forms, purchase orders, and labels, as shown in Table 6-4.

In addition to these specific reports, there are four folders of forms:

- Disbursement Checks
- 1099 Forms
- Labels - Vendors
- Purchase Orders

Each of the folders contains a selection of forms that are print-only— you can print them, but you can't see them on the screen. The reports and forms you haven't seen are described next.

Vendor List	Vendor Master File List
Vendor Ledgers	Purchase Order Register
Purchase Journal	Check Register
Cash Requirements	Aged Payables
Cash Disbursements Journal	Purchase Order Journal
Purchase Order Report	

TABLE 6-4 Accounts Payable Reports

Printing Vendor Labels

You can print labels with your vendor addresses. These are convenient for automating the payment process. As with the checks, you can print an alignment form by clicking Align rather than OK. This lets you align the labels on your printer before printing. Peachtree Accounting lets you specify vertical and horizontal offsets through the program, rather than having to manually adjust the forms in the printer.

You can edit the address label formats or create new ones using the Forms Designer. For more information on the Forms Designer, see Chapter 12.

Printing 1099s

At the end of the calendar year, you will need to print 1099 forms for all contract and qualifying vendors. A 1099 is required only for unincorporated professional help. This is also a calendar year requirement of the IRS. 1099s are due to vendors by January 31 of each year and are due (with a 1096 cover sheet) to the IRS by February 28th. You can print two kinds of 1099s: 1099-MISC and 1099-INT.

Using Management Tools

As you read in Chapter 5, Peachtree Accounting has a selection of management tools to help you manage your business. These management tools are located in the Action Items/Event Log Options window and also include the four analysis tools in the Business Manager Series: the Cash Manager, the Collection Manager, the Payment Manager, and the Financial Manager. The management tools that relate directly to Accounts Payable are in the Action Items and Event Log Options window, the Cash Manager and the Payments Manager. The Action Items and Event Log Options window and the analysis tools in the Business Manager Series are discussed in detail in Chapter 13.

Summary

In this chapter, you saw how to set up Accounts Payable and vendor defaults for payment terms; set up and maintain vendor records; add, modify, and delete vendor invoices and purchase orders; select invoices for payment; create checks; post Accounts Payable transactions; and print reports. In the next chapter, you'll learn how use the Payroll Setup Wizard to set up payroll and employee defaults, enter and maintain employee and sales rep records, edit payroll tax tables, run payroll checks, print reports, and post payroll transactions.

Payroll

7

In this chapter, you'll learn how to use the Payroll Setup Wizard to set up payroll and employee defaults, set up and maintain payroll tax tables, enter employee and sales rep records, select employees for payment and run payroll checks, and print payroll reports and tax forms.

In Chapter 6, you saw how to set up and use Accounts Payable functions: adding vendors, entering purchase orders, and issuing payments. In this chapter, you'll learn how to set up payroll and employee defaults, edit payroll tax tables, enter and maintain employee and sales rep records, run payroll checks, print payroll reports, and post payroll transactions.

Generating a payroll is one of the most time-consuming tasks in any business. There are many details to keep track of—employee information, time sheets, and state and federal government regulations and requirements. There is also the tedious task of writing out the checks. Nevertheless, you must do this job right, or you'll risk complaints from employees and penalties from the government.

For all these reasons, payroll is a main motive for companies to switch to computerized accounting systems. Peachtree Accounting's Payroll feature will simplify your payroll processing tremendously while reducing errors and automatically integrating all the payroll information into the General Ledger.

The steps for setting up and using the Payroll feature are as follows:

1. Set up payroll and employee defaults.
2. Edit payroll tax tables.
3. Add, modify, and delete employees and sales representatives.
4. Select employees for payment.
5. Print payroll checks.
6. Print payroll reports.
7. Post payroll transactions.

Setting Up Payroll Defaults

The first step in setting up Payroll is to set up your payroll defaults. There are two classes of payroll default information: initial defaults and employee defaults. The initial defaults include defaults for the state, locality (local region), and locality tax rate; the unemployment percent for your company; whether you want to deduct for 401(k) plans and record employee meals and tips; and the General Ledger accounts for gross pay, tax liability, and tax expense. Employee defaults are defaults for the employee records, such as general employee information, pay levels, and employee and employer information.

Entering Initial Payroll Defaults

The very first time you set up payroll defaults, you need to enter the initial defaults using the Payroll Setup Wizard unless you copied your payroll defaults when you were setting up your company. Choose Setup Checklist from the Maintain menu, then select Employee Defaults. Peachtree displays the Payroll Setup Wizard window, shown in Figure 7-1. Click Next to display the Initial Payroll Setup window, shown in Figure 7-2.

N O T E : If employee defaults have already been established or you copied employee defaults from an existing company during New Company Setup, the Initial Payroll Setup process is skipped and Peachtree displays the Payroll Setup Wizard—Tax Table Version window.

You've seen how to select an option from the Setup Checklist in previous chapters when you entered the General Ledger, Accounts Receivable, and Accounts Payable defaults. If the Setup Checklist is not already displayed,

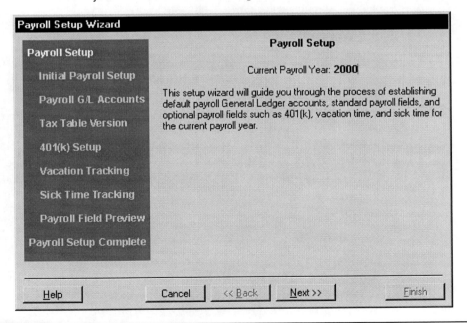

FIGURE 7-1   Payroll Setup Wizard window

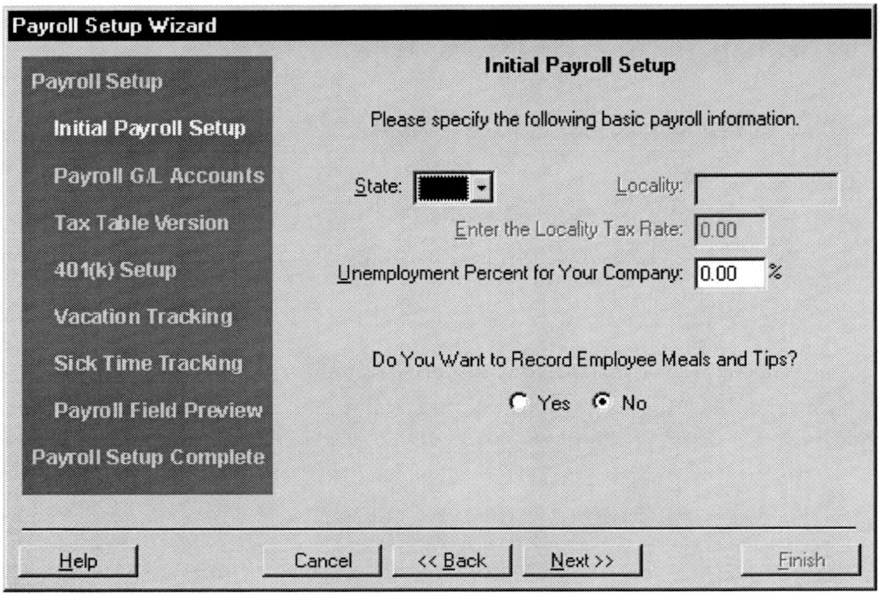

FIGURE 7-2 Payroll Setup Wizard—Initial Payroll Setup window

select the Setup Checklist option from the Maintain menu. From the Setup Checklist, select Employee Defaults. (You can also reach this window by selecting the Default Information option from the Maintain menu, then selecting Employees from the submenu or selecting Payroll Setup Wizard from the Payroll navigational aid.) The Initial Payroll Setup window appears, shown in Figure 7-3 with sample data for Big Business, Inc.

If you didn't choose to copy the payroll defaults from a sample company when you set up your company, you will need to enter the payroll defaults now. Check with your accountant if you're not sure what you need to enter for payroll defaults in this window.

State Enter the two-letter code for the state in which your business is located.

Locality Select the locality from the drop-down list. (The Locality and Enter the Locality Tax Rate fields are not available for all states. Please check with your state and local revenue departments for information regarding local tax regulations.)

Enter the Locality Tax Rate Enter the tax rate for the locality you selected.

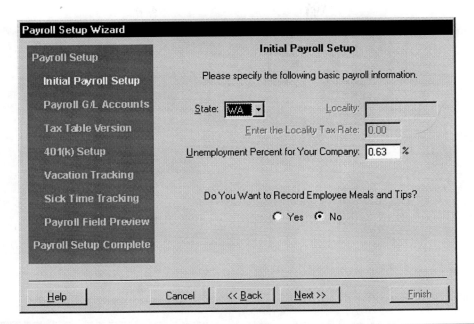

FIGURE 7-3 Sample data in the Payroll Setup Wizard—Initial Payroll Setup window

Unemployment Percent for Your Company   Enter the percentage of the employer-paid unemployment taxes required for your company by your state. You can override this in the company payroll tax tables for the appropriate SUI tax. See "Editing Company Tax Tables" later in this chapter for more information.

Do You Want to Record Employee Meals and Tips?   Click Yes or No. This will appear on employee W-2 forms. You can change this for each employee if necessary in the EmployEE fields on the Employee Defaults window.

When you have finished entering Initial Payroll Setup information, click Next to open the Payroll G/L Accounts window, shown in Figure 7-4.

Gross Pay Acct   Enter the General Ledger expense account for gross pay. If you are using a sample client chart of accounts included with Peachtree Accounting, use 77500, the Wages Expense account. (The Wages Expense account is the only account that cannot be changed in the defaults after you have completed the Initial Payroll Setup.)

Tax Liability Acct   Enter the General Ledger account for Federal Payroll Taxes Payable. If you are a small business that has a single General Ledger

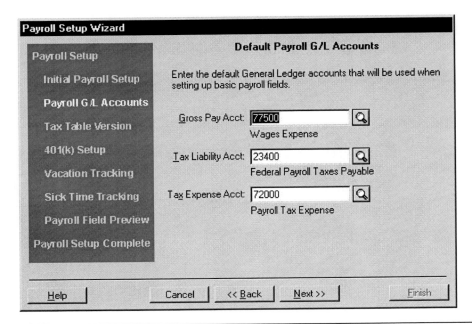

FIGURE 7-4   Payroll Setup Wizard—Default Payroll G/L Accounts window

account for tracking Federal Payroll Taxes Payable, use that account for all of the Tax Liability Acct fields. If you are using separate General Ledger accounts for FUTA, FICA, and state taxes, enter any General Ledger tax liability account. You'll change this later in the Employee Defaults window.

Tax Expense Acct   Enter the General Ledger account for Payroll Tax Expense.

When you are satisfied with your entries, click Next.

When you have finished entering Payroll G/L Accounts information, click Next to open the Payroll Tax Table Information window as shown in Figure 7-5. The window displays the currently installed version of the global tax table. Verify that this table is the most current version available by visiting Peachtree's Web site at *http://www.peachtree.com*.

 N O T E :   The first four digits of the global tax table number represent the tax year associated with your tax tables.

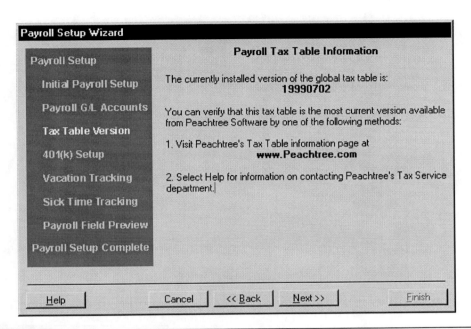

FIGURE 7-5 Payroll Setup Wizard—Payroll Tax Table Information window

Click Next to enter your 401(k) Setup Information as shown in Figure 7-6. You have three options. Click the appropriate option.

401(k) Plan Not Offered   If you click this option, you have completed the 401(k) Setup Information.

401(k) Plan, Employee Contributions Only   If you click this option, you will have to fill in the current federal 401(k) deduction limit and select the 401(k) liability account.

401(k) Plan, Employee Contributions with Matching Employer Contribution   If you click this option, you will have to fill in the current federal 401(k) deduction limit and select the 401(k) liability account and the 401(k) expense account.

Click Next to begin entering company information for tracking vacation time, as shown in Figure 7-7. You have three options. Click the appropriate option.

Vacation Time Not Tracked   If you select this option, you have completed the Tracking Vacation Time information.

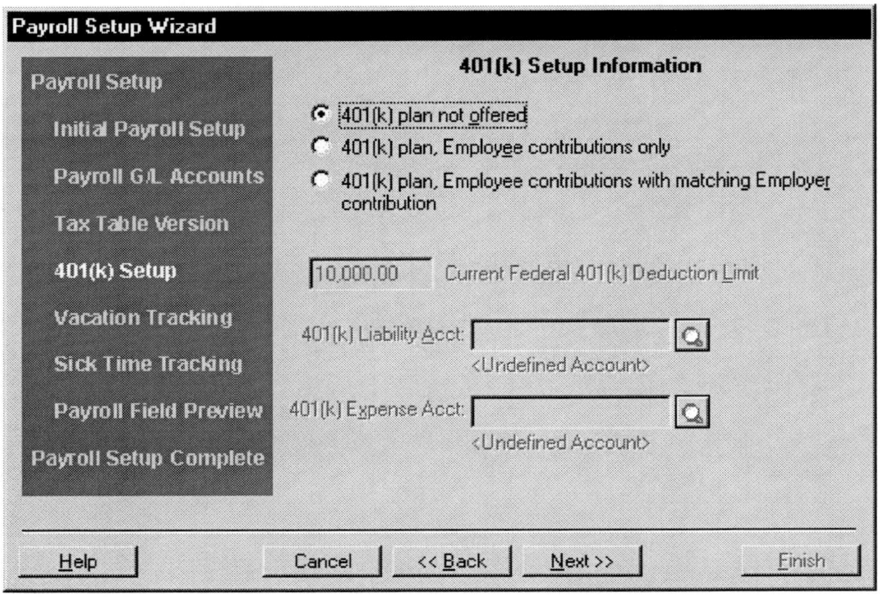

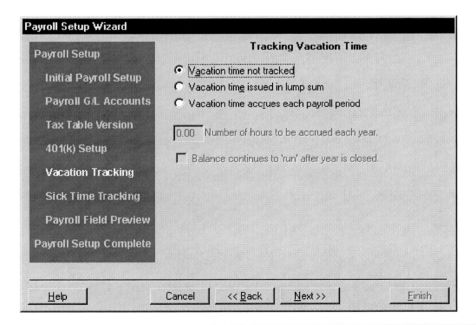

FIGURE 7-6   Payroll Setup Wizard—401(k) Setup Information window

FIGURE 7-7   Payroll Setup Wizard—Tracking Vacation Time window

Vacation Time Issued in Lump Sum   If you select this option, you establish a default payroll field for all employees. In addition you can separately modify each employee who requires a unique setup.

Vacation Time Accrues Each Payroll Period   If you select this option, you establish a default payroll field for all employees. In addition, you can separately modify each employee who requires a unique setup. You need to specify the number of hours to be accrued each year and click the checkbox to specify that the balance continues to run after the year is closed.

Click Next to begin entering company information for tracking sick time as shown in Figure 7-8. You have three options. Click the appropriate option.

Sick Time Not Tracked   If you click this option, you have completed the Tracking Sick Time information.

Sick Time Issued in Lump Sum   If you select this option, you establish a default payroll field for all employees. In addition, you can separately modify each employee who requires a unique setup.

Sick Time Accrues Each Payroll Period   If you select this option you establish a default payroll field for all employees. In addition, you can separately modify each employee who requires a unique setup. You need to specify the number of hours to be accrued each year and click the checkbox to specify that the balance continues to run after the year is closed.

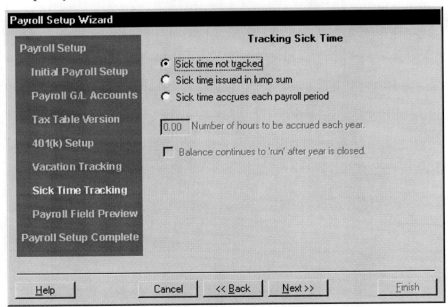

FIGURE 7-8   Payroll Setup Wizard—Tracking Sick Time window

Click Next to view a summary of the options you have selected in the Payroll Field Preview window, as shown in Figures 7-9 and 7-10. Figure 7-9 shows the EmployEE Fields tab, and Figure 7-10 shows the EmployER Fields tab.

Click Next to open the Payroll Setup Complete window, as shown in Figure 7-11. Click Finish to set the payroll defaults you have chosen using the Payroll Setup Wizard.

You are now ready to begin entering employee defaults.

Entering Employee Defaults

After you have entered the initial payroll defaults using the Payroll Setup Wizard, the Employee Defaults window appears with sample entries, as shown in Figure 7-12. If you have already entered the initial payroll defaults in the Initial Payroll Setup window, or if you used payroll defaults from a sample company, the Employee Defaults window will appear directly when you select Employee Defaults from the Setup Checklist or when you select the Default Information option from the Maintain menu and then select Employees from the submenu.

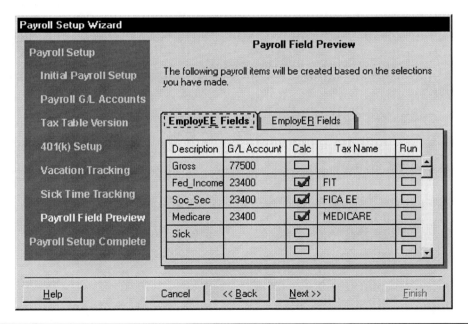

FIGURE 7-9 Payroll Setup Wizard—Payroll Field Preview window showing the EmployEE Fields tab

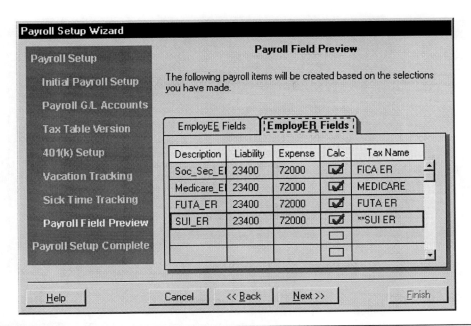

FIGURE 7-10 Payroll Setup Wizard—Payroll Field Preview window showing the EmployER Fields tab

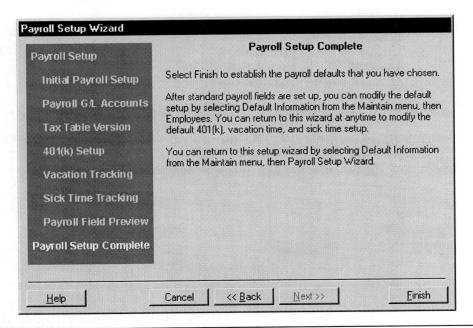

FIGURE 7-11 Payroll Setup Wizard—Payroll Setup Complete window

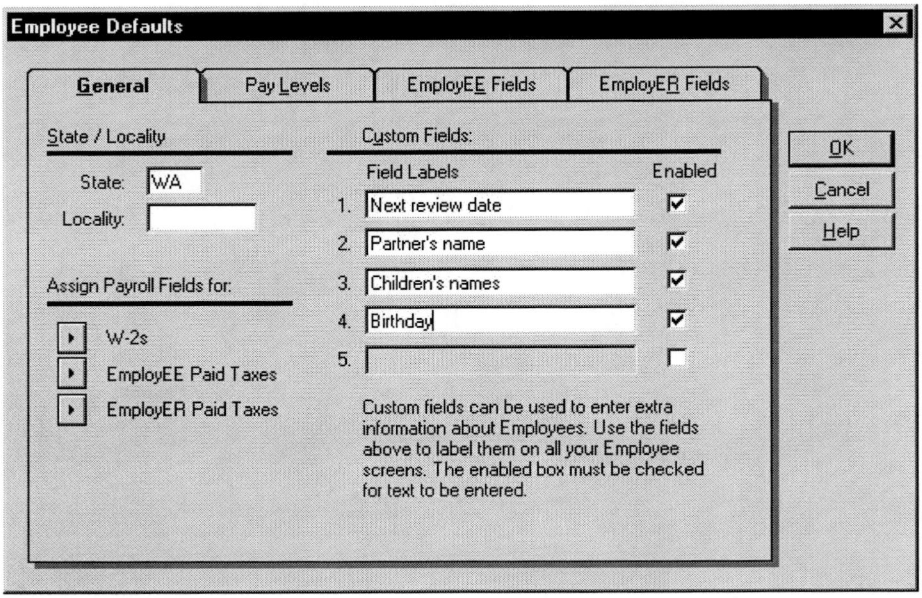

FIGURE 7-12 Employee Defaults window

Like the customer and vendor default windows, the Employee Defaults window has four tabs: General, Pay Levels, EmployEE Fields, and EmployER Fields. The General tab appears as the default. You enter general default information for employees in this tab.

State Enter the default state of residence for employees. (Figure 7-12 shows the State field already filled in.) The information you enter here goes to the Maintain Employee/Sales Rep window. If you have payroll in multiple states or localities, leave this field blank and let the information you enter on the Maintain Employees/Sales Reps window determine which tax table will be used for a specific employee.

Locality Enter the locality (local region) in which the company is located. If you have multiple divisions in different cities, be sure to use the appropriate locality.

Assign Payroll Fields for W-2s Click this button to set up the payroll fields for W-2s. The Assign Payroll Fields for W-2s window appears (shown in Figure 7-13). The fields in this window correspond to the federal W-2 form. (Some of this information is also used to create the federal 941 forms.) The fields in the window are identified with the number of the corresponding box on the W-2 form.

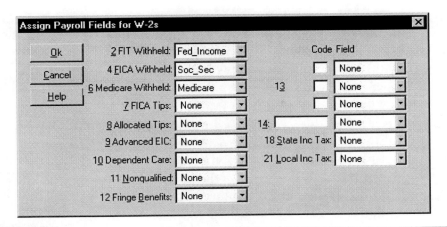

FIGURE 7-13 Assign Payroll Fields for W-2s window

Payroll information is identified by field names, such as Fed_Income and Soc_Sec. By selecting one of the field names from the drop-down list, you tell Peachtree Accounting to print the corresponding information in the field on the W-2 form. If you need to set up additional fields for the W-2, you can do this through the EmployEE Fields and EmployER Fields tabs in the Employee Defaults window, discussed later in this section. Field 14 is a custom field. You can enter your own label for this field.

When you're satisfied with your answers, click OK to return to the Employee Defaults window, as shown in Figure 7-12.

Assign Payroll Fields for EmployEE Paid Taxes   Click this button to set up the payroll fields for employee paid taxes. The Assign Payroll Fields for Employee Paid Taxes window appears (shown in Figure 7-14).

If you need to set up state tax deductions for employees for disability, unemployment, or training tax, you identify the payroll fields in this window by clicking the down arrow and selecting from the drop-down list. Not all states

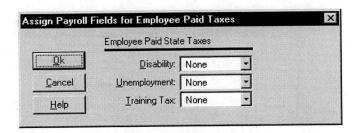

FIGURE 7-14 Assign Payroll Fields for Employee Paid Taxes window

require these deductions. Check your state and locality regulations to establish requirements for employee portions of applicable taxes. Some states offer the option of employer/employee splits on certain taxes, or let the employer choose to pay 100 percent of the tax liability.

When you're satisfied with your answers, click OK to return to the Employee Defaults window.

Assign Payroll Fields for EmployER Paid Taxes   Click this button to set up the payroll fields for employer paid taxes. The Assign Payroll Fields for Employer Paid Taxes window appears (shown in Figure 7-15).

You select the fields to appear on the federal 940 form for FUTA and for the corresponding quarterly federal payroll tax forms. When you're satisfied with your answers, click OK to return to the Employee Defaults window.

Custom Fields   As with the customer and vendor custom fields, you set default labels to track employee information such as spouse's name, number of children, and so on. Click the Enabled box to enable or disable the corresponding field label. If the Enabled box is not checked, the field label will not appear in the Employee Defaults window. Enter up to five categories in the field labels. The information in these fields is used for headings in the Maintain Employees/Sales Reps window (discussed later in this chapter), as well as on some of the payroll reports.

When you are satisfied with your entries, click the Pay Levels tab. The Pay Levels tab appears, as shown in Figure 7-16.

You use the Pay Levels tab to set the levels of employee pay. You can enter up to ten different employee rates for both hourly and salaried employees. You can enter descriptions for standard pay, overtime pay, bonuses, or other types of pay. (The descriptions shown in Figure 7-16 are the defaults, but you can add other types if you want.) Note that you don't enter the specific pay rates in

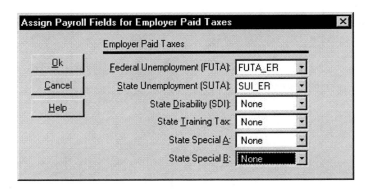

FIGURE 7-15   Assign Payroll Fields for Employer Paid Taxes window

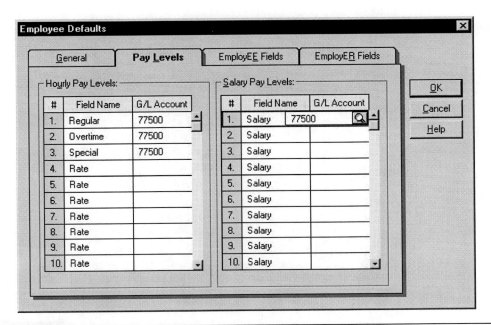

FIGURE 7-16 Employee Defaults window with the Pay Levels tab displayed

this tab, only the classes of pay (such as regular, overtime, or salary). Specific pay rates are set for each employee in the employee's record.

Enter the descriptions for the pay type in the fields in the Field Name column and the corresponding General Ledger accounts in the G/L Account fields. (The G/L Account field has a drop-down list so you can select an account from the chart of accounts.)

When you are satisfied with your entries, click the EmployEE Fields tab. The EmployEE Fields tab appears, as shown in Figure 7-17.

The EmployEE Fields tab lets you set and calculate the employee gross pay. You can enter payroll deductions and allowances, amounts such as tips (which are tracked for calculating taxes but are not posted to the General Ledger), and tax withholding for the employees' W-2s. (The entries in Figure 7-17 are the standard defaults.) You can also set up additional fields for payroll accumulations, such as 401(k) deductions, payroll savings programs, and vacation and sick time.

Field Name   Enter the name of the payroll field. This can be up to 11 alphanumeric characters.

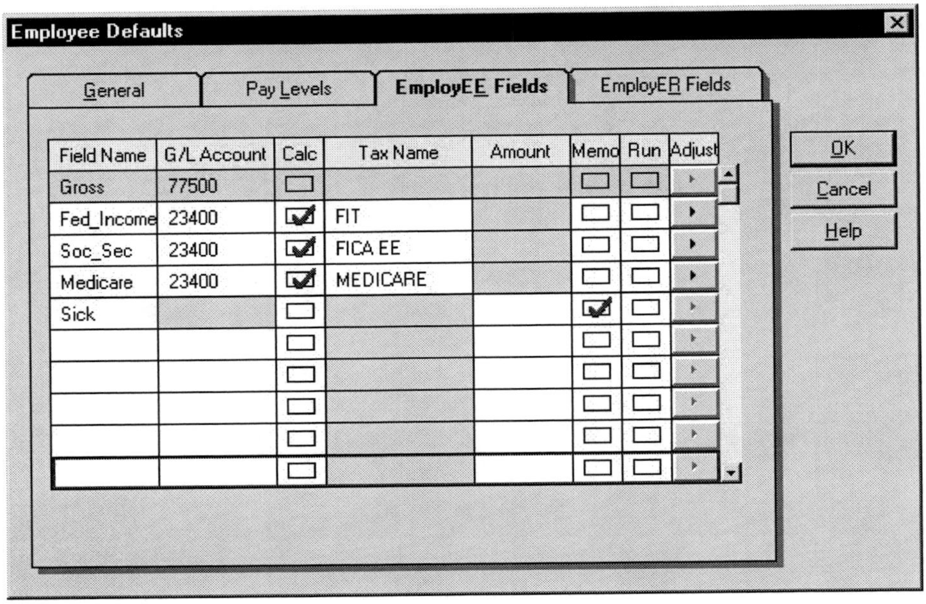

FIGURE 7-17 Employee Defaults window with the EmployEE Fields tab displayed

G/L Account   Enter the General Ledger account number. Peachtree Accounting will not post this information to the General Ledger if you check the corresponding Memo box.

Calc   Check the Calc box if Peachtree Accounting can calculate this information from the adjusted gross pay and the payroll tax tables. Don't check this box if you want to use a flat rate amount. (See the "Setting Up Payroll Tax Tables" section later in this chapter for more information on calculations.)

Tax Name   Enter the name of the tax table to use. You can select this from the drop-down list. You must have checked the corresponding Calc box to use this field. For information on the specific calculation options and a table of the various options, see the "Setting Up Payroll Tax Tables" section later in this chapter.

Amount   Enter a flat rate amount here. Enter a positive number for an income amount and a negative number for deductions. The amount entered will be the amount per pay period. You will only enter an amount if you don't make an entry in the corresponding Tax Name field.

Memo Check this box if you don't want this information to be posted to the General Ledger—for example, for noncash benefits such as tips and meals.

Run Check this box if you don't want Peachtree Accounting to zero the account when you close the payroll year. You would carry over account balances for things like accumulated vacation and sick leave.

Adjust Click this button to identify the fields you want to use to calculate the gross. The Calculate Adjusted Gross window appears, as shown in Figure 7-18.

You check the boxes for each of the fields you want to use in the calculation, then click OK to close the window. Peachtree Accounting will add the checked fields to calculate the adjusted gross. If you want to perform more complicated calculations, you will need to set up a tax table. See the "Setting Up Payroll Tax Tables" section later in this chapter for more information.

When you are satisfied with your entries in the EmployEE Fields tab, click the EmployER Fields tab. The EmployER Fields tab appears, as shown in Figure 7-19. (The entries shown in Figure 7-19 are the default entries.)

The EmployER Fields tab is similar to the EmployEE Fields tab. In the EmployER Fields tab, you set up employer deduction categories.

Field Name Enter the name of the payroll field. This can be up to 11 alphanumeric characters.

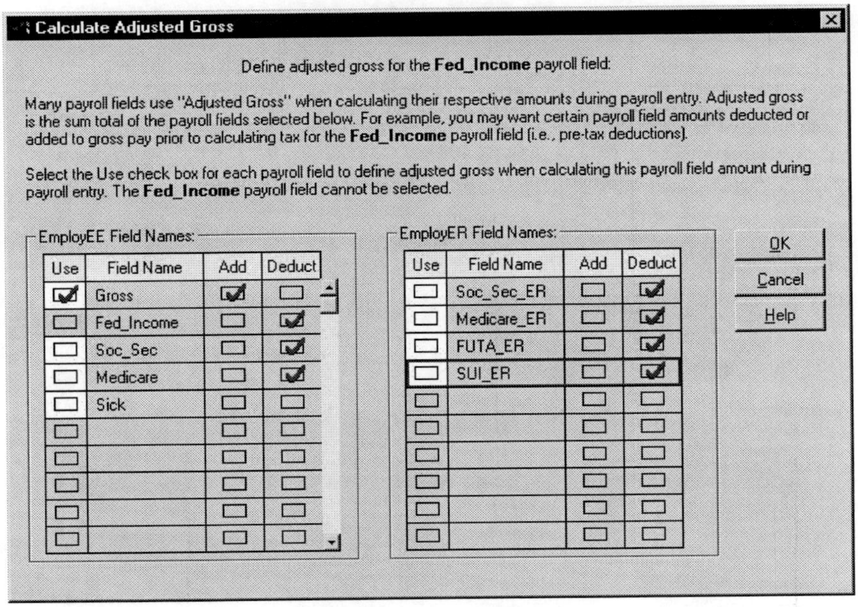

FIGURE 7-18 Calculate Adjusted Gross window

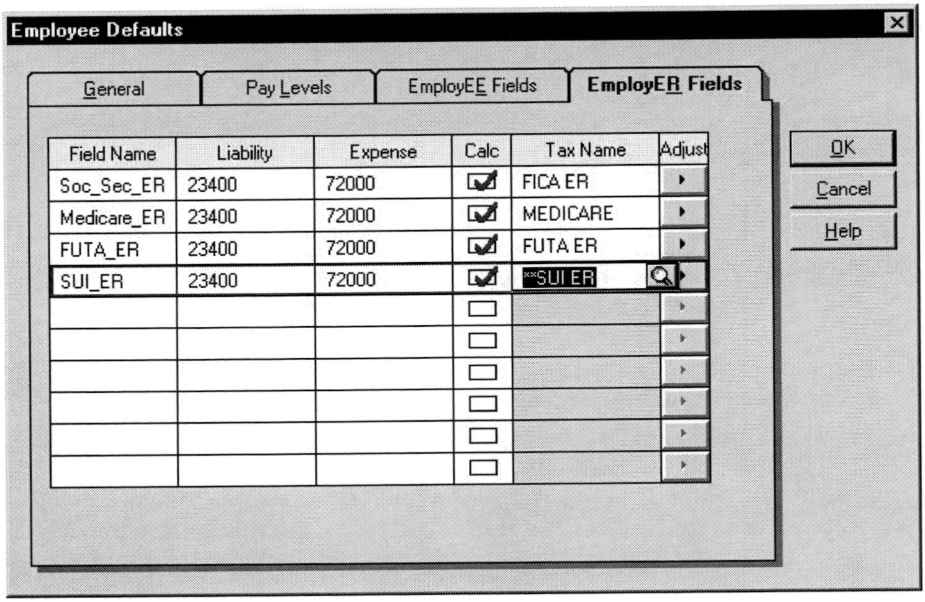

FIGURE 7-19 Employee Defaults window with the EmployER Fields tab displayed

Liability   Enter the General Ledger liability account for the field.

Expense   Enter the General Ledger expense account for the field.

Calc   Check the Calc box if Peachtree Accounting can calculate this information from the adjusted gross pay and the payroll tax tables. Don't check this box if you want to use a flat rate amount.

Tax Name   Enter the name of the tax table to use. You can select this from the drop-down list. You must check the corresponding Calc box in order to use this field. For information on the specific calculation options and a table of the various options, see the "Setting Up Payroll Tax Tables" section later in this chapter.

Adjust   Click this button to identify the fields you want to use to calculate the gross. The Calculate Adjusted Gross window appears, as shown earlier in Figure 7-18. When you have made your selections, click OK to close this window.

   When you are satisfied with all your entries in the Employee Defaults window, click OK. As usual, Peachtree Accounting will ask if you want to mark this task as completed on the Setup Checklist. If you choose Yes, Peachtree puts a checkmark next to the item to indicate that you've completed this portion of the setup.

Setting Up Payroll Tax Tables

The next step in setting up payroll is to set up your tax tables. The term "tax table" is misleading, because a tax table is actually an individual calculation, such as the employer's Social Security deduction. Tax tables are used as the Tax Name for entering calculations in fields. You use tax tables to calculate and accumulate amounts in the Assign Payroll Fields for W-2s window, the Assign Payroll Fields for Employee Paid Taxes window, the Assign Payroll Fields for Employer Paid Taxes window, and the EmployEE Fields and EmployER Fields tabs of the Employee Defaults window.

There are two types of tax tables supplied with Peachtree Accounting. The global tax tables focus on federal, state, and local taxes. These are used by all companies in Peachtree Accounting. Peachtree Accounting ships with tax tables that reflect the current state and federal tax and withholding rates. You can buy upgrades from Peachtree for subsequent tax years or create them yourself if you prefer.

Company tax tables are special tax tables that you use for creating custom calculations for local taxes and company-specific tax tables. You can use company tax tables to accumulate amounts for employees and employers, such as employee stock purchase amounts, employer matching amounts, garnishments, vacation time, and special commissions and bonuses. (Company tax tables will not be overwritten when loading a tax update from Peachtree Accounting.)

CAUTION: Creating and customizing tax table formulas and calculations can be difficult if you're not used to working with spreadsheets or database formulas. Creating tax tables can also involve some simple programming. If you are not comfortable with the process of creating formulas, consider contacting Peachtree or a local Peachtree third-party support organization to customize your tax tables for you. Call Peachtree Software at (770) 492-6310 for information on customizing tax tables. Call (800) 626-0941 for information on the Peachtree Resource Center referral line nearest to you.

Editing Company Tax Tables

If you want to customize your company's tax tables, start by backing up your company's data. Also make a copy of the Peachtree Accounting global tax tables file, taxtable.dat. This way, if you make an error, you can restore the information safely. See Chapter 13 for more information on backing up data. (Tax tables are located in your PEACHW directory.)

Start by selecting Payroll Tax Tables from the File menu. Next, select Edit Company from the submenu. The Maintain Company Payroll Tax Tables window appears. (This task does not appear on the Setup Checklist.)

Figure 7-20 shows the window with the tax table displayed for calculating the employer's contributions for Washington state unemployment insurance for 1999.

The buttons in the toolbar for the Maintain Company Payroll Tax Tables window are shown in Table 7-1.

Enter information in the lower part of the window for the tax table you are creating or modifying.

Tax ID Enter a tax table ID in this field. To edit an existing tax table, select the name from the list. To create a new tax table, enter a new tax table ID.

Filing Status Select the appropriate filing status. If this is for all employees, select All Statuses from the drop-down list. If you choose something other

Payroll tax tables

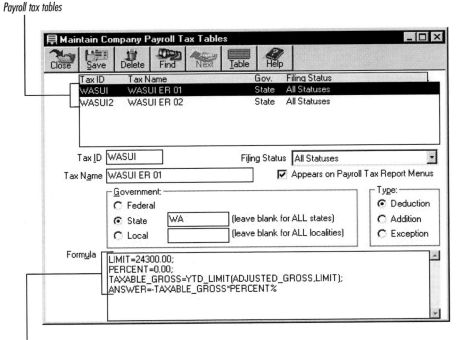

Formula for calculating employer SUI

FIGURE 7-20 Maintain Company Payroll Tax Tables window

BUTTON	NAME	DESCRIPTION
Close	Close	Close the window without saving the information.
Save	Save	Save the current tax table.
Delete	Delete	Delete the current tax table.
Find	Find	Find the next tax table.
Next	Next	Find the next tax table with the information you entered for the last "find."
Table	Table	Display the calculation table (for example, where there is a cutoff amount after which a tax rate changes or is fulfilled, such as FUTA).
Help	Help	Get help on this window.

TABLE 7-1 Toolbar Buttons in the Maintain Company Payroll Tax Tables Window

than All Statuses for the tax table, Peachtree Accounting will check that the employee's filing status qualifies for this calculation, such as a state head of household deduction rate.

Tax Name A name actually has two parts: the calculation name (the name that will appear in the drop-down lists of Tax Names), followed by the last two digits of the calendar year. For example, to create a name for employee 401(k) distributions for 1999—for which you just created a tax table ID of 401(k)—you might enter a tax table ID such as "401(k) EE 97" in this field.

 T I P : Use the suffix EE for employee tax tables and ER for employer tax tables to keep the two types of calculations distinct.

Appears on Payroll Tax Report Menus Check this box if you want the calculation to appear on the Payroll Tax report menu and have the related Payroll field appear on the Exception report.

Government Enter the tax authority. If this is a state or local tax authority, enter the state or locality in the appropriate fields. If you have multiple state or local tax authorities, leave this field blank.

Type   Click the appropriate radio button to identify this tax table as a deduction, an addition, or an exception. Deductions can only be negative numbers, and additions can only be positive numbers. If you want to show both positive and negative numbers (for example, for vacation time or salary draws), the field should be an exception.

Formula   Enter the formula for the tax table.

 C A U T I O N :   Creating formulas can be complex if you're not used to programming or writing spreadsheet formulas. Detailed information for creating formulas appears in the Peachtree Accounting manual. If you're still uncomfortable creating formulas on your own, you should strongly consider getting help from Peachtree Accounting or from a Peachtree Support Center.

When you're satisfied with your entries, click Close. Peachtree Accounting saves the tax table in the company data files stored on your hard disk.

Editing Global Tax Tables

The procedures for editing company and global tax tables are the same. Follow the directions in the previous section for editing the company tax tables.

 C A U T I O N :   Because editing the global tax table can damage the integrity of your payroll calculations for all the companies in Peachtree Accounting, you should avoid making changes or additions to the global tax tables unless specifically directed to do so by Peachtree Accounting or your company's accountant.

Loading New Tax Tables

If you subscribe to Peachtree's tax service, you will receive a tax table update floppy disk accompanied by a booklet with installation instructions. (If you purchased Peachtree Accounting within three months of a change in the tax tables or if you received damaged tax tables for some reason, you can download new tax tables from the Peachtree Web site at *http://www.peachtree.com*. You will need a password and access information, which can be obtained from your Peachtree support representative.) The update floppy disk includes a setup program that will automatically install the new global tax tables and payroll forms.

You can use the default drive and filename or enter a different drive and filename. When you are satisfied with your entry, click OK to start loading the tax tables from the disk. Remember that company tax tables will not be overwritten when loading a tax update from Peachtree Accounting, but any changes you may have made to your company's tax tables will also have to be updated for the current year, as shown earlier in the "Editing Company Tax Tables" section.

Entering Employee and Sales Rep Records

Once you've set up your payroll and employee defaults, you're ready to start entering records for employees and sales reps. You must enter employee or sales rep information for each person who works for your company as an employee or a sales rep. A sales representative does not have to be an employee.

Employee and sales rep records are similar to the customer and vendor records you entered earlier in Accounts Receivable and Accounts Payable. Once you have entered employee and sales rep information, you can enter employee and sales rep beginning balances.

 N O T E : For simplicity, all references to entering, modifying, or deleting employee records will also refer to sales rep records, unless otherwise noted.

Entering an Employee or Sales Rep

There are five types of information you enter to set up an employee or sales rep: general information, custom fields, pay information, employee fields, and employer fields. You also need to enter a beginning balance for the employee or sales rep. This section shows you how to enter all this information.

Entering General Employee Information

From the Setup Checklist, click the Employee Records item. (You can also select Employee/Sales Reps directly from the Maintain menu.) The Maintain Employee/Sales Reps window appears with the General tab already selected (shown in Figure 7-21, with sample employee information).

Enter information for an employee as follows:

Employee ID Enter the employee ID. Employee IDs can be up to 20 characters long and can contain any characters except the asterisk (*), the question mark (?), or the plus sign (+).

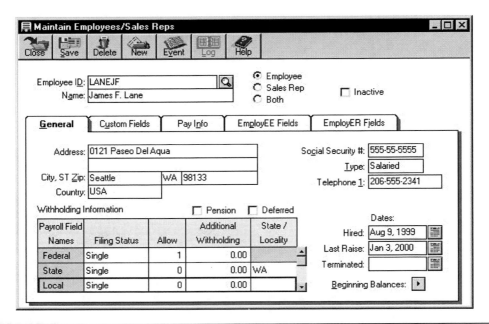

FIGURE 7-21 Maintain Employees/Sales Reps window showing the General tab

A good way to create employee IDs is to use the last name followed by the first and middle initials. For example, James F. Lane would become LANEJF. If there is a chance of two employees having the same last name and initials, you can append a number, such as LANEJF001. Using the first few letters of the employee's name gives you a reasonably intuitive way of looking up the employee in the company file. As with customer and vendor IDs, employee IDs are case sensitive, so Peachtree Accounting treats the employee IDs LANEJF and lanejf differently. You may want to set a policy that all letters in employee IDs be entered as capital letters.

Whatever you choose as an employee ID system, be sure that it can expand with the business. All the payroll transactions you enter for an employee are keyed to the employee ID. Once you set up an employee, you cannot change the employee ID without deleting the old employee and setting up a new employee. Also remember that Payroll sorts employees on reports in order of the employee ID.

C A U T I O N : Employee IDs cannot be changed. If you make a mistake when entering an employee ID, you will have to delete the employee ID and enter a new one.

Name   Enter the employee's name. You can enter up to 30 characters in this field. Payroll will list the employee name as you have entered it on employee checks, W-2 forms, and reports.

Employee   Clicking this radio button will include this employee in the employee reports. The employee will also be accessible through the Select for Payroll Entry and Payroll Entry windows.

Sales Rep   Clicking this radio button will include this person on all the sales representative reports. A sales representative does not have to be an employee. A sales representative is not accessible through the Select for Payroll Entry and Payroll Entry windows.

Both   Clicking this radio button will include this employee on all the employee reports as well as all the sales representative reports. The employee will also be accessible through the Select for Payroll Entry and Payroll Entry windows.

Inactive   Check this box to set the employee to inactive status. Although you can update the name and address information, Peachtree Accounting will warn you if you try to post a transaction to an inactive employee. When you close the payroll year, Peachtree Accounting will delete the employee records for all inactive employees with no outstanding transactions. You should set employees to inactive instead of deleting them so that you can run W-2s or other reports at year-end processing.

Peachtree Accounting lets you purge employees at any time. Purging employees is discussed in Chapter 13.

Address   Enter the employee's address (not including the city, state, and ZIP code). If you only have one line of address information, enter it on the first line and leave the second line blank.

City, ST Zip   Enter the city, state, and ZIP code for this address.

Country   Enter the country for this address. You may also leave this field blank.

Social Security #   Enter the employee's Social Security number.

Type   This custom field allows you to group employees so you can print checks or reports for an entire class of employees. You can enter up to eight characters to identify the type of employee. For smaller companies, types such as FULL (for full-time employees), PART (for part-time employees), and TEMP (for temporary employees) may be adequate. For larger companies with many employees, you may want to use masking (described in Chapter 4,) to create detailed employee types. Like all type fields in Peachtree Accounting, the information is case sensitive.

Telephone   Enter the telephone number for the employee.

Withholding Information   Enter the appropriate tax information for the employee's federal, state, and local filing status. Options for each field are available in each field's drop-down list.

Allow   Enter the number of allowances for the federal, state, and local filing statuses. If the employee is exempt from withholding for a category, enter 99 for the allowances.

Additional Withholding   Enter an amount for employee additional withholding, if any.

You won't need to enter local withholdings often. You can enter other information in this field—such as an employee's 401(k) or employee stock purchase percentage—and then use this information in a calculation in a custom tax table, as described briefly in the "Setting Up Payroll Tax Tables" section earlier.

State/Locality   Enter the two-digit code for the state and locality. This will be printed on the W-2 forms.

Pension   Entering a check in this box will cause Peachtree Accounting to mark the Pension box on the employee's W-2 form.

Deferred   Entering a check in the box will cause taxes to be deferred for this employee. Deferred income can include such things as dependent care (129) deductions, family insurance (125) deductions, 401(k) plans, and other qualified deferred bonuses and compensation.

Hired   Enter the employee's hire date. Click the Calendar button or right-click in this field to display the date-selection calendar.

Last Raise   Enter the date the employee last received a raise. (If the employee has not received a raise yet, leave this field blank.) Click the Calendar button or right-click in this field to display the date-selection calendar.

Terminated   Enter the employee's last working date. Click the Calendar button or right-click in this field to display the date-selection calendar.

Entering Employee Custom Fields

After you have entered the general employee information, click the Custom Fields tab. The Custom Fields tab appears, as shown in Figure 7-22. (You'll see how to enter a beginning balance for employees and sales reps later.) As the figure shows, the field labels entered earlier as part of the employee defaults information appear on this window.

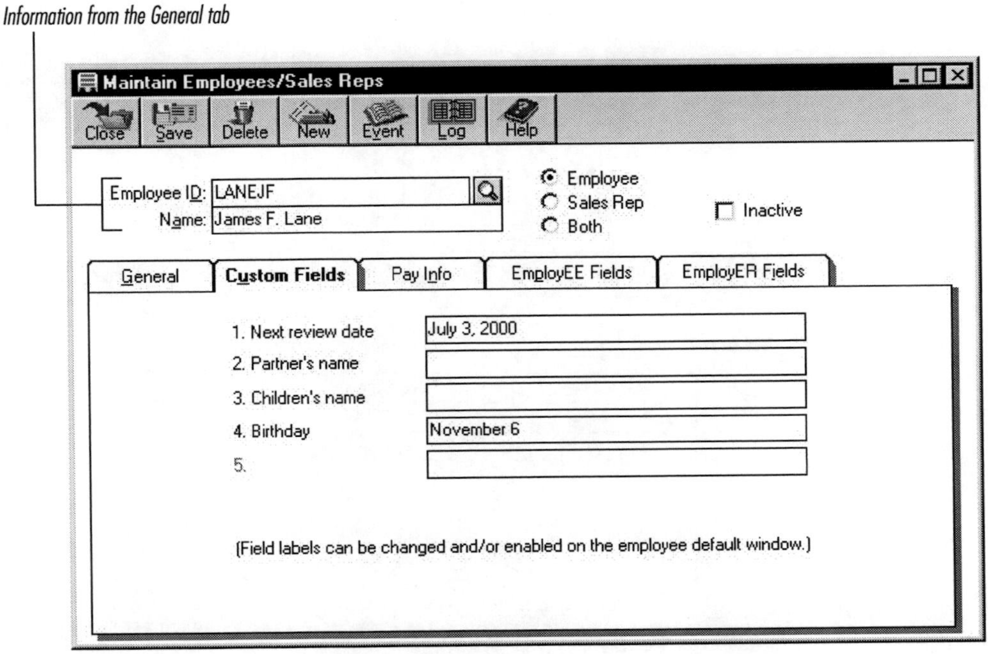

Information from the General tab

FIGURE 7-22 Maintain Employees/Sales Reps window showing the Custom Fields tab

As with customer and vendor records, the employee information in the top part of the tab is carried forward from the information you entered in the General tab. You can work with this employee, select another one, or change the name and inactive information for the employee from this tab.

Enter the custom field information for the employee here, exactly as you entered custom field information for customer records in Chapter 4.

Entering Pay Info Information

Click the Pay Info tab. The Pay Info tab appears, as shown in Figure 7-23.

The Pay Info tab lets you set the pay method, the pay frequency, hourly billing rate, and hours per pay period the employee is eligible for.

Pay Method   Select the pay type for the employee from the drop-down list: Salary, Hourly – Hours per Pay Period, or Hourly – Time Ticket Hours (the latter is available only in Peachtree Complete Accounting for Windows). The pay method you select here will determine the options in the description fields below.

Information from the General tab

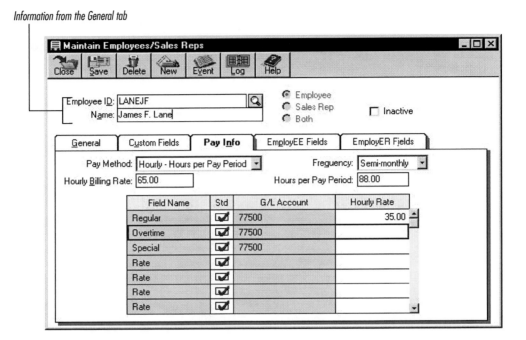

FIGURE 7-23 | Maintain Employees/Sales Reps window showing the Pay Info tab

Frequency   Select the paycheck frequency from the drop-down list: weekly, biweekly, semi-monthly, monthly, or annually. The frequency you select here is used in calculating payroll taxes.

Hourly Billing Rate   Enter the hourly billing rate for the employee. This is the rate your customers will be billed for the employee's time when you use time tickets to pass on expenses. (This field is only available in Peachtree Complete Accounting for Windows.)

The lower half of the window contains the pay types you set up earlier in the Pay Levels tab of the Employee Defaults window.

Field Name   This is the field name you entered in the Pay Levels tab of the Employee Defaults window. This field is display-only.

Std   When this box is checked, Peachtree Accounting uses the default General Ledger account you entered in the Pay Levels tab of the Employee Defaults window. Click this box to remove the check if you want to enter a different General Ledger account in the G/L Account field.

G/L Account The default account number is the General Ledger account you entered in the Pay Levels tab of the Employee Defaults window. If you want to enter another General Ledger account, clear the corresponding Std box and select an account from the drop-down list.

Hourly Rate Enter the default hourly or salaried rate for this employee for this pay type. If an employee doesn't qualify for a pay type, leave the rate for that pay type blank. When entering salary rates, make sure the salary rate matches the pay frequency. For example, if the employee is making $36,000 annual salary and the pay frequency is monthly, the basic salary rate should be $3,000.

Entering EmployEE Field Information

Click the EmployEE Fields tab. The EmployEE Fields tab appears, as shown in Figure 7-24.

The EmployEE Fields tab lets you set specific deduction amounts for the employee that differ from the default payroll deductions you set up in the EmployEE Fields tab of the Employee Defaults window. However, you cannot

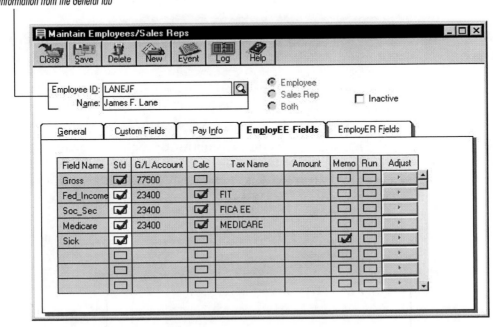

FIGURE 7-24 Maintain Employees/Sales Reps window showing the EmployEE Fields tab

add new types of payroll deductions; you can do that only through the Employee Defaults window.

Field Name   This is the name of the payroll field. This field is display-only.

Std   When this box is checked, Peachtree Accounting uses the default payroll information you entered in the EmployEE Fields tab of the Employee Defaults window. Click this box to remove the check and enter a different General Ledger account or calculation.

G/L Account   The default account number is the General Ledger account you entered in the EmployEE Fields tab of the Employee Defaults window. If you want to enter another General Ledger account, uncheck the corresponding Std box and select an account from the drop-down list.

N O T E :   If the Memo box is checked, Peachtree Accounting will not post information for this payroll field to the General Ledger. You would use this account for noncash benefits such as tips and meals.

Calc   Check the Calc box if Peachtree Accounting can calculate this information from the payroll tax tables.

Tax Name   The default tax table is the tax table you entered in the EmployEE Fields tab of the Employee Defaults window. If you want to enter another tax table, uncheck the corresponding Std box and select a tax table from the drop-down list. (For information on the specific calculation options and a table of the various options, see the "Setting Up Payroll Tax Tables" section earlier in this chapter.)

Amount   This field shows the amount for the employee deduction or allowance you entered in the EmployEE Fields tab of the Employee Defaults window. To enter an amount, you must have first unchecked the corresponding Std and Calc boxes.

Putting It to Work

Some employees are exempt from 401(k) or other standard deductions. You may also have local or state taxes that some employees may not be required to pay because they live in a different city, county, or state. Here's how to set up an employee's record so he or she doesn't pay selected taxes:

1. From the Maintain menu, select Employees/Sales Reps. The Maintain Employees/Sales Reps window appears, as shown earlier in Figure 7-21.

2. Enter the employee's ID in the Employee ID field, or use the drop-down list to select the employee's ID from the list of IDs.

3. Click the EmployEE Fields tab to display the EmployEE Fields tab, shown in Figure 7-24.

4. Uncheck the Std and Calc fields for the calculations you want to remove for this employee. (The Tax Name disappears when both fields are unchecked.)

5. Now click the EmployER Fields tab to display the EmployER Fields tab, shown in Figure 7-25.

6. Uncheck the Std and Calc fields for the appropriate calculations on the window you want to remove for this employee. Clicking the Std and Calc fields in this tab removes any employer contribution for the calculations. (The Tax Name disappears when both fields are unchecked.)

7. Click Save to save the changes to this employee, then click Close.

Memo   If this box is checked, information for this payroll field is not posted to the General Ledger. This field is display-only.

Run   If this box is checked, Peachtree Accounting will not zero the account when you close the payroll year. This field is display-only.

Adjust   Click this button to identify the fields you want to use to calculate the adjusted gross. The Calculate Adjusted Gross window appears, as shown earlier in Figure 7-18. You check the boxes for each of the fields you want to use in the calculation, and Peachtree Accounting adds those fields to calculate the information. (You must uncheck the Std box to use this feature.)

Entering EmployER Field Information

Click the EmployER Fields tab. The EmployER Fields tab appears, as shown in Figure 7-25.

The EmployER Fields tab lets you set specific employer tax amounts for the employee different from the default tax amounts you set up in the EmployER Fields tab of the Employee Defaults window. To replace an entry, click the Std box and change the tax table referred to in the Tax Name field. However, you cannot add new types of payroll taxes; you can only do that through the Employee Defaults window.

Information from the General tab

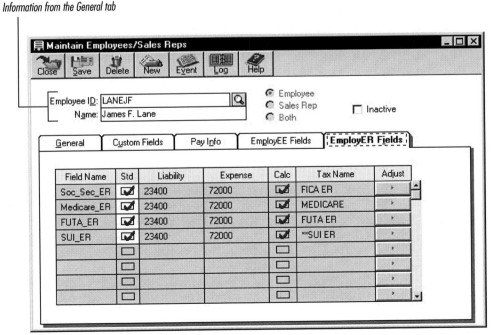

FIGURE 7-25   Maintain Employees/Sales Reps window showing the EmployER Fields tab

Field Name   This is the name of the payroll field. This field is display-only.

Std   When this box is checked, Peachtree Accounting uses the default information you entered in the EmployER Fields tab of the Employee Defaults window. Click this box to remove the check and enter a different General Ledger liability or expense account, or a different calculation.

Liability   The default liability account is the General Ledger account you entered in the EmployER Fields tab of the Employee Defaults window. If you want to enter another General Ledger account, uncheck the corresponding Std box and select an account from the drop-down list.

Expense   The default expense account is the General Ledger account you entered in the EmployER Fields tab of the Employee Defaults window. If you want to enter another General Ledger account, uncheck the corresponding Std box and select an account from the drop-down list.

Calc   Check the Calc box if Peachtree Accounting can calculate this information from the payroll tax tables.

Tax Name   The default tax table is the tax table you entered in the EmployER Fields tab of the Employee Defaults window. If you want to enter another tax table, uncheck the corresponding Std box and select a tax table from the drop-down list. (For information on the specific calculation options and a table of the various options, see the "Setting Up Payroll Tax Tables" section earlier in this chapter.)

Adjust   Click this button to identify the fields you want to use to calculate the gross. The Calculate Adjusted Gross window appears, as shown earlier in Figure 7-18. You check the boxes for each of the fields you want to use in the calculation, and Peachtree Accounting adds those fields to calculate the information. (You must uncheck the Std box to use this feature.)

Entering Employee Beginning Balances

As the last step to setting up an employee, you enter the employee's beginning balance. To enter a beginning balance for an employee, go to the General tab in the Maintain Employees/Sales Reps window, and click Beginning Balances. The Employee Beginning Balances window appears. You can go directly to the Employee Beginning Balances window by selecting Employee Y-T-D Earnings and Withholdings from the Setup Checklist, but this is probably not as convenient as clicking Beginning Balances. Figure 7-26 shows this window with sample information already entered.

You enter beginning balances for the employee in this window. You can enter beginning balances for an employee at any time, even after posting

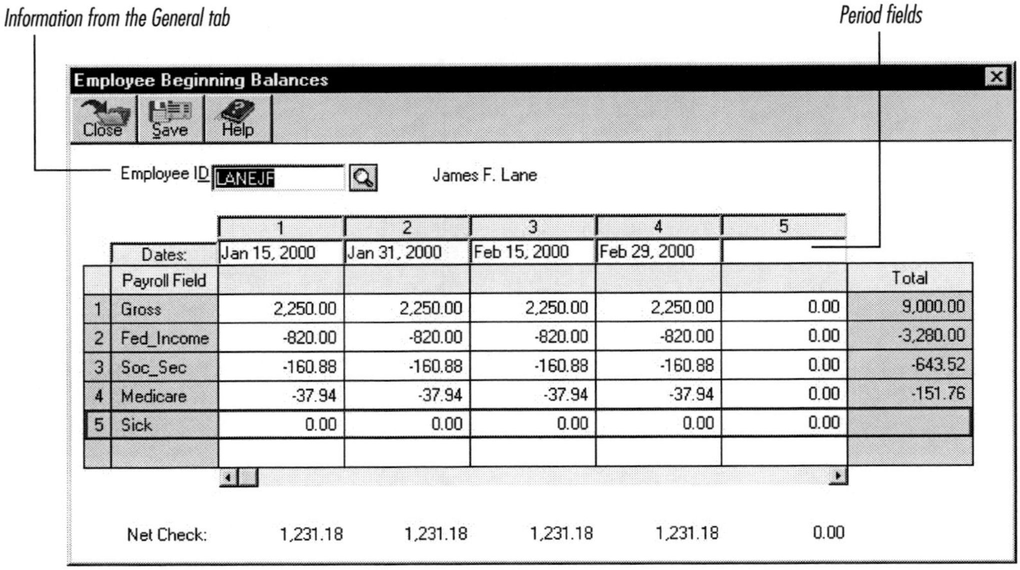
Information from the General tab
Period fields
Employee Beginning Balances
Close
Save
Help
Employee ID LANEJF
James F. Lane
1
2
3
4
5
Dates:
Jan 15, 2000
Jan 31, 2000
Feb 15, 2000
Feb 29, 2000
Payroll Field
Total
1 Gross 2,250.00 2,250.00 2,250.00 2,250.00 0.00 9,000.00
2 Fed_Income -820.00 -820.00 -820.00 -820.00 0.00 -3,280.00
3 Soc_Sec -160.88 -160.88 -160.88 -160.88 0.00 -643.52
4 Medicare -37.94 -37.94 -37.94 -37.94 0.00 -151.76
5 Sick 0.00 0.00 0.00 0.00 0.00
Net Check: 1,231.18 1,231.18 1,231.18 1,231.18 0.00

FIGURE 7-26 Employee Beginning Balances window

a transaction for the employee, but this is not recommended for a clear audit trail. If this is a new employee with no prior activity, you won't need to enter a beginning balance.

Dates Enter the dates of the pay periods for which you want to enter beginning balances.

Payroll Field Enter the beginning balance amounts for the period for the employee fields. (These fields are determined by the entries you've made on the EmployEE Field tab for this employee record.)

If you're entering an employee at a time other than the start of the year, you will need to enter employee payroll information so you can run quarterly and end-of-year reports. Probably the most effective way to enter employee payroll data is to combine the data through the end of the most recent quarter and enter that as a single pay period. Then enter any subsequent period information as separate periods of data. For example, if your pay periods are semi-monthly and you are entering data in Peachtree Accounting as of August 1, you would combine the information from January 1 through June 30 into a single period, then enter the data for the periods ending July 15 and July 31 as two separate periods. Entering prior payroll data this way reduces the number of payroll periods you have to enter from 14 to 3.

When you're satisfied with the information you've entered, click Save at the top of the window. To close the Employee Beginning Balances window and return to the Maintain Employees/Sales Reps window, click Close at the top of the window.

Modifying Employee Records

Once you've entered an employee record, you can modify it. Modifying an employee record is easy. All you have to do is display the employee record in the Maintain Employees/Sales Reps window by entering the employee ID in the Employee ID field. You can then change any of the employee information except for the Employee ID itself. If you want to change the Employee ID for an employee, you will have to delete the employee and then re-enter the information under the new employee ID.

Deleting Employee Records

You can delete an employee record by selecting an employee record and then clicking Delete at the top of the screen. Peachtree Accounting asks you if you're sure you want to delete this record. Click Yes to delete the employee record.

C A U T I O N : You cannot delete employees with any transactions in the current year. Instead, set the employee to inactive by clicking the Inactive box in the General tab of the employee's record. Peachtree Accounting will then purge the employee when you close the payroll year.

Printing an Employee List

Now that you've entered the employee information, you can print a report of the employees to verify the information you've entered. The Employee List is a list of employees with employee address, Social Security number, filing status, and pay type.

To print the Employee List, select Payroll from the Reports menu. The Select a Report window appears with the Payroll option selected. Next, select the Employee List from the list, and click Print or Screen at the top of the window. Enter the information in the report selection windows and click OK. The Employee List appears on the screen or is sent to the printer. Figure 7-27 shows a sample of this report.

Big Business, Inc.
Employee List

Filter Criteria includes: Report order is by ID.

Employee ID Employee	Address line 1 Address line 2 City ST ZIP	SS No	Fed Filing Status	Pay Type
ANDERSONKB Karen B. Anderson	6741 Chandler Blvd. Apt. 12-E Bothell, WA 98036 USA	814-24-5220	Married	Salaried
BILLINGSND Nancy D. Billings	1523 Carmelian Seattle, WA 98103 USA	340-13-0247	Married	Hourly
FITZGERALDR Ronda G. Fitzgerald	1814 Eastlake Ave E. Seattle, WA 98103 USA	905-10-1147		Hourly
FRANKLINJL John L. Franklin	4119 Interlander Blvd.	999-65-4309	Single	Salaried
JOHNSONPR Pamela Johnson	1924 Rosalyn Summers Blvd. Apt. 2A Bothell, WA 98036 USA	021-50-2436	Married	Salaried
LANEJF James F. Lane	0121 Paseo Del Aqua Seattle, WA 98133 USA	555-55-5555	Single	Hourly

FIGURE 7-27 Employee List report

The employee records are now complete, and you'll be able to add, update, and delete employee records as necessary. Payroll setup is also complete; you are now ready to generate payroll checks.

Running Payroll

The previous sections in this chapter showed how to enter payroll defaults, add and maintain employee and sales rep records, and set up tax tables. You are now ready to enter payroll information, select employees to pay, and create payroll checks.

Although setting up payroll information is somewhat time-consuming, running paychecks is actually fairly simple. You select the employees for payment, make any adjustments and enter information for manually created paychecks, verify the information, and save or post the paycheck. You then print the paychecks. Finally, you print payroll reports to provide a hard copy audit trail.

TIP: The steps for creating payroll checks are very similar to the steps for paying vendors. If you have not already gone through Chapter 6 you may want to review it now.

Selecting Employees for Payment

Selecting employees for payment is very similar to the process of selecting vendors for payment. There are two ways to select employees for payment. The first (and easier) is to use the Select for Payroll Entry window, which lets you select employees based on selection criteria you enter. The second is to use the Payroll Entry window, which lets you select individual employees for payment, modify amounts, and print individual checks. You will probably want to use the Select for Payroll Entry window to select a group of employees and then use the Payroll Entry window to modify or delete individual employee paychecks.

To select employees for payment, choose the Select for Payroll Entry option from the Tasks menu. The Select Employees – Filter Selection window appears, as shown in Figure 7-28.

Pay End Date   Enter the cutoff date to include employee time tickets for in the payroll calculations. Peachtree Complete Accounting for Windows will include all time tickets up to and including this date. (This field only shows in Peachtree Complete Accounting for Windows.)

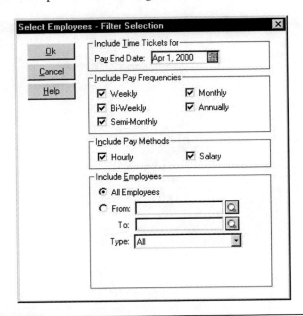

| **FIGURE 7-28** | Select Employees – Filter Selection window |

Include Pay Frequencies   Peachtree Accounting includes all employees for the selected pay frequencies.

Include Pay Methods   Peachtree Accounting includes hourly, salaried, or both types of employees, depending on your selections.

Include Employees   If you select All Employees, Peachtree Accounting will pay all employees. You can enter a range of employees by specifying a start and stop employee in the From and To fields. You can also pay all employees of a given type by entering the employee type in the Type field. If you select a type other than All, Peachtree Accounting displays additional fields as appropriate for entering ranges of employee types.

When you're satisfied with your entries, click OK to select the employees to pay. The Select Employees to Pay window appears, as shown in Figure 7-29.

Table 7-2 shows the toolbar buttons that appear in the Select Employees to Pay window.

Check Date   Enter the date you want Peachtree Accounting to print on the employee checks. The default for this field is the first day of the current accounting period if you are not in the same period as the system date. Otherwise, it defaults to the system date.

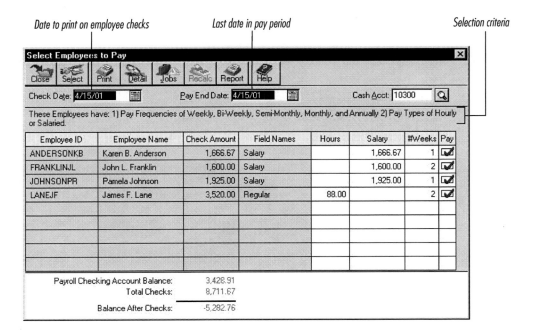

Date to print on employee checks   *Last date in pay period*   *Selection criteria*

Select Employees to Pay

Close | Select | Print | Detail | Jobs | Recalc | Report | Help

Check Date: 4/15/01   Pay End Date: 4/15/01   Cash Acct: 10300

These Employees have: 1) Pay Frequencies of Weekly, Bi-Weekly, Semi-Monthly, Monthly, and Annually 2) Pay Types of Hourly or Salaried.

Employee ID	Employee Name	Check Amount	Field Names	Hours	Salary	#Weeks	Pay
ANDERSONKB	Karen B. Anderson	1,666.67	Salary		1,666.67	1	☑
FRANKLINJL	John L. Franklin	1,600.00	Salary		1,600.00	2	☑
JOHNSONPR	Pamela Johnson	1,925.00	Salary		1,925.00	1	☑
LANEJF	James F. Lane	3,520.00	Regular	88.00		2	☑

Payroll Checking Account Balance:	3,428.91
Total Checks:	8,711.67
Balance After Checks:	-5,282.76

FIGURE 7-29   Select Employees to Pay window

BUTTON	NAME	DESCRIPTION
Close	Close	Close the window without saving the changes.
Select	Select	Return to the Select Employees to Pay – Filter Selection window to select employees.
Print	Print	Print checks for the selected employees in the amounts shown in this window.
Detail	Detail	Show detail amounts for the selected employee (you can also double-click an employee line item for this).
Jobs	Jobs	Distribute labor to jobs.
Recalc	Recalc	Recalculate account balances.
Report	Report	Preview report.
Help	Help	Get help on this window.

TABLE 7-2   Toolbar Buttons in the Select Employees to Pay Window

Pay End Date   Enter the last date in the pay period. The default for this field is the first day of the current accounting period if you are not in the same period as the system date. Otherwise, it defaults to the system date.

Cash Acct   Enter the General Ledger account ID for the appropriate cash account. The default for this field is the last cash account you used in Peachtree Accounting.

The lower portion of the window shows the employees you selected to pay. The Employee ID, Employee Name, Check Amount, and Field Names fields are display-only.

Hours   Peachtree Accounting enters the default hours for the pay period if the employee is hourly. Peachtree Accounting determines the paycheck amount by multiplying the hours by the hourly rate, then making the calculations and distributions to the General Ledger accounts for withholding and any other accumulations you set up in the employee record.

Salary   Peachtree Accounting enters the default salary amount for the pay period if the employee is salaried. Peachtree Accounting determines the paycheck amount by using the base paycheck amount and making the calculations and distributions to the General Ledger accounts for withholding and any other accumulations you set up in the employee record.

#Weeks   Peachtree Accounting displays the number of weeks in the pay period for the employee: 1 for weekly employees, 2 for biweekly and semi-monthly employees, 4 for monthly employees, and 52 for annual employees.

Pay   This checkbox lets you select or deselect the employee for payment on this check run. The default is for the employees appearing in this window to be selected for payment, but you can manually deselect some of the employees by unchecking the Pay checkbox for the employee.

Payroll Checking Account Balance   The current cash balance in the checking account appears in this field. This field is display-only. If the field displays question marks, click Recalc. Peachtree Accounting will calculate the cash in the checking account and display the amount in the field.

Total Checks   The total of the paychecks selected for payment appears in this field. As you select and deselect checks with the Pay checkbox, Peachtree Accounting updates the total in this field. This field is display-only.

Balance After Checks   Peachtree Accounting displays the cash balance in the checking account less the total checks in the window. This field is display-only.

N O T E :   You can select paychecks for payment and print checks even if the total disbursements will leave you with a negative cash balance.

You can click Detail at the top of the window or double-click a line item to see transaction detail and enter adjustments. Figure 7-30 shows the Select Employees to Pay – Detail window with sample data for an hourly employee.

You can make adjustments to the amounts in this window. When you click OK, Peachtree Accounting transfers these amounts to the Select Employees to Pay window for the employee.

You can enter labor distributions to jobs by clicking Jobs at the top of the Select Employees to Pay window. The Labor Distribution to Jobs window appears, as shown in Figure 7-31.

You can use this window to distribute the labor costs for a given employee to up to ten different jobs. To enter a distribution, double-click the line you want to distribute costs from, or click Add to insert a blank line to add another line of information. Enter a job ID in the Job field, then enter the number of hours

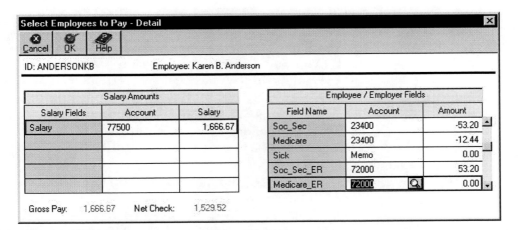

FIGURE 7-30 Select Employees to Pay – Detail window

in the Hours field; if salaried, enter the dollar amount. You cannot enter more than the total hours for the employee in the distributions.

You can use the Add and Remove buttons to add and remove individual line items. When you are satisfied with your entries, click OK to return to the Select Employees to Pay window. The totals for the employee will be unaffected, but labor distributions will appear on the employee's pay stub. The Labor Distribution to Jobs window has slightly different fields for hourly employees, but the process for making distributions is the same.

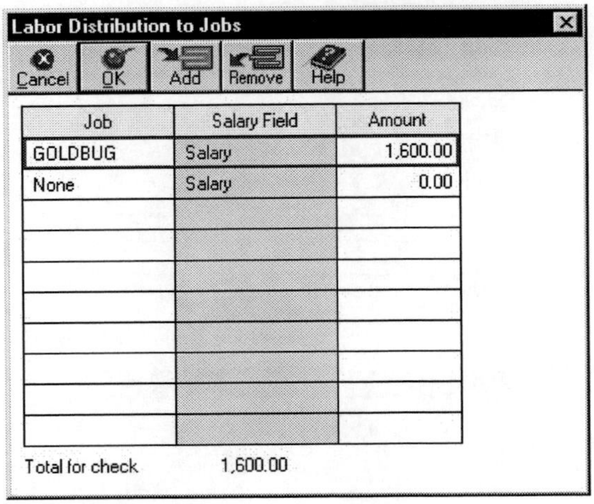

FIGURE 7-31 Labor Distribution to Jobs window

Printing Checks

When you are satisfied with the information you have entered, click Print to start printing paychecks. You may also print a pre-check register by clicking on Report. Peachtree Accounting displays the Print Forms window, shown in Figure 7-32.

Select the payroll check you want to print and click OK. Peachtree Accounting then displays the Print Forms window for the payroll check you've selected (shown in Figure 7-33) and lets you print either a practice form (for alignment purposes), or the real checks.

When you click Real, Peachtree Accounting prompts you for the first check number in the print run (as shown in Figure 7-34).

Peachtree Accounting tracks the check numbers. After you've entered a check number, the first time you print checks of any kind, Peachtree Accounting tracks the check numbers from then on. You can change the check number from the default as necessary. Click OK to start printing paychecks.

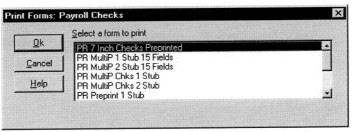

FIGURE 7-32   Print Forms window for payroll checks

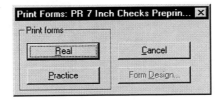

FIGURE 7-33   Print Forms window for a payroll check

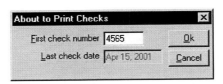

FIGURE 7-34   About to Print Checks window

When Peachtree Accounting has finished printing the checks, it asks you if the checks printed properly and if it's okay to update the Payroll Journal. Click Yes if the checks printed correctly; otherwise, click No.

Entering Individual Payments

Normal payroll check runs happen regularly on specific calendar dates, making them easy to plan for. You will probably select most of your employees for payment using the Select for Payments option discussed in the previous section. However, you may want to create individual paychecks from time to time, for example, when an employee is terminated or receives a bonus paycheck on a date other than a standard pay date. Preprinted checks (and other preprinted forms discussed in this chapter) can be obtained from Peachtree. A catalog of preprinted-stock is included in the Peachtree Accounting package, or you can phone Peachtree Forms directly at (800) 61-PEACH for information.

Start by selecting Payroll Entry from the Tasks menu. Figure 7-35 shows the Payroll Entry window with a sample employee selected.

The Payroll Entry window is very similar to the Payments window in Accounts Payable. There is one new button on this window, as shown here:

BUTTON	NAME	DESCRIPTION
Journal	Journal	Display the Accounting Behind the Screens window.

Employee ID   Enter the employee ID in the field. When you select the employee ID, Peachtree Accounting enters the employee name and address, and the payroll information in the lower half of the window.

Pay to the Order Of   This shows the name and address of the employee as entered in the employee record. This field is display-only.

Check Number   Leave this field blank to include the check in the check run. When you prepare to run checks, Peachtree Accounting will see that this field is blank and will include the check as part of the check run. If you are recording a check after the check has been written (logging a manual check), enter the check number in this field.

Date   Enter the date for the paycheck in this field. Peachtree Accounting displays the date of the first day in the current account period as the default, if you are not in the same period as the system date. Otherwise, it defaults to the system date. Click the Calendar button or right-click in this field to display the date-selection calendar.

Check Amount   Peachtree Accounting calculates this field for you based on the amounts you enter in the lower half of the screen. This field is display-only.

Check amount   Adjustments to gross payment amounts

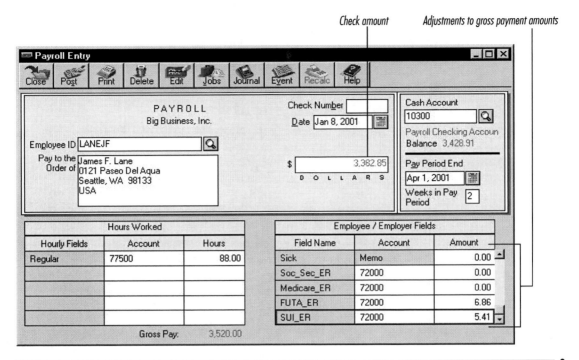

FIGURE 7-35   Payroll Entry window

Cash Account   This is the default General Ledger account to pay checks from, such as a cash or payroll account.

Pay Period End   Enter the last date in the pay period for this paycheck.

Weeks in Pay Period   Peachtree Accounting displays the number of weeks in the pay period for the employee: 1 for weekly employees, 2 for biweekly and semi-monthly employees, 4 for monthly employees, and 52 for annual employees. You can change this field if necessary; for example, if you're paying an employee severance through a specific date.

The fields in the lower half of the screen are identical to the detail fields you saw earlier on the Select Employees to Pay – Detail window in Figure 7-30. You can make manual adjustments to the General Ledger accounts and the pay amounts in these fields.

You can print the paycheck directly from the Payroll Entry by clicking Print at the top of the window or through the normal check printing procedure. You can also click Post to save the changes you've made to the employee's pay amounts. Then, when you select the employee as part of a group of employees, the revised pay amounts will appear on the paycheck. This technique is useful if you need to modify a number of employee check amounts, but don't want to print checks until you've done all of them.

Voiding Checks

The process for voiding paychecks is identical to the process for voiding checks in Accounts Payable. Start by selecting Void Checks from the Tasks menu. The Choose a Cash Account window appears, as shown in Figure 7-36.

Account ID   Enter the ID of the General Ledger account used for creating the checks. The account name appears in the field below the Account ID field.

Click OK to display the Void Existing Checks window (shown in Figure 7-37).

Select the check you want to void and click Void (or double-click the line item). The second Void Existing Checks window appears (shown in Figure 7-38).

| **FIGURE 7-36** | Choose a Cash Account window |

Check selected for voiding

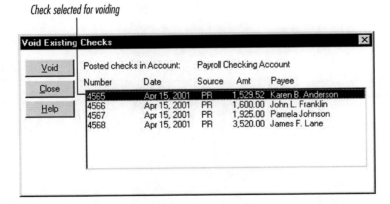

| **FIGURE 7-37** | Void Existing Checks window |

| **FIGURE 7-38** | Second Void Existing Checks window |

The Following Check Will Be Voided As Of   Peachtree Accounting displays a default date for voiding the check. You can enter any date in this field that is not earlier than the start of the current accounting period.

Click OK to void the check. Peachtree Accounting then returns you to the first Void Existing Check window and updates the list of checks to remove the line for the voided check. You can continue voiding checks by selecting checks and clicking Void. Click Close when you're done.

After you have printed paychecks, you will want to print payroll reports to provide hard copy documents for your audit trail, such as a Check Register and a Payroll Journal. The following section shows you how to print payroll reports.

Printing Payroll Reports

Most of the work you do in Payroll is actually related to creating printed checks, reports, and forms. You've already seen how to print an Employee List. Table 7-3 shows a list of the other payroll reports in Peachtree Accounting.

In addition to the list of reports in Table 7-3, there are six folders of forms you can print:

- Payroll Checks
- Federal Form W-2
- Federal Form 940

REPORT	DESCRIPTION
Employee List	Employee information, including address, Social Security number, withholding status, and pay type.
Check Register	Employee information, including the most recent payroll check number, check date, employee name, and check amount.
Payroll Journal	Payroll information printed in journal format.
Payroll Tax Report	Employee pay information, showing gross pay and taxable amounts.
Exception Report	Employee pay information that differs from the amounts calculated by Peachtree Accounting.
Payroll Register	Payroll information for employees for selected period.
Current Earnings Report	Detailed employee payroll information for the current (or other specified) period.
Quarterly Earnings Report	Detailed employee payroll information for the quarter.
Yearly Earnings Report	Detailed employee payroll information for the year.

TABLE 7-3   Payroll Reports

- Federal Form 941
- State Qtrly Payroll
- Labels – Employees

Each of the folders contains a selection of reports that are print-only—you can print them, but you can't see them on the screen.

Check Register

The Check Register contains employee information, including the most recent payroll check number, check date, employee name, and check amount. You should print a Check Register immediately after you print paychecks for your permanent hard copy documents.

To print the Check Register, select Payroll from the Reports menu. Next, select the Check Register from the list and click Screen or Print at the top of the window. Enter the information in the report selection windows and click OK. The Check Register appears on the screen or is sent to the printer. Figure 7-39 shows a sample of this report.

Payroll Journal

The Payroll Journal report gives you payroll information in journal format.

To print the Payroll Journal, select Payroll from the Reports menu and select the Payroll Journal from the list. Click Screen or Print at the top of the window, enter the information in the report selection windows, and click OK. The Payroll Journal appears on the screen or is sent to the printer. Figure 7-40 shows a sample of this report.

Big Business, Inc.
Check Register
For the Period From Apr 15, 2001 to Apr 23, 2001
Filter Criteria includes: Report order is by Check Date. Report is printed in Detail Format.

Reference	Date	Employee	Amount
4565	4/15/01	Karen B. Anderson	1,529.52
4566	4/15/01	John L. Franklin	1,600.00
4567	4/15/01	Pamela Johnson	1,925.00
4568	4/15/01	James F. Lane	3,520.00
		4/15/01 thru 4/23/01	8,574.52
		4/15/01 thru 4/23/01	8,574.52

FIGURE 7-39 Check Register report

Big Business, Inc.
Payroll Journal
For the Period From Apr 15, 2001 to Apr 30, 2001
Filter Criteria includes: Report order is by Check Date. Report is printed in Detail Format.

Date Employee	GL Acct ID	Reference	Debit Amt	Credit Amt
4/15/01	77500	4565	1,666.67	
Karen B. Anderson	23400			71.51
	23400			53.20
	23400			12.44
	23400			53.20
	72000		53.20	
	10300			1,529.52

FIGURE 7-40 Payroll Journal report

Payroll Tax Report

The Payroll Tax report provides tax information for individual tax calculations that have an upper limit (such as FICA, FUTA, and Medicare) for the specified quarter. The report lists the employee's pay information, showing gross pay, taxable gross, excess gross, and tax amounts for the selected tax calculation.

To print the Payroll Tax report, select Payroll from the Reports menu, select the Payroll Tax Report from the list, and click Screen or Print at the top of the window. Enter the information in the report selection windows, and click OK. You must specify the tax ID and the quarter for which to generate the report in the report selection windows.

The Payroll Tax report appears on the screen or is sent to the printer. Figure 7-41 shows a sample of this report.

Big Business, Inc.
Payroll Tax Report
As of Jun 30, 2001
(WASUI ER)

Filter Criteria includes: Report order is by ID.

Employee ID Employee	SS No	Weeks	Gross	Taxable Gross	Excess Gross	Tax Amount
FRANKLINJL John L. Franklin	999-65-4309	2	1,600.00	1,600.00		
JOHNSONPR Pamela Johnson	021-50-2436	1	1,925.00	1,925.00		
LANEJF James F. Lane	555-55-5555	2	3,520.00	3,520.00		
	Total:		7,045.00	7,045.00		

FIGURE 7-41 Payroll Tax report

Putting It to Work

The Payroll Tax report is a very useful report. In the Filter tab, you can select a wide range of tax IDs to report on. However, in addition to the standard federal taxes, you may also have set up state or local tax IDs that you want to run the report for. Here's how to add payroll tax IDs to the drop-down list of tax IDs:

1. From the File menu, select the Payroll Tax Tables option, then select Edit Company from the submenu. The Maintain Company Payroll Tax Tables window appears (shown earlier in Figure 7-20).
2. Select the tax ID from the list.
3. Check the Appears on Payroll Tax Report Menu box.
4. Click Save to save the entry.

It's important to note that because the Payroll Tax report calculates the tax paid toward a limit, the formula for the selected tax ID must have a limit, a percent, and a taxable_gross calculation (such as the Washington state UI calculation in Figure 7-20). If the formula doesn't have these elements, you may need to rework the formula. Detailed information for creating formulas appears in the Peachtree Accounting manual. However, if you're uncomfortable creating formulas on your own, you should strongly consider getting help from Peachtree Accounting or from a Peachtree Resource Center.

Exception Report

The Exception report lists every employee with a withholding amount different than the amount calculated by Peachtree Accounting for the specified tax. The Exception report shows employee information with taxable gross, amount withheld, amount calculated, and the difference between the calculated and withheld amounts.

To print the Exception report, select Payroll from the Reports menu, select the Exception report from the list, and click Screen or Print at the top of the window.

Entering the report selection criteria for this report is different from the other reports you've printed. In the Filter tab for this report, you must specify the tax you want to check (such as Social Security or FUTA), and you must specify the quarter for which to generate the report in the report selection windows. You can also have Peachtree Accounting automatically prepare correcting journal entries and post them back to the Payroll Journal. If you click the Prepare correcting entries box in the Filter tab, you must specify the tax ID in the Tax to Adjust To field to which you want Peachtree Accounting to post these journal entries. If you are using batch method entry, be sure to post the Payroll Journal immediately after running this report.

When you are satisfied with your entries, click OK. The Exception report appears on the screen or is sent to the printer. Figure 7-42 shows a sample of this report.

Payroll Register

The Payroll Register report lets you verify the posting accounts and amounts. To print the Payroll Register, select Payroll from the Reports menu, choose the Payroll Register from the list, and click Screen or Print at the top of the window. In the Filter tab for this report, enter the General Ledger cash account ID you

Big Business, Inc.
Exception Report
As of Jun 30, 2000

Filter Criteria includes: Report order is by Name. Report is printed for SUI_ER.

Employee ID Employee	SS No ST	Qt	Taxable Gross	Amt Withheld	Calculated A	Difference
LANEJF	555-55-55	1	12,520.00	-5.41	0.00	5.41
James F. Lane	WA	2	3,520.00	0.00	0.00	0.00
	Total		16,040.00	-5.41	0.00	5.41
FRANKLINJL	999-65-43	1	0.00	0.00	0.00	0.00
John L. Franklin	WA	2	1,600.00	0.00	0.00	0.00
	Total		1,600.00	0.00	0.00	0.00

FIGURE 7-42   Exception report

Big Business, Inc.
Payroll Register
For the Period From Apr 15, 2001 to Apr 30, 2001
Filter Criteria includes: Report order is by Check Date. Report is printed in Detail Format.

Employee ID Employee SS No Reference Date	Pay Type	Pay Hrs	Pay Amt	Amount	Gross Sick SUI_ER	Fed_Income Soc_Sec_ER	Soc_Sec Medicare_ER	Medicare FUTA_ER
ANDERSONKB Karen B. Anderson 814-24-5220 4565 4/15/01	Salary		1,666.67	1,529.52	1,666.67	-71.51 -53.20	-53.20	-12.44

FIGURE 7-43 Payroll Register report

used to print the payroll checks, and the date range. When you are satisfied with your entries, click OK. The Payroll Register appears on the screen or is sent to the printer. Figure 7-43 shows a sample of this report.

Earnings Reports

Peachtree Accounting provides three different earnings reports: the Current Earnings report, Quarterly Earnings report, and Yearly Earnings report. The Current Earnings report (shown in Figure 7-44) lists the detailed employee payroll information for the current (or other) period. Each of the distributions that appear on the employee's check appears on this report. The Quarterly Earnings report (shown in Figure 7-45) lists the same information and provides

Big Business, Inc.
Current Earnings Report
For the Period From Apr 15, 2001 to Apr 30, 2001
Filter Criteria includes: Report order is by Employee ID. Report is printed in Detail Format.

Employee ID Employee SS No	Date Reference	Amount	Gross Sick SUI_ER	Fed_Income Soc_Sec_ER	Soc_Sec Medicare_ER	Medicare FUTA_ER
Beginning Balance for Karen B. Anderson		7,753.34	8,333.35	-580.01		
ANDERSONKB Karen B. Anderson 814-24-5220	4/15/01 4565	1,529.52	1,666.67	-71.51 -53.20	-53.20	-12.44
Total 4/15/01 thru 4/30/01		1,529.52	1,666.67	-71.51 -53.20	-53.20	-12.44

FIGURE 7-44 Current Earnings report

Big Business, Inc.
Quarterly Earnings Report
For the Period From Jan 1, 2001 to Mar 31, 2001
Filter Criteria includes: Report order is by Employee ID. Report is printed in Detail Format.

Employee ID Employee SS No	Date Reference	Amount	Gross Sick SUI_ER	Fed_Income Soc_Sec_ER	Soc_Sec Medicare_ER	Medicare FUTA_ER
LANEJF James F. Lane 555-55-5555	1/8/01	3,382.85	3,520.00 -5.41	-71.51	-53.20	-12.44 -6.86
LANEJF James F. Lane 555-55-5555	1/15/01 BEGBAL	1,231.18	2,250.00	-820.00	-160.88	-37.94
LANEJF James F. Lane 555-55-5555	1/31/01 BEGBAL	1,231.18	2,250.00	-820.00	-160.88	-37.94
LANEJF James F. Lane 555-55-5555	2/15/01 BEGBAL	1,231.18	2,250.00	-820.00	-160.88	-37.94

FIGURE 7-45 Quarterly Earnings report

quarterly subtotals. The Yearly Earnings report (not shown) is similar to the Quarterly Earnings report, except that it gives the employee's information for the year to date.

To print an earnings report, select Payroll from the Reports menu. Choose the appropriate earnings report from the list, and click Screen or Print at the top of the window. In the Filter tab for this report, enter the General Ledger cash account ID you used to print the payroll checks, and the date range. When you are satisfied with your entries, click OK. The report appears on the screen or is sent to the printer.

Printing Employee Labels

You can print labels with your employees' addresses. These are convenient for mailing W-2 forms or company announcements. As with the checks, you can print an alignment form by clicking Align rather than OK. This lets you align the labels on your printer before printing. Peachtree Accounting lets you specify vertical and horizontal offsets through the program rather than having to manually adjust the forms in the printer.

You can edit the address label formats or create new ones. For more information on the Forms Designer, see Chapter 12.

Printing W-2s, 940s, and 941s

At the end of the year, you will need to print W-2 forms for all employees. You can print three kinds of W-2 forms: double-wide, four per page, or standard. There are also two kinds of 940 forms and three kinds of 941 forms. All of these reports will require preprinted stock, which you can order directly from Peachtree Accounting or purchase from many office and stationery supply stores. You may want to try printing a few sample forms on plain paper to determine which preprinted form stock you prefer.

Printing State Quarterly Payroll Reports

Peachtree Accounting comes with a few quarterly payroll reports for specific states. You can print these reports to fulfill quarterly reporting requirements for these states.

Posting Payroll Transactions

Posting Payroll transactions is much the same as posting other types of accounting transactions in Peachtree Accounting. The posting process debits Payroll and credits the cash account for the net amount of the checks. Peachtree Accounting also updates individual employee totals for the period and year.

To post information, select System from the Tasks menu, then select Post from the submenu to display the Post window. Click the checkbox for All Journals (the default) to post all transactions, or click the checkboxes for the various journals—such as the Cash Receipts Journal and the General Journal—to post to just those journals. Click OK to post the transactions. Peachtree Accounting displays the progress for posting to each journal on the screen.

You can also unpost transactions from selected journals or all journals. Unposting removes posted transactions from the General Ledger for the current period and periods forward. You can then edit or delete these transactions, then repost them. To unpost transactions, select System from the Tasks menu, then select Unpost from the submenu to display the Unpost window. (The Unpost window is identical to the Post window.) Choose the journals you want to unpost transactions from and click OK to begin unposting.

Using Management Tools

As you read in previous chapters, Peachtree Accounting has a selection of management tools to help you manage your business. These are the Action Items/Event Log Options and the four Analysis tools: the Cash Manager, the Collection Manager, the Payment Manager, and the Financial Manager. The management tools that relate directly to payroll are the Action Items and Event Log Options, the Cash Manager, and the Payments Manager. The Action Items/Event Log Options and the Analysis tools are discussed in detail in Chapter 13.

Summary

In this chapter you saw how to set up payroll and employee defaults, edit payroll tax tables, enter and maintain employee and sales rep records, run payroll checks, print payroll reports, and post payroll transactions. In the next chapter, you'll learn about inventory: how to set up and maintain inventory defaults, enter and maintain item records, create assemblies, and print inventory reports.

Inventory

In this chapter, you'll learn how to set up inventory defaults, set up and maintain inventory records, create and maintain assemblies, and print a variety of inventory reports.

BASICS

- How to set up inventory defaults
- How to set up inventory item records
- How to print inventory reports

& BEYOND

- How to set up bills of materials
- How to make adjustments to inventory
- How to update prices
- How to build and break down assemblies

In the last chapter, you saw how to set up payroll and employee defaults, edit payroll tax tables, enter and maintain employee and sales rep records, run payroll checks, print payroll reports, and post payroll transactions. In this chapter, you'll learn about inventory: how to set up and maintain inventory defaults, enter and maintain item records, create assemblies, and print inventory reports.

Even if you don't stock physical inventory, you can set up inventory items for services, labor charges, and even description-only items to make it faster to fill out invoices, quotes, and purchase orders.

Setting Up Inventory Defaults

The first step in setting up Inventory is to set up your inventory defaults. Compared to the defaults for Accounts Receivable, Accounts Payable, and Payroll, setting up inventory defaults is very simple. If you haven't done so already, you should set up the business and the General Ledger (see Chapters 2, 3, and 4). You should also familiarize yourself with the procedures described in Chapters 5 and 6, which are very similar to the procedures in this chapter.

When you set your inventory defaults, you will determine the General Ledger accounts for costs on stock items, non-stock items, shipping, labor, and other things like tax types, shipping methods, and custom fields.

You've seen how to select an option from the Setup Checklist in previous chapters. If the Setup Checklist is not already displayed, select the Setup Checklist option from the Maintain menu. From the Setup Checklist, click the Inventory Defaults item. (You can also display this window by selecting the Default Information option from the Maintain menu, then selecting the Inventory Items option from the submenu.) The Inventory Item Defaults window appears with the GL/Accts Costing tab already selected (shown in Figure 8-1). As with other defaults, inventory item defaults (except custom fields) can be overridden for any one inventory item in the inventory item record.

The GL Accts/Costing tab in the Inventory Item Defaults window is where you enter the default General Ledger accounts for the inventory items and costs. Peachtree Accounting only tracks costing methods (FIFO, LIFO, and average) for stock and assembly items. You must also identify a default account for tracking freight charges (which are entered in the Quote, Sales Order, and Sales/Invoicing windows in Accounts Receivable). If you're not sure what default accounts and costing method to use, check with your accountant. Costing methods are discussed a little later in this chapter.

When you are satisfied with your entries, click the Taxes/Shipping tab. Within this tab are the Item Tax Type and Ship Methods tables, as shown in Figure 8-2, complete with default entries.

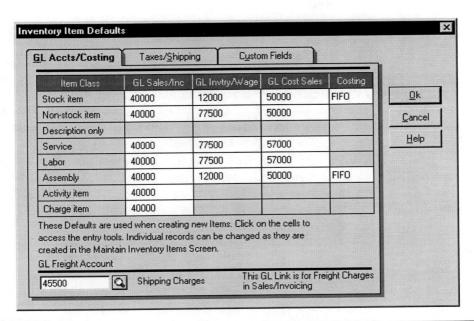

FIGURE 8-1 Inventory Item Defaults window showing the GL Accts/Costing tab

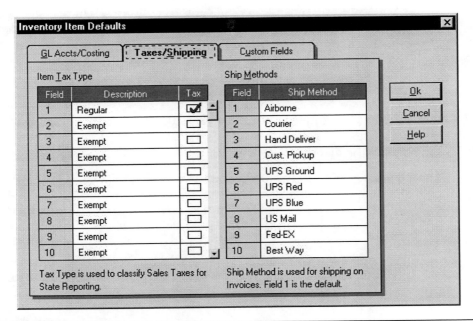

FIGURE 8-2 Inventory Item Defaults window showing the Taxes/Shipping tab

You use the Taxes/Shipping tab to set the levels and types of taxation as well as the shipping methods.

In the Item Tax Type section of the tab, you enter the classes of taxation. (Specific tax rates are not entered in this tab; they are entered as part of the customer record, as described in Chapter 5.) For example, many states have a general sales tax, but food items are taxed differently or not at all. Similarly, wholesale purchases of items used in the construction of items for resale are usually exempt, but some specific items may have a special use or sales tax.

Enter the descriptions for the tax type in the fields under the Description column, such as RAM CHIP TAX or EXEMPT. You can enter up to 25 different tax rates. Check the Tax box to set the corresponding tax type as the default. When entering individual inventory item records, you can override this tax type with any of the other tax types in the list. (Checking the Tax box identifies this inventory item as a taxable item. The item will appear in the Taxable column of the Taxable/Exempt Sales report in the Accounts Receivable reports.)

In the Ship Methods section of the tab, you identify up to ten different shipping methods, such as UPS BLUE, FED EX, US MAIL, and so on. These shipping methods show up in the Accounts Receivable and Accounts Payable windows.

When you are satisfied with your entries, click the Custom Fields tab. The Custom Fields tab appears, as shown in Figure 8-3, with sample entries.

The Custom Fields tab lets you set default labels for tracking specific inventory item information that you enter in the Maintain Inventory Items window for each inventory item. (The Maintain Inventory Items window is discussed later in this chapter.) For example, you may want to set up custom fields for alternate vendors for the item, the account rep, the preferred brand, or recommended shipping method.

Field Labels   Enter up to five categories in the fields here. The information in these fields is used for headings in the Maintain Inventory Item window, as well as in some of the inventory reports.

Enabled   Click the box to enable or disable the Field Label. If the Enabled box is not checked, the field label will not appear in the Custom Fields tab of the Maintain Inventory Items window. The Enabled box must also be checked for you to enter text in the associated Field Labels field.

When you are satisfied with your entries, click OK. As usual, Peachtree Accounting will ask if you want to mark this task as completed on the Setup Checklist. If you choose Yes, Peachtree puts a check mark next to the item to indicate that you've completed this portion of the setup.

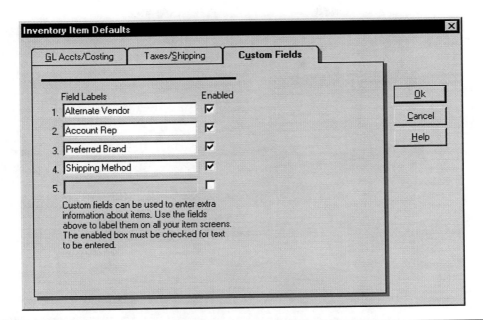

FIGURE 8-3 Inventory Item Defaults window showing the Custom Fields tab

Setting Up and Maintaining Inventory Item Records

Once you've set up your inventory defaults, you're ready to start entering inventory item information. Inventory items help you classify stock items as well as services, standard labor charges, and nonstock items.

Entering an Inventory Item Record

There are four types of information you enter to set up an inventory item record: general inventory item information, custom fields, history, and bill of materials information. You can also set up beginning balances for the inventory item. This section shows you how to enter all this information.

Entering General Inventory Item Information

From the Setup Checklist, click the Inventory Items and Assembly Records item. (You can also display this window by selecting the Inventory Items option from the Maintain menu.) The Maintain Inventory Items window appears with the General tab already selected (shown in Figure 8-4).

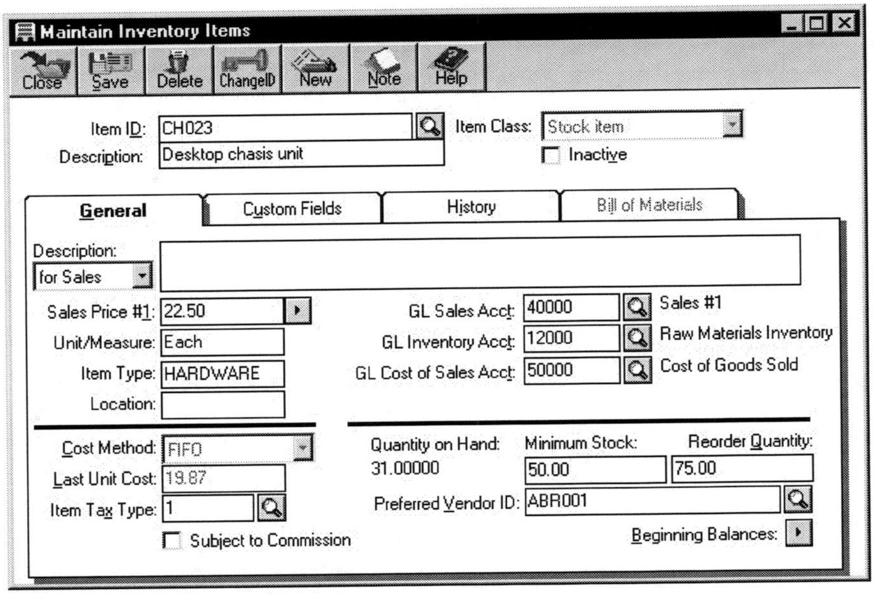

FIGURE 8-4 Maintain Inventory Items window showing the General tab

Enter information for an inventory item as follows:

Item ID Enter the inventory item ID. Inventory item IDs can be up to 20 characters long and can contain any characters except an asterisk (*), a question mark (?), or a plus sign (+). As with other IDs in Peachtree Accounting, inventory item IDs are case sensitive, so Peachtree Accounting treats the inventory item IDs RAM001 and ram001 differently. You may want to set a policy that all letters in inventory item IDs be entered as capital letters.

Description Enter the inventory item's name. You can enter up to 30 characters in this field. This description appears in the inventory windows for quick reference. The information you enter in the detailed description field (located just below this field) appears on the Accounts Receivable and Accounts Payable windows, reports, and forms.

Item Class Enter the item class in this field. You can enter any of the inventory item classes shown in Table 8-1.

Inactive Check this box to set the inventory item to inactive status. Although you can update the information for the inventory item, Peachtree Accounting will warn you if you try to sell an inactive inventory item. When you close the

INVENTORY ITEM CLASS	DESCRIPTION OF CLASS
Stock item	Use this for standard stock items. Peachtree Accounting tracks all related inventory information, including quantities, costs, low stock points, unit prices, and so on. It also makes cost-of-goods entries in the General Ledger. (Be careful: if you designate an inventory item as a "stock item," you cannot change it to any other inventory item class.)
Non-stock item	Use this for any item you don't normally stock. Peachtree Accounting doesn't calculate quantities or costs for you as it does for stock items, but it does print the quantities, descriptions, and unit prices on invoices. Peachtree Accounting always assumes that a non-stock item is available when creating invoices.
Description only	Use this for repetitive phrases you want to enter on invoices, quotes, or purchase orders, such as "Thank you for your business." Peachtree Accounting prints only the description.
Service	Use this to set up a service as an inventory item, such as a one-hour consultation. (Be careful: if you select Service as the item class, some of the fields in the General tab, such as the Minimum Stock and the Reorder Quantity fields, will disappear.)
Labor	Use this to set up a labor inventory item, such as a standard service intake fee.
Assembly	Use this to create and track an assembly, which is composed of other inventory items. Building assemblies is discussed later in this chapter in the next "Putting It to Work" section. (Be careful: if you designate an inventory item as an "assembly item," you cannot change it to any other inventory item class.)
Activity (Peachtree Complete Accounting version only)	Use this for activities related to any services being performed for a customer or job that will be tracked on employee or vendor time tickets for billing a customer for reimbursable expenses over and above the standard cost of sales. (Be careful: if you designate an inventory item as an "activity item," you cannot change it to any other inventory item class.)
Charge (Peachtree Complete Accounting version only)	Use this for expenses related to any services being performed for a customer or job that will be tracked on employee or vendor time tickets for billing a customer for reimbursable expenses over and above the standard cost of sales. (Be careful: if you designate an inventory item as a "charge item," you cannot change it to any other inventory item class.)

TABLE 8-1   Classes of Inventory Items

fiscal year, Peachtree Accounting will delete the inventory item records for all inactive inventory items that are not attached to a current transaction or an active job, customer, or vendor.

N O T E : Peachtree Accounting lets you purge inventory items at any time. Purging is discussed in Chapter 13.

For Sales/For Purchases   Select either For Sales or For Purchases from this drop-down box to determine how the description you enter in the Description field is used.

Description   Enter a detailed description for the inventory item of up to 160 characters. Depending on what you select in the Sales/Purchases field, this description will appear on different windows, receipts, and forms. If you selected For Sales, the detailed description will appear on Quotes, Sales Orders, Sales/Invoicing, and Receipts windows, reports, and forms. If you selected For Purchases, the detailed description will appear on Purchase Orders, Purchases/Receive Inventory, and Payments windows, reports, and forms. (If you leave the For Purchases detailed description blank, Peachtree Accounting will use the detailed description you entered for the For Sales option.)

Sales Price   Enter the sales price for the item. This amount appears in the sales journal whenever you enter this item ID on a transaction. You can enter amounts to the thousandth of a penny (for example, $35.16078) if you need to track the cost of goods this closely. (You must first set up the global options in Peachtree Accounting and the options in the Currency tab of the Regional Settings Properties window in the Windows 98 Control Panel as appropriate to allow this many decimal places.)

Depending on your needs for pricing levels, you can enter up to five sales prices in this field for different customers by clicking the button to the right of the field and making entries in the Multiple Pricing window (not shown). These prices correspond to the pricing levels you set for the customer in the customer's invoice defaults. Enter the prices in ascending or descending order so they're easier to find.

Unit/Measure   Enter the appropriate unit of measure for this inventory item—for example, EACH, UNITS, BOX, CASE, or GROSS.

Item Type   This is a custom field in which you can enter up to eight characters to identify the type of inventory item. This field allows you to group inventory items for reports. For example, all inventory items related to office supplies might have an inventory item type of SUPPLIES. This field is case sensitive.

Location   Enter up to ten characters describing the location of the item, such as MAIN WHSE, AISLE 15, SHED 3, or BIN 15. This information appears on some of the inventory reports, such as the Physical Inventory and Stock Status reports.

GL Sales Account   Enter the sales account to credit for this inventory item.

GL Inventory Account   Enter the inventory account for this inventory item. (Use this field only for stock items.) Peachtree Accounting debits this account for purchases and credits this account for the cost of sales.

GL Salary and Wages Account   Enter the salary and wages account to debit for this inventory item. (This field only appears when you have selected Service or Labor as the inventory item class.)

GL Cost of Sales Account   Enter the cost of sales account to debit when this inventory item is sold. If you sell a stock item that you don't currently have in stock (such as for a backordered item), Peachtree Accounting does not post the cost of goods information. If the inventory item is a nonstock item, Peachtree Accounting uses this account as the default expense account for purchases.

> **C A U T I O N :** Although you are not prohibited from selling stock you don't have on hand (so that the stock on hand becomes negative), you may have problems with cost of goods information as a result. When the stock on hand is negative, Peachtree Accounting creates a system cost adjustment that appears on the Inventory Adjustment Journal. The only way to subsequently eliminate this entry is to date the purchases of stock prior to the sale, then unpost and post the purchase journal followed by the sales journal.

Cost Method   You can select one of three costing methods, as shown in Table 8-2. (The Cost Method field appears only for stock and assembly inventory items. You can't change the costing method once you have saved the inventory item record.)

> **C A U T I O N :** You generally won't use more than one type of costing method. If you're not sure about which type of costing method your business should use, check with your accountant or tax attorney. Some states mandate particular costing methods for businesses with certain classifications or sales volumes.

COSTING METHOD	DESCRIPTION
FIFO	An acronym for "First In, First Out," FIFO costing tracks the price for stock items as the actual cost of the item. In FIFO costing, when you sell an item, Peachtree Accounting costs the item as if you had sold the items you received first.
LIFO	An acronym for "Last In, First Out," LIFO costing tracks the price for stock items as the actual cost of the item. In LIFO costing, when you sell an item, Peachtree Accounting costs the item as if you had sold the items you received most recently.
Average Cost	Average costing tracks the cost for stock items as the average cost times the quantity of items you sold. The average cost is recalculated each time you buy or sell more of an inventory item.

TABLE 8-2   Costing Methods

Last Unit Cost   Enter the last unit cost of the stock, non-stock, labor or service item. This field can be changed after saving the item for non-stock, Labor or Service item classes only. Stock items are updated by the system and cannot be changed after saving.

Item Tax Type   Select the inventory item tax type from the list of tax types you set up earlier in the Inventory Item Defaults window.

Subject to Commission   Check this box if the sales rep receives a commission for selling this item. (This will affect the Accounts Receivable Sales History reports.)

Quantity on Hand   Peachtree Accounting displays the quantity on hand as of the end of the current period based on previous quantities on hand, the quantities sold through the Sales/Invoicing window, and the quantities purchased through the Purchases window. This display-only field only appears for stock and assembly items.

Minimum Stock   Enter the mandatory reorder point for this inventory item. You use this only for stock items.

Reorder Quantity   Enter the standard reorder point for this inventory item. You use this only for stock items.

Preferred Vendor ID   Enter the vendor ID for the vendor from whom you purchase this item.

Entering Inventory Item Beginning Balances

After entering the information in the General tab, click the Beginning Balances button. The Inventory Beginning Balances window appears (shown in Figure 8-5).

Entering beginning balances for inventory items is slightly different from other beginning balances you've entered. To enter beginning balances, select the inventory item from the lower part of the Inventory Beginning Balances window. The inventory item appears in the top of the window. In Figure 8-5, sample inventory item information has already been entered, but no beginning balances have been entered yet. You can enter beginning balances at any time when entering the inventory items.

Quantity   Enter the quantity you have on hand of the specific inventory item.

Unit Cost   Enter the beginning unit cost for the inventory item. You can have Peachtree Accounting calculate this amount by leaving this field blank and entering an amount in the Total Cost field. Depending on your costing method, you may need to consult with your accountant or your tax attorney to determine the correct cost to enter in this or the next field.

Total Cost   Enter the total cost for the beginning quantity of the inventory item. You can have Peachtree Accounting calculate this amount by leaving this field blank and entering an amount in the Unit Cost field.

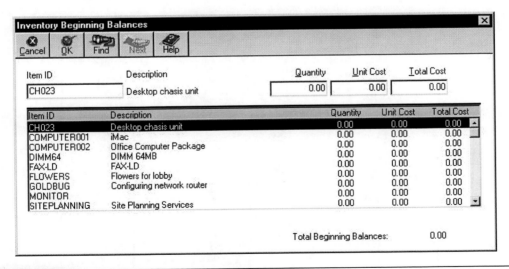

FIGURE 8-5   Inventory Beginning Balances window

Total Beginning Balances This field displays the total cost of the inventory items.

CAUTION: As with customer and vendor beginning balances, the total beginning balances must equal the total inventory beginning balances amount you entered in the General Ledger. If these two amounts are different, Peachtree Accounting will not be able to balance the books. As a result, you may want to enter all of your inventory beginning balances at once to make it easier to check your inputs instead of doing them one at a time.

When you are done entering beginning balances for inventory items, click OK to return to the General tab in the Maintain Inventory Items window.

Entering Inventory Item Custom Fields

After you have entered the general inventory item information, click the Custom Fields tab. The Custom Fields tab appears, as shown in Figure 8-6. As with other records, the inventory item information in the top part of the tab is carried forward from the information you entered in the General tab. You can work with this inventory item, select another one, or change the name and inactive status information for the inventory item from this tab.

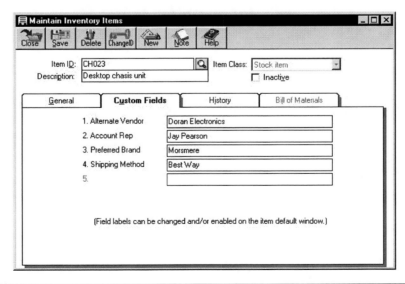

FIGURE 8-6 Maintain Inventory Items window showing the Custom Fields tab

Enter the custom field information for the inventory item here, exactly as you entered custom field information for other types of records in earlier chapters.

Entering History Information

When you are satisfied with the entries in the Custom Fields tab, click the History tab. The History tab appears, as shown in Figure 8-7.

The History tab lets you examine the history of a selected inventory item. The information in this window is display-only. When you first enter the inventory item in Peachtree Accounting, the History tab will have no data. Peachtree Accounting updates this tab based on the sales and purchases for this inventory item.

Entering Bill of Materials

Click the Bill of Materials tab. The Bill of Materials tab appears, as shown in Figure 8-8. (A sample bill of materials list appears in this figure.)

The Bill of Materials tab lets you build a bill of materials for assembly-type inventory items. The bill of materials you enter in this tab tells Peachtree Accounting which components and in which quantity comprise the assembly.

Print Components on Invoice   Check this box to have the individual components in the assembly print on the invoice as line items. The components that appear on the invoice will have quantities equal to the quantity of the

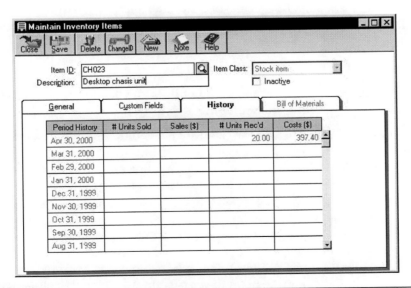

FIGURE 8-7   Maintain Inventory Items window showing the History tab

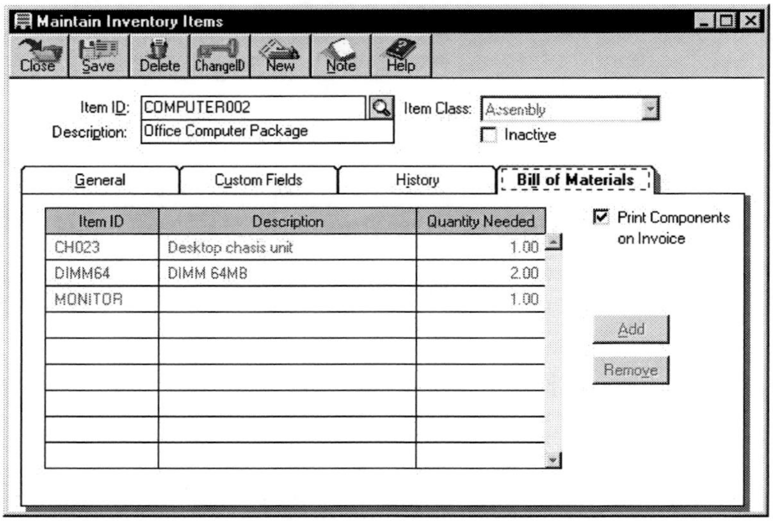

FIGURE 8-8   Maintain Inventory Items window showing the Bill of Materials tab

component in one assembly times the number of assemblies on the invoice. Peachtree Accounting leaves the price blank for the individual components.

To enter items in the lower half of the tab, click Add and position the cursor in the first available line. You can only enter items in the lower half of the tab if the inventory item class on the General tab is Assembly.

Enter the information as follows:

Item ID   Enter the ID for the item.

Description   Peachtree Accounting fills in the default description for the inventory item. You can modify this if you want.

Quantity Needed   Enter the quantity needed for an individual assembly. You can insert a line item at a specific location by positioning the cursor and clicking Add. Peachtree Accounting adds a line above the selected line item. To remove an item, highlight the line item and click Remove.

When you're satisfied with the bill of materials information, you can save the inventory item record by clicking Save at the top of the window. You can add notes to the inventory items (just like adding notes to other records as described in earlier chapters) by clicking on the Note button and entering information in the Inventory Item Note window (not shown). This information does not show up on any of the reports, but you can make notes to yourself regarding the inventory item.

You can enter additional inventory item records by clicking New at the top of the window (to clear the entries in the fields) and then entering new information.

Once you enter a bill of materials, you can't change it. However, you may want to change your assemblies at times to reflect updates to an assembly's part list or the parts' suppliers. To use the standard Bill of Materials features would require you to have inventory items for each revision of your assembly. As an alternative, Peachtree Complete Accounting for Windows Release 6.0 and 7.0 users can use the Memorize Transaction feature for more flexibility. Here's how:

1. From the Tasks menu, select Sales/Invoicing. The Sales/Invoicing window appears.

2. Create a memorized transaction that includes each component in the assembly. This memorized transaction will reflect all the parts for the items in the assembly with the appropriate quantities and prices. Be sure to add any service or labor charges related to the actual assembly, installation, or configuration.

3. Save the memorized transaction.

4. If you use quotes or sales orders, you should set up matching memorized transactions in these windows as well.

When you sell something that would be an assembly, you can simply use the memorized transaction as the basis for the customer invoice. When you need to make changes to this assembly for any reason, you can modify the memorized transaction appropriately. You have greater flexibility, and you also don't need to build or unbuild assemblies.

Modifying Inventory Item Records

Once you've entered an inventory item record, you can modify it. Modifying an inventory item record is easy. First, display the inventory item record in the Maintain Inventory Items window by entering the inventory item ID in the Item ID field. You can then change any of the inventory item information including the item ID itself.

Deleting Inventory Item Records

You can delete an inventory item record by selecting a record and then clicking the Delete button at the top of the window. Peachtree Accounting asks you if you're sure you want to delete this record. Click Yes to confirm.

CAUTION: You cannot delete an inventory item record if there are previous transactions against the inventory item. In such a case, you may want to flag the inventory item as inactive. Activity will not be entered for the inventory item without Peachtree Accounting warning you that the inventory item is inactive and asking you if you want to post activity to the inventory item.

Printing Inventory Item Reports

Now that you've entered the inventory item information, you can print a variety of reports to verify the information you've entered. Peachtree Accounting has a suite of reports for verifying inventory item information:

Item List   Shows inventory items with ID, description, class, type, and quantity on hand.

Item Master List   Lists detailed information for inventory items (this report prints in landscape instead of portrait mode).

Inventory Valuation Report   Lists the value and the average cost of the inventory items you have in stock. (The Average Cost column on the Inventory Valuation report will have data only if the cost method is Average.)

Assembly List   Shows each assembly and lists the component inventory items.

To print each of the reports, select Inventory from the Reports menu. The Select a Report window appears with the Inventory option selected. Next, select the appropriate report from the list by double-clicking or by highlighting the report and selecting the Screen or Print button at the top of the window. Enter the information in the report selection windows and click OK. The report appears on the screen or is sent to the printer. Figures 8-9, 8-10, 8-11, and 8-12 show samples of these reports for selected inventory item information. Note that Service class items do not have a quantity on hand in the Item List report.

The inventory item information is now complete. You'll be able to add, update, and delete inventory item records as necessary. You are now ready to enter inventory item adjustments and build assemblies, as discussed in the next section. Before you continue, make sure the total inventory beginning balances match the inventory amount you entered in the General Ledger.

Making Inventory Adjustments

Once you've established your inventory, you need to periodically verify the Peachtree Accounting records against actual inventory. Peachtree Accounting provides a report to help you take inventory: the Physical Inventory List (shown in Figure 8-13). The Physical Inventory List creates a worksheet for checking actual inventory against the information stored in Peachtree Accounting.

Once you have taken inventory, you will probably need to make adjustments to the quantities on hand recorded in Peachtree Accounting. To do this, select Inventory Adjustments from the Tasks menu. The Inventory Adjustments window appears, as shown in Figure 8-14.

Big Business, Inc.
Item List

Filter Criteria includes: Report order is by ID.

Item ID	Item Description	Item Class	Active?	Item Type	Qty on Hand
CH023	Desktop chasis unit	Stock item	Active	HARDWA	40.00
COMPUTER001	iMac	Stock item	Active	HARDWA	8.00
COMPUTER002	Office Computer Package	Assembly	Active	HARDWA	14.00
DIMM64		Stock item	Active	SERVICE	
FAX-LD	FAX-LD	Stock item	Active		
FLOWERS	Flowers for lobby	Stock item	Active	SERVICE	
GOLDBUG	Configuring network router	Stock item	Active		
LUNCH		Charge item	Active		
MONITOR		Stock item	Active	HARDWA	20.00
POSTAGE	POSTAGE STAMPS	Charge item	Active		
TELEPHONE CHARG		Stock item	Active		
TRAINING	Training	Activity item	Active	SERVICE	
TRAINING MATERI	Training Materials	Activity item	Active		

FIGURE 8-9 Item List report

Big Business, Inc.
Item Master List

Filter Criteria includes: Report order is by ID. Report is printed with Truncated Long Descriptions.

Item ID Item Description	Description for Sales	Item Class Item Type Cost Method Tax Type Commission Unit Preferred Vendor I	Qty on Hand Min Stock Reorder Qty Sales Acct Inv Acct COS Acct	Sales Price#1 Sales Price#2 Sales Price#3 Sales Price#4 Sales Price#5
CH023 Desktop chasis unit		Stock item HARDWARE FIFO Regular No Each ABR001	40.00 50.00 75.00 40000 12000 50000	22.50 24.25 25.75 26.50 28.10
COMPUTER001 iMac		Stock item HARDWARE FIFO Regular No	8.00 40000 12000 50000	1995.00 2009.95 2019.95 2025.00 2049.95

FIGURE 8-10 Item Master List report

Big Business, Inc.
Inventory Valuation Report
As of Apr 30, 2000

Filter Criteria includes: 1) Stock/Assembly. Report order is by ID. Report is printed with Truncated Long Descriptions.

Item ID Item Class	Item Description	Unit	Cost Met	Qty on Hand	Item Value	Avg Cost	% of Inv Valu
CH023 Stock item	Desktop chasis unit	Each	FIFO	40.00	397.40		7.98
COMPUTER001 Stock item	iMac	Each	FIFO	8.00			
COMPUTER002 Assembly	Office Computer Package	Each	FIFO	14.00			
DIMM64 Stock item	DIMM 64MB	Each	FIFO	106.01	960.48		19.29

FIGURE 8-11 Inventory Valuation report

Big Business, Inc.
Assembly List

Filter Criteria includes: 1) Assembly. Report order is by ID.

Item ID	Item Description	Component ID	Component Description	Qty Needed
COMPUTER002	Office Computer Package	CH023	Desktop chasis unit	1.00
COMPUTER002	Office Computer Package	DIMM64	DIMM 64MB	2.00
COMPUTER002	Office Computer Package	MONITOR		1.00

FIGURE 8-12   Assembly List report

Big Business, Inc.
Physical Inventory List
As of Apr 30, 2000

Filter Criteria includes: 1) Stock/Assembly. Report order is by ID. Report is printed with Truncated Long Descriptions.

Item ID	Item Description	Unit	Location	Count	By
CH023	Desktop chasis unit	Each			
COMPUTER001	iMac	Each			
COMPUTER002	Office Computer Package	Each			
DIMM64	DIMM 64MB	Each			
FAX-LD	FAX-LD	Each			

FIGURE 8-13   Physical Inventory List

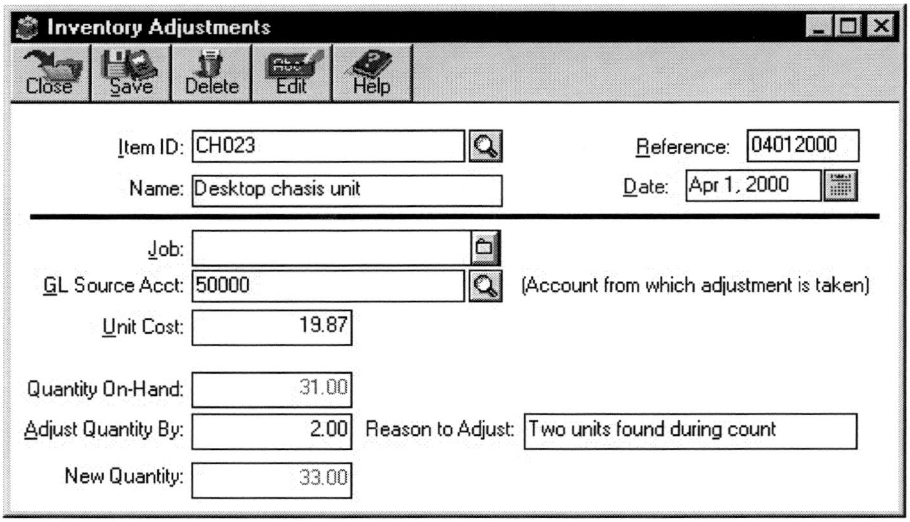

FIGURE 8-14 Inventory Adjustments window

You can only make adjustments to stock or assembly inventory items. Changes to your inventory are costed as if they were a purchase for zero dollars, but the average cost is updated.

Item ID   Enter the inventory item ID in this field.

Name   Peachtree Accounting enters this information from the inventory item record. This field is display-only.

Reference   Enter a reference of up to eight characters. Although an entry in this field is not required, it is good business practice to enter a unique reference for auditing your inventory adjustments. A simple reference system is to use an eight-character date followed by two digits for the number of the inventory adjustment that day, such as "1125199903" or "0108200024."

Date   Peachtree Accounting displays the first day of the accounting period as the default for this field if your system date is not in the accounting period in which you are working; otherwise, it defaults to the system date. Enter the date the change in inventory took place or the date the physical inventory took place. Click Calendar or right-click in this field to display the Peachtree Accounting date-selection calendar.

Job   Enter the job ID to which to apply the change in inventory, if necessary.

GL Source Acct Enter the General Ledger source account to debit (if the inventory is decreased) or credit (if the inventory is increased). Decreases or increases in the inventory will debit or credit the inventory item's account appropriately.

Unit Cost Peachtree Accounting displays the current cost for the inventory item as determined in the inventory item record. You can change this if necessary.

Quantity On-Hand Peachtree Accounting displays the current quantity on hand before the adjustment is entered. This field is display-only.

Adjust Quantity By Enter the amount to adjust the inventory item by (a decrease in inventory should be entered as a negative number). You can add or subtract portions of a unit, such as when you are adjusting for a damaged assembly from which you can salvage individual inventory items.

New Quantity Peachtree Accounting displays the new quantity after the adjustment. This field is display-only.

Reason to Adjust Enter up to 37 characters for the reason for the adjustment, such as damaged, theft, misassembled, salvaged, or found in storage.

When you are satisfied with your entries, click Save. You can check your entries by running another Item List (shown earlier in Figure 8-9) and comparing it to the information from your physical inventory.

Updating Prices

If you have Peachtree Complete Accounting, you can update prices with the new Maintain Item Prices window.

Select Item Prices from the Maintain menu. The Maintain Item Prices – Filter Selection window appears. From this window you can select a single item, a range of items, or all inventory items. Enter or select a range of items you want to adjust, as shown in Figure 8-15.

Filter These are the fields you are allowed to filter on. You cannot change or add to these.

Type The choices depend on the filter field. If you select Range, you can enter a beginning record and an ending record in the From and To boxes.

From and To These fields are available if you select Range. Enter the beginning record and the ending record.

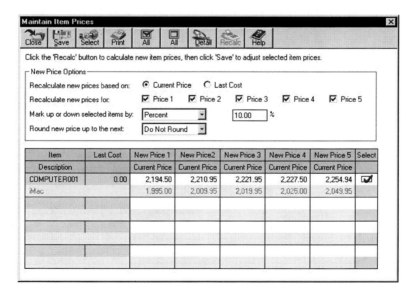

Maintain Item Prices - Filter Selection

Select items for price adjustment, then click 'OK'.

Filter	Type	From	To
Item Class	Equal to	All	
Item ID	All		
Item Type	All		
Preferred Vendor	All		
Location	All		
Item Tax Type	All		
Active/Inactive	Equal to	Active	
G/L Sales Account	All		
Item Cost	All		

OK Cancel Help

FIGURE 8-15 Maintain Item Prices – Filter Selection window

When you are finished, select OK to display the Maintain Item Prices window as shown in Figure 8-16. In this example, we are marking the item up 10 percent for all price classes.

Recalculate New Prices Based On Select the Current Price or Last Cost radio button to recalculate new prices based on the current sales price or the last cost sales price.

Maintain Item Prices

Close Save Select Print All All Detail Recalc Help

Click the 'Recalc' button to calculate new item prices, then click 'Save' to adjust selected item prices.

New Price Options

Recalculate new prices based on: ⦿ Current Price ◯ Last Cost

Recalculate new prices for: ☑ Price 1 ☑ Price 2 ☑ Price 3 ☑ Price 4 ☑ Price 5

Mark up or down selected items by: Percent 10.00 %

Round new price up to the next: Do Not Round

Item	Last Cost	New Price 1	New Price2	New Price 3	New Price 4	New Price 5	Select
Description		Current Price	Current Price	Current Price	Current Price	Current Price	
COMPUTER001	0.00	2,194.50	2,210.95	2,221.95	2,227.50	2,254.94	☑
iMac		1,995.00	2,009.95	2,019.95	2,025.00	2,049.95	

FIGURE 8-16 Maintain Item Prices window

Recalculate New Prices For Select each price level that you want to recalculate new prices for.

Mark Up or Down Selected Items By Choose either Amount or Percent as the markup method. If you select Amount, enter the amount as a positive or negative dollar amount. If you select Percent, enter the amount as a positive or negative percentage. (For example, enter 10.00 for a 10 percent markup.)

Round New Price Up to the Next Choose Dollar or Specific Cent if you want to round item prices up to a specific currency level.

TIP: You can use this feature to round all prices up to the 95-cent price level, such as 5.95, 7.95, 11.95, and so on.

Item Peachtree Accounting enters this information from the Maintain Item Prices – Filter Selection window. This field is display-only.

Last Cost Peachtree Accounting enters this information from the Maintain Item Prices – Filter Selection window. This field is display-only.

New Price 1 Through New Price 5 These are prices you originally set up.

Select Check this box to have the option to recalculate this item.

Building and Breaking Down Assemblies

The final task for inventory management in Peachtree Accounting is to track the individual inventory items used in assemblies when you build or break down assemblies. For example, Big Business, Inc.'s basic vendor service package, COMPUTER002, is comprised of three different inventory items. When you build a COMPUTER002 assembly, you decrease the quantity of the individual inventory items that make up the package. Similarly, if you break down an assembly into its component parts, the quantity of individual inventory items is increased accordingly. Breaking down an assembly is also a necessary step in modifying the components that make up the assembly.

To build or break down assemblies, select Assemblies from the Tasks menu. The Build/Unbuild Assemblies window appears, as shown in Figure 8-17.

You can use this window to make changes in the inventory when you build or break down assemblies.

Item ID Enter the inventory item ID in this field.

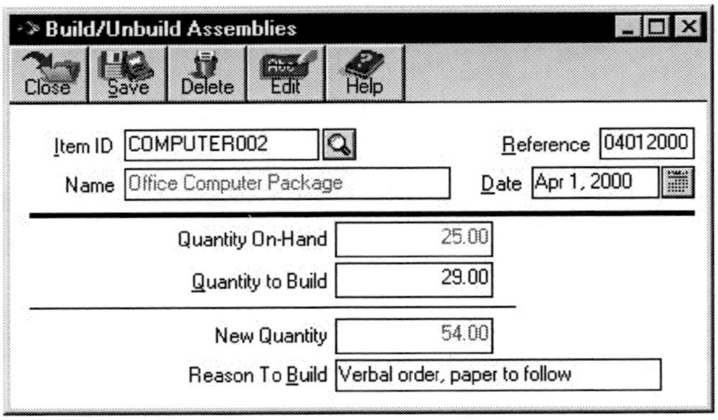

FIGURE 8-17 Build/Unbuild Assemblies window

Name Peachtree Accounting enters this information from the inventory item record. This field is display-only.

Reference Enter a reference of up to 12 characters.

Date Enter the date the change in inventory took place or the date the physical inventory took place. Click Calendar or right-click in this field to display the Peachtree Accounting date-selection calendar.

Quantity On-Hand Peachtree Accounting displays the current quantity on hand before the adjustment is entered. This field is display-only.

Quantity to Build Enter the quantity of the item to build or break down. If you are breaking down an assembly, the quantity should be entered as a negative number. You cannot build more assembly items than you have the individual inventory items for. You also cannot break down more assembly items than you have on hand.

New Quantity Peachtree Accounting displays the new quantity after the assembly has been built or broken down. This field is display-only.

Reason To Build Enter up to 37 characters for the reason for building or breaking down the assembly, such as "Fulfillment of Goldbug Job," "No longer sold," "Changing components," or "Preparing for holiday."

When you are satisfied with your entries, click Save.

You can use the Physical Inventory List as part of your inventory setup to get a complete and accurate statement of your company's inventory items. Here's how:

1. Enter your inventory items as described earlier in this chapter, but don't enter any beginning balances yet.
2. Print a Physical Inventory List.
3. Do a physical inventory. Make note of any inventory items that are inaccurately described, have the wrong part number, or are missing from the inventory list.
4. Make corrections to the inventory item entries in Peachtree Accounting as necessary.
5. Enter the inventory quantities on hand through the Beginning Balances window.

By taking a physical inventory at the time you set up your inventory items, you will make sure you have the descriptions and part numbers correct as well as minimize the need for adjusting entries to your inventory.

Printing Other Inventory Reports

In addition to the inventory reports you saw earlier in this chapter, Peachtree Accounting comes with a number of other inventory reports, which are described in Table 8-3. Figures 8-18 and 8-19 show samples of two of the inventory reports.

REPORT	DESCRIPTION
Assemblies Adjustment Journal	Shows the assembly adjustment information in journal format.
Inventory Adjustment Journal	Shows the inventory adjustment information in journal format.
Item Costing Report	Lists the costing information for inventory items.
Cost of Goods Sold Journal	Lists the costs of goods sold in journal format.
Item Price List	Lists the inventory items with the quantity on hand and the related sales prices.
Inventory Profitability Report	Shows inventory items with the number of units sold, the cost, the gross profit, inventory adjustments, and the percentage of the total.
Inventory Stock Status Report	Shows inventory items, the quantity on hand, and the reorder point for each inventory item.
Inventory Unit Activity Report	Shows activity for inventory items for the selected period.
Inventory Reorder Worksheet	Lists inventory items and their minimum stock amounts in a worksheet format to identify inventory items that need to be reordered.

TABLE 8-3   Other Inventory Reports

Big Business, Inc.
Item Price List

Filter Criteria includes: Report order is by ID. Report is printed with Truncated Long Descriptions.

Item ID	Item Description	Tax Type Commission	Unit	Sales Price#1 Sales Price#2 Sales Price#3 Sales Price#4 Sales Price#5	Qty on Hand
CH023	Desktop chassis unit	Regular No	Each	22.50 24.25 25.75 26.50 28.10	31.00
COMPUTER001	iMac	Regular No	Each	1995.00 2009.95 2019.95 2025.00 2049.95	8.00

FIGURE 8-18   Items Price List of Big Business, Inc.

Big Business, Inc.
Inventory Stock Status Report
As of Apr 30, 2000

Filter Criteria includes: 1) Stock/Assembly. Report order is by ID. Report is printed with Truncated Long Descriptions.

Item ID Item Description	Item Class	Unit	Qty on Hand	Min Stock	Reorder Qty	Location
CH023 Desktop chassis unit	Stock item	Each	31.00	50.00	75.00	
COMPUTER001 iMac	Stock item	Each	8.00	20.00	25.00	

FIGURE 8-19   Inventory Stock Status Report of Big Business, Inc.

Summary

In this chapter, you saw how to set up inventory defaults, set up and maintain inventory item records, make adjustments to inventory, update prices, and build or break down assemblies. You also saw how to print a variety of inventory reports. In the next chapter, you'll see how to set up job defaults, create and maintain jobs, and print job reports. You'll also see how to use job costing with inventory to provide a detailed and accurate picture of your business at each stage of the manufacturing process.

Job Costing

B A S I C S

- How to set up job defaults
- How to set up job records
- How to print job reports

B E Y O N D

- How to set up and maintain job phases
- How to set up and maintain job cost codes

In this chapter, you'll see how to set up job cost defaults, create and maintain job cost records, and print job cost reports.

In the last chapter, you saw how to set up inventory, set up and maintain inventory items, make adjustments to inventory, update prices, and build or break down assemblies. You also saw how to print a variety of inventory reports. In this chapter, you'll see how to set up job defaults, create and maintain jobs, phases, and cost codes, and print job reports.

 NOTE: Although both Peachtree Accounting for Windows and Peachtree Complete Accounting for Windows allow you to set up jobs, only Peachtree Complete Accounting for Windows has phases and cost codes.

Understanding Jobs

A *job* is a project your company is undertaking to which you want to assign expenses or income. For example, if your company is doing a complete site analysis and preparation for a customer prior to installing equipment at their site, you might want to set up a job for this so that costs can be tracked and passed on to the customer. You might also set up a job that is strictly internal to your company—for example, if you change your filing system and you want to accurately assess costs and labor expenses.

Assigning a transaction to a job does not affect the General Journal or any of the accounting information. Assigning the transaction to a job simply lets you extract the information for the job and report it.

Each job is identified by a unique job ID. Peachtree Accounting lets you assign a job ID, for tracking purposes, to almost any transaction. You can assign job IDs to any of the following types of transactions:

- General Journal
- Inventory adjustments
- Payments
- Purchase orders
- Purchases/receive inventory
- Quotes
- Receipts
- Sales/invoicing
- Time tickets and expense tickets (available only in Peachtree Complete Accounting for Windows)

Labor costs can also be assigned to a job ID through the Payroll Entry and the Select Employees to Pay windows.

Tracking job data is a valuable analysis tool. You can create an estimate for a job based on your initial understanding of the project. Then, as the project progresses, you can measure your actual costs against your estimated costs. This can identify potential cost overruns before they become serious and will also give you internal data to measure areas in your company that may not be as efficient as they could be.

Setting Up Job Defaults

The only job defaults you need to set up are custom fields. From the Setup Checklist, click the Job Defaults item. (You can also display this window by selecting Default Information from the Maintain menu, then selecting the Jobs option from the submenu.) The Job Defaults window appears (shown in Figure 9-1).

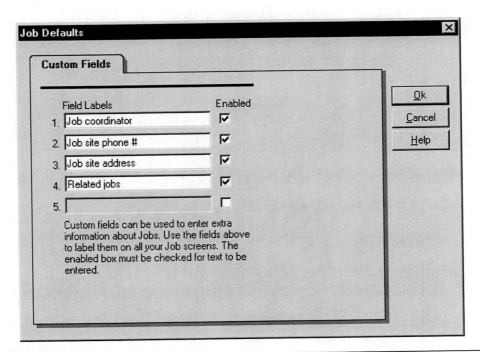

FIGURE 9-1   Job Defaults window

The Custom Fields tab for the job defaults is identical to the Custom Fields tabs you saw when setting up defaults for the other sections of Peachtree Accounting. You use the custom fields in the Job Defaults to set default labels for tracking specific job information that you enter for each job in the Maintain Jobs window. (The Maintain Jobs window is discussed later in this chapter.) For example, you may want to set up custom fields for alternate contacts for the job coordinator, the job site phone number or address, or related jobs.

Field Labels   Enter up to five categories in the fields here. The information in these fields is used as headings in the Maintain Jobs window as well as in some of the jobs reports.

Enabled   Click the box to enable or disable the Field Label. If the Enabled box is not checked, the field label will be grayed out in the Custom Fields tab of the Maintain Jobs window. The Enabled box must also be checked for you to enter text in the associated Field Label field.

When you are satisfied with your entries, click OK. As usual, Peachtree Complete will ask if you want to mark this task as completed on the Setup Checklist. If you choose Yes, Peachtree puts a check mark next to the item to indicate that you've completed this portion of the setup.

Setting Up and Maintaining Job Records

Once you've set up your job defaults, you're ready to start entering job information. You've already seen how jobs are used for tracking Accounts Receivable, Accounts Payable, and Payroll expenses in Chapters 5, 6, and 7. You will now see how to enter job records.

Entering a Job Record

Setting up jobs in Peachtree Complete is very simple. This section shows you how to enter all the general and custom field information.

Entering General Job Information

From the Setup Checklist, click the Job Records item. (You can also display this window by selecting Job Costs from the Maintain menu and then Jobs from the submenu.) The Maintain Jobs window appears with the General tab already selected (shown in Figure 9-2).

Job ID   Enter the job ID. Job IDs can be up to 20 characters long, and they can contain any characters except an asterisk (*), a question mark (?), or

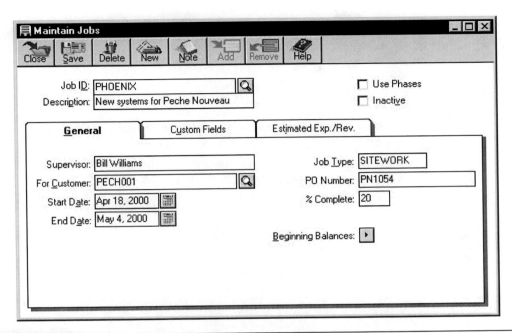

FIGURE 9-2   Maintain Jobs window showing the General tab

a plus sign (+). As with other IDs in Peachtree Complete, job IDs are case sensitive, so Peachtree Complete treats the job IDs INSTALL001 and install001 differently. You may want to set a policy that all letters in job IDs be entered as capital letters.

C A U T I O N :   Job IDs cannot be changed. If you make a mistake when entering a job ID, you will have to delete the job ID and enter a new one.

Description   Enter a description for the job. You can enter up to 30 characters in this field. This description appears in list boxes in other windows and in some reports.

Use Phases   Check this box to use phases with this job. Phases are discussed later in this chapter. (This field does not appear in Peachtree Accounting for Windows.)

C A U T I O N : If you have already set up estimates for the job (as described later in this chapter) and you uncheck the Use Phases box, you will lose any estimated expenses or revenues you entered previously on the Estimated Exp./Rev. tab.

Inactive   Check this box to set the job to inactive status. Peachtree Complete will warn you if you try to post a transaction to an inactive job.

Peachtree Accounting lets you purge jobs at any time. However, if a job is connected to a current transaction or a transaction that is connected to an active customer or vendor, it will not be purged. Purging jobs is discussed in Chapter 13.

Supervisor   Enter the supervisor's name.

For Customer   Enter the customer ID for the customer related to this job. This lets you track expenses and charge them back to the customer.

Start Date   Enter the starting date for the job.

End Date   Enter the anticipated end date for the job.

Job Type   This is a custom field in which you can enter up to eight characters to identify the type of job. This field allows you to group jobs for reports, and it is case sensitive.

PO Number   Enter the customer's purchase order number for the job.

% Complete   Enter the percentage complete for the job. You can update this field at any time.

Entering Job Beginning Balances

After entering the information in the General tab, click the Beginning Balances button. The Job Beginning Balances window appears (shown in Figure 9-3 with sample beginning balance information).

N O T E : Because Peachtree Accounting for Windows does not support phases or cost codes, the Job Beginning Balances window in Peachtree Accounting for Windows looks like the one shown in Figure 9-4. The other fields are the same as those in the window shown in Figure 9-3.

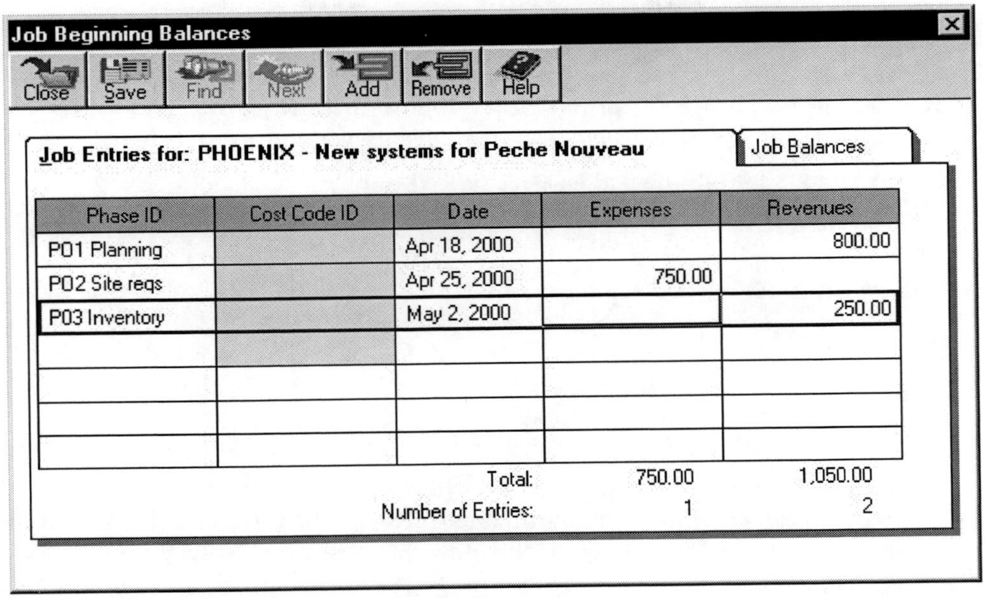

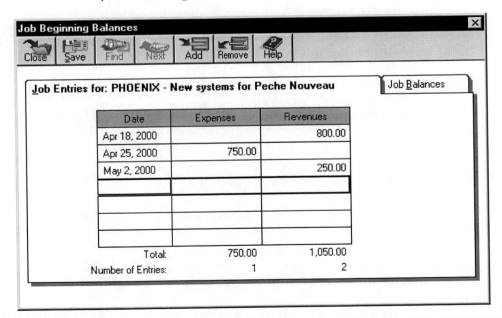

FIGURE 9-3 Job Beginning Balances window showing the Job Entries tab in Peachtree Complete Accounting

FIGURE 9-4 Job Beginning Balances window showing the Job Entries tab in Peachtree Accounting for Windows

Enter the beginning balance information as follows:

Phase ID   If the job is using phases, enter the phase ID. (This field does not appear in Peachtree Accounting for Windows.) If the job does not use phases, this field will be grayed out. Phases are discussed later in this chapter.

If you are going to use phases, or phases and cost codes, with this job, you must set these up for the job before entering beginning balances. Setting up phases and cost codes is discussed later in this chapter.

Cost Code ID   Enter the cost code ID for this phase ID, if any. (This field does not appear in Peachtree Accounting for Windows.) If the phase ID you specified in the associated Phase ID field does not use cost codes, this field will be grayed out. (Cost codes are discussed later in this chapter.)

Date   Enter the beginning date for the cost code or phase.

Expenses   Enter the expense amount for this cost code or phase. The expense amount or revenue amount (in the next field) is the difference between the total expenses and revenues for this phase or cost code. You can only enter an expense amount or a revenue amount. If you enter both an expense amount and a revenue amount on the same line, Peachtree Complete Accounting will only save the last entry you make on that line.

Revenues   Enter the revenue amount for this cost code or phase.

Total   These display-only fields show the totals for the expenses and revenues you've entered for this job.

Number of Entries   These display-only fields show the total number of entries in the Expenses and Revenues fields.

You can enter beginning balances at any time when entering the jobs. You can enter beginning balance information for another job by clicking the Job Balances tab (shown in Figure 9-5). The total of the beginning balances for the jobs appears at the bottom of the tab. Select the job from the lower part of the Job Beginning Balances window. The job information appears in the top of the window. Click the Job Entries tab to enter beginning balances for the selected job.

When you are done entering beginning balances for jobs, click OK to save the information and return to the General tab in the Maintain Jobs window.

Keep in mind that job beginning balances are not entered in the General Ledger. The value of any transactions that have been entered and distributed to a job should not be included in the beginning balance figure, as these amounts will already be included in the information on the Job Cost reports. Only those amounts that will not be distributed through normal transaction entries should be entered through the Job Beginning Balances window.

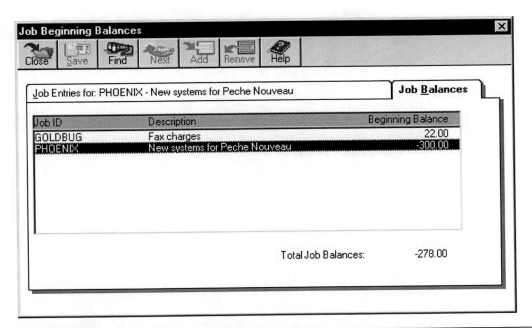

FIGURE 9-5 Job Beginning Balances window showing the Job Balances tab

When you are satisfied with your entries, click Save. (Clicking Close will close the window without saving your entries; you will not be prompted to save your entries either.)

Entering Job Custom Fields

After you have entered the information on the General tab, click the Custom Fields tab. The Custom Fields tab appears, as shown in Figure 9-6. As with other records, the job information in the top part of the tab is carried forward from the information you entered in the General tab. You can work with this job, select another one, or change the name and inactive information for the job from this tab.

Enter the custom field information for the job here, exactly as you entered custom field information for other types of records in earlier chapters.

Entering Estimated Expenses and Revenues

After you have entered the information on the Custom Fields tab, click the Estimated Expenses/Revenue tab. The Estimated Expenses/Revenue tab appears, as shown in Figure 9-7.

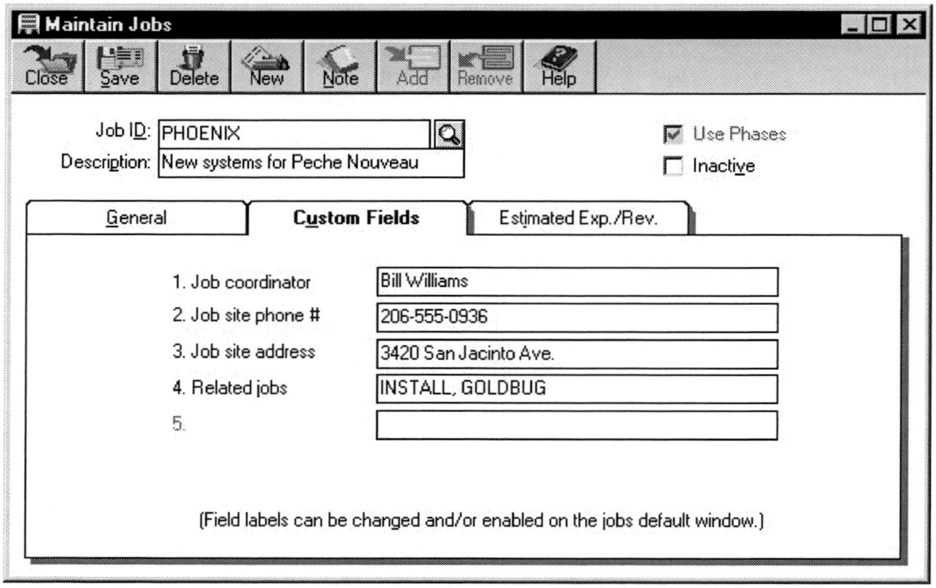

FIGURE 9-6 Maintain Jobs window showing the Custom Fields tab

You use the Estimated Expenses/Revenues tab to enter estimated costs and revenues for a job. Once you have entered your estimates, you can track actual costs and revenues against the estimates for cost control and for project tracking. Figure 9-7 shows the Estimated Expenses/Revenues tab if you aren't using phases (shown here with the Use Phases checkbox unchecked). Enter your estimates for the expenses and revenues in the Expenses and Revenues fields. When you are satisfied with your entries, click Save. (Clicking Close will close the window without saving your entries.)

You can also enter estimates for phases and cost codes. (You see how to set up phases and cost codes later in this chapter.) To enter estimates for phases and cost codes, the Use Phases field must be checked, as shown in Figure 9-8. If you have already entered estimates in the Expenses and Revenues fields, they will be erased when you check the Use Phases box in this tab. Unlike the Job Beginning Balances window shown earlier in Figure 9-3, you can enter both expense and revenue amounts on the same line, although this is not recommended.

The top half of the tab is the same as on the previous two tabs. Enter the estimate information in the fields in the bottom portion of the tab as follows:

Phase ID Enter the phase ID or right-click in the field to select from a drop-down list of phase IDs.

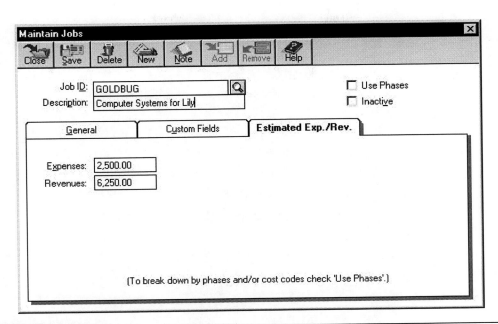

FIGURE 9-7 Maintain Jobs window showing the Estimated Expenses/Revenues tab

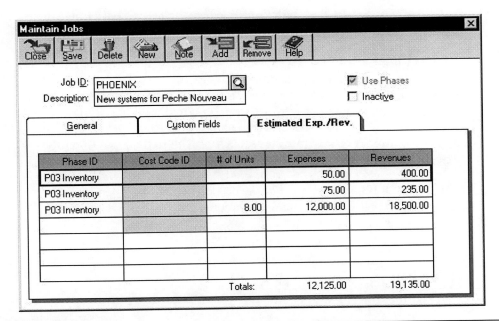

FIGURE 9-8 Maintain Jobs window showing the Estimated Exp./Rev. tab with the Use Phases field checked

Cost Code ID   Enter the cost code ID or right-click in the field to select from a drop-down list of cost code IDs. The cost code IDs you can select will depend on the phase ID specified in the associated field. If the phase ID you selected does not have any associated cost code IDs, the cost code ID field will be grayed out. You can only enter a phase and cost code combination once in this window for a given job.

# of Units   Enter the number of units for this phase and cost code. This field is for informational purposes only; units can be hours of labor, permits, systems, or assemblies.

Expenses   Enter the estimated expense for this phase and cost code.

Revenues   Enter the estimated revenue for this phase and cost code.

T I P : If you do not want to track revenues by phase and/or cost code, create a phase called Revenue and use it for your revenues.

Totals   These display-only fields show the running totals for all estimated expenses and revenues.

When you are satisfied with your entries, click Save. (Clicking Close will close the window without saving your entries.)

Entering Phases

You've seen in the previous sections how to enter basic job information. Many jobs will be simple and straightforward, requiring little in the way of detailed steps. However, some jobs require more detailed tracking of individual parts of the project. For example, installing a computer network at an office may require a number of separate steps, each of which must be done in order. The following is an example of the steps such a job would require:

1. Planning the project.
2. Creating a site requirement document.
3. Purchasing the necessary materials.
4. Creating the systems for the client's site.
5. Installing the systems.
6. Testing and debugging the systems.
7. Training the client's personnel.

If your jobs have this level of complexity, you may want to set up phases to track individual steps. *Phases* identify the individual parts of a project. By dividing the job into different phases, you can track the steps required for completion for each phase as well as the associated expenses and revenues for each phase. You can set up phases and then use them to track job cost information. Keep in mind that phases are not tied to specific jobs; any phase can be applied to any job. As a result, you should take some time to plan your phases carefully so you can use them on a wide array of jobs effectively.

To enter a phase record, select Jobs Costs from the Maintain menu and then Phases from the submenu. The Maintain Phases window appears, as shown in Figure 9-9.

Enter the phase information as follows:

Phase ID   Enter the phase ID. Phase IDs can be up to 20 characters long, and they can contain any characters except an asterisk (*), a question mark (?), or a plus sign (+). Right-click in this field to display a list of the phase IDs already entered. It's a good idea to have a naming system for phases so that all phases start with the same letter, such as "P01," "P02," and so on, followed by a word or two identifying the phase. If you have different groups of phases, you may want to use different first letters.

Description   Enter a description for this phase. Table 9-1 shows the sample phases for Big Business, Inc.

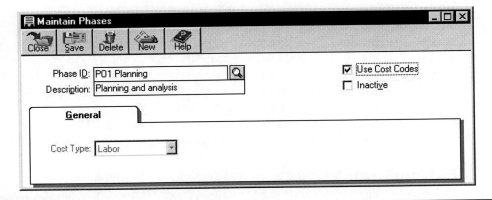

FIGURE 9-9   Maintain Phases window

PHASE	DESCRIPTION
01 Planning	Initial project planning
02 Site Requirements	Site requirement document
03 Inventory	Inventory purchasing
04 Assembly	Material preparation and assembly
05 Site preparation	Site preparation
06 Installation	Installation of systems
07 Testing	System testing and debugging
08 Training	Training of client personnel

TABLE 9-1   Sample Phases and Descriptions

Use Cost Codes   Check this box if you want to use cost codes with this phase. (Cost codes are described later in this chapter. You don't need to have your cost codes set up in advance to check this box.)

Inactive   Check this box to set the phase to inactive status. Peachtree Complete will warn you if you try to post a transaction to an inactive phase. If a phase is connected to an active job, Peachtree Complete Accounting will not let you purge the phase. Purging phases is discussed in Chapter 13.

Cost Type   Select the cost type from the drop-down list: Labor, Materials, Equipment, Subcontractor, or Other. Cost types provide a basic level of detail for assigning classes of expense to a phase. If you checked the Use Cost Codes box earlier in this window, the Cost Types window will be grayed out.

If you are setting up a number of similar phases, display the phase you want to copy from, then change the information in the Phase ID and Description fields appropriately. When you are satisfied with the information as you've entered it, click Save. The information you didn't change is a copy of the original phase. This is particularly handy if you have extensive cost codes associated with a specific phase.

When you are satisfied with your entries, click OK to save the phase.

Entering Cost Codes

Peachtree Complete Accounting for Windows offers an additional level of detail for tracking job costs: cost codes. *Cost codes* let you specify costs or tasks within a phase. Where one job can have many phases, one phase can have many cost codes. Keep in mind that not all phases require the detail that using cost codes provides. You can choose to have cost codes for some phases and not for others, as your business requires.

As with phases, cost codes aren't tied to specific phases or jobs; any cost code can be applied to any phase. The cost codes you create should be as generic as possible so that you can apply them to each job you do. This will help you standardize the cost codes and phases that comprise each job and make it easier for you to repeat your processes from job to job. In turn, this will help your company get better at delivering jobs quickly and without problems.

Table 9-2 shows you a typical set of cost codes for Big Business, Inc.'s phase for installing computers at a client site.

Note that the costs for materials and labor are broken out separately, letting you track each cost as an individual item. The code "06" before each cost code number shows that this cost code will tend to be associated with this phase; however, you could also use the "ConfiguringL" cost code elsewhere where computers are configured, such as in Big Business, Inc.'s phases for computer assembly and testing. Using sequential numeric headers in phase and cost code IDs is particularly useful when printing reports, as you can easily sort your phase and cost codes in numeric order.

To enter a cost code, select Jobs Costs from the Maintain menu and then Costs from the submenu. The Maintain Cost Codes window appears, as shown in Figure 9-10.

Enter the cost code information as follows:

Cost ID   Enter the cost ID. Cost IDs can be up to 20 characters long, and they can contain any characters except an asterisk (*), a question mark (?), or a plus sign (+). Right-click in this field to display a list of the cost IDs already entered. As with phases, it's a good idea to have a naming system for cost codes so that all cost codes start with the same letter, such as "C01," "C02," and so on, followed by a word or two identifying the code. If you have different groups of cost codes, you may want to use different first letters. Alternatively, you might start the cost code with the numbers identifying the phase they're closely linked to.

Description   Enter a description for this cost code.

PHASE	COST CODE	DESCRIPTION	COST TYPE
06 Installation	0601-CablingM	Cabling	Materials
	0602-CablingL	Labor laying cable	Labor
	0603-ComputersM	Computers for client	Materials
	0604-ComputersL	Labor	Labor
	0605-ConnectingL	Connecting network	Labor
	0606-ConfiguringL	Configuring computers	Labor

TABLE 9-2   Sample Cost Codes

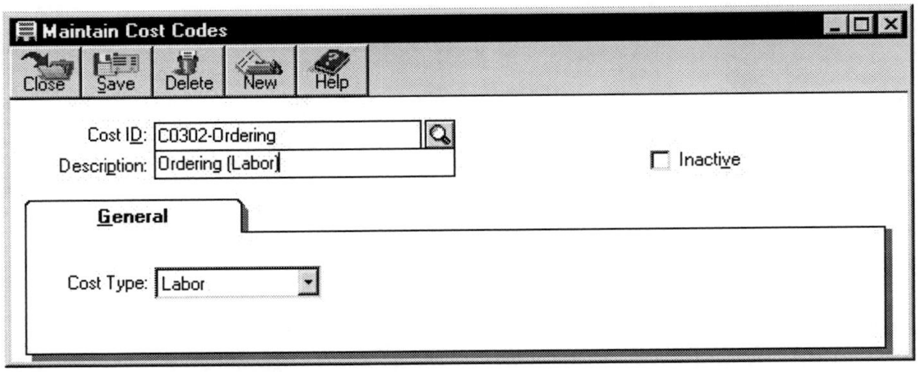

FIGURE 9-10 Maintain Cost Codes window

Inactive Check this box to set the cost code to inactive status. Peachtree Complete will warn you if you try to post a transaction to an inactive cost code. If a cost code is connected to an active phase, Peachtree Complete Accounting will not let you purge the cost code. Purging cost codes is discussed in Chapter 13.

Cost Type Select the cost type from the drop-down list: Labor, Materials, Equipment, Subcontractor, or Other. Cost types provide a basic level of detail for assigning classes of expense to a phase or cost code.

When you are satisfied with your entries, click OK to save the cost code.

Modifying Jobs, Phases, and Cost Codes

Once you've entered a job record, a phase, or a cost code, you can modify it.

Modifying a job record is easy. First, display the job record in the Maintain Jobs window by entering the job ID in the Job ID field. You can then change any of the job information except for the job ID itself. If you want to change the job ID, you will have to delete the job and then reenter the information under the new job ID.

You can similarly modify phases and cost codes by displaying the phase or cost code in the Maintain Phases or Maintain Cost Codes windows and modifying the information. As with jobs, if you want to change the phase ID or cost code ID, you will have to delete the phase or cost code and then reenter the information under the new ID.

Most people think about jobs as having something to do with construction projects, installation of products, or consulting services. In this book, for example, you have seen how Big Business Inc. is setting up computers for LilyPod Systems and providing training to the staff. However, there are many other uses for jobs in Peachtree Accounting related to tracking accounting transactions, time, expenses, and reimbursable expenses for a specific project.

For example, realtors can set up a job for a specific property or parcel of land they're selling. Payments on the property can be applied to that property, as can commissions paid out. Printers and typesetters can establish large printing jobs as separate jobs in Peachtree Accounting so the expenses for each phase can be tracked easily. Lawyers will have many uses for jobs, such as the administration of trust funds or an account for a legal action. Time and expense information can be tracked for the job (and with even greater detail using phases and cost codes, if necessary) and detailed reports can be produced for audit purposes.

As you consider how you might use jobs in your company, think about how you sell your products and services. If you find that you tend to do specific kinds of business where expenses are reimbursed or time and costs are passed on to the customer, you may be able to set up a job to track the financial transactions for this activity more effectively.

One of the most common modifications you may need to make is to reclassify a transaction from one job, phase, or cost code to another. You use the General Journal to reclassify a transaction or part of a transaction from one account to another. For example, if you have posted information to a phase incorrectly, you can make a General Journal entry to the same account with a debit and credit to the same account. Enter the correct job, phase, or cost code information on the debit line and the job, phase, or cost code information that needs to be reclassified on the credit line. This transaction will not affect the General Ledger, but it will apply the transaction amount to the correct job, phase, or cost code. For more information on making entries in the General Journal, see Chapter 4.

Deleting Job Records, Phases, and Cost Codes

You can delete a job record, phase, or cost code by selecting the record and then clicking the Delete button at the top of the window. Peachtree Complete asks you if you're sure you want to delete this record. Click Yes to confirm.

CAUTION: You cannot delete a job record if there are previous transactions against the job. In such a case, you may want to flag the job as inactive so activity is not entered for the job (without, of course, Peachtree Complete warning you that the job is inactive and asking you if you want to post activity to the job).

Printing Job Reports

Once you have set up your jobs, phases, and cost codes, you can track any expense or revenues related to a job by entering the job ID in the appropriate Job field in the transaction window. As you have seen in previous chapters, almost all transaction windows have a Job field for each line item. By entering a job ID in this field, you tell Peachtree Accounting to track the expense or revenue for that job. This information can then be extracted and printed on the job reports.

There are no tasks directly associated with jobs, so once you have entered the job records, you can run the job reports. Peachtree Complete has a dozen standard job reports, as shown in Table 9-3.

The Job List and Job Master File List (shown in Figures 9-11 and 9-12) are useful for verifying the job records you have just entered.

REPORT	DESCRIPTION
Job List	Shows basic job information.
Job Master File List	Shows job information from the Maintain Jobs window.
Phase List	Shows phases with description, cost types, and if the phase uses cost codes.
Cost Code List	Shows cost codes and associated cost types.
Job Ledger	Shows jobs with transaction activity and the outstanding balance.
Job Register	Shows job information, including description, customer ID, activity, balance, and status.
Job Profitability Report	Shows jobs with activity, balances, estimated revenues, and amount remaining for the job.
Unbilled Job Expense	Shows jobs, customer ID, and transaction information that has not been applied to an invoice using the Reimbursable Expenses feature.
Job Estimates	Shows the estimates for a job.
Estimated Job Expenses	Shows detailed information on job estimates compared to actual expenses.
Estimated Job Revenue	Shows detailed information on job estimates compared to actual revenue.
Job Costs by Type	Shows estimated versus actual expenses and estimated versus actual units.

TABLE 9-3   Job Reports

Big Business, Inc.
Job List

Filter Criteria includes: Report order is by Description.

Job ID	Job Description	Starting	Ending	For Customer	PO Number	% Complete
GOLDBUG	Computer Systems for Lily	4/18/00	4/25/00	LILY001		100
PHOENIX	New systems for Peche Nouveau	4/18/00	5/4/00	PECH001	PN1054	20

FIGURE 9-11   Job List

Big Business, Inc.
Job Master File List

Filter Criteria includes: Report order is by Description.

Job ID Job Description Supervisor For Customer Job Type	Job coordinator Job site phone # Job site address Related jobs Starting Ending	Active?	Est Revenues	Est Expenses
PHOENIX New systems for Peche Nouveau Bill Williams PECH001 SITEWORK	Connie Brenden 425-555-8176 Bellevue LilyPod 4/18/00 5/4/00	Yes		24,000.00

FIGURE 9-12   Job Master File List

If you have entered phases or cost codes, you can use the Phase List and the Cost Code List (shown in Figures 9-13 and 9-14) to check your entries.

In addition, the other reports will show you the transactions for jobs, the relative profitability, and unbilled expenses. The remaining job reports are shown in Figures 9-15 through 9-22.

Big Business, Inc.
Phase List

Filter Criteria includes: 1) Types. Report order is by ID.

Phase ID	Phase Description	Cost Type	Cost Codes?	Active?
P01 Planning	Planning and analysis	Labor	No	Yes
P02 Site reqs	Site Requirements	Labor	No	Yes
P03 Inventory	Inventory Process		Yes	Yes
P04 Assembly	Computer Assembly		Yes	Yes
P05 Site Preparation	Site Preparation	Labor	No	Yes
P06 Installation	Installation of equipment		Yes	Yes

FIGURE 9-13   Phase List

Big Business, Inc.
Cost Code List

Filter Criteria includes: 1) Types. Report order is by Description.

Cost Code ID	Cost Code Description	Cost Type	Active?
C0401	Assembly	Labor	Yes
C0402	Assembly	Materials	Yes
C0601	Cabling	Materials	Yes
CO301	Inventory received	Materials	Yes
CO302	Ordering	Labor	Yes
CO303	Ordering	Materials	Yes
C0302-Ordering	Ordering (Labor)	Labor	Yes

FIGURE 9-14 Cost Code List

Big Business, Inc.
Job Ledger Report
For the Period From Apr 1, 2000 to Apr 30, 2000

Filter Criteria includes: Report order is by ID.

Job ID	Phase ID	Cost Code ID	GL Acct ID	Trx Dat	Trans Description	Jrnl	Trans Ref	Amount	Totals
GOLDBUG				4/1/00	Balance Fwd			22.00	
			40000	4/1/00	Lily Pod Systems - Copying and report charges	SJ	123489	-47.96	
				4/1/00	Lily Pod Systems - Copying and repro charges	SJ	123489	-47.96	
			58000	4/10/00	Copying and repro charges	GENJ	00-2232	-47.96	
				4/10/00	Copying and repro charges	GENJ	00-2232	47.96	
									-73.92
GOLDBUG	**Total**								**-73.92**
PHOENIX	P01 Planning			4/18/00		CRJ	BegBal	-800.00	
									-800.00

FIGURE 9-15 Job Ledger Report

Big Business, Inc.
Job Register
For the Period From Apr 1, 2000 to Apr 30, 2000

Filter Criteria includes: Report order is by ID.

Job ID Job Description For Customer	Phase ID	Cost Code ID	GL Acct ID	Amount	Totals	Progress Statu
PHOENIX New systems for Peche No PECH001	P01 Planning			-800.00		In progress
					-800.00	
	P02 Site reqs			750.00		
					750.00	
PHOENIX Total					-50.00	

FIGURE 9-16   Job Register

Big Business, Inc.
Job Profitability Report
For the Period From Apr 1, 2000 to Apr 30, 2000

Filter Criteria includes: Report order is by ID.

Job ID	Phase ID	Cost Code ID	GL Acct ID	Actual Exp.	Exp. Totals	Rev. Totals	Profit $	Profit
GOLDBUG				22.00				
			58000	-47.96				
				47.96				
					22.00			
GOLDBUG	Total				22.00		-22.00	
PHOENIX	P01 Planning					800.00		
PHOENIX	P02 Site reqs			750.00				
					750.00			
PHOENIX	Total				750.00	800.00	50.00	6.25
Report	Total				772.00	800.00	28.00	3.50

FIGURE 9-17   Job Profitability Report

Big Business, Inc.
Unbilled Job Expense
For the Period From Apr 1, 2000 to Apr 30, 2000

Filter Criteria includes: Report order is by ID.

Job ID For Customer	GL Acct ID	Phase ID	Cost Code ID	Jrnl	Trans Ref	Trx Dat	Trans Description	Activity
GOLDBUG LILY001	58000			GE	00-2232	4/10/00	Copying and repro charges	47.96
								47.96
GOLDBUG Total								47.96
Report Total								47.96

FIGURE 9-18   Unbilled Job Expense

Big Business, Inc.
Job Estimates
As of Apr 30, 2000

Filter Criteria includes: Report order is by ID.

Job ID Job Description For Customer	Phase ID	Cost Code ID	Est. Exp. Units	Est. Expenses
GOLDBUG Computer Systems for Lily LILY001				2,500.00
GOLDBUG	Total			2,500.00
PHOENIX New systems for Peche Nouve PECH001	P01 Planning P02 Site reqs P03 Inventory P04 Assembly	CO301 C0401	10.00	2,000.00 6,000.00 1,000.00 15,000.00
PHOENIX	Total		10.00	24,000.00
Report	Total		10.00	26,500.00

FIGURE 9-19   Job Estimates

Big Business, Inc.
Estimated Job Expenses
As of Apr 30, 2000

Filter Criteria includes: Report order is by ID.

Job ID	Phase ID	Cost Code ID	Est. Exp. Units	Act. Exp. Units	Diff. Exp. Units	Est. Expenses	Act. Expenses
GOLDBUG						2,500.00	69.96
GOLDBUG	**Total**					**2,500.00**	**69.96**
PHOENIX	P01 Planning					2,000.00	
	P02 Site reqs					6,000.00	750.00
	P03 Inventory	CO301	10.00		-10.00	1,000.00	
	P04 Assembly	C0401				15,000.00	
PHOENIX	**Total**		**10.00**		**-10.00**	**24,000.00**	**750.00**
Report	**Total**		**10.00**		**-10.00**	**26,500.00**	**819.96**

FIGURE 9-20 Estimated Job Expenses

Big Business, Inc.
Estimated Job Revenue
As of Apr 30, 2000

Filter Criteria includes: Report order is by ID.

Job ID	Phase ID	Cost Code ID	Est. Revenue	Act. Revenue	Diff. Revenue
GOLDBUG			6,250.00	47.96	-6,202.04
GOLDBUG	**Total**		**6,250.00**	**47.96**	**-6,202.04**
PHOENIX	P01 Planning			800.00	800.00
	P02 Site reqs				
	P03 Inventory	CO301			
	P04 Assembly	C0401			
PHOENIX	**Total**			**800.00**	**800.00**
Report	**Total**		**6,250.00**	**847.96**	**-5,402.04**

FIGURE 9-21 Estimated Job Revenue

Big Business, Inc.
Job Costs by Type
As of Apr 30, 2000

Filter Criteria includes: Report order is by ID.

Job ID	Cost Type	Est. Exp. Units	Act. Exp. Units	Diff. Exp. Units	Est. Expenses	Act. Expenses	Diff. Expenses
PHOENIX	Labor				23,000.00	750.00	-22,250.00
	Materials	10.00		-10.00	1,000.00		-1,000.00
	Equipment						
	Subcontractor						
	Other						
PHOENIX	**Total**	**10.00**		**-10.00**	**24,000.00**	**750.00**	**-23,250.00**
Report	**Total**	**10.00**		**-10.00**	**24,000.00**	**750.00**	**-23,250.00**

FIGURE 9-22   Job Costs by Type

Summary

In this chapter, you saw how to set up job defaults, create and maintain jobs, phases, and cost codes, and print job reports. In the next chapter, you'll enter assets, set depreciation schedules, and print fixed asset reports.

Time & Billing

10

In this chapter, you'll learn how to enter time tickets, time sheets, and expense tickets and how to print time and expense reports.

The previous chapter showed you how to set up job defaults; create and maintain jobs, phases, and cost codes; and print job reports. This chapter shows you how to enter, modify, and delete time and expense tickets and how to print Time & Billing reports.

Peachtree Complete Accounting's Time & Billing lets you track the time your company's employees and managers spend and the expenses they incur for specific jobs and activities. You can then use this information to bill customers, identify areas for cost improvements, and refine your company's internal processes. It's important to note that not everyone will need to use Peachtree Complete Accounting's Time & Billing features. You should examine your company's requirements carefully, as you may not need to create the level of detail that Time & Billing offers you.

Time Tickets and Time Sheets

Time & Billing has no defaults or options to set up, so you can start entering time and billing information right away. The first kind of information you can enter is a time ticket. *Time tickets* and *time sheets* record any activity measured in units of time (usually hours). Time tickets are used to record activities one activity at a time, whereas time sheets do so on a weekly basis. Time-based activities can be any of the following:

- Any kind of labor or service
- Consultation
- Design
- Planning
- Phone calls with clients

You will usually track billable time, but you may also want to track non-billable time just so you can identify possible areas of improvement.

Entering Time Tickets

To enter a time ticket, select the Time/Expense option from the Tasks menu, then select Time Tickets from the submenu. The Time Tickets window appears, as shown in Figure 10-1 with a typical time ticket entered. (The default option is for the Daily time ticket tab to appear in this window, but Peachtree Complete Accounting will remember whichever tab you used last and display that one the next time you use the Time Tickets window.)

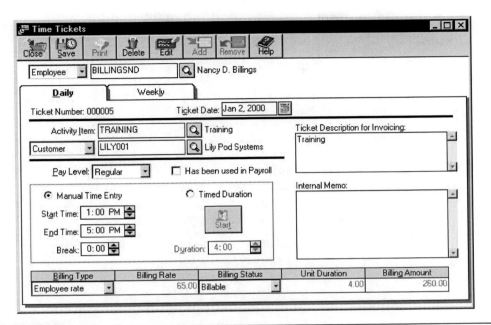

FIGURE 10-1 Time Tickets window with the Daily tab displayed

To enter information on a time ticket, fill in the fields as follows:

Employee/Vendor Select Employee or Vendor in this field to specify whether this is an employee or vendor time ticket—that is, whether an employee of your company or a vendor hired by the company is doing the activity being recorded. For example, having your company's engineers draw up a plan for modifying a customer's machine shop would be an employee activity; hiring a contract engineer to do the same thing would be a vendor activity. Both activities may be passed on to the customer, but employee time tickets can be used for payroll entry.

Employee/Vendor ID Enter the employee ID or vendor ID (depending on what you've selected in the preceding field). Right-click in this field to display the standard drop-down list of employees or vendors. When you enter an ID in this field, the employee's or vendor's name appears to the right of this field.

Ticket Number This display-only field shows the ticket number. Peachtree Complete Accounting for Windows automatically assigns the ticket number starting at 1. If you are also using expense tickets (discussed later in this chapter), the number you see here will be the next number in sequence after the last time ticket or expense ticket.

Ticket Date   The default date is the current system date. You can enter a date for the two fiscal years currently open as well as for the preceding fiscal year. This feature lets you enter hours generated in the previous fiscal year that are going to be billed to a client this fiscal year.

Activity Item   Enter an activity item in this field or right-click to select from the list of activity items. Activity items identify what task the time was spent on. If an activity item does not appear in the list, click New Records at the bottom of the list to display the Maintain Inventory Items window so you can enter a new item. Be sure to use an Item Class of Activity Item. For more information on entering new inventory items, see Chapter 8.

Customer/Job/Administrative   Select Customer, Job, or Administrative in this field. Select Customer if you are doing this for a customer and there is no job set up in Job Costing that would contain this activity. Select Job if you are doing this for a job, phase, or cost code that has already been set up in Job Costing. Select Administrative if this activity is purely administrative and is not associated with either a customer or a job.

If you select Administrative, Peachtree Complete Accounting automatically sets the status in the Billing Status field to Non-Billable.

Customer/Job ID   Enter the customer or job ID in this field (depending on your selection in the preceding field). If you selected Administrative in the preceding field, the Customer/Job ID field does not appear.

Pay Level   Select a pay level from the drop-down list. Pay levels are determined in the Pay Info tab of the Maintain Employees window (described in Chapter 7.) If the employee is set up with a pay type of Hourly Time Ticket Hours, Peachtree Complete Accounting uses the hours you enter here for payroll entry for that employee. If the employee is salaried, the information you enter here is used only for reporting purposes. If you have not set up pay levels with defined rates in the Maintain Employees window, no pay levels will appear in this field. If you leave this field blank, you will not be able to use the hours you enter here for payroll entry.

If you selected Vendor in the Customer/Vendor field earlier, this field does not appear.

Has Been Used in Payroll   Peachtree Complete Accounting checks this box when the time ticket is applied to an employee's paycheck during payroll entry. If this box is not checked, Peachtree Complete Accounting lets you apply this time ticket to an employee's paycheck.

N O T E : Hourly employees must be set up with the Hourly Time Ticket Hours payment method in the Pay Info tab of the Maintain Employees window. Salaried employees have a field for entering an hourly billing rate. For more information, see Chapter 7.

Checking this box before the hours have been applied prevents Peachtree Complete Accounting from including the hours on this time ticket during payroll calculation. You might do this if the hours are in dispute with the customer or you do not wish to issue payment to the employee until you have received money from the customer.

You can uncheck this box even if Peachtree Complete Accounting has checked it to show that the hours have been applied and then apply the hours a second time during payroll entry, but this may cause problems later when reconciling your time ticket entries.

If you selected Vendor in the Customer/Vendor field earlier, this field does not appear.

Manual Time Entry Select this if you are entering a time ticket after the activity has occurred. (Use Timed Duration to time an activity in progress.)

Start Time Enter the start time for this activity in HH:MM AM/PM format. There are actually three parts to this field: the hours, the minutes, and the AM/PM sections. You can enter the information by typing it into each subfield, or you can use the arrows to the right of the field to change the value of the subfield.

End Time Enter the ending time for this activity in HH:MM AM/PM format. The ending time for an activity can go into a second day (such as an activity that started at 11:15 PM on November 13 and ended at 8:30 AM on November 14), but the time span for an activity cannot exceed 23 hours and 59 minutes. If you have an activity that is 24 hours or more in one continuous stretch, break it into two separate time entries, or use the time sheet (described later) to enter the hours for this activity. As with the Start Date, you can enter information by typing it into each of the three subfields or use the arrows to the right of the field to change the value of the subfield.

Break Enter the total break time (if any) for the activity. Breaks would be any time spent away from the activity. The break time is subtracted from the total time between the starting and ending times entered previously. As with the Start Date and End Date, you can enter information by typing it into each of the two subfields or use the arrows to the right of the field to change the value of the subfield.

Timed Duration　Select this if you want Peachtree Complete Accounting to time the activity as you are performing it. Click Start below this field to start the timer. You can start and stop the timer while you are working; Peachtree Complete Accounting will continue timing from where you last stopped the timer. As with the Start Date and End Date, you can enter information by typing it into each of the three subfields or use the arrows to the right of the field to change the value of the subfield.

Ticket Description for Invoicing　Enter up to 160 characters of comments in this field. These comments will appear on the invoice created with this time ticket.

Internal Memo　Enter up to 2,000 characters of information about this time ticket. The information in this field is for detailed internal information on the time ticket. This memo does not appear on the invoice or employee paycheck, although you can display this information by clicking Detail in the Apply Time/Reimbursable Expenses window (described in Chapter 5). You can press CTRL-J in this field to insert a line break for a new line.

Billing Type　Select the billing type from the list.

- Select Employee Rate if this is a time ticket for an employee. Peachtree Complete Accounting will use the billing rate previously set up for this employee in the Maintain Employees window to calculate the billing amount. (If you selected Vendor in the Employee/Vendor field earlier, the Employee Rate option does not appear.)
- Select Activity Rate to use the billing rate that was previously set up for this activity in the Maintain Inventory Items window to calculate the billing amount. Although Peachtree Complete Accounting uses the customer's default pricing level to determine which activity item billing rate to use as the default, you can select any of the billing rates in the Billing Rate field.
- Select Override Rate to override the predetermined billing rate for the employee or activity item.
- Select Flat Fee to charge a flat fee regardless of the time on the time ticket. You can still use the duration on the time ticket for reporting hours worked on a project and for an employee's payroll entry.

If you selected Administrative in the Customer/Job/Administrative field earlier, the Billing Type field does not appear.

Billing Rate　Enter the billing rate in the field. Peachtree Complete Accounting uses this to calculate the billing amount.

Depending on your answer in the preceding field, this rate may already be filled in for you. You can accept the entry or change it.

The billing rate for employees is determined by the billing rate established in the Maintain Employees window for the employee. To adjust the billing rate for an employee, you must adjust the basic billing rate for the employee in the Maintain Employees window as described in Chapter 7.

The billing rate for activities is determined by the billing rates established in the Maintain Inventory Items window for the activity item. To adjust the billing rates for an activity item, you must adjust the basic billing rates for the activity item in the Maintain Inventory Items window as described in Chapter 8.

If the entry in the preceding field is Override Rate, you must enter an override billing rate in this field. Also, if you selected Flat Fee in the preceding field or Administrative in the Customer/Job/Administrative field, this field is not available.

Billing Status   Enter the billing status in this field: Billable, Non-Billable, No Charge, or Hold.

A status of Billable (the default) lets you apply the time ticket to customer invoices. A status of Non-Billable prevents you from applying the time ticket to customer invoices. (Non-Billable is the default option if you selected Administrative in the Customer/Job/Administrative field.) If you selected Administrative in the Customer/Job/Administrative field, you can change the billing status from Non-Billable to Billable, but you will not be able to apply the time ticket to any customer invoice because you cannot associate the time ticket with a customer or job.

A status of Hold prevents you from applying the time ticket to customer invoices until you change the time ticket status to Billable. A status of No Charge zeros out the Billing Amount field regardless of entries in the Billing Type or Billing Rate field. You can apply No Charge time tickets to customer invoices.

Unit Duration   This display-only field shows the time in Duration in decimal format. To change the entry in this field, you must change the entry in Duration.

Billing Amount   Peachtree Complete Accounting calculates this field as the product of the billing rate times the unit duration for the Employee Rate, Activity Rate, or Override Rate billing type. If the billing type is Flat Fee, enter the amount in this field. Peachtree Complete Accounting uses the billing amount when applying time tickets to sales invoices. If the Billing Status is set to No Charge, the billing amount is zero regardless of the other entries.

NOTE: The billing amount must be zero or greater. To enter a credit to a customer for time, use the credit memo process described in Chapter 5.

When you are satisfied with your entries, click Save.

Entering Time Sheets

The advantages to entering time on a time ticket rather than a time sheet are that you can enter starting and ending times (rather than a duration) and comments about a specific activity. In addition, the time ticket has a timer built in so you can time an activity directly.

However, there are several advantages to entering time on a time sheet as well. While each time ticket records only a single activity in a day, a time sheet can record many activities in a day on a single record. Time tickets will only let you enter time less than 24 hours; time sheets will let you enter larger blocks of time.

To enter information on a time sheet rather than a time ticket, click the Weekly tab in the Time Tickets window. The Weekly tab of the Time Tickets window appears as shown in Figure 10-2.

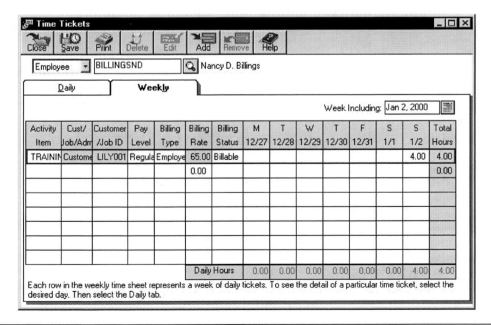

FIGURE 10-2   Time Tickets window with the Weekly tab displayed

Each row on the time sheet is used to enter the information for a single activity item, billing type, rate, and amount. (The fields in the Weekly tab are very similar to those you saw earlier in the Daily tab.) In Figure 10-2, you can see how the time ticket shown in Figure 10-1 appears in this tab.

To enter a time sheet, fill out the fields as follows:

Employee/Vendor   Select Employee or Vendor in this field to specify whether this is an employee or vendor time ticket—that is, whether an employee of your company or a vendor hired by the company is doing the activity being recorded.

Employee/Vendor ID   Enter the employee ID or vendor ID (depending on what you've selected in the preceding field). Right-click in this field to display the standard drop-down list of employees or vendors. When you enter an ID in this field, the employee's or vendor's name appears to the right of this field.

Week Including   Click the calendar button to the right of the Date field to choose a date. Peachtree displays the week (Monday through Sunday) that includes the selected date.

Activity Item   Enter an activity item in this field or right-click to select from the list of activity items. Activity items identify what task the time was spent on. If an activity item does not appear in the list, click New Records at the bottom of the list to display the Maintain Inventory Items window so you can enter a new item. Be sure to use an Item Class of Activity Item. For more information on entering new inventory items, see Chapter 8.

Customer/Job/Administrative   Select Customer, Job, or Administrative in this field. Select Customer if you are doing this for a customer and there is no job set up in Job Costing that would contain this activity. Select Job if you are doing this for a job, phase, or cost code that has already been set up in Job Costing. Select Administrative if this activity is purely administrative and is not associated with either a customer or a job.

If you select Administrative, Peachtree Complete Accounting automatically grays out the Customer/Job ID, Billing Type, and Billing Rate fields and sets the status in the Billing Status field to Non-Billable.

Customer/Job ID   Enter the customer or job ID in this field (depending on your selection in the preceding field). If you selected Administrative in the preceding field, Peachtree Complete Accounting grays out the Customer/Job ID field.

Pay Level   Select a pay level from the drop-down list. Pay levels are determined in the Pay Info tab of the Maintain Employees window (described in Chapter 7). If the employee is set up with a pay type of Hourly Time Ticket Hours, Peachtree

Complete Accounting uses the hours you enter here for payroll entry for that employee. If the employee is salaried, the information you enter here is only used for reporting purposes. (Time tickets for salaried employees can be used as reimbursable expenses, but will not appear on the salaried employee's payroll.) If you have not set up pay levels with defined rates in the Maintain Employees window, no pay levels will appear in this field. If you leave this field blank, you will not be able to use the hours you enter here for payroll entry.

If you selected Vendor in the Customer/Vendor field earlier, Peachtree Complete Accounting grays out the Pay Level field.

Billing Type   Select the billing type from the list.

- Select Employee Rate if this is a time ticket for an employee. Peachtree Complete Accounting will use the billing rate previously set up for this employee in the Maintain Employees window to calculate the billing amount. (If you selected Vendor in the Employee/Vendor field earlier, the Employee Rate option does not appear.)
- Select Activity Rate to use the billing rate that was previously set up for this activity in the Maintain Inventory Items window to calculate the billing amount. Although Peachtree Complete Accounting uses the customer's default pricing level to determine which of the activity items billing rates to use as the default, you can select any of the billing rates in the Billing Rate field.
- Select Override Rate to override the predetermined billing rate for the employee or activity item.
- Select Flat Fee to charge a flat fee regardless of the time on the time ticket. You can still use the duration on the time ticket for reporting hours worked on a project and for an employee's payroll entry.

If you selected Administrative in the Customer/Job/Administrative field earlier, Peachtree Complete Accounting grays out the Billing Type field.

Billing Rate   Enter the billing rate in the field. Peachtree Complete Accounting uses this to calculate the billing amount.

Depending on your answer in the preceding field, this rate may already be filled in for you. You can accept the entry or change it.

The billing rate for employees is determined by the billing rate established in the Maintain Employees window for the employee. To adjust the billing rate for an employee, you must adjust the basic billing rate for the employee in the Maintain Employees window as described in Chapter 7.

The billing rate for activities is determined by the billing rates established in the Maintain Inventory Items window for the activity item. To adjust the billing rates for an activity item, you must adjust the basic billing rates for the activity item in the Maintain Inventory Items window as described in Chapter 8.

If the entry in the preceding field is Override Rate, you must enter an override billing rate in this field.

If you selected Flat Fee in the preceding field or Administrative in the Customer/Job/Administrative field, Peachtree Complete Accounting grays out the Billing Rate field.

Billing Status   Enter the billing status in this field: Billable, Non-Billable, No Charge, or Hold.

A status of Billable (the default) lets you apply the time ticket to customer invoices. A status of Non-Billable prevents you from applying the time ticket to customer invoices. (Non-Billable is the default option if you selected Administrative in the Customer/Job/Administrative field.) If you selected Administrative in the Customer/Job/Administrative field, you can change the billing status from Non-Billable to Billable, but you will not be able to apply the time ticket to any customer invoice because you cannot associate the time ticket with a customer or job.

A status of Hold prevents you from applying the time ticket to customer invoices until you change the time ticket status to Billable. A status of No Charge zeros out the Billing Amount field regardless of entries in the Billing Type or Billing Rate field. You can apply No Charge time tickets to customer invoices.

Daily Durations   Enter the duration for the activity item in each applicable daily column. As with the time durations on the daily time tickets earlier, you cannot enter a time duration of greater than 23 hours and 59 minutes converted to decimal format; however, if you have a span of hours across several days, you can enter successive quantities of hours for a single activity time on the succeeding days.

Total Hours   Peachtree Complete Accounting displays the total hours of duration for the activity item in this field.

Daily Hours   Peachtree Complete Accounting displays the total hours for this day in this row.

When you click Save, Peachtree Complete Accounting uses the information you enter on the weekly time sheet to create individual daily time tickets that identify the specific information for that day. You can then display the corresponding daily time ticket and edit the information—for example, by adding a memo or by including starting and ending times.

Figure 10-3 shows the Weekly tab with information added for an employee working on the TRAINING activity item. Figure 10-4 shows one of the

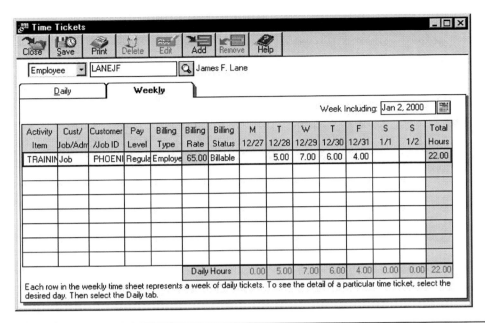

FIGURE 10-3   Time Tickets window with the Weekly tab displayed showing sample data

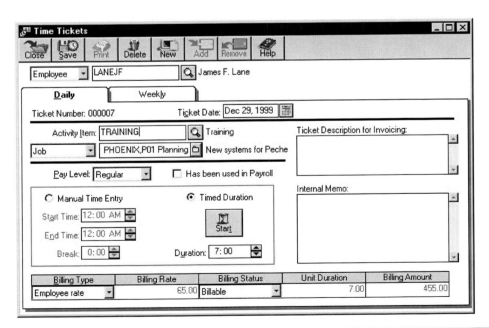

FIGURE 10-4   Corresponding daily information for the second day's entry in Figure 10-3

corresponding daily time tickets created by Peachtree Complete Accounting after you save the information. Note that there is no invoicing or memo information in Figure 10-4.

Be aware that Peachtree Complete Accounting does not create time tickets if the duration for any given day is zero hours. Moreover, time tickets you create through the Daily tab that are saved with zero hours of time do not appear on the Weekly tab.

Modifying Time Tickets and Time Sheets

Once you've entered a time ticket or time sheet, you can modify it. Modifying time tickets and time sheets is easy. From the Daily tab of the Time Tickets window, click Edit Records. The standard Edit Records window appears (not shown). Select the record you want to edit by double-clicking it or highlighting the record and clicking OK. Peachtree Complete Accounting displays the record in the Daily tab.

T I P : If you're working with weekly time sheets, a fast way of selecting a specific time ticket is to highlight a single duration on the Weekly tab, then switch to the Daily tab. The time ticket for the corresponding entry in the Weekly tab will be displayed in the Daily tab.

Once you have displayed the record in the Daily tab, you can change any of the information. When you are satisfied with your entries, click Save to save the record and update the totals. When you save the time ticket, Peachtree Complete Accounting assigns a new time ticket number. (If the ticket has already been used in Sales/Invoicing, you can't edit the time ticket because it has already been applied to an invoice.)

Deleting Time Tickets

You can delete a time ticket by selecting the time ticket record as you did when modifying a time ticket and then clicking Delete at the top of the window. Peachtree Complete Accounting asks you if you're sure you want to delete this time ticket. Click Yes to delete the time ticket.

To delete a time ticket that has been used in Sales/Invoicing, delete the corresponding invoice in Accounts Receivable, and then recreate it without using the information on the time ticket that you want to delete. Deleting the invoice will remove the "Has been used in Sales/Invoicing" flag from the corresponding time tickets. You can then use these time tickets in another invoice, or you can modify or delete them. If you want to delete time tickets that have already been used in Sales/Invoicing, you must purge the time tickets. The purging process is described in Chapter 13.

Expense Tickets

Where time tickets record the time necessary to perform activities, expense tickets record how company resources are used. Typical expensed items include:

- Photocopies
- Long distance calls
- Other office supplies
- Mileage
- Filing and recording fees
- Postage
- Faxes
- Charges for online services
- Floppy disks, toner cartridges, and other computer supplies

In Chapter 5, you saw how to enter reimbursable expenses. You can use reimbursable expenses to enter information for billing the customer for expensed items. However, using expense tickets will provide you with a much greater level of detail for the information entered, as well as a wider variety of reports showing what expenses have been entered and how. Furthermore, you can only use reimbursable expenses with jobs; you can use expense tickets on their own without assigning expenses to a specific job.

Time tickets are useful to many different types of businesses. Temporary employment agencies use time tickets to make payroll entries for each temporary employee's hours with a particular client or multiple clients. Similarly, other businesses that track hours worked or billable hours—such as law firms, architectural firms, consultancies, and accounting companies—can benefit from using time tickets.

Using time tickets can make your payroll more accurate and easier to generate (by using time ticket entries rather than hourly wage entries in the Payroll windows). An additional advantage of using time tickets is that you can also use them to generate bills to clients for reimbursable time expenses, simply by making the appropriate entries for reimbursable expenses (as described in Chapter 5).

Entering Expense Tickets

To enter an expense ticket, select the Time/Expense option from the Tasks menu, then select Expense Tickets from the submenu. The Expense Tickets window appears, as shown in Figure 10-5 with a sample expense ticket already entered.

To enter information on an expense ticket, fill in the fields as follows:

Employee/Vendor Select Employee or Vendor in this field to specify whether this is an employee or vendor expense ticket.

Employee/Vendor ID Enter the employee ID or vendor ID (depending on what you've selected in the preceding field). Right-click in this field to display the standard drop-down list of employees or vendors. When you enter an ID in this field, the employee's or vendor's name appears to the right of this field.

Ticket Number This display-only field shows the ticket number. Peachtree Complete Accounting for Windows automatically assigns the ticket number starting at 1. If you are also using time tickets (discussed earlier in this chapter), the number you see here will be the next number in sequence after the last time ticket or expense ticket.

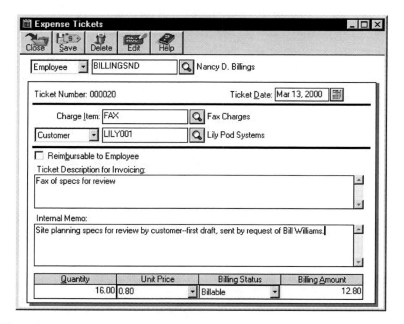

FIGURE 10-5 Expense Tickets window

Ticket Date   The default date is the current system date. You can enter a date for the two fiscal years currently open as well as for the preceding fiscal year. This feature lets you enter hours generated in the previous fiscal year that are going to be billed to a client this fiscal year.

Charge Item   Enter a charge item in this field or right-click to select from the list of charge items. Charge items identify what task the time was spent on. If a charge item does not appear in the list, click New Records at the bottom of the list to display the Maintain Inventory Items window so you can enter a new item. Be sure to use an Item Class of Charge Item. For more information on entering new inventory items, see Chapter 8.

Customer/Job/Administrative   Select Customer, Job, or Administrative in this field. Select Customer if you are doing this for a customer and there is no job set up in Job Costing that would contain this charge. Select Job if you are doing this for a job, phase, or cost code that has already been set up in Job Costing. Select Administrative if this activity is purely administrative and is not associated with either a customer or a job.

   If you select Administrative, Peachtree Complete Accounting automatically sets the status in the Billing Status field to Non-Billable.

Customer/Job ID   Enter the customer or job ID in this field (depending on your selection in the preceding field). If you selected Administrative in the preceding field, the Customer/Job ID field does not appear.

Reimbursable to Employee   Check this box to identify this expense as a reimbursable expense. Reimbursable expenses are tracked for reporting purposes only and are listed on the Reimbursable to Employee Expense report.

   If you selected Vendor in the Employee/Vendor field, this field does not appear.

Ticket Description for Invoicing   Enter up to 160 characters of comments in this field. These comments will appear on the invoice created with this time ticket.

Internal Memo   Enter up to 2,000 characters of information about this time ticket. The information in this field is for detailed internal information on the time ticket. This memo does not appear on the invoice or employee paycheck, although you can display this information by clicking Detail in the Apply Time/Reimbursable Expenses window (described in Chapter 5). You can press CTRL-J in this field to insert a line break for a new line.

Quantity   Enter the quantity of the item (if appropriate).

Unit Price   Select the unit price that was previously set up for this activity in the Maintain Inventory Items window to calculate the billing amount.

Although Peachtree Complete Accounting uses the customer's default pricing level to determine which of the charge item's unit prices to use as the default, you can select any of the unit prices in the Unit Price field. You can enter a different amount, which will override the current unit price.

Billing Status   Enter the billing status in this field: Billable, Non-Billable, No Charge, or Hold.

A status of Billable (the default) lets you apply the expense ticket to customer invoices. A status of Non-Billable prevents you from applying the expense ticket to customer invoices. (Non-Billable is the default option if you selected Administrative in the Customer/Job/Administrative field.) If you selected Administrative in the Customer/Job/Administrative field, you can change the billing status from Non-Billable to Billable, but you will not be able to apply the expense ticket to any customer invoice because you cannot associate the expense ticket with a customer or job.

A status of Hold prevents you from applying the expense ticket to customer invoices until you change the expense ticket status to Billable. A status of No Charge zeros out the Billing Amount field regardless of entries in the Billing Type or Billing Rate field. You can apply No Charge expense tickets to customer invoices.

Billing Amount   Peachtree Complete Accounting calculates this field as the product of the quantity times the unit price. You can enter a different amount in this field to override the calculation, but Peachtree Complete Accounting will adjust the Unit Price field appropriately.

When you are satisfied with your entries, click Save.

Modifying Expense Tickets

Once you've entered an expense ticket, you can modify it. Modifying expense tickets is easy. From the Expense Tickets window, click Edit Records. The standard Edit Records window appears (not shown). Select the record you want to edit by double-clicking it or highlighting the record and clicking OK. Peachtree Complete Accounting displays the record in the Expense Tickets window. You can change any of the information. When you are satisfied with your entries, click Save to save the record. When you save the modified expense ticket, Peachtree Complete Accounting assigns a new expense ticket number. (If the ticket has already been used in Sales/Invoicing, you can't edit the expense ticket because it has already been applied to an invoice.)

Deleting Expense Tickets

You can delete an expense ticket by selecting the expense ticket record as you did when modifying an expense ticket and then clicking Delete at the top of the window. Peachtree Complete Accounting asks you if you're sure you want to delete this expense ticket. Click Yes to delete the expense ticket.

To delete an expense ticket that has been used in Sales/Invoicing, delete the corresponding invoice in Accounts Receivable and then recreate it without using the information on the expense ticket you want to delete. Deleting the invoice will remove the "Has been used in Sales/Invoicing" flag from the corresponding expense tickets. You can then use these expense tickets in another invoice, or you can modify or delete them. If you want to delete expense tickets that have already been used in Sales/Invoicing, you must purge the expense tickets. The purging process is described in Chapter 13.

Printing Time & Billing Reports

Peachtree Complete Accounting Time & Billing comes with an extensive array of reports. These reports are described in Table 10-1.

Figures 10-6 through 10-15 show samples of each of these reports.

REPORT	DESCRIPTION
Time Ticket Register	Lists all time tickets
Expense Ticket Register	Lists all expense tickets
Tickets Recorded By	Lists all time tickets sorted by employee or vendor
Reimbursable Employee Expense	Lists expense tickets flagged as reimbursable employee expenses
Employee Time	Shows the time entered on time tickets for each employee and the associated billing status
Payroll Time Sheet	Shows the time entered on time tickets for each employee for a specified payroll period
Aged Tickets	Lists any tickets that have not been billed to customers and associated aging information
Ticket Listing by Customer	Lists tickets and billing amounts for each customer
Tickets Used in Invoicing	Lists tickets billed to a customer
Tickets by Item ID	Lists tickets by item ID

TABLE 10-1   Time & Billing Reports

Big Business, Inc.
Time Ticket Register
For the Period From Apr 1, 2000 to Apr 30, 2000
Filter Criteria includes: Report order is by Ticket Number.

Ticket Number	Ticket Date	Recorded by ID	Item ID	Completed for ID	Billing Status	Billing Amount
000037	4/3/00	LANEJF	TRAINING	GOLDBUG	Billable	260.00
000038	4/4/00	LANEJF	TRAINING	GOLDBUG	Billable	325.00
000039	4/5/00	LANEJF	TRAINING	GOLDBUG	Billable	260.00
000040	4/6/00	LANEJF	TRAINING	GOLDBUG	Billable	455.00
000041	4/7/00	LANEJF	TRAINING	GOLDBUG	Billable	585.00

FIGURE 10-6   Time Ticket Register

Big Business, Inc.
Expense Ticket Register
For the Period From Apr 1, 2000 to Apr 30, 2000
Filter Criteria includes: Report order is by Ticket Number.

Ticket Number	Ticket Date	Recorded by ID	Item ID	Completed for ID	Billing Status	Billing Amount
000042	4/3/00	BILLINGSND	FAX	LILY001	Billable	9.60
000043	4/3/00	ANDERSONKB	POSTAGE		Non-billable	6.40
000044	4/5/00	FRANKLINJL	LUNCH	KRELL	Billable	25.90
000045	4/6/00	JOHNSONPR	FAX	LILY001	No Charge	

FIGURE 10-7   Expense Ticket Register

Big Business, Inc.
Tickets Recorded By
For the Period From Apr 1, 2000 to Apr 30, 2000
Filter Criteria includes: Report order is by Recorded by ID.

Recorded by ID / Recorded by Name	Employee/Vendor	Ticket Number	Ticket Date	Ticket Type	Item ID	Billing Amount
ANDERSONKB / Karen B. Anderson	Employee	000043	4/3/00	Expense	POSTAGE	6.40
BILLINGSND / Nancy D. Billings	Employee	000042	4/3/00	Expense	FAX	9.60
FRANKLINJL / John L. Franklin	Employee	000044	4/5/00	Expense	LUNCH	25.90
JOHNSONPR / Pamela Johnson	Employee	000045	4/6/00	Expense	FAX	
LANEJF / James F. Lane	Employee	000037	4/3/00	Time	TRAINING	260.00
		000038	4/4/00	Time	TRAINING	325.00
		000039	4/5/00	Time	TRAINING	260.00
		000040	4/6/00	Time	TRAINING	455.00
		000041	4/7/00	Time	TRAINING	585.00

FIGURE 10-8   Tickets Recorded By

Big Business, Inc.
Reimbursable Employee Expense
For the Period From Apr 1, 2000 to Apr 30, 2000

Filter Criteria includes: Report order is by Employee ID.

Employee ID Employee Name	AR-Used?	For Customer ID	Item ID Item Description	Billing Amount	Total Billing
ANDERSONKB Karen B. Anderson	No	<No ID Assigned>	POSTAGE POSTAGE STAMPS	6.40	
					6.40
FRANKLINJL John L. Franklin	No	KRELL Krell Office Systems	LUNCH	25.90	
					25.90
					32.30

FIGURE 10-9 Reimbursable Employee Expense

Big Business, Inc.
Employee Time
For the Period From Apr 1, 2000 to Apr 30, 2000

Filter Criteria includes: Report order is by Employee ID. Report is printed in Detailed Format.

Employee ID Employee Name	Billing Status	Unit Duration	Billing Amount
ANDERSONKB Karen B. Anderson	Billable	8.00	600.00
BILLINGSND Nancy D. Billings	Billable	10.00	650.00
	Billable	12.00	780.00
	Billable	8.00	520.00
	Billable	7.00	455.00
	Billable	12.00	780.00
LANEJF James F. Lane	Billable	4.00	260.00
	Billable	8.00	520.00
	Billable	5.00	325.00
	Billable	4.00	260.00
	Billable	7.00	455.00
	Billable	9.00	585.00

FIGURE 10-10 Employee Time

Big Business, Inc.
Payroll Time Sheet
As of Jan 2, 2000

Filter Criteria includes: Report order is by Employee ID.

Employee ID Employee Name Pay Method Frequency	Ticket Number	Ticket Date	PR-Used?	Unit Duration	Total Unit Duration
LANEJF	000010	12/27/99	No	5.00	
James F. Lane	000022	12/27/99	No	5.00	
Hourly - Hours per Pay Period	000006	12/28/99	No	5.00	
Semi-monthly	000011	12/28/99	No	7.00	
	000023	12/28/99	No	6.00	
	000007	12/29/99	No	7.00	
	000012	12/29/99	No	6.00	
	000024	12/29/99	No	4.00	
	000008	12/30/99	No	6.00	
	000013	12/30/99	No	4.00	
	000025	12/30/99	No	5.00	
	000009	12/31/99	No	4.00	
	000014	12/31/99	No	6.00	
	000026	12/31/99	No	7.00	
	000021	1/2/00	No		
					77.00

FIGURE 10-11 Payroll Time Sheet

Big Business, Inc.
Aged Tickets
As of Apr 30, 2000

Filter Criteria includes: Report order is by For Customer ID. Report is printed in Detailed Format.

For Customer ID	Ticket Number	0-30	31-60	61-90	Over 90 days	Billing Amount	Total Billing
PECH001	000006				325.00	325.00	
	000007				455.00	455.00	
	000008				390.00	390.00	
	000009				260.00	260.00	
	000010				325.00	325.00	
	000011				455.00	455.00	
	000012				390.00	390.00	
	000013				260.00	260.00	
	000014				390.00	390.00	
	000015		325.00			325.00	
	000016		455.00			455.00	
	000017		390.00			390.00	
	000018		260.00			260.00	
	000019		390.00			390.00	
	000047	650.00				650.00	
	000048	780.00				780.00	
	000049	520.00				520.00	
	000050	455.00				455.00	
	000051	780.00				780.00	
	000052	600.00				600.00	
		3,785.00	1,820.00		3,250.00		8,855.00

FIGURE 10-12 Aged Tickets

Big Business, Inc.
Ticket Listing by Customer
For the Period From Apr 1, 2000 to Apr 30, 2000
Filter Criteria includes: Report order is by For Customer ID. Report is printed Summarized By: Item ID.

For Customer ID For Customer Description	Item ID	Item Description	Billing Amount
<No ID Assigned>	POSTAGE	POSTAGE STAMPS	13.89
			13.89
KRELL Krell Office Systems	LUNCH		25.90
			25.90
LILY001 Lily Pod Systems	FAX TRAINING	Fax Charges Training	9.60 2,405.00
			2,414.60
PECH001 Peche Nouveau	TRAINING	Training	3,785.00
			3,785.00

FIGURE 10-13 Ticket Listing by Customer

Big Business, Inc.
Tickets Used in Sales Invoicing
For the Period From Apr 1, 2000 to Apr 30, 2000
Filter Criteria includes: Report order is by For Customer ID.

For Customer ID For Customer Description	Invoice Number	Ticket Number	Item ID Item Description	Billing Amount
LILY001 Lily Pod Systems	123489	000041	TRAINING Training	585.00
	123489	000042	FAX Fax Charges	9.60
	123489	000045	FAX Fax Charges	11.92
	123489	000053	TRAINING Training	520.00

FIGURE 10-14 Tickets Used in Sales Invoicing

Big Business, Inc.
Tickets by Item ID
For the Period From Apr 1, 2000 to Apr 30, 2000
Filter Criteria includes: Report order is by Item ID. Report is printed in Detailed Format.

Item ID Item Description	Ticket Number Ticket Date	Recorded by ID	Unit Duration	Billing Amount	Total Billing
FAX Fax Charges	000042 4/3/00	BILLINGSND		9.60	
	000055 4/3/00	ANDERSONKB		9.60	
	000045 4/6/00	JOHNSONPR		11.92	
					31.12
LUNCH	000044 4/5/00	FRANKLINJL		25.90	
					25.90
POSTAGE POSTAGE STAMPS	000043 4/3/00	ANDERSONKB		13.89	
					13.89

FIGURE 10-15 Tickets by Item ID

Summary

Not everyone who uses Peachtree Complete Accounting will want to use the Time & Billing features, but you can always incorporate them after your basic accounting practice is in place. In this chapter, you've seen how to enter, modify, and delete time and expense tickets and how to print Time & Billing reports. In the next chapter, you'll see how to enter assets, set depreciation schedules, and print fixed asset reports.

Fixed Asset Management

B A S I C S

- How to set up Peachtree Fixed Assets
- How to enter fixed assets
- How to dispose of fixed assets
- How to print fixed asset reports

B E Y O N D

- How to calculate depreciation
- How to post depreciation

In this chapter, you'll learn about the basics of fixed assets management, how to enter fixed asset records, how to dispose of fixed assets, how to calculate and post depreciation, and how to print fixed asset management reports.

In Chapter 10 you saw how to set up time and billing defaults, enter and maintain time and billing information, and print time and billing reports. In this chapter, you will learn how to enter assets, set depreciation schedules, and print fixed asset reports.

Why Should You Use Peachtree Fixed Assets?

You should use Peachtree Fixed Assets to track your fixed assets. *Fixed assets* are any asset with a useful life of more than one year: furniture, computers, software, fixtures, machinery, equipment, buildings, and vehicles. Fixed assets can also be intangibles, such as patents and copyrights. All of these can either be depreciated over their useful life (a period defined by the IRS) or expensed (per Section 179 of the tax code) in whole or in part up to the limits set by the IRS.

 C A U T I O N : Fixed assets management and depreciation can be confusing. In addition, regulations on fixed assets and the way in which the regulations can be applied change fairly frequently. If you are not familiar with setting up and maintaining fixed assets and depreciation schedules, you should discuss this with your CPA. Altering the depreciation tables incorrectly or misclassifying assets can result in substantial last-minute expenses for CPA time.

Setting Up Peachtree Fixed Assets for Your Company

Because Peachtree Fixed Assets is a separate application from Peachtree Complete Accounting for Windows, you need to start it separately. To start the application, select Start on the Windows 98 taskbar, then select Programs. Then from the Peachtree Complete Accounting group folder, select the Peachtree Fixed Assets icon. Alternatively, you can double-click on the program icon.

When you start the application, you will see the standard startup window. From the File menu select Open Company. Select the company you wish to open and click OK.

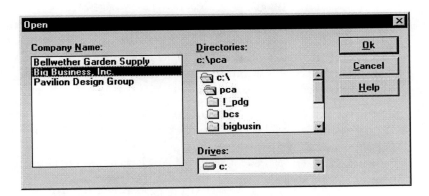

The first time you open a company in Peachtree Fixed Assets, you need to enter some basic information. The Maintain Company Calendar window is displayed, as shown in Figure 11-1.

The Maintain Company Calendar window lets you identify the last month of your fiscal year, the conversion date, and short tax years.

Month Fiscal Year Ends Enter the month the fiscal year ends. The default month is December.

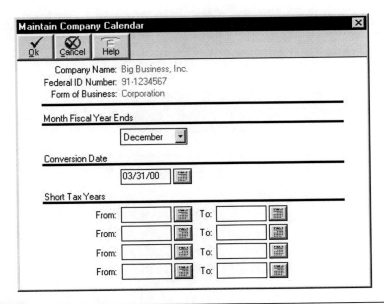

FIGURE 11-1 Maintain Company Calendar window

Conversion Date   Enter the date you switch your fixed asset management over to Peachtree Fixed Assets. You should know the accumulated depreciation for all company assets on this date. The application uses this date in the As Of (Date) field in the Asset Maintenance window and also uses this date to calculate the year-to-date and life-to-date depreciation values.

Short Tax Years   Enter the short tax year dates. You need to enter short tax year information if you have a tax year of less than 12 months. Short tax years most frequently occur in a company's first or last year of operation, or if your company changes its fiscal year. Peachtree Fixed Assets matches the depreciation period to the appropriate short tax year to determine the fiscal year-end. If you are not sure if you need to use short tax years, check with your accountant.

When you are satisfied with your entries, click OK. Peachtree Fixed Assets saves the information. You now need to select which books to use. Books are depreciation tables that contain information about how to depreciate assets.

Select Company Books from the Maintain menu. The Maintain Company Books window appears (shown in Figure 11-2).

Select the books you want to use for your assets. Selecting the books you need for your business is complex. Peachtree Fixed Assets supplies commonly accepted default values for various fields in the Asset Maintenance window for the books you have selected, but changes made in one book may not be automatically reflected in the other books. Be sure to check with your accountant on how to select books.

When you are satisfied with your entries, click OK.

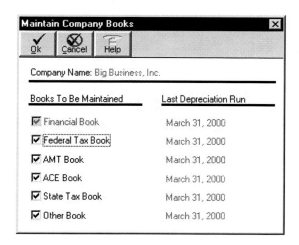

FIGURE 11-2   Maintain Company Books window

Setting Up and Maintaining Fixed Asset Records

You are now ready to start entering information for specific fixed assets. Entering fixed assets may require a substantial amount of information gathering, including taking physical inventory before you start. If you have many fixed assets, take time to prepare before you begin.

Entering Fixed Asset Records

Once you have entered the appropriate information in the Maintain Company Calendar and Maintain Company Books windows, you are ready to enter assets.

To enter a fixed asset record, select Assets from the Maintain menu. The Asset Maintenance – Financial Book window appears (shown in Figure 11-3).

The Asset Maintenance window is divided into three portions. The top portion is information about the asset across all the depreciation books. The middle portion lets you select a different book to enter information about the asset for that book. The bottom portion of the window contains information for

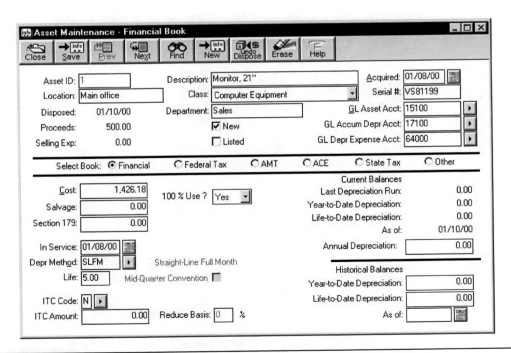

FIGURE 11-3   Asset Maintenance – Financial Book window

the asset for that specific book. (Although this is probably going to be the same for all the books for most assets, there may be differences.)

Table 11-1 shows you a list of the buttons in the Asset Maintenance window and what they're used for.

To enter a fixed asset, fill in the fields in the Asset Maintenance window as follows:

Asset ID   Enter an asset ID number between 1 and 999999999 in this field. Peachtree Fixed Assets supplies the next number in sequence as the default entry for this field. (Once you enter an asset ID, you cannot modify it. You must delete the asset entry and re-enter it with the new asset ID.)

BUTTON	NAME	DESCRIPTION
Close	Close	Closes the window and the current fixed asset without saving the information
Save	Save	Saves (posts) the information in the fields
Prev	Prev	Displays the previous fixed asset record
Next	Next	Displays the next fixed asset record
Find	Find	Finds a specific fixed asset
New	New	Clears the window to enter a new fixed asset
Dispose	Dispose	Displays the Dispose of Asset window to enter disposal information for an asset
Erase	Erase	Erases the current transaction
Help	Help	Gets help on the Asset Maintenance window

TABLE 11-1   Toolbar Buttons in the Asset Maintenance window

If you don't have a lot of assets, using the default asset ID is probably sufficient. However, if you have a lot of assets or anticipate adding a lot of assets in the next 6-12 months, you may want to set up a coding system for your asset IDs to make browsing and reporting easier. When you browse for assets (described later in this chapter) or print asset reports, Peachtree Fixed Assets sorts the information by asset ID. If you plan your asset IDs so that assets are sorted into logical groups, you will save yourself time in the future.

Creating a plan for asset IDs is similar to creating account ID masks (discussed in Chapter 4). Some different ways in which you could create groups of asset IDs include the following:

- Create blocks of asset IDs for types of assets (000xxxxxx for buildings and real estate, 001xxxxxx for cars, trucks, and related equipment, and so on)
- Enter the four-digit year of the acquisition followed by the asset number (199900001, 199900002, 199900003)
- Enter a division number, or both division and department numbers, followed by the asset number (for example, for division 41, department 6, the first asset ID would be 041060001)

Depending on the number of assets you have, you may want to combine the ID coding ideas above. However, since you can also sort your assets by acquisition date and the department to which the assets are assigned, you will probably not need a complex asset ID system.

Description   Enter up to 30 characters to describe the asset.

Acquired   Enter the date the asset was acquired. Peachtree Fixed Assets fills in the current date as the default and uses the date you enter here to fill in the In Service field (located farther along in this window).

Location   Enter up to 24 characters specifying the location for the asset.

Class   Select from one of the classes of fixed asset in this field. Peachtree Fixed Assets lists 39 different property types, shown in Table 11-2.

Selecting the right class of asset is important, because Peachtree Fixed Assets uses the class to determine the asset's depreciation method and life. If none of the classes seem to fit the asset you are entering, use the Other Asset class.

Peachtree Fixed Assets uses the class you select to determine default values for the Listed, Life, and Depreciation Method fields. It also sets up defaults for the GL Asset, GL Accumulated Depreciation, and GL Depreciation Expense accounts, if you have already set up accounts for this class. Peachtree Fixed Assets uses the information you enter for the General Ledger accounts as the

Agricultural Structure	Land	Real Property – Low Income Housing
Airplane – Commercial	Land Improvement	Real Property – Nonresidential
Airplane – Noncommercial	Leasehold Improvement	Real Property – Residential Rental
Amortized Expense	Mach & Equip – Construction	Taxi
Automobile	Mach & Equip – Farm	Telephone Equipment
Bus	Mach & Equip – Manufacturing	Tools, Special Manufacturing
Calculator/Copier	Mach & Equip – Trades & Services	Tractor Unit
Computer Equipment	Nondepreciable	Trailer/Trailer – Mounted Container
Computer Software	Office Equipment	Tree – Fruit/Nuts
Farm Building	Other Asset	Truck – Heavy
Furniture & Fixtures	Other Personal Property	Truck – Light
Intangible Asset, Other	Qualified Technological Equipment	Typewriter
Intangible Asset, Section 197	Railroad Grading and Tunnel Bores	Water Transportation

TABLE 11-2   Property types in the Class field

default the next time you select that class. Like all default information, you can change this as necessary for any fixed asset.

Serial #   Enter a serial number for the asset of up to 15 characters.

Disposed   This display-only field shows the date an asset was disposed of, traded, or sold.

Department   Enter, at your option, a department of up to 15 characters. This is the department that owns the asset. You can sort by the Department field when browsing and on some Fixed Asset reports. Even if you don't have departments, you can use this field as an optional sorting field.

GL Asset Acct   Enter the General Ledger asset account for this asset. This General Ledger account will vary depending on the asset class you've selected. For example, for a car, you'd probably use the Automobiles account, whereas for desks and chairs, you'd probably use the Furniture and Fixtures account. (The sample chart of accounts included with Peachtree Complete Accounting for Windows has the General Ledger asset accounts in the 14700 to 16900 range.)

You cannot enter a new account directly from this field as you did with other General Ledger account fields in Peachtree Complete Accounting for Windows. To enter a new General Ledger account, you must start the Peachtree Complete Accounting program and enter the account from there. Peachtree Complete Accounting posts to the GL Asset account (as well as the GL Accum Depr and GL Depr Expense accounts you enter later) when you calculate depreciation.

When you enter the first asset for a class of assets, Peachtree Fixed Assets uses the General Ledger accounts you previously entered to establish the default for the subsequent entries for that class. For the Depreciation Method, Life, Listed, and Mid-Quarter Convention fields, Peachtree Complete Accounting uses standard values based on the item class.

Proceeds　This display-only field shows the proceeds from the disposal of an asset.

New　Check this box to show that the asset was purchased new rather than used. Peachtree Fixed Assets checks this field as the default.

GL Accum Depr Acct　Enter the General Ledger accumulated depreciation account for this asset. This General Ledger accumulated depreciation account will vary depending on the asset class you've selected. For example, for a car, you'd probably use the Accumulated Depreciation – Automobiles account, and so on. (The sample chart of accounts included with Peachtree Complete Accounting for Windows has the accumulated depreciation accounts in the 17000 to 17600 range.) Peachtree Fixed Assets uses this accumulated depreciation account when you post accumulated depreciation to the General Ledger in Peachtree Complete Accounting for Windows.

You cannot enter a new account directly from this field as you did with other General Ledger account fields in Peachtree Complete Accounting for Windows. To enter a new General Ledger account, you must start the Peachtree Complete Accounting program and enter the account from there.

Selling Exp　This display-only field shows the cost of disposing of an asset.

Listed　Check this box to show that the asset is considered as listed property. (Listed property is property that is not used fully for business, such as a passenger automobile.) Peachtree Fixed Assets leaves this box unchecked as the default except when you've selected the Automobile or Truck – Light asset class.

If you check this box, Peachtree Fixed Assets will print the asset in Section 5 of the Form 4562 Worksheet. See IRS Publication 946 for more information on listed property.

GL Depr Expense Acct   Enter the General Ledger depreciation expense account for this asset. (The sample chart of accounts included with Peachtree Complete Accounting for Windows has the depreciation expense accounts in the 64000 range.) Peachtree Fixed Assets uses this depreciation expense account when you post depreciation expenses to the General Ledger in Peachtree Complete Accounting for Windows.

You cannot enter a new account directly from this field as you did with other General Ledger account fields in Peachtree Complete Accounting for Windows. You have to enter the new account in Peachtree Complete Accounting beforehand (the same rules apply from the previous note).

Select Book   When you first set up an asset, the information will be saved in the Financial book and in any other books you have specified in the Maintain Company Books window (shown earlier in Figure 11-2). Once you have saved this information, you can then make any adjustments for these books by selecting the book in this field. If a book is not available for this asset, the radio button will be grayed out. By default, the first book you enter information for is the Financial book. You must set up this book before you can enter information for the other five books.

Table 11-3 shows the six books and what they're used for.

You may not have access to all six books. If any of the above six books are grayed and not available in the Maintain Assets window, make sure the book has been selected in the Maintain Company Books window. When access is turned off, Fixed Assets still maintains the books, but it doesn't allow changes to default information.

BOOK	WHAT IT'S USED FOR
Financial	Financial statements
Federal Tax	Depreciation calculation
AMT	Alternative Minimum Tax accelerated depreciation
ACE	Adjusted Current Earnings tax depreciation
State Tax	State depreciation calculation (if applicable)
Other	Personal or real property using SLFM depreciation

TABLE 11-3   Books and How They're Used

To select a different book (after you have set up the first book for the asset), click the radio button. The depreciation method may change depending on the book you've selected.

You can now fill in or change any of the book information for this book in the lower portion of the Asset Maintenance window.

Cost   Enter the dollar value of the asset when you first acquired it. Peachtree Fixed Assets uses this amount to determine the asset's depreciable basis. The depreciable basis is usually determined as follows:

> Asset cost
> – Salvage value
> – Section 179 expense
> – Investment tax credit (ITC) reduction
> --
> = Adjusted cost
>   × Business use %
> --
> =   Asset's depreciable basis

N O T E : The depreciable basis can vary based on the depreciation method you use for the asset.

You can have separate costs for an asset in each book (although Peachtree Fixed Assets warns you whenever you enter a cost different from another book). If you have not checked the AMT, ACE, and/or State Tax books in the Maintain Company Books window (shown earlier in Figure 11-2), the application sets the asset costs for these books to be equal to the asset costs in the Federal Tax book. Similarly, if the Federal Tax and Other books are not checked, the application sets the asset costs for these books to be equal to the asset costs in the Financial book.

For additional information, check the Help files accompanying the Peachtree Fixed Assets program.

Salvage   Enter the salvage value of the asset in this field. The salvage value is the estimated worth of the asset at the end of its useful life. Straight-line depreciation uses the salvage value for determining the asset's depreciable basis, as do several other depreciation methods. ACRS, MACRS, and ADS depreciation methods ignore salvage value for the purposes of calculating depreciation.

Section 179   Enter the Section 179 deduction in this field. Section 179 of the tax code, as described in IRS Publication 946, lets you expense some or all of the cost of some qualified property instead of treating it as a capital expense.

This lets you deduct some or all of the cost of an asset in a single year instead of taking deductions for depreciation over the asset's recovery period.

The maximum allowable annual deduction for Section 179 expense for property placed in service is $17,500. A taxpayer who places qualified zone property in an enterprise zone may be eligible for an additional deduction of $20,000. You can spread the deduction among several qualifying items. The deduction is limited to the lesser of the cost of the personal property or your income generated in the trade or business. If the total amount invested in Section 179 property exceeds $200,000, the deduction calculation is limited. For every dollar invested above $200,000, the Section 179 deduction is reduced by the same amount and therefore no Section 179 deduction is allowed once the investment exceeds $217,500.

 N O T E : Check with your CPA for the current maximum allowable annual deduction for Section 179 expense.

100% Use?   Select No in this field if this asset is not used at all times for business. The Business Use Percentage window (shown in Figure 11-4) appears.

In the first Effective Dates field, enter the first day of the fiscal year, such as 1/1/00 (you can also right-click in the field to bring up the standard Peachtree calendar). In the corresponding Percent field, enter the percentage of time this asset is used for business. For example, if the asset is used 75 percent for business use and 25 percent for personal use, enter 75% in the Percent field. If the percentage the asset is used for business use changes at a later date, you can enter a new effective date and a new percentage.

FIGURE 11-4   Business Use Percentage window

When you are satisfied with your entries in this field, click OK.

In Service   Enter the date the asset was placed in service. Peachtree Fixed Assets puts the date from the Acquired field (earlier in this window) in the In Service field as a default. Although the date from the In Service field is usually the same as the Acquired field, you might buy an asset at the end of one fiscal year and put it into service at the beginning of the next year. The IRS considers property as being "in service" in the tax year the asset is first ready and available for specified business use. After you enter the asset information, if you change the in-service date, the application makes sure the depreciation method is still valid with respect to the new in-service date and issues a warning message if it isn't.

Depr Method   Select a depreciation method for the asset. Peachtree Fixed Assets enters a default depreciation method based on the asset's class and the date you acquired it. You can use the default method or click the arrow to the right of the field to display the Select Depreciation Method window (shown in Figure 11-5).

The list of the depreciation methods shown in this window contains all the depreciation methods for the selected book. Select a depreciation method and click OK.

If you select a declining balance depreciation method from this window, Peachtree Fixed Assets displays the Declining Balance Percentage window, shown in Figure 11-6.

Peachtree Fixed Assets supplies a default percentage to use for the current declining balance percentage. You can accept the default or enter a new percentage. When you are satisfied with your entry, click OK.

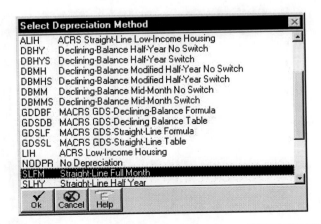

FIGURE 11-5   Select Depreciation Method window

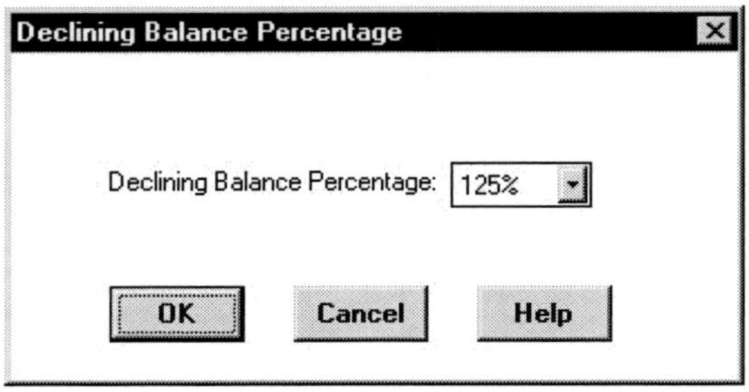

Declining Balance Percentage

Declining Balance Percentage: 125%

OK   Cancel   Help

FIGURE 11-6 Declining Balance Percentage window

Life   Enter the years of life for the asset in this required field. An asset can have a life of up to 99.99 years. Peachtree Fixed Assets enters a default life for the asset based on the asset's class and the date the asset was placed in service.

If you change the entry for this field, be sure that the asset life you are specifying is in compliance with the IRS and GAAP guidelines. (See IRS Publication 946 or your CPA for more information.)

If you have not checked the AMT, ACE, and/or State Tax books in the Maintain Company Books window (shown earlier in Figure 11-2), Peachtree Fixed Assets sets the asset life for these books to be equal to the asset life in the Federal Tax book. If the Federal Tax book is not checked, the application sets the asset life for this book to be equal to the default asset life for this class of asset. If the Other book is not checked, the application sets the asset life for this book to be equal to the asset life in the Financial book.

Mid-Quarter Convention   Check this box if you want to calculate depreciation for this asset using the mid-quarter convention. You can check or uncheck this box at any time for an asset. Check with your accountant or the IRS to make sure you are using the mid-quarter convention in compliance with IRS regulations for the asset.

ITC Code   Enter a one-character letter to identify the Investment Tax Credit (ITC) the asset qualifies for (the default is "N," for No Investment Tax Credit). Click the arrow to the right of the field to display the Select I.T.C. Code window (shown in Figure 11-7).

Select the appropriate ITC code from the list and click OK.

ITC Amount   Enter the dollar amount of the ITC taken on this asset in this field.

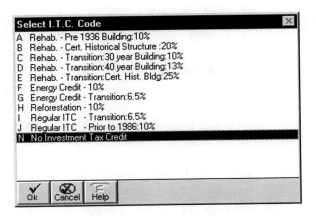

FIGURE 11-7 Select I.T.C. Code window

N O T E : Assets placed in service after December 31, 1985, are no longer eligible for most forms of investment tax credit. See IRS Form 3468 instructions or talk to your CPA for more information on investment tax credits.

Reduce Basis Enter the Investment Tax Credit Basis Reduction percentage (from 0 to 999) in this field. For certain types of qualified ITC property, the asset's basis must be reduced by the percentage you enter in this field, multiplied by the amount entered in the ITC Amount field. Peachtree Fixed Assets enters a default percentage based on the ITC code you entered in the ITC Code field.

Last Depreciation Run (Current Balances) This display-only field shows the depreciation amount, as calculated by Peachtree Fixed Assets, the last time you ran depreciation (based on the as-of date).

Year-to-Date Depreciation (Current Balances) This display-only field shows the depreciation amount for the current year, as calculated by Peachtree Fixed Assets, the last time you ran depreciation for the period (based on the as-of date).

Life-to-Date Depreciation (Current Balances) This display-only field shows the depreciation amount, as calculated by Peachtree Fixed Assets, the last time you ran depreciation for the life of the asset (based on the as-of date).

As of (Current Balances) This display-only field shows the date you last calculated the depreciation.

Annual Depreciation   Enter the annual depreciation amount in this field only if you specified a depreciation method of USER in the Depr Method field. This field is a display-only field for all other depreciation methods, showing the annual depreciation amount for the year of the last depreciation run.

Year-to-Date Depreciation (Historical Balances)   Enter the amount of the year-to-date depreciation (as of the conversion date) for an asset that has been fully or partially depreciated using a different depreciation method or another fixed assets management package. Peachtree Fixed Assets uses the amounts you enter in this field and in the following Life-to-Date Depreciation field to determine if depreciation needs to be adjusted in the first calculation. Peachtree Fixed Assets recalculates the depreciation and compares them to the amounts in these two fields and then adjusts the depreciation amounts as necessary.

The Year-to-Date Depreciation and the Life-to-Date Depreciation fields are used to store historical balances, as of the conversion date. Enter the conversion date in the As Of field if you are converting your fixed asset management to Peachtree Fixed Assets from another program, or if you are changing the method you use to calculate depreciation for this asset and you don't want to recalculate prior depreciation history.

If you are setting up Peachtree Fixed Assets from the beginning of the current tax year, enter an amount of zero dollars in the Year-to-Date Depreciation field and the amount of the asset's accumulated depreciation, as of the end of the previous tax year, in the Life-to-Date Depreciation field. You would then enter the ending date for the tax year in the As Of field. You would also enter an amount of zero dollars in the Year-to-Date Depreciation field if the asset was placed in service after the ending date of the last period for which you calculated depreciation using your previous fixed asset management software.

Life-to-Date Depreciation (Historical Balances)   Enter the accumulated depreciation (as of the conversion date) for an asset that has been fully or partially depreciated using a different depreciation method or another fixed assets management package. Enter an amount of zero dollars in the Life-to-Date Depreciation field if the asset was placed in service after the ending date of the last period for which you calculated depreciation using your previous fixed asset management software. For more information, see the comments in the preceding section describing the Year-to-Date Depreciation field.

As of (Historical Balances)   Enter the conversion date for an asset that has been fully or partially depreciated using a different depreciation method or another fixed assets management package. (This is the date the figures for year-to-date and life-to-date depreciation represent.) Peachtree Fixed Assets uses the Conversion Date you entered in the Maintain Company Calendar window (shown earlier in Figure 11-1) as the default date in this field. You would leave this field blank if the asset was placed in service after the ending date of the last period for which you calculated depreciation using your previous fixed asset management software. For more information, see the comments in the earlier section describing the Year-to-Date Depreciation field.

When you are satisfied with your entries, click Save to save the fixed asset information.

Modifying Fixed Assets Records

You can modify fixed asset records by displaying them in the Asset Maintenance window and changing the information. To display a record to edit, you first browse for fixed asset records. Browsing for fixed asset records is very similar to using the Edit windows shown in earlier chapters. You can sort assets in the browse window by any of the following criteria:

- Acquired Date
- Asset ID
- Asset Class
- Department
- GL Asset Account
- GL Accumulated Depreciation Account
- GL Expense Account
- Location

To browse assets, select the method to sort by from the Browse menu. The Asset Browse window appears, as shown in Figure 11-8. (Even if you selected one sort for the Browse menu, you can display the assets in a different order by selecting a different option in the Sort By field at the top of the window.)

Select an asset by highlighting the asset and clicking Detail, or simply by double-clicking the detail line. Peachtree Fixed Assets displays the asset information in the Asset Maintenance window. You can then change any of the fixed asset information except for the asset ID itself. If you want to change the asset ID, you will have to delete the fixed asset record and then re-enter the information under the new asset ID.

	Asset ID	Description	Status	Acquired	Class	GL Asset Acct	GL Accum Acct	GL Expense Acc
1	14	Telephone Switch	Active	12/13/99	Telephone Equipment	15100	17100	64000
2	15	Supply Cabinet	Active	12/13/99	Furniture & Fixtures	15100	17100	64000
3	2	Computer	Active	12/15/99	Computer Equipment	15100	17100	64000
4	3	Computer	Active	12/15/99	Computer Equipment	15100	17100	64000
5	4	Computer	Active	12/15/99	Computer Equipment	15100	17100	64000
6	5	Computer	Active	12/15/99	Computer Equipment	15100	17100	64000
7	6	Monitor, 21"	Active	12/15/99	Computer Equipment	15100	17100	64000
8	7	Monitor, 21"	Active	12/15/99	Computer Equipment	15100	17100	64000
9	8	Monitor, 21"	Active	12/15/99	Computer Equipment	15100	17100	64000
10	9	Modular desks (4)	Active	12/15/99	Furniture & Fixtures	15100	17100	64000
11	10	Office Chairs (4)	Active	12/15/99	Furniture & Fixtures	15100	17100	64000
12	11	LaserJet 2100M	Active	12/15/99	Computer Equipment	15100	17100	64000
13	12	Fax Machine	Active	12/15/99	Computer Equipment	15100	17100	64000
14	13	Filing Cabinets (4)	Active	12/20/99	Furniture & Fixtures	15100	17100	64000
15	1	Monitor, 21"	Active	01/08/00	Computer Equipment	15100	17100	64000

FIGURE 11-8   Asset Browse window

 CAUTION: Changing the Class field in the top portion of the Asset Maintenance window or any of the fields in the bottom portion of the Asset Maintenance window may affect the way Peachtree Fixed Assets calculates depreciation for the asset.

Once you have displayed a record in the Asset Maintenance window, you can use the Prev and Next buttons at the top of the Asset Maintenance window to scroll through fixed asset records.

If you're entering a lot of similar assets at once, you can use the Browse window to speed up the process. Start by entering the first asset in the Asset Maintenance window and then clicking Save. Next, click New in the Asset Maintenance window to clear the fields. Open the Browse window and double-click on the asset listing. Peachtree Fixed Assets will issue a warning saying that you have modified the current record but not saved it. Click No on the warning. The information for the selected asset is displayed in the fields of the Asset Maintenance window. You can change the asset ID, the date the asset was acquired, and any other information, then save the new asset record. This is particularly helpful if you are entering a list of similar assets acquired on the same date.

Deleting Fixed Asset Records

You can delete a fixed asset record by selecting the record and displaying it in the Asset Maintenance window, then clicking the Erase button at the top of the window. Peachtree Fixed Assets asks you if you're sure you want to delete this record. Click Yes to confirm.

Although you can delete a fixed asset record at any time, it's usually preferable to dispose of an asset so that a record of the asset remains in Peachtree Fixed Assets. You should delete only incorrect fixed asset records that have not yet had depreciation calculated. You should also be sure that the total of your asset accounts on your company's balance sheet is always equal to the totals on the fixed assets Asset List report.

Disposing of Fixed Assets

Disposing of a fixed asset tells Peachtree Fixed Assets that you have sold or otherwise retired the fixed asset from service. To dispose of a fixed asset, you should follow these steps:

1. Create the necessary General Journal entries in Peachtree Complete Accounting.
2. Remove the fixed asset from Peachtree Fixed Assets (through the Asset Maintenance window).
3. Remove the fixed asset's accumulated depreciation from all the books in Peachtree Complete Accounting.

Creating the General Journal Entries

Because Peachtree Fixed Assets does not create General Ledger entries, you need to provide the financial information related to the disposal of a fixed asset in Peachtree Complete Accounting for Windows yourself.

First, if you sold the asset, enter the cash you received in the Receipts window (select Receipts from the Tasks menu in Peachtree Complete Accounting for Windows as described in Chapter 5). As you debit the cash account for the money you received, you need to credit the Gain/Loss on Sale of Assets account (standard in the Peachtree Complete Accounting charts of accounts). The Gain/Loss on Sale of Assets account is an expense account you use for any moneys you receive for selling fixed assets, as well as for any expenses associated with the sale, such as advertising, shipping, or transfer of licenses associated with a fixed asset. (If you are disposing of a number of fixed assets regularly, you may want to split the

Gain/Loss on Sale of Assets account into separate income and expense accounts: Gain on Sale of Assets and Loss on Sale of Assets.)

However you track the income and expenses associated with disposing of fixed assets, you should be consistent in your procedures so you can reconcile your General Ledger entries in Peachtree Complete Accounting for Windows with the disposition of fixed assets information in Peachtree Fixed Assets.

Disposing of the Fixed Asset

To dispose of a fixed asset in Peachtree Fixed Assets, display the fixed asset's record in the Asset Maintenance window and then click Dispose at the top of the window. The Dispose of Asset window appears (shown in Figure 11-9).

Fill in the fields as follows:

Date of Disposal   Enter the date you are disposing of the asset.

Proceeds   Enter the cash you received (if any) as a result of the disposition of the fixed asset.

Selling Expense   Enter the selling expense (if any) incurred in the disposition of the fixed asset.

Reason   Enter the reason you are disposing of the fixed asset.

Partial Disposal   Check this box if this is a partial rather than a full disposal of the fixed asset. Partial disposal usually happens if you have purchased a

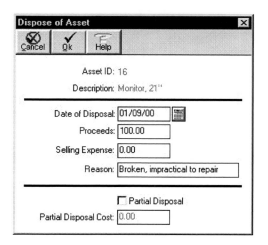

FIGURE 11-9   Dispose of Asset window

group of assets (such as computers or cars) and you are disposing of a few of the assets within the group, but not the entire group of fixed assets.

Partial Disposal Cost   Enter the cost basis for the partial disposal of this asset, which will generally be the percentage of the original cost for the specific fixed assets in the group you are disposing. For example, if you bought eight computers as a group for $15,000 and you are disposing of three of them, the partial disposal cost would be 3/8ths of $15,000, or $5,625.

When you are satisfied with your entries, click OK. To finish disposing of the fixed asset in Peachtree Fixed Assets, click Save. The Dispose button changes to an Undo Dispose button (which is the way you can tell the fixed asset has been disposed of). You can undo an asset you've disposed of by displaying the fixed asset's record in the Asset Maintenance window and clicking Undo Disposal. Peachtree Fixed Assets asks if you want to undo the disposal. Click Yes to reactivate the fixed asset's record.

Removing the Accumulated Depreciation

The final step in disposing of the fixed asset is to print the Asset Disposition report in Peachtree Fixed Assets. (Printing reports in Peachtree Fixed Assets is discussed later in this chapter.) Print the report twice, sorted first by the GL Asset account and then by the GL Accum Depreciation account.

Using these reports, you create entries in the Peachtree Complete Accounting for Windows General Journal that credit the fixed asset account, debit the accumulated depreciation account, and make any final adjustments to the Gain/Loss on Sale of Assets account for the Net Book Value of the fixed asset you have disposed. These final entries remove the fixed asset's cost from your books and the life-to-date depreciation.

You should make an entry in Peachtree Fixed Assets as soon as you have disposed of a fixed asset. If you don't keep your fixed asset records current and record disposals, you may calculate depreciation for fixed assets you have already disposed of, which will require you to make adjustments to the accumulated depreciation and depreciation expense in Peachtree Complete Accounting for Windows.

If you calculated depreciation for an asset you disposed of in the same business year, display the fixed asset's record in the Asset Maintenance window and make a note of the Year-to-Date Depreciation and Life-to-Date Depreciation amounts, then go through the procedure for disposing of a fixed asset in Peachtree Fixed Assets. Now subtract the new Year-to-Date Depreciation amount in the Asset Maintenance window from the Year-to-Date Depreciation amount you wrote down a moment ago. Create a General Journal entry in

Peachtree Complete Accounting for Windows that debits the appropriate General Ledger Accumulated Depreciation account with the remainder and credits the appropriate Depreciation Expense account with the remainder. The reason for this is that once an asset is disposed of, it will not be included with the assets for which depreciation will be calculated. You will need to manually book the depreciation for this one asset for the month in which it is disposed.

Calculating Depreciation

Once you have entered all of your fixed asset records and made any appropriate adjustments, you can calculate the depreciation. Peachtree Fixed Assets lets you calculate depreciation for any date range, and for one, several, or all of the books.

Before you begin, make sure that your fixed asset records are up to date and that all assets acquired or disposed of in the period have been duly recorded in Peachtree Fixed Assets as well as in Peachtree Complete Accounting for Windows. Also check that Peachtree Fixed Assets and Peachtree Complete Accounting are in balance by reconciling the fixed asset accounts in the Peachtree Complete Accounting for Windows General Ledger with the fixed asset accounts on the Depreciation–Projection report in Peachtree Fixed Assets. (The Depreciation–Projection report is discussed later in this chapter.) If the balances for each fixed asset account don't match, you probably failed to enter an asset in either Peachtree Complete Accounting or Peachtree Fixed Assets. Asset information is entered in Peachtree Complete Accounting either with the actual purchase transaction or the asset's beginning balance.

It is a good idea to back up your data before calculating depreciation. This way, if you need to recalculate depreciation later, you can just restore the data files, make any entries for new or disposed fixed assets, and calculate depreciation again. Information on backing up your data appears in Chapter 13 To calculate depreciation, select Calculate Depreciation from the Tasks menu. The Calculate Depreciation window (shown in Figure 11-10) appears.

Select the books you want to calculate depreciation for by checking the appropriate boxes in the window. Enter the ending date for the month you're calculating depreciation through as a cutoff date. When you are satisfied with your entries, click OK. Peachtree Fixed Assets calculates the depreciation (this may take a few moments depending on the number of fixed assets and the books you have selected to calculate depreciation for).

When you run the Calculate Depreciation process, Peachtree Fixed Assets checks for assets placed in service in the current year. If the Mid-Quarter Convention can apply, Peachtree Fixed Assets asks if you want to apply the

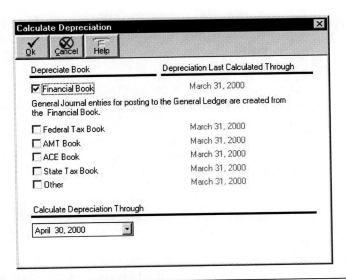

FIGURE 11-10 Calculate Depreciation window

Mid-Quarter Convention. If you say Yes, Peachtree Fixed Assets automatically checks this field for each asset that meets the Mid-Quarter Convention rules.

Recalculating Depreciation

Earlier in the discussion on entering assets in the Asset Maintenance window, you read how changing asset information can affect the way depreciation is calculated. You may need to recalculate depreciation to take into account retroactive changes to a fixed asset's information if any of the following is true:

- If you had corrected errors in the fixed asset record
- If you were out of balance with respect to the fixed asset and depreciation accounts in Peachtree Complete Accounting
- If you had disposed of a fixed asset, but had not recorded the disposal in Peachtree Fixed Assets

C A U T I O N : Recalculating depreciation is done exclusively through the Asset Maintenance window. The Calculate Depreciation option on the Peachtree Fixed Assets Tasks menu is only done once a quarter.

When you recalculate depreciation for a fixed asset, Peachtree Fixed Assets uses either the in-service date or the as-of date in the Asset Maintenance window, whichever is later. You can force Peachtree Fixed Assets to recalculate using the in-service date by deleting the as-of date.

You can recalculate depreciation back to the last time you calculated depreciation, to the end of the preceding fiscal year, or all the way back to the date the fixed asset was placed in service. The depth to which you choose to recalculate depends on why you are recalculating depreciation, the value of the fixed asset, and the amount by which you expect the recalculated depreciation to change as a result. If you are not sure, talk to your accountant for more information on how and when you should recalculate depreciation.

Posting Depreciation

When you calculate the depreciation in Peachtree Fixed Assets for the Financial book, the application creates the General Journal entries that are posted to Peachtree Complete Accounting. Peachtree Fixed Assets creates separate General Journal entries for each month for which depreciation is calculated. These entries connect the depreciation information in Peachtree Fixed Assets to the company's General Ledger in Peachtree Complete Accounting for Windows.

 N O T E : You must post each month. The General Journal entry information is written to the Peachtree Fixed Assets file fapost.dat. This file is not appended to; it is overwritten each time.

Before you post depreciation to Peachtree Complete Accounting for Windows, print a Depreciation–General Journal Entries report in Peachtree Fixed Assets. (The Depreciation–General Journal Entries report is discussed later in this chapter.) Verify your entries on the report. It is also a good idea to back up your Peachtree Fixed Assets and Peachtree Complete Accounting data before posting to the General Ledger. This way, if something goes wrong, you can just restore the Peachtree Fixed Assets and Peachtree Complete Accounting data files, make any corrections necessary, and repost the depreciation to the Peachtree Complete Accounting General Ledger.

To post the Peachtree Fixed Assets General Journal entries to Peachtree Complete Accounting, select Post to General Ledger from the Tasks menu in

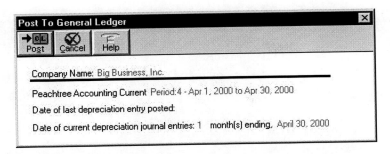

FIGURE 11-11 Post To General Ledger window

Peachtree Fixed Assets. The Post To General Ledger window (shown in Figure 11-11) appears.

The Post To General Ledger window has no fields for entering information. You should simply verify that the current period and the range of the months you are about to post are correct. (To post for a different month or a different range of months, you would need to use the Calculate Task option on the Tasks menu to calculate depreciation for a different set of dates.)

When you are satisfied with the information in the window, click Post. Peachtree Fixed Assets posts the General Journal entries. (This may take a few minutes depending on the number of entries you are posting.) Check your work by verifying the balances for Cost, Accumulated Depreciation, and Year-to-Date Depreciation, as shown on the Depreciation–Expense report in Peachtree Fixed Assets, against the balances for Fixed Asset, Accumulated Depreciation, and Depreciation Expense account shown on the General Ledger report in Peachtree Complete Accounting.

Printing Peachtree Fixed Assets Reports

Peachtree Fixed Assets has 14 standard reports, as shown in Table 11-4.

Figures 11-12 through 11-17 show a partial selection of the reports available in Peachtree Fixed Assets.

 NOTE: Some of the report options available in Peachtree Complete Accounting for Windows, such as the forms design options, are not available in Peachtree Fixed Assets.

REPORT	DESCRIPTION
Acquisition	Lists the assets you have acquired between the specified dates
Asset Listing	Lists the selected assets on file for a specified book
Depreciation–Expense	Lists asset information, depreciation information from the most recent depreciation calculation, and the year-to-date and life-to-date depreciation
Depreciation–General Journal Entries	Lists the General Journal entries ready for posting to Peachtree Complete Accounting for Windows
Depreciation–Projection	Lists the projected asset depreciation for the as-of date you specify
Depreciation–Schedule	Lists the annual depreciation of assets through the end of the specified year, for a specified book
Depreciation–Adjustment	Lists the life-to-date depreciation you have entered for the conversion balances and compares it to the life-to-date depreciation calculated by Peachtree Fixed Assets, through the conversion date for a specified book for all assets for which you have entered a conversion date
Dispositions	Lists the assets you have disposed of between the specified dates for a specified book
Form 4562	Lists the information you need (in worksheet format) for completing IRS Form 4562
Sale of Property	Lists the information you need (in worksheet format) for completing IRS Form 4797
Investment Tax Credit	Lists the tax credits (in summary worksheet format) recorded for the Federal Tax book, for the current fiscal year, for completing IRS Form 3468
I.T.C. Recapture	Lists information for completing IRS Form 4255, Recapture of Investment Credit, on the recaptured ITC resulting from the early disposition of tax credit property
Alt Min Tax	Lists information for completing IRS Form 4626, Alternative Minimum Tax: Corporations; and IRS Form 6251, Alternative Minimum Tax: Individuals on Alternative Minimum Tax adjustments and preference items required for depreciation
FASB 109	Lists information for determining the Deferred Tax asset or liability as required under FASB 109

TABLE 11-4   Peachtree Fixed Assets reports

```
                              Big Business, Inc.
                       A C Q U I S I T I O N   R E P O R T
                           For: Financial Book
                                From  to

Select: All      Sub-Total By: Asset ID
Asset ID    Description          Serial No.    Acquired  Method Life      Cost           Accum. Depr.
--------    -----------          ----------    --------  ------ ----   -----------       -----------
       1   Monitor, 21"         VS81199       01/08/00   SLFM   5.0     1,426.18              95.08
       2   Computer             R1493401      12/15/99   SLFM   5.0     2,285.44             190.45
       3   Computer             R1593402      12/15/99   SLFM   5.0     2,285.44             190.45
       4   Computer             R1593407      12/15/99   SLFM   5.0     2,285.44             190.45
       5   Computer             R1593409      12/15/99   SLFM   5.0     2,285.44             190.45
       6   Montor, 21"          VS81200       12/15/99   SLFM   5.0     1,426.18             118.85
       7   Monitor, 21"         VS81201       12/15/99   SLFM   5.0     1,426.18             118.85
       8   Monitor, 21"         VS81202       12/15/99   SLFM   5.0     1,426.18             118.85
       9   Modular desks (4)                  12/15/99   SLFM   7.0     8,070.74             480.40
      10   Office Chairs (4)                  12/15/99   SLFM   7.0     2,232.77             132.90
      11   LaserJet 2100M       LP772140      12/15/99   SLFM   5.0       915.00              76.25
      12   Fax Machine          2137562       12/15/99   SLFM   5.0       243.16              20.26
      13   Filing Cabinets (4)                12/20/99   SLFM   7.0       859.25              51.15
      14   Telephone Switch     0048902       12/13/99   SLFM   7.0     6,234.00             371.07
      15   Supply Cabinet       18704TZ       12/13/99   SLFM   7.0       204.05              12.15
      16   Monitor, 21"         VS81199       01/08/00   SLFM   5.0     1,426.18              95.08

                                                                     -------------     -------------
Grand Totals       Assets: 16                                          35,031.63          2,452.69
-----------------------------------------------------------------------------------------------------
```

FIGURE 11-12 Acquisition report (partial view)

```
                              Big Business, Inc.
                     A S S E T   L I S T I N G   R E P O R T
                           For: Financial Book
                         Period Ending: April 30, 2000

Select: All      Sub-Total By: Asset ID
=====================================================================================================
Asset ID    Description          Serial No.  Acquired  Method Life      Cost           Accum. Depr.
--------    -----------          ----------  --------  ------ ----   -----------       -----------
       1   Monitor, 21"         VS81199     01/08/00   SLFM   5.0     1,426.18              95.08
       2   Computer             R1493401    12/15/99   SLFM   5.0     2,285.44             190.45
       3   Computer             R1593402    12/15/99   SLFM   5.0     2,285.44             190.45
       4   Computer             R1593407    12/15/99   SLFM   5.0     2,285.44             190.45
       5   Computer             R1593409    12/15/99   SLFM   5.0     2,285.44             190.45
       6   Montor, 21"          VS81200     12/15/99   SLFM   5.0     1,426.18             118.85
       7   Monitor, 21"         VS81201     12/15/99   SLFM   5.0     1,426.18             118.85
       8   Monitor, 21"         VS81202     12/15/99   SLFM   5.0     1,426.18             118.85
       9   Modular desks (4)                12/15/99   SLFM   7.0     8,070.74             480.40
      10   Office Chairs (4)                12/15/99   SLFM   7.0     2,232.77             132.90
      11   LaserJet 2100M       LP772140    12/15/99   SLFM   5.0       915.00              76.25
      12   Fax Machine          2137562     12/15/99   SLFM   5.0       243.16              20.26
      13   Filing Cabinets (4)              12/20/99   SLFM   7.0       859.25              51.15
      14   Telephone Switch     0048902     12/13/99   SLFM   7.0     6,234.00             371.07
      15   Supply Cabinet       18704TZ     12/13/99   SLFM   7.0       204.05              12.15
      16   Monitor, 21"         VS81199     01/08/00   SLFM   5.0     1,426.18              95.08

                                                                   -------------     -------------
Grand Totals       Assets: 16                                        35,031.63          2,452.69
=====================================================================================================
```

FIGURE 11-13 Asset Listing report (partial view)

```
                                   Big Business, Inc.
                            D E P R E C I A T I O N   E X P E N S E
                                   For: Financial Book
                                Period Ending: April 30, 2000

Select: All     Sub-Total By: Asset ID
=================================================================================================
Asset ID    Description      In Serv:  Method  Life      Cost      Adjustments  Period Depr    YTD Depr
--------    -----------      --------  ------  ----   ------------  -----------  -----------  ------------
      1  Monitor, 21"        01/08/00  SLFM    5.0      1,426.18       0.00         23.77         95.08
      2  Computer            12/15/99  SLFM    5.0      2,285.44       0.00         38.09        152.36
      3  Computer            12/15/99  SLFM    5.0      2,285.44       0.00         38.09        152.36
      4  Computer            12/15/99  SLFM    5.0      2,285.44       0.00         38.09        152.36
      5  Computer            12/15/99  SLFM    5.0      2,285.44       0.00         38.09        152.36
      6  Montor, 21"         12/15/99  SLFM    5.0      1,426.18       0.00         23.77         95.08
      7  Monitor, 21"        12/15/99  SLFM    5.0      1,426.18       0.00         23.77         95.08
      8  Monitor, 21"        12/15/99  SLFM    5.0      1,426.18       0.00         23.77         95.08
      9  Modular desks (     12/15/99  SLFM    7.0      8,070.74       0.00         96.08        384.32
     10  Office Chairs (     12/15/99  SLFM    7.0      2,232.77       0.00         26.58        106.32
     11  LaserJet 2100M      12/15/99  SLFM    5.0        915.00       0.00         15.25         61.00
     12  Fax Machine         12/15/99  SLFM    5.0        243.16       0.00          4.05         16.21
     13  Filing Cabinets     12/20/99  SLFM    7.0        859.25       0.00         10.23         40.92
     14  Telephone Switc     12/13/99  SLFM    7.0      6,234.00       0.00         74.21        296.86
     15  Supply Cabinet      12/13/99  SLFM    7.0        204.05       0.00          2.43          9.72
     16  Monitor, 21"        01/08/00  SLFM    5.0      1,426.18       0.00         23.77         95.08
                                                     -------------  -----------  -----------  ------------
    Grand Totals:                                      35,031.63       0.00        500.04      2,000.19
 Assets: 16

               Section 179   :                                        0.00
```

FIGURE 11-14 Depreciation—Expense report (partial view)

```
                                   Big Business, Inc.
                          D E P R E C I A T I O N   S C H E D U L E
                                   For: Financial Book
                                 Through Year End 2000

Select: All     Sub-Total By: Asset ID
=================================================================================================
Asset ID  Description      In Serv:  Method  Life      Cost      Year Ending   YTD Depr.    Accum Depr
--------  -----------      --------  ------  ----   ------------  ------------  ------------  ----------
      1  Monitor, 21"      01/08/00  SLFM    5.0      1,426.18     12/31/00        285.24        285.

      2  Computer          12/15/99  SLFM    5.0      2,285.44     12/31/99         38.09         38.
                                                                   12/31/00        457.09        495.

      3  Computer          12/15/99  SLFM    5.0      2,285.44     12/31/99         38.09         38.
                                                                   12/31/00        457.09        495.

      4  Computer          12/15/99  SLFM    5.0      2,285.44     12/31/99         38.09         38.
                                                                   12/31/00        457.09        495.

      5  Computer          12/15/99  SLFM    5.0      2,285.44     12/31/99         38.09         38.
                                                                   12/31/00        457.09        495.

      6  Montor, 21"       12/15/99  SLFM    5.0      1,426.18     12/31/99         23.77         23.
                                                                   12/31/00        285.24        309.

      7  Monitor, 21"      12/15/99  SLFM    5.0      1,426.18     12/31/99         23.77         23.
                                                                   12/31/00        285.24        309.
```

FIGURE 11-15 Depreciation—Schedule report (partial view)

```
                           Big Business, Inc.
                        D I S P O S E D   A S S E T S
                           For: Financial Book
                               From  to

Select: All     Sub-Total By: Asset ID
==================================================================================
Asset ID  Description     In Serv:  Disposed     Cost     Accum. Depr.  Net Proceeds   Book Value
--------  -------------   --------  --------  -----------  ------------  ------------  ------------  ---
       1 Monitor, 21"    01/08/00  01/10/00   1,426.18       0.00         500.00       1,426.18
                                            -----------  ------------  ------------  ------------  ---
   Grand Total:          Assets: 1            1,426.18       0.00         500.00       1,426.18
==================================================================================
```

FIGURE 11-16 Disposed Assets report (partial view)

```
                              Big Business, Inc.
                         F A S B   1 0 9   R E P O R T
                       For Assets in Service as of: 12/31/00

                 --------------- Balances as of 12/31/00 -------------- ------- Variances as of 12/31/00---

  Asset ID        Financial        Federal         AMT            ACE       Fin - Fed    Fed - AMT    AMT -
     2          Method Life     Method Life    Method Life    Method Life
                SLFM    5.0      GDSDB  5.0     ADSDB  5.0     ADSDB  5.0
                -------------   -------------  -------------  -------------  ------------ -------------- -------
Cost               2,285           2,285          2,285          2,285           0            0
Section 179            0               0              0              0           0            0
Salvage Value          0               0              0              0           0            0
ITC Basis Adj.         0               0              0              0           0            0
Curr. YTD Depr.      457             731            582            582        -274          148
Prior Acc. Depr.      38             457            342            342        -419          114
                -------------   -------------  -------------  -------------  ------------ -------------- -------
Remaining Basis    1,790           1,097          1,359          1,359         693         -262

---------------------- Projected Depreciation ------------------------  -----Projected Recovery of Varianc
12/31/01            457             438            408            408          18           30
----------------------------------------------------------------------------------------------------
Totals              457             438            408            408          18           30
==================================================================================
```

FIGURE 11-17 FASB 109 report (partial view)

Summary

Entering and using fixed asset information can be confusing. If you have any questions, talk to your accountant about the best way to enter and classify your company's fixed assets. A little time up front may save you large amounts of CPA time when filing your tax returns.

With this chapter, you have completed the setup of your information in Peachtree Complete Accounting for Windows. The remaining two chapters in this book show you how to use the advanced features of Peachtree Complete Accounting for Windows. Chapter 12 shows you how to use Peachtree Complete Accounting's report design features to create customized reports for your company. Chapter 13 shows you how to perform management-level tasks such as reconciling accounts, closing financial periods, and using the Action Items, Action Items and Events Log Options, and the Analysis tools.

12

Customizing Reports

B A S I C S

- Understanding reporting concepts
- How to plan report changes
- How to add and change columns
- How to customize financial statements

B E Y O N D

- How to change report formats
- How to copy report information to a spreadsheet

In this chapter, you'll learn how to create, modify, and print custom reports and financial statements. You'll also be introduced to customizing forms and using Peachtree Report Writer for more advanced reports.

In the preceding chapter, you saw how to enter assets, set depreciation schedules, calculate depreciation, post depreciation information to the General Ledger, and print fixed asset reports. In this chapter, you will learn how to create customized reports and financial statements.

 C A U T I O N : Creating and customizing financial reports and forms can be difficult if you're not used to working with spreadsheets or database formulas. If you are not comfortable with the process of creating or customizing financial reports, consider contacting Peachtree or a local Peachtree third-party support organization to customize your reports and forms for you. Call Peachtree technical support at (770) 492-6311 for information on customizing reports. Call (800) 626-0941 for information on the Peachtree Support Center nearest to you.

Understanding Basic Reporting Concepts

Peachtree Accounting comes with an extensive variety of reports, financial statements, and forms (reports and financial statements can be displayed on the screen or printed, while forms can only be printed), but you may want to create your own customized ones. This chapter shows you how to do this using Peachtree Accounting's report design features.

You are strongly encouraged to follow GAAP (Generally Accepted Accounting Practices) when designing all your financial reports and statements. This means that assets should precede liabilities and equity. Although you may want reports primarily for internal use, accountants, bankers, and auditors all expect reports and statements in a standardized form. Check with your accountant for more information on GAAP as it applies to report design.

You can use customized reports and financial statements for many different things, including:

- Vendor and transaction information
- Checks
- State and local tax reports
- Inventory reports for physical inventory and logging

Customizing Reports

Although the reports that come with Peachtree Complete are probably adequate for your needs, most of the time you will want to customize existing reports. This involves doing things such as adding and moving fields, changing column headings, and customizing titles. This section will show you how to customize an existing report. Later on in this chapter, you'll see how to create a new report.

The first step in customizing an existing Peachtree report is to select the report most similar to the report you want to create. You can then change or add other parts of the report as needed. This lets you take advantage of existing headings and titles as well as some of the filtering options.

Planning Your Changes

Peachtree Accounting provides you with extensive flexibility for producing the widest possible range of reports and forms.

Each report and form has different requirements. Planning your reports in advance will save you a great deal of time and effort. You have to define the titles and headings, columns of data, report breaks, subtotals, and totals.

As you plan your report, you will find it helpful to consider the following questions:

- Who will use this report? Is this report strictly for internal use, or will the report be released to people outside the company? Is the report information confidential or restricted in any way?
- How often will you need to print the report: daily, weekly, monthly, quarterly, or annually? Will the report be printed on a printer or just displayed on the screen? Will the report be arranged in landscape or portrait mode? Will the report require special paper stock such as checks or W-2s?
- What titles, headings, instructions, and labels need to be on the report? What accounting information do you want on the report? What calculations do you need to perform? What will trigger subtotals and totals?

Gathering this information may take some time, but you will find that creating your report is quicker and easier if you take the time up front to plan what you want to do.

If you are making extensive changes or matching a report or a form to preprinted stock, you may find it helpful to lay out the report on paper. One of the easiest ways to do this is with a *printout design form*, a form with a grid of rectangles representing the possible positions of text on a printed page. You can buy printout design forms at most office supply stores. The advantage of using printout design forms is that you can sketch your report layout by hand and see what the report will look like before you build it in Peachtree Accounting.

When you're designing a report or form, print the text titles, headings, and labels on the printout design form where they should appear on the final report.

For alphanumeric information such as inventory item descriptions and customer names, fill the spaces in with Xs to show where the information will appear. For numeric information such as amounts, enter 9s. Be sure to allow the maximum number of characters in the item, as well as commas, decimal points, and dollar signs.

TIP: Many numbers, such as phone numbers, Social Security numbers, and postal codes, should be treated as alphanumeric information rather than numeric because the fields may contain special characters such as parentheses, hyphens, or letters.

Once you have adequately planned your changes, you are ready to customize your reports. (For simple experimentation and minor changes, you probably don't need to plan extensively.)

Start by clicking on the Reports menu and a menu option (such as Accounts Receivable, Accounts Payable, or General Ledger) to display the Select a Report window for that family of reports. Select a report from the list. You can use any of the standard Peachtree Accounting reports or a report you created yourself. Click the Design button to display the report in Design mode. (If you have already displayed a report on your screen by using the Screen button, you can still go into Design mode by clicking the Design button.) Figure 12-1 shows the Employee List report in Design mode.

The examples in this section show you how to make changes to the Employee List report from Payroll.

Adding and Changing Columns

The simplest change you can make to the report format is to change the column widths on an existing report. Use the lines next to the headers as handles to change the column size or position. To expand or shrink the column, click and drag the line to the right of the column. The column will expand and shrink as you drag the line. To shift a column's position, click and drag the line to the left of the column. The column (and all the columns to the right) moves to the new location on the page.

As you move the columns around on the screen, you may see a vertical dotted line appear in between columns. This dotted line shows where Peachtree Accounting is putting a page break. Any information to the right of the dotted line prints on another page. One way to eliminate an inconvenient page break, if you have just one or two columns, is to change the page orientation from

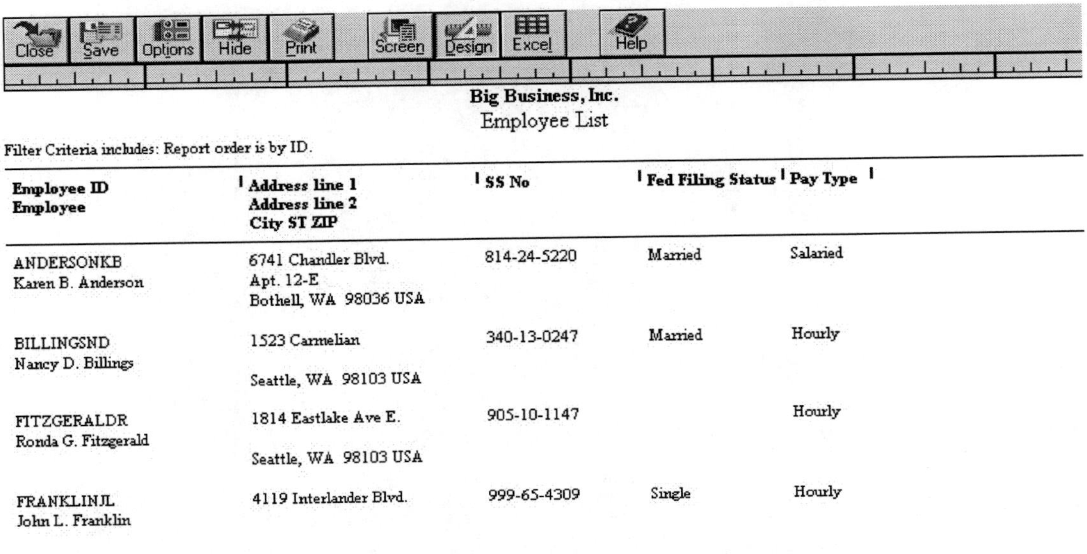

FIGURE 12-1 Employee List report in Design mode

portrait to landscape (to be discussed later this chapter in the "Changing the Report Format" section).

CAUTION: Although you can change the report fields and format, you cannot change the filter options for reports. If you are making substantial changes to a report, make sure that the filter options for the existing report include the options you want to use in the new report.

You can also add fields or change the order of the information through the Fields tab in the Report Options window. Click the Options button to display the standard Report Options window for the report. Figure 12-2 shows the Fields tab for the Payroll Employee List.

The Fields tab shows all the fields you can include on the report. A check mark in the Show field tells Peachtree Accounting to include that field on the report. In the example in Figure 12-2, the fields come from the Maintain Employees window.

Show Check the Show box to include the corresponding field on the report.

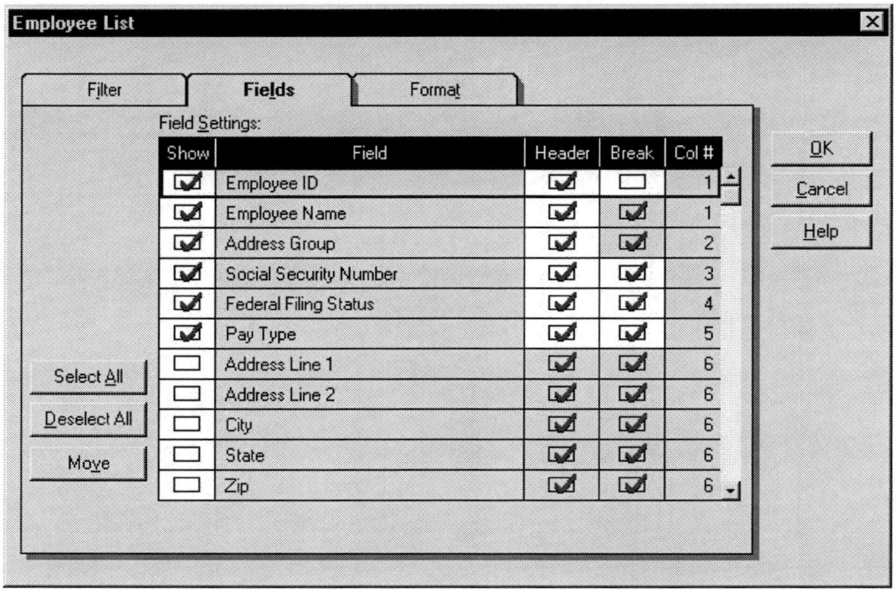

FIGURE 12-2 Fields tab for the Payroll Employee List

Field This field identifies the field to include; it is display-only.

Header Check the Header box to have Peachtree Accounting include a header on the report.

Break Check the Break box to have Peachtree Accounting break out a separate column for the item. If this box is not checked, Peachtree Accounting will stack the information below the previous item. For example, after unchecking the Break box for the SS No and Fed Filing Status fields for the report shown earlier in Figure 12-1, Peachtree Accounting stacks these three data items in the same column, as shown in Figure 12-3.

Col # The Col # field shows the order in which the information will appear on the report. If you have several fields that will display in the same column—in other words, they are stacked because they don't have the Break box checked—the column number will be the same for all of them.

You can also move columns around on the report. For example, to move the Pay Type column to the first position on the report, highlight the Pay Type line and click the Move button. Then click the line you want the Pay Type column to be inserted in front of—in this example, the Employee ID line. Peachtree Accounting reorders the columns. This technique lets you rearrange the order

Big Business, Inc.
Employee List

Filter Criteria includes: Report order is by ID.

Employee ID	Address line 1	SS No	
Employee	Address line 2	Fed Filing Status	
	City ST ZIP	Pay Type	
ANDERSONKB	6741 Chandler Blvd.	814-24-5220	
Karen B. Anderson	Apt. 12-E	Married	
	Bothell, WA 98036 USA	Salaried	
BILLINGSND	1523 Carmelian	340-13-0247	
Nancy D. Billings		Married	
	Seattle, WA 98103 USA	Hourly	
FITZGERALDR	1814 Eastlake Ave E.	905-10-1147	
Ronda G. Fitzgerald			
	Seattle, WA 98103 USA	Hourly	
FRANKLINJL	4119 Interlander Blvd.	999-65-4309	
John L. Franklin		Single	
		Hourly	

FIGURE 12-3 Customized Employee List with stacked employee information

in which the columns of data appear on the report. The technique for moving columns shown earlier in "Customizing the Report Format" simply changes the widths of the columns on the page.

Changing the Report Format

To change the report format, start by clicking the Format tab in the Report Options window. Figure 12-4 shows the Format tab for the Employee List.

You can change the default printer for a specific report or form. For example, if you have checks queued up on a dedicated printer, you may want to set the default printer information for that printer. Similarly, you may need to change a report from portrait to landscape so that all the columns print on one page. Although you can specify landscape mode for a particular form or report, Peachtree Accounting does not save this option when you save the form or report. To print the form or report in landscape mode, you will need to change to landscape mode in the Format tab each time you print the form or report.

To change the printer settings, click the button in the Default Printer section. The standard Windows 98 Print Setup dialog box appears (as shown in Figure 12-5).

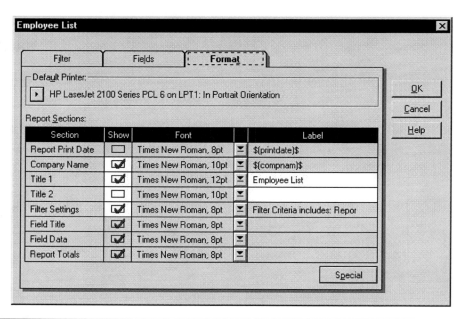

FIGURE 12-4   Format tab for the Employee List

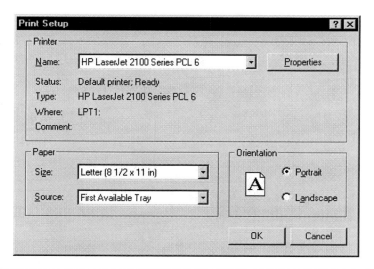

FIGURE 12-5   Windows Print Setup dialog box

You can use this dialog box to change the printer settings, the default printer, the page orientation (portrait or landscape), and so on. Any changes you make to the orientation, the printer you want to use, paper size, and so on, will remain when you save the report, provided that you switch from the Default Printer to the Specific Printer under the Format tab in the Windows Print Setup dialog box. (Portrait and landscape modes also remain when you select Specific Printer.)

The Report Sections area in the lower half of the Format tab lets you specify which titles are printed and how they are printed. The predefined text for the titles appears in the Label column shown in Figure 12-4. You can only change the items that are white. Items that are gray cannot be changed.

Section The Section field lists the parts of the report you can change. This field is display-only. The line items are described in Table 12-1.

You can change only the font styles for the Report Print Date, the Company Name, the Filter Settings, the Field Title, the Field Data, and the Report Totals.

Show Check the Show box to include the corresponding field on the report. Like the Fields tab, shown earlier in Figure 12-2, you can click the Show box for the various line items to include or exclude the item from the report.

Font The default font appears in the Font field. You can change the font for any of the lines by clicking the down arrow. The standard Windows Font dialog box appears (as shown in Figure 12-6).

LINE ITEM	DESCRIPTION
Report Print Date	Prints the system date and time in the upper-left corner of the report (this only appears on printed reports).
Company Name	Prints the company name. This information comes from the company information you set up in Chapter 3.
Title 1	Prints the report title (which you can enter in the Label field) or a special code. Special codes are described later in this section.
Title 2	Prints a second title line (which you can enter in the Label field).
Filter Settings	Prints the report selection options chosen in the Filter tab.
Field Title	Prints the field titles in the report header.
Field Data	Prints the body of the report (the actual report "information"), except the totals.
Report Totals	Prints totals for any "total" or "amount" field.

TABLE 12-1 Report Sections

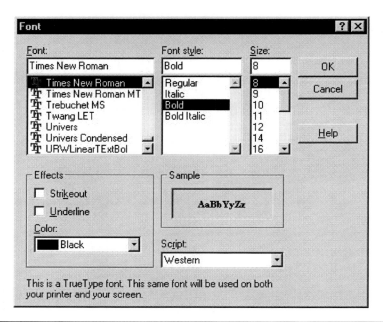

FIGURE 12-6 Windows Font dialog box

From this dialog box, you can select a different font, style, or size. A sample of the font appears in the lower-right corner of the dialog box.

Label Enter the label to print on the report. You can enter text or a special code. *Special codes* are predefined options that let you print such things as the company name, the current accounting period, and today's date. (Table 12-2 lists the special codes and what appears on the report when you use them.)

To enter a special code, highlight a white Label field and then click Special at the bottom of the tab. The Insert Special Code window appears, as shown in Figure 12-7.

You can select any of the special codes from this window. You can also mix special codes and text. For example, you could create a label $(**begdate**)$ **to** $(**enddate**)$, which would print the beginning date, the word "to," and the ending date.

Big Business, Inc.
Employee List
Period 4, Apr 1, 2000 to Period 4, Apr 30, 2000

SPECIAL CODE	WHAT APPEARS ON THE REPORT
$(compname)$	The company name as it is entered in the Company Name field on the Maintain Company Information window.
$(currper)$	The current accounting period and the dates. For example, if this is the third accounting period and the period is for March 2000, this would appear as "Period 3, 3/1/00 to 3/31/00" on the report.
$(begdate)$	The beginning date for the current accounting period. For example, if this is the third accounting period and the period is for March 2000, this would appear as "Period 3, Mar 1, 2000" on the report.
$(enddate)$	The ending date for the current accounting period. For example, if this is the third accounting period and the period is for March 2000, this would appear as "Period 3, Mar 31, 2000" on the report.
$(date)$	Today's date. For example, if today's date is March 21, 2000, this would appear as "Mar 21, 2000" on the report.
$(asofdate)$	The as-of date for the report. For example, if the as-of date is March 15, 2000, this would appear as "Mar 15, 2000" on the report.

TABLE 12-2   Special Codes

When you are satisfied with the entries you have made to the tabs, click OK. Peachtree Accounting displays the report on the screen with your modifications.

When you click the Save button, Peachtree Accounting displays the Save As window, as shown in Figure 12-8.

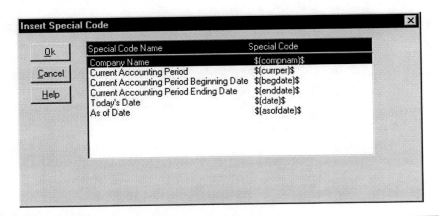

FIGURE 12-7   Insert Special Code window

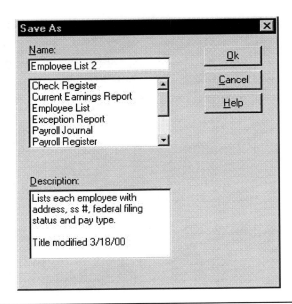

FIGURE 12-8 Save As window

Enter information as follows:

Name   Enter a name for the new report. This name should reflect the name of the report upon which this report is based. Entering a name for an existing custom report or form will overwrite the report or form. (You cannot overwrite the standard reports and forms that come with Peachtree Accounting.)

Description   Enter a description of the report. As with many other memo and description fields, you can press CTRL-J to insert a line break. It's a good idea to enter the date the report was created or modified and a brief comment about the changes to the report in this field to keep track of changes you've made.

When you save a report with a different name, you should also change the wording of the Title 1 label (refer back to Figure 12-4), which is used to print the report name, to reflect the change.

Enter the name of the report as you'd like it to appear in the list of reports on the Select a Report window, add any text you want in the Description field, and click OK. Figure 12-9 shows the Payroll Report List with a new report, Employee List 2, added. The triangle on the report icon shows that this is a custom report.

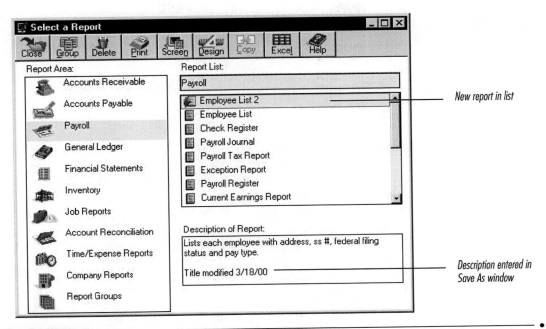

New report in list

Description entered in
Save As window

FIGURE 12-9 Payroll Report List showing an additional report

Understanding Financial Statements

Peachtree Accounting comes with a group of predefined financial statements.
Financial statements are a special kind of report you can display on the screen
or print on the printer. The predefined financial statements are described in
Table 12-3.

Printing Financial Statements

You can print financial statements like any other report. Start by selecting Financial
Statements from the Reports menu. Then select the particular financial statement
from the report list. The Report Options window for financial statements is slightly
different from the other Report Options windows, as shown in Figure 12-10.

Select the report options and click OK. The financial statement appears on
the screen or prints on the printer appropriately. Figure 12-11 shows part of a
sample Balance Sheet.

FINANCIAL STATEMENT	DESCRIPTION
Balance Sheet	Standard balance sheet
Income Stmnt	Income statement with income and expenses as an amount and also as a percentage of the total income for the current period and year-to-date
Cash Flow	Cash flow for the current period and year-to-date
Stmnt Changes	Changes in the company's financial position for the current period and year-to-date
Income 2 yrs	Income and expenses for the current period and year-to-date for previous and current year
Income/Budgets	Current period and year-to-date income and expenses contrasted with the budgeted amounts
GL Account Summary	Beginning balance, account activity, and ending balance for each General Ledger account
Retained Earnings	Statement of retained earnings for the current period and year-to-date
Income/Earnings	Income statement and statement of retained earnings for the current period and year-to-date

TABLE 12-3   Financial Statements

Customizing Financial Statements

Customizing financial statements can be extremely complex if you're not used to programming or working with spreadsheets or databases. Most users won't need or want to make extensive changes to the financial statements provided with Peachtree Accounting. If you are interested in experimenting with customizing financial statements on your own, you can find detailed information on financial statements in the Peachtree Accounting manual. If, after reading the documentation and experimenting a little, you're still uncomfortable customizing financial statements on your own, you should consider getting help from Peachtree Accounting or from a Peachtree Support Center.

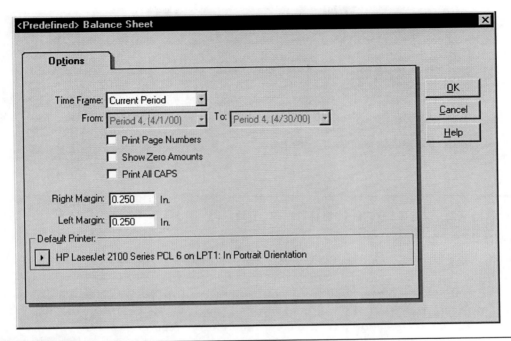

FIGURE 12-10   Report Options window for Financial Statements—Balance Sheet

Big Business, Inc.
Balance Sheet
April 30, 2000

ASSETS

Current Assets		
Petty Cash	$	250.00
Cash on Hand		35,713.05
Regular Checking Account		13,606.85
Payroll Checking Account		3,428.91
Savings Account		12,636.74
Special Account		3,002.04
Investments-Money Market		3,764.52
Accounts Receivable		<665.39>
Raw Materials Inventory		4,377.62
Total Current Assets	76,114.34	

FIGURE 12-11   Balance Sheet

C A U T I O N : The financial statements are in the standard formatted style expected by financial institutions, boards of directors, the IRS, and so on. Peachtree Accounting has set up these reports based on the account types. For example, the Balance Sheet lists information in a particular order, starting with assets, current assets, and fixed assets, then continuing with liabilities and equity. Similarly, the Profit and Loss/Income Statement is formatted in the order of account types, income, cost of goods (where applicable), and expenses. If you make changes to any of these statements, be sure to maintain the order in which the information is presented.

Creating Custom Reports and Forms with Peachtree Report Writer

Peachtree Accounting for Windows and Peachtree Complete Accounting for Windows come with a wide variety of reports and procedures, but you may want to add reports that fulfill your company's unique reporting requirements. Peachtree Report Writer is an add-on product sold by Peachtree that expands and augments your ability to create and modify reports. Peachtree Report Writer comes with more than 30 report and label formats for tasks such as sales analysis, vendor analysis, job tracking, payroll, and inventory analysis. You can use Peachtree Report Writer to create new reports, labels, and forms. To order Peachtree Report Writer, contact your Peachtree Support Center or order directly from Peachtree by calling (800) 247-3224. For additional detailed information on using Peachtree Report Writer, you can also look at *Peachtree Complete Business Toolkit* (Osborne/McGraw-Hill, 1998).

Customizing Forms

In the preceding chapters, you've seen how to print a variety of forms, such as invoices, purchase orders, statements, labels, checks, letters, and W-2s. Although Peachtree Accounting offers an extensive array of forms, you may want to customize some of them. For example, you may have a preprinted check that does not match the Peachtree Accounting check form, or you may want to add your company's logo to statements, invoices, or purchase orders.

Like financial statements, customizing forms can be extremely complex if you're not used to programming or working with spreadsheets or databases. Because forms are used most frequently with preprinted stock, you won't need to customize them frequently. You can find detailed information on customizing forms in the Peachtree Accounting manual. If, after reading the documentation and

You aren't limited to viewing your reports and financial statements on the screen or printing them on the printer. You can also copy the information and work with it further in a spreadsheet. Here's how:

1. Select the report or financial statement you want to use as the source for your data.
2. Display the report or financial statement on the screen.
3. Select Copy from the Edit menu. This copies the information on the report to the Windows clipboard.
4. Start your spreadsheet program.
5. Open the spreadsheet into which you want to paste the information.
6. Position the cursor at the appropriate insertion point, then select Paste from the spreadsheet's Edit menu. The report data appears in the spreadsheet. Figure 12-12 shows an example of cutting and pasting information from the Balance Sheet into a Microsoft Excel spreadsheet. (Keep in mind that you will have to format the information after you paste it into the spreadsheet.)

You can use this technique to copy information from any report or financial statement you can display on the screen.

	A	B	C	D	E	
1	Big Business, Inc.					← Report heading information
2	Balance Sheet					
3	April 30, 2000					
4						
5	ASSETS					
6						
7	Current Assets					
8	Petty Cash	$	250.00			
9	Cash on Hand		35,713.05			
10	Regular Checking Account		13,606.85			
11	Payroll Checking Account		3,428.91			
12	Savings Account		12,636.74			
13	Special Account		3,002.04			
14	Investments-Money Market		3,764.52			
15	Accounts Receivable		<665.39>			
16	Raw Materials Inventory		4,377.62			
17	Total Current Assets				$ 76,114.34	

Report data points to rows 7–17.

FIGURE 12-12 Balance Sheet information pasted into a Microsoft Excel spreadsheet

experimenting a little, you're still uncomfortable customizing forms on your own, you should strongly consider getting help from Peachtree Accounting or from a Peachtree Support Center.

If you decide to customize your own forms, keep in mind that the most common error is to add or delete lines in the detail area of the form and then have either no command lines or multiple command lines, resulting in the data not printing at all or printing twice. You may simply prefer to have someone else do the work for you. Many Peachtree Support Centers offer report- and form-design services. There are several vendors' coupons in the back of this book that will provide you with a discount on report and form design.

Summary

Peachtree Accounting offers many features for creating and customizing reports, financial statements, and forms. This chapter has only touched on some of the possibilities. You are encouraged to experiment and see how you can best take advantage of Peachtree Accounting's reporting features.

In the next and final chapter, you will see how to perform a variety of system and maintenance tasks and to use various management tools and procedures in Peachtree Accounting to complete the accounting cycle.

Management Tools and Procedures

13

In this chapter, you'll learn how to back up and restore data, reconcile accounts, change and close periods, use management tools, and exchange data with other programs.

The tools and procedures covered in this chapter are for functions that you generally won't need to perform every day. You will learn how to back up your data and programs, reconcile your accounts against your bank statements, import and export data, close periods, and use the various management tools in the Peachtree Accounting Manager Series to plan and track your accounting information.

Backing Up and Restoring Company Data

To back up your data means to copy it from your computer's hard disk to floppy disks or tapes. Backing up is a task nobody likes to do. It's generally slow, it's tedious, and it seems to serve little useful purpose. Nevertheless, if you don't back up your data and files on a regular basis, you're going to eventually lose massive amounts of work.

If you back up your data, you can then restore it from the backup copy in case your data gets damaged. There are many ways your data might get damaged, including:

- **Hardware failures**   These could include a read/write failure, a bad sector on the hard disk, or a hard-disk head crash.
- **Software failures**   A software problem could cause Peachtree Accounting or your system software to read or write incorrect data.
- **Network problems**   These could include lost network packets, net connection problems, and network software failures.
- **Power surges**   Power surges can cause hard disk and software problems.
- **Viruses**   Viruses can damage existing data, cause errors when reading or writing data, and can occasionally cause hardware problems.

In addition, you may want to be able to restore your data to recreate a picture of your company's financial state on a given date.

The chance of your data getting damaged is fairly small, but problems do happen eventually, so you should back up your data regularly. A good rule of thumb is to perform a backup at least every week or so if you are only entering a few transactions a day or every day if you are entering many transactions. If you're using a network in your office, you are probably already having backups done on a nightly basis, but this isn't always the case. Check with your network administrator for more information. Make sure that all the files in the company directory are being backed up.

As you determine your backup policy, keep in mind that you may be required by law to keep a certain number of backups showing the company's financial records. Corporate financial records are required for at least three years and may be required as a permanent part of your company's records. Check with your CPA or tax attorney for more information on your reporting and record requirements.

TIP: If you find yourself saying, "I don't have time to back up my Peachtree Accounting files," stop immediately and back up your files. The amount of time it takes to back up your files is minimal compared to the amount of time and effort it can take to recreate your company's financial records in the event that your data is damaged or lost. Companies have gone out of business when their computerized accounting data was lost because of a hardware or software failure with no backup.

There are two ways to back up your Peachtree Accounting data: you can use the Peachtree Accounting backup feature, or you can use the backup programs supplied with Windows 98. This section will show you how to back up your data in either of these ways.

Backing Up with Peachtree Accounting

To use Peachtree Accounting's internal backup procedure, select Back Up from the File menu. The Back Up Company window appears, as shown in Figure 13-1.

Remind Me When I Haven't Backed Up In ... Days   Check the box and use the up or down arrow to specify in number of days when you want to be prompted to back up your data.

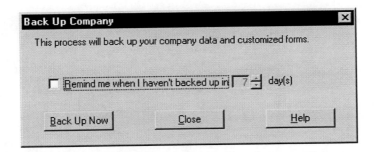

FIGURE 13-1   Back Up Company window

N O T E : Peachtree Accounting will display a reminder message when you close or exit the program when the specified number of days has elapsed.

Back Up Now   Click the Back Up Now button and specify where you want to back up your data. Peachtree Accounting starts copying files to the drive and directory you specified in Destination.

Close   Click Close if you are not prepared to back up data at this time.

Help   Click Help for more information on backing up company data.

After you click the Back Up Now button, Peachtree Accounting will display the Save Backup for Big Business, Inc. As: window, shown in Figure 13-2. Backup files are saved with the .ptb extension.

Tips for Backing Up Your Data Files

The default destination is the company subdirectory (in a file called PTBackup.ptb), which is in the directory containing your Peachtree Accounting directory. You can change this destination to another drive and directory by clicking on the down arrow and selecting the drive and directory, such as (A:) to back up to diskette or (D:) to back up to another hard drive. You can also change the file name, for instance using the date. For February 12, 2000, you could use 021200.

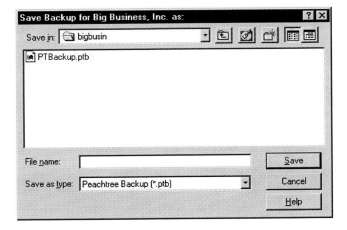

FIGURE 13-2   Save Backup for Big Business, Inc. As: window

Backing up to your hard drive will save a copy of the files while you work on them. However, if the hard drive crashes or the computer itself is damaged or stolen, both the original files and the backup files will be lost. Therefore, it is safest to make regular backups to a zip drive, a server, a writable CD, floppy disks, or tape and store them away from the computer (as a safeguard against fire or theft).

 C A U T I O N : For safety, you should make periodic backups of all of your Peachtree Accounting data files to a zip drive, a server, a writable CD, floppy disks, tape, or other removable media and store them offsite.

If you have more files than will fit on a single floppy disk, Peachtree Accounting will prompt you for another disk. If this happens, insert another floppy disk for Peachtree Accounting to continue backing up.

 T I P : If you are not sure of the sizes of your files, you can use the File Statistics command located on the Help menu to view the size of each of the data files.

Back up to your hard disk only if you are making a quick backup before performing a process that could potentially damage or corrupt your data, such as importing data from another file.

If you want to back up several companies at once, use the Windows Backup program.

 T I P : You may want to zip (compress) your files before you store them.

Backing Up Using the Windows 98 Backup Program

The second way to back up your data is to use the backup program that ships with Windows 98.

There are several advantages to using the Windows 98 Backup program:

- You can back up both data files and Peachtree Accounting program files.
- You can verify the backup to detect any errors in the backed-up files.
- You can back up to tape drives.
- You can back up with additional security to prevent unauthorized users from restoring the backup.

Start the Windows Backup program by clicking Start, then selecting Programs, then Accessories, then System Tools. Click Backup to start the Backup program.

The first time you start the Windows 98 Backup program, the Welcome to Microsoft Backup displays a message prompting you to select from Create A New Backup Job, Open An Existing Backup Job, or Restore A Backup Job. Select Create A New Back Job and click OK. The Backup Wizard prompts you to select Back Up My Computer or Back Up Selected Files, Folders, And Drives. Select Back Up Selected Files, Folders, And Drives. Click Next. The Backup window appears, as shown in Figure 13-3, with the Big Business data files already selected. You specify the files to be backed up by checking the box to the left of the folder or filename.

 C A U T I O N : Always back up all the Peachtree Accounting data files for a company whenever you back up files! If you back up part of a company's data files and then restore them later, you may have partial transactions or mismatched data that is impossible to reconcile.

Your Peachtree Accounting data files are usually stored in a folder within the PEACHW directory that looks like a shortened version of the company's name; for example, as previously shown in Figure 13-3, the Big Business, Inc., data files are stored in the BIGBUSIN folder.

If you're not sure what the name of the directory for the company is, you can find out by opening the company in Peachtree Accounting, then select File Statistics from the Help menu. At the top of the File Statistics window (not shown),

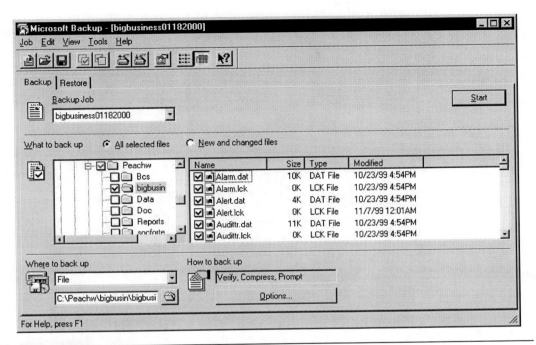

FIGURE 13-3 Microsoft Backup – [bigbusiness01182000]

Peachtree Accounting will display a title that reads "Data File Statistics for" followed by the name of the directory for the company. (Each company will have its own directory.) You can then select this directory in the backup program.

Select the files and folders you want to back up by clicking the checkbox to the left of the file or folder in either pane of the window.

The Peachtree Accounting data files all have filenames ending in .dat. Custom forms you've created are stored in the PEACHW directory, not the company directory.

When you are satisfied with your selections, click Start in the upper-right corner of the Backup program window. A dialogue box will appear and prompt you to save the backup job before you begin. Click Yes. The Save Backup Job As window appears, as shown in Figure 13-4.

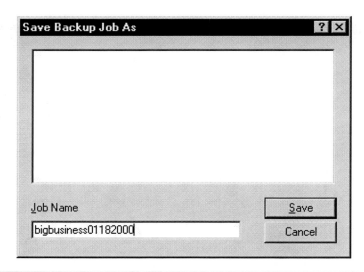

FIGURE 13-4 Save Backup Job As window

Enter the job name. Enter a name like "bigbusiness01182000" and click Save. The Backup program starts backing up files. (If you need more detailed information on the Windows 98 Backup program, click Help in the Windows 98 Backup program or refer to the documentation that accompanies your copy of Windows 98.) You will be prompted if you are about to overwrite an existing backup job. If that happens you will have the option of overwriting or canceling. When your job is complete, the Microsoft Backup dialogue box is displayed, as shown in Figure 13-5.

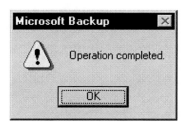

FIGURE 13-5 Microsoft Backup window

Once you've created customized reports and forms, it's a good idea to back them up, both as insurance against hard drive failure and also for historical tracking of your report modifications. Peachtree Accounting stores your custom reports and financial statements in the subdirectory for a specific company—custom reports and financial statements only apply to the company you've created them for—but custom forms are global, applying to all the companies you've set up. Backing up your company's files will also back up all your custom reports and financial statements.

The files for standard and custom forms appear (usually) in the directory where your Peachtree Accounting software has been installed.

You can copy form files directly from Windows to a floppy disk if you want. All custom forms and many of the standard forms have filenames that start with three letters that identify the type of form, followed by five numbers, followed by the file extension .frm., for example abc12345.frm.

You can back up specific forms by identifying the forms' filenames, or you can simply back up all form files (*.frm) in your directory.

> **TIP:** Using *.frm specifies that all files ending in .frm will be backed up.

You should consider backing up the entire Peachtree Accounting directory and all its subdirectories periodically. For archival purposes, this will guarantee that you have a current copy of the Peachtree Accounting software so you can recreate your company's accounting picture if necessary.

> **CAUTION:** Always back up all the Peachtree Accounting data files for a company whenever you back up files! If you back up part of a company's data files and then restore them later, you may have partial transactions or mismatched data that is impossible to reconcile.

Backing Up Using Another Backup Program

You may prefer to use a backup program other than the Windows Backup program, such as the backup program included with Norton Desktop for Windows or the backup program for your computer's tape drive. See the documentation for your backup program for details on how to configure and back up information on your hard disk.

Restoring Data

You will not usually have to restore data on your computer unless you're recovering from a hardware or software failure or are restoring files from a previous period.

CAUTION: It is a good policy to back up your existing files just before restoring files (if possible). If the backup you are restoring from is physically damaged or includes damaged or corrupted data, you could partially overwrite the data files on your hard disk and then have no data files at all.

Restoring Data Files from a Floppy disk

To restore the files from a simple copy, select Restore from the File menu. The Backup File window appears (as shown in Figure 13-6).

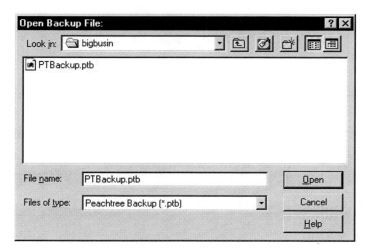

FIGURE 13-6   Open Backup File window

Specify the name of the file you want to restore in the File Name field. This will be the same drive and directory you specified when you backed up the files earlier. Click Open to start restoring the files. Peachtree Accounting will warn you that you're going to overwrite files before starting the restore. As mentioned earlier, be sure that you've backed up your files immediately before restoring (if possible).

Restoring Files from a Windows 98 Backup

If you used the Windows 98 Backup program to back up your files, you will need to use the Windows 98 Backup program to restore them as well.

Start the Windows 98 Backup program as you did earlier: click Start, then select Programs, then Accessories, then System Tools. Click Backup to start the Backup program.

Select Restore Backed Up Files, as shown in Figure 13-7, and click OK. The Restore Wizard appears, as shown in Figure 13-8. Specify the location you would like the files restored from, then click Next. The Select Backup Sets window appears. As you can see from Figure 13-9, assigning meaningful names and dates to the backup sets can make it easy to find a particular backup set.

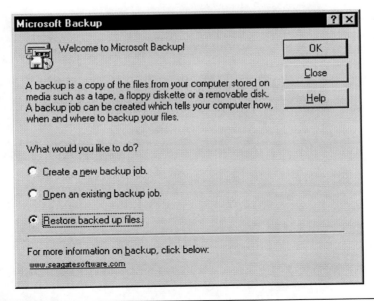

FIGURE 13-7 Microsoft Backup window – Restore Backed Up Files

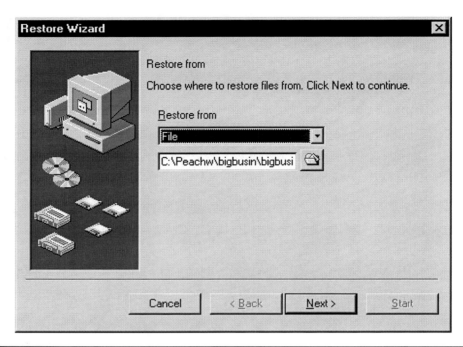

FIGURE 13-8   Restore Wizard window – Restore From

When you are satisfied with your selections, as shown in Figure 13-10, click Next.

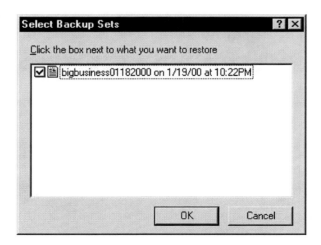

FIGURE 13-9   Select Backup Sets window allows you to specify the file you want restored

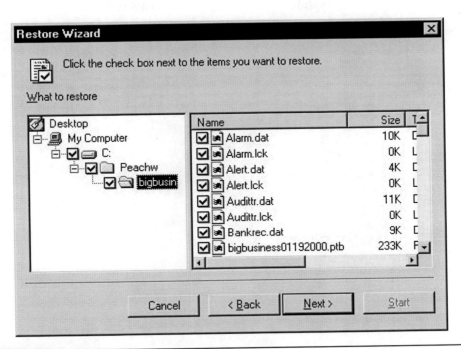

FIGURE 13-10 Restore Wizard window shows the files selected

If you have configured the Windows 98 Backup program to restore files to alternate locations, you will have the opportunity to specify the destination for the restored files in the Where To Restore window, as shown in Figure 13-11.

Before Windows restores your files, you have three options, as shown in Figure 13-12. Windows recommends selecting the first option ("Do not replace the file on my computer"). Make your selection and then click Start.

Windows starts restoring your files. You will almost always want to restore your files to the same directory you backed up from. When finished, Windows displays Operation Completed, as shown in Figure 13-13.

For more detailed information on the Windows 98 Backup program, click Help in the Windows 98 Backup program or refer to the documentation that accompanies your copy of Windows 98.

Restoring Files with Another Backup Program

To restore files with another backup program, make your selections in the Restore Company Data Files window and follow the appropriate procedure for restoring files with the program. When you are finished, Peachtree Accounting requires you to click OK to continue.

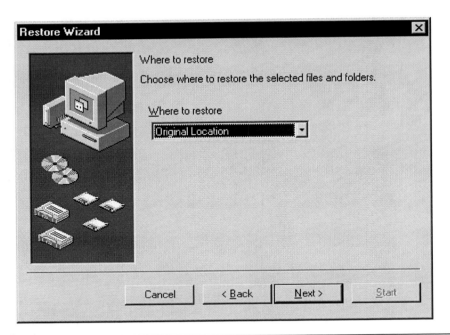

FIGURE 13-11 Restore Wizard window – Where To Restore

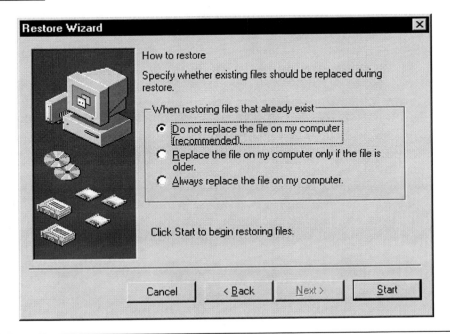

FIGURE 13-12 Restore Wizard window – When Restoring File That Already Exist

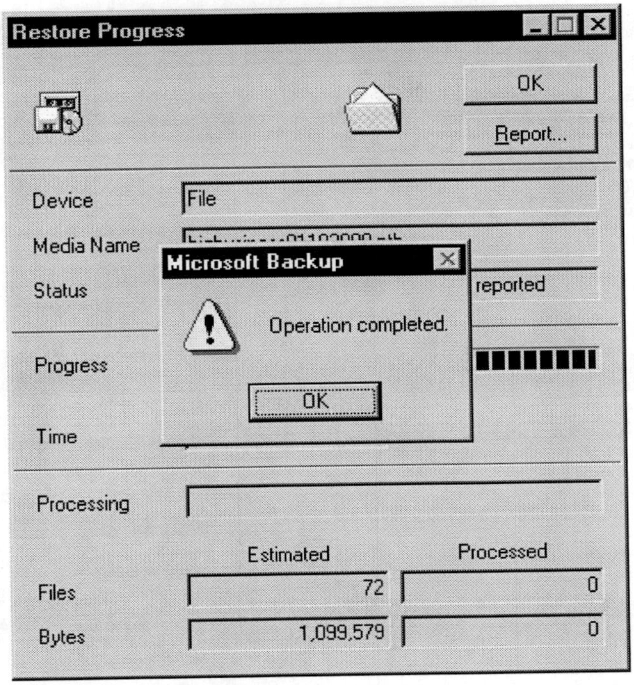

FIGURE 13-13 Restore Progress window

Account Reconciliation

The account reconciliation function lets you reconcile your checking statement against the checks, deposits, and General Journal entries you've recorded in Peachtree Accounting. (If your company is set up for batch posting, you must post your accounts before you reconcile to ensure that you have complete information when you reconcile.)

Reconciling Your Accounts

Reconciling your accounts and your bank statement in Peachtree Accounting is very much like reconciling your accounts and bank statement on paper. To reconcile your accounts, select Account Reconciliation from the Tasks menu. The Account Reconciliation window appears (as shown in Figure 13-14).

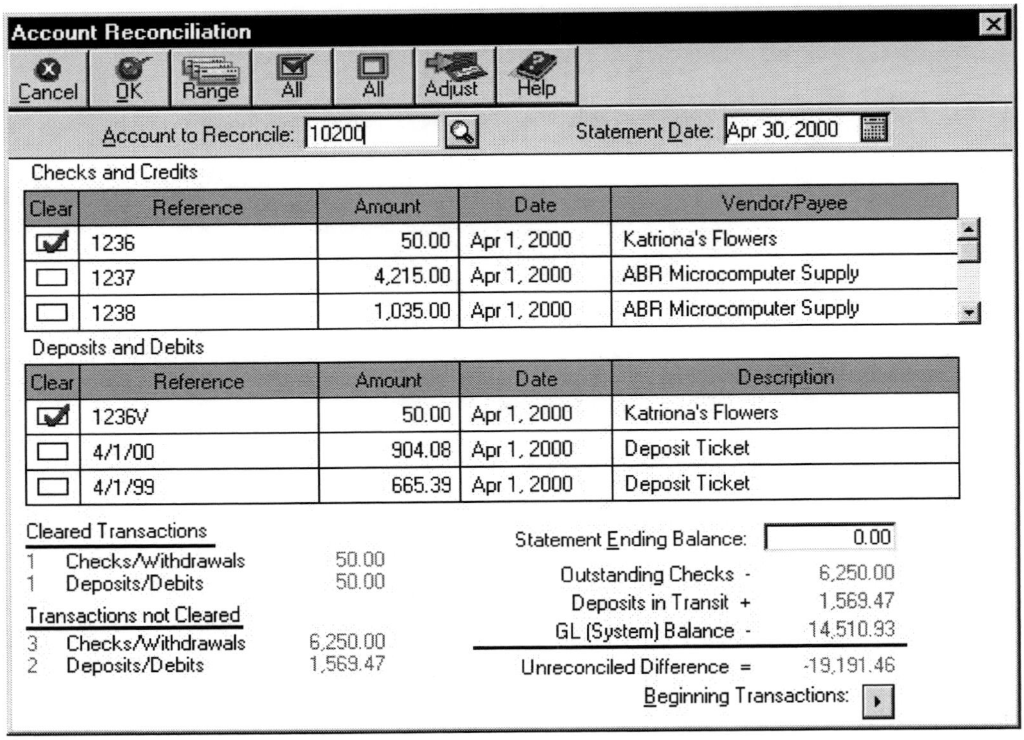

FIGURE 13-14 Account Reconciliation window

Take a moment to look at the buttons at the top of this window, shown in Table 13-1.

Account to Reconcile Enter the General Ledger account to reconcile. The default for this field is the first Cash account in your chart of accounts.

Statement Date Enter the bank statement's closing date (this must be within the current accounting period). Click the Calendar button or right-click in this field to display the date-selection calendar.

Clear Mark this checkbox to clear the check or deposit from the total.

Reference This is the reference number for the check that was entered as part of the transaction or the date of the deposit ticket. This field is display-only.

Amount This is the amount of the check or deposit. This field is display-only.

Date This is the date of the check or deposit. This field is display-only.

BUTTON	NAME	DESCRIPTION
Cancel	Cancel	Cancels the current operation
OK	OK	Makes the changes on the window
Range	Select Range	Lets you select a range of checks
All	Select All	Checks the Clear boxes for all the items
All	Deselect All	Unchecks the Clear boxes for all the items
Adjust	Adjust	Allows an adjusted transaction to be entered
Help	Help	Displays the online help on this window

TABLE 13-1 Toolbar Buttons on the Account Reconciliation Window

Vendor/Payee   This is the payee for the check. This field is display-only.

Description   This is the description for the check entered as part of the original transaction, usually either "Deposit Ticket," or whatever was entered in the Description field of the General Journal entry. This field is display-only.

Statement Ending Balance   Enter the ending balance shown on the bank statement in this field.

Outstanding Checks   This is the total of the unreconciled outstanding checks in Peachtree Accounting. As you clear checks by checking the Clear box, the total is reduced. This field is display-only.

Deposits in Transit   This is the total of the unreconciled deposits in Peachtree Accounting. As you clear deposits by checking the Clear box, the total is reduced. This field is display-only.

GL (System) Balance This is the balance for the selected account. This field is display-only.

Unreconciled Difference This is the unreconciled difference between the various totals.

To reconcile your accounts, start by entering the ending balance shown on the bank statement in the Statement Ending Balance field in the lower-right corner of the window. Mark the Clear box for each item that matches the statement. As you do so, the Outstanding Checks and Deposits in Transit fields are reduced appropriately.

You can use Select Range, Select All, and Deselect All to quickly check or uncheck Clear boxes. When you click Select Range, the Clear Range window appears, as shown in Figure 13-15.

Enter the range of checks to clear in the Clear Checks From and To fields. Peachtree Accounting checks the Clear boxes in the specified range.

When you have cleared all the transactions, the amount in the Unreconciled Difference field should be zero. This shows that the ending balance on the statement, less all outstanding checks and plus all outstanding deposits, is equal to the balance for the General Ledger account in Peachtree Accounting.

Making Adjusting Entries

If there are unresolved discrepancies when all the outstanding checks and deposits are reconciled, you may need to make adjusting journal entries. You may want to make adjusting journal entries for unrecorded checks or deposits, bank service charges for checking or overdrafts, and accounting errors. To make an adjusting entry to the account, click Adjust. The Additional Transactions window appears (as shown in Figure 13-16).

Enter the information in the field for a withdrawal or a deposit. The information is debited or credited against the account displayed in the Cash Account field, and Peachtree Accounting makes an entry in the General Journal.

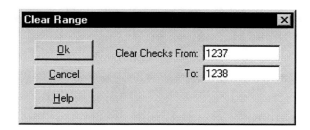

FIGURE 13-15 Clear Range window

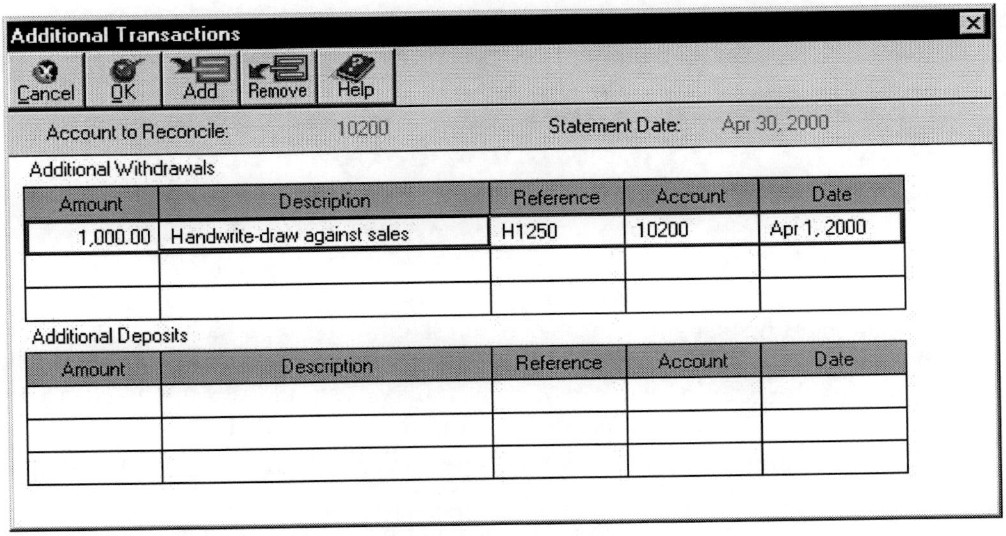

Additional Transactions					
Cancel	OK	Add	Remove	Help	

Account to Reconcile: 10200   **Statement Date:** Apr 30, 2000

Additional Withdrawals

Amount	Description	Reference	Account	Date
1,000.00	Handwrite-draw against sales	H1250	10200	Apr 1, 2000

Additional Deposits

Amount	Description	Reference	Account	Date

FIGURE 13-16   Additional Transactions window

Account to Reconcile   This is the account for which adjustments are being posted. This field is display-only.

Statement Date   This is the bank statement date you entered in the Account Reconciliation window. This field is display-only.

Amount   Enter the amount for the transaction.

Description   Enter up to 30 alphanumeric characters to describe the transaction.

Reference   Enter up to 20 alphanumeric characters as a reference for the transaction (such as a check number, a deposit ID, or a deposit date).

Account   Enter the account number for the transaction. (The account in the Account to Reconcile field is the account against which the other half of the journal entry is posted.)

Date   Enter the date of the transaction.

The Additional Transactions window lets you add and remove transactions with Add and Remove at the top of the window. When you are satisfied with your entries, click OK to post the entries to the General Journal and return to the Account Reconciliation window. If, after closing this window, you realize an adjustment was in error, you can find the transaction using the Edit Records feature for the General Journal window and then delete the adjusting entry. For more information on deleting General Journal entries, see Chapter 4.

Printing Account Reconciliation Reports

Peachtree Accounting has a variety of reports to help you reconcile your accounts. Table 13-2 shows a list of the Account Reconciliation reports in Peachtree Accounting.

The Account Reconciliation report (shown in Figure 13-17) is a report in statement format showing the current bank balance, all detail entries for transactions in the reconciliation, and the totals for the accounts. This report is a valuable part of your printed audit trail; you should run it whenever you reconcile your accounts and save it with the other printed documents of record.

The Account Register report shows you all the transactions for a selected General Ledger account, as shown in Figure 13-18.

The Deposits in Transit report (shown in Figure 13-19) shows the outstanding deposits, checks, or other deposit transactions.

The Outstanding Checks report shows the outstanding checks, as shown in Figure 13-20.

REPORT	DESCRIPTION
Account Register	Lists the transactions for a selected account
Account Reconciliation	Prints a report of the account reconciliation information in statement format
Deposits in Transit	Lists the outstanding deposits that have not yet been recorded at the bank
Outstanding Checks	Lists the outstanding checks that have not yet cleared the bank
Other Outstanding Items	Lists any other outstanding items (such as transfers to or from the account through the General Journal) that have not yet been cleared
Bank Deposit Report	Lists bank deposits

TABLE 13-2   Account Reconciliation Reports

Big Business, Inc.
Account Reconciliation
As of Apr 30, 2000
10200 - Regular Checking Account
Bank Statement Date: April 30, 2000

Filter Criteria includes: Report is printed in Detail Format.

Beginning GL Balance				19,191.46
Add: Cash Receipts				1,569.47
Less: Cash Disbursements				<6,250.00>
Add <Less> Other				
Ending GL Balance				14,510.93
Ending Bank Balance				
Add back deposits in transit				
	Apr 1, 2000	4/1/00	904.08	
	Apr 1, 2000	4/1/99	665.39	
Total deposits in transit				1,569.47

FIGURE 13-17 Account Reconciliation report

Big Business, Inc.
Account Register
For the Period From Apr 1, 2000 to Apr 30, 2000
10200 - Regular Checking Account

Filter Criteria includes: Report order is by Date.

Date	Trans No	Type	Trans Desc	Deposit Amt	Withdrawal Am	Balance
			Beginning Balance			19,191.46
4/1/00	1236	Withdrawal	Katriona's Flowers		50.00	19,141.46
4/1/00	1236V	Withdrawal	Katriona's Flowers		-50.00	19,191.46
4/1/00	1237	Withdrawal	ABR Microcomputer Supply		4,215.00	14,976.46
4/1/00	1238	Withdrawal	ABR Microcomputer Supply		1,035.00	13,941.46
4/1/00	1239	Withdrawal	ABR Microcomputer Supply		1,000.00	12,941.46
4/1/00	4/1/00	Deposit	B. C. Consulting	904.08		13,845.54
4/1/00	4/1/99	Deposit	B. C. Consulting	665.39		14,510.93
			Total	**1,569.47**	**6,250.00**	

FIGURE 13-18 Account Register report

Big Business, Inc.
Deposits in Transit
As of Apr 30, 2000
10200 - Regular Checking Account
Filter Criteria includes: 1) Uncleared Transactions; 2) Deposits. Report order is by Number.

Trans No	Date	Reference	Trans Desc	Trans Amt	Deposit Amt
4/1/00	4/1/00	Ck# 5614	B. C. Consulting	904.08	904.08
4/1/99	4/1/00	Ck# 5614	B. C. Consulting	665.39	665.39
			Total	**1,569.47**	**1,569.47**

FIGURE 13-19 Deposits in Transit report

Big Business, Inc.
Outstanding Checks
As of Apr 30, 2000
10200 - Regular Checking Account
Filter Criteria includes: 1) Uncleared Transactions; 2) Checks. Report order is by Number.

Trans No	Date	Trans Desc	Trans Amt
1237	4/1/00	ABR Microcomputer Supply	-4,215.00
1238	4/1/00	ABR Microcomputer Supply	-1,035.00
1239	4/1/00	ABR Microcomputer Supply	-1,000.00
		Total	**-6,250.00**

FIGURE 13-20 Outstanding Checks report

The Other Outstanding Items report shows outstanding miscellaneous items such as General Journal transfers and other information (as shown in Figure 13-21).

The final Account Reconciliation report, the Bank Deposit report, shows bank deposits for the period (as shown in Figure 13-22).

Changing and Closing Accounting Periods

You can use Peachtree Accounting to post transactions to any accounting period within the fiscal year by changing the accounting period. Changing the accounting period is a simple process. (Accounting periods were originally discussed in Chapter 3.)

Big Business, Inc.
Other Outstanding Items
As of Apr 30, 2000
10100 - Cash on Hand
Filter Criteria includes: 1) Uncleared Transactions; 2) Others. Report order is by Number.

Trans No	Date	Trans Desc	Trans Amt	Balance
	4/1/00	Krell Office Systems	2,197.58	2,197.58
	4/1/00	Krell Office Systems	86.72	2,284.30
11507	4/1/00	Krell Office Systems	2,197.58	4,481.88
123489	4/1/00	Lily Pod Systems	21,940.52	26,422.40
XFER04012000	4/1/00	Xfer to Money Market	-1,000.00	25,422.40
		Total	**25,422.40**	

FIGURE 13-21 Other Outstanding Items report

At the end of the fiscal or the payroll year, you must close the year. Closing closes the books for the year. The closing process involves posting journals, printing year-end reports for the audit trail, and (optionally) changing your accounting periods for the next fiscal year. Peachtree Accounting also performs a variety of maintenance tasks at closing, such as purging cleared transactions, employees, purchase orders, and other inactive information. (If you are using the Payroll features in Peachtree Accounting, you must close the payroll year before you can close the fiscal year.)

Big Business, Inc.
Bank Deposit Report
For the Period From Apr 1, 2000 to Apr 30, 2000
10100 - Cash on Hand
Filter Criteria includes: Report order is by Deposit Ticket ID. Report is printed in Detail Format.

Deposit Ticket ID	Date	Reference	Description	Amount
4/1/2000	4/1/00	Ck #2065	Krell Office Systems	-2,197.58
			Total Deposit	**-2,197.58**
			Total Deposits for the Period	**-2,197.58**

FIGURE 13-22 Bank Deposit report

Changing the Accounting Period

You need to change the accounting period whenever the current period changes or you want to post to an accounting period in the fiscal year prior to the current period. Peachtree Accounting allows you to enter transactions to future accounting periods.

 C A U T I O N : Be sure to back up your company data before changing the accounting period!

To change the accounting period, select System from the Tasks menu, then select the Change Accounting Period option from the System submenu. The Change Accounting Period window appears, as shown in Figure 13-23.

Select the accounting period from the drop-down list and click OK. Peachtree Accounting asks you if you want to print reports before continuing. Click Yes to display the Print Reports window (shown in Figure 13-24).

The reports and reporting periods are listed in the window. Peachtree Accounting will print each report that has the Print? checkbox marked. When you are satisfied with your entries, click OK. Peachtree Accounting prints the selected reports to the default printer. Printing the complete list of reports may take a while, but it's a good idea to print a complete set of reports for your audit trail each time you change your accounting period.

Depending on the reports you selected, Peachtree Accounting may ask if you want to post journal information during the reporting processing. Click Yes to post the journal information. This feature ensures that all current year data has been included. (If you switch to a previous accounting period, Peachtree Accounting will not ask if you want to print reports.)

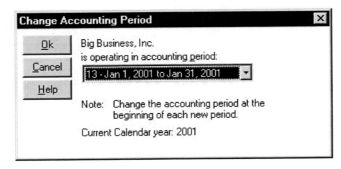

FIGURE 13-23 Change Accounting Period window

Print Reports ✕

The following reports should be printed before the Accounting Period is closed.

Report Name	Reporting Period	Print?
General Ledger	3 - Mar 1, 2000 to Mar 31, 2000	☑

Ok
Cancel
Help

FIGURE 13-24 Print Reports window

Closing the Payroll Year

When you close the payroll year, Peachtree Accounting closes out (zeroes out) the year-to-date payroll totals on all pay levels and EE and ER fields for each employee and the 1099 vendors listed in Accounts Payable.

C A U T I O N : Be sure to back up your company data immediately before closing the payroll year! If you discover after closing the payroll year that you need to make changes to the data in that year, your only option is to restore the data you backed up before you closed, make the changes to that data, and then reconstruct the information you added after you closed the year. (This would be necessary because the new information would not be included in the backed-up data.)

Preparing to Close the Payroll Year

Before you close the payroll year, you must print the following payroll reports:

- Current Earnings report
- Quarterly Earnings report
- Yearly Earnings report

- Payroll Tax report
- Payroll Journal
- State Quarterly Forms (optional)

Peachtree Accounting does not let you select these reports from a window as you did when you changed the accounting period earlier. You must select each of these reports from the Select a Report window in the Payroll section.

After you have printed the reports, verify your payroll information. You may need to make or edit entries through the Payroll Entry window. (For more information on printing Payroll reports and using the Payroll Entry window, see Chapter 7.) When all the payroll information is correct, print the following forms from the Reports menu in the Payroll group:

- Federal Form 940
- Federal Form 941
- Federal Form W-2
- Federal Form W-3

When you have verified the information on these reports and forms, you can install the payroll tax tables (if you have purchased them) or update the payroll tax tables yourself. Basic information on the payroll tax tables appears in Chapter 7. You can then print the W-2s for employees and the 1099s for qualifying 1099 vendors. (1099 forms are part of the Accounts Payable reports. For information on printing Accounts Payable reports, see Chapter 6.)

Closing the Year-to-Date Payroll Totals

Once you have printed your reports, you are ready to close the payroll year.

To close the payroll year, select System from the Tasks menu, then select the Close Payroll Year option from the System submenu. The Close Year window appears, as shown in Figure 13-25.

If you click Backup from the Close Year window, Peachtree Accounting displays the Back Up Company window (shown at the beginning of this chapter in Figure 13-1). You can perform a backup from this window as described earlier in the "Backing Up and Restoring Company Data" section. If you click Continue, Peachtree Accounting will continue without making a backup.

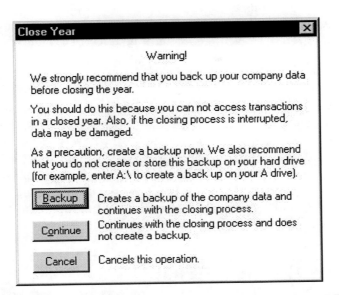

Close Year

Warning!

We strongly recommend that you back up your company data before closing the year.

You should do this because you can not access transactions in a closed year. Also, if the closing process is interrupted, data may be damaged.

As a precaution, create a backup now. We also recommend that you do not create or store this backup on your hard drive (for example, enter A:\ to create a back up on your A drive).

Backup	Creates a backup of the company data and continues with the closing process.
Continue	Continues with the closing process and does not create a backup.
Cancel	Cancels this operation.

FIGURE 13-25 Close Year window

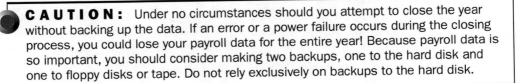

C A U T I O N : Under no circumstances should you attempt to close the year without backing up the data. If an error or a power failure occurs during the closing process, you could lose your payroll data for the entire year! Because payroll data is so important, you should consider making two backups, one to the hard disk and one to floppy disks or tape. Do not rely exclusively on backups to the hard disk.

When the backup is done, Peachtree Accounting displays the Close Calendar Year window.

When you are satisfied, click OK. Peachtree Accounting closes the payroll year. Keep in mind that closing the payroll year in Peachtree Accounting does not purge closed entries in the Payroll Journal or inactive employees. To purge this information, you must run the Purge Old Transactions/Inactives option as described later in this chapter in the section "Purging Information."

It's important to note that you can carry selected payroll totals forward from the previous year for any of the EmployEE calculations. For example, you wouldn't want to close out accrued vacation at the end of the year with the other values. To tell Peachtree Accounting to carry a total forward, you must check the appropriate Run checkbox on the EmployEE tab in the Employee Defaults window (described in Chapter 7).

After Closing the Payroll Year

As a final step to the closing process, you should make changes to any of the state or local tax tables to update them for the new payroll year.

If Peachtree Accounting cannot find a specific tax table for the new year when it prints a report or form, it displays a message that it can't find a specific calculation. Note the calculation Peachtree Accounting can't find, then update the payroll tax tables accordingly. See the "Setting Up Payroll Tax Tables" section in Chapter 7 for more information.

Closing the Fiscal Year

Closing the fiscal year is similar to the process for closing the payroll year. Closing the fiscal year will zero all income, expense, cost of goods, and Equity-Gets Closed account types and post them to your retained earnings account on the balance sheet. Peachtree Accounting summarizes the General Ledger, customer history, and vendor history data for the year, and optionally purges all closed entries in the journals, as well as any customers, vendors, inventory items, and jobs flagged as inactive. All accounts marked as inactive will also be purged at this time.

This process effectively closes the books for the year. Once this is completed, all entry corrections or adjusting journals are locked out. If you are scheduled for an audit for your tax reports or for a general review by your accounting service or CPA, do not close the books until all adjusting entries have been entered and verified by your CPA. You cannot make changes to a closed year, but you can keep the previous year's books open and move forward with later accounting periods while you're assembling the data for the fiscal year closing. Peachtree Accounting keeps up to two fiscal years open (a maximum of 26 accounting periods), so it's not necessary to close the fiscal year until the end of the following year.

Be sure to back up your company data immediately before closing the fiscal year! If you discover after closing the fiscal year that you need to make changes to the data in that year, your only option is to restore the data you backed up before you closed, make the changes to that data, and then reconstruct the information you added after you closed the year. (This would be necessary because the new information would not be included in the backed-up data.)

When you close a year, you may still want to view detailed information such as customer ledgers and invoices for a while after the closing and before you've purged the details. Here's how:

1. Select the appropriate process from the Tasks menu, such as Purchase Orders.
2. From the task window, click Edit Records.
3. In the Show field, select All Transactions from the drop-down list.
4. Select the transaction you want to view.

To close the fiscal year, select System from the Tasks menu, then select the Close Fiscal Year option from the System submenu. The Close Year window appears (shown earlier in Figure 13-25). If you click Backup, Peachtree Accounting displays the Back Up Company window (shown at the beginning of this chapter in Figure 13-1). You can perform a backup from this window, as described earlier in the "Backing Up and Restoring Company Data" section. If you click Continue, Peachtree Accounting will continue without making a backup.

CAUTION: Under no circumstances should you attempt to close the year without backing up the data. If an error or a power failure occurs during the closing process, you could lose your financial data for the entire year! Because this data is so important, you should consider making two backups, one to the hard disk and one to floppy disks or tape. Do not rely exclusively on backups to the hard disk.

When the backup is done, Peachtree Accounting asks if you want to print reports. These reports are a valuable part of your printed audit trail, and you should save them with the other printed documents of record. When you click Yes, the Print Reports window appears, as shown in Figure 13-26.

The reports and reporting periods are listed in the Print Reports window. Note that these reports are different from those that appeared in the Print Reports window shown earlier in Figure 13-24. Peachtree Accounting will print each report that has the Print? checkbox checked. When you are satisfied with your entries, click OK. Peachtree Accounting prints the selected reports to the default printer. Printing the complete list of reports may take a while, but it's a good idea to print a complete set of reports for your audit trail each time you close the fiscal year.

Depending on the reports you selected, Peachtree Accounting may ask if you want to post journal information during the reporting processing. Click Yes to post the journal information. This feature ensures that all current year data has been included.

When the reports have finished spooling to the printer, the Close Fiscal Year Window will display and you can optionally change the accounting periods for the upcoming fiscal year.

When Peachtree Accounting has completed closing the year, you can purge transactions. For audit purposes, always print reports before purging. Although

	Print Reports			
	The following reports should be printed before the Fiscal Year is closed.			
	Report Name	Reporting Period	Print?	
	General Ledger	Fiscal Year Dec 31, 2000	☑	
	General Journal	4 - Apr 1, 2000 to Apr 30, 2000	☑	
	General Journal	5 - May 1, 2000 to May 31, 2000	☑	
	General Journal	6 - Jun 1, 2000 to Jun 30, 2000	☑	
	General Journal	7 - Jul 1, 2000 to Jul 31, 2000	☑	
	General Journal	8 - Aug 1, 2000 to Aug 31, 2000	☑	
	General Journal	9 - Sep 1, 2000 to Sep 30, 2000	☑	
	Cash Receipts Journal	4 - Apr 1, 2000 to Apr 30, 2000	☑	
	Cash Disbursements Journal	4 - Apr 1, 2000 to Apr 30, 2000	☑	

FIGURE 13-26 Print Reports window

purging transactions is not required at this time and may be done at a later time, it may speed up system response. The first Purge Guide window appears (as shown in Figure 13-27).

Depending on the number of records to purge, the range of records to look for, and how fast your computer or network is, the purging process may take quite some time. Therefore, schedule a purge process overnight or even over a weekend. You can also purge records in smaller ranges, such as quarters or months.

Peachtree Accounting steps you through the purging process. There are roughly ten screens (only the first of which is shown in Figure 13-27) that will show you everything you need to know about purging transactions. You can choose to purge quotes, purchase orders, account reconciliation transactions, and reimbursable expenses for all or part of the year. For each type of transaction, enter the date through which you want to purge the transactions. All transactions outside the range will remain in the company's data files.

Although activating the purge log is not recommended by Peachtree Accounting, you may want to turn on the purge logging feature before you purge transactions. If you need to troubleshoot the purging process, the purge.log is very valuable. The purge.log generates a rather bulky file—you should have at least 50 MB or more of free space before activating. You will need to edit the paw70.ini file to activate the purge log.

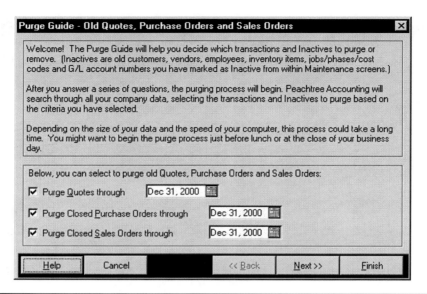

FIGURE 13-27 First Purge Guide window

Exit Peachtree Accounting, select Start, then select Run. Type **paw70.ini** in the command line and select OK. Notepad displays the Peachtree Accounting configuration file. In the options section of the file type **PurgeLog=Yes** (Yes activates the purge log, while No deactivates the purge log.) Save your file, then exit. After you successfully purge your data, deactivate the purge log.

C A U T I O N : If your purge log is too large for Notepad, use WordPad instead. From WordPad, navigate to the purge.log file, which is located in your company data directory.

When you are satisfied with the entries you have made in the purge guide, Peachtree Accounting purges the selected transactions and completes the year-end processing.

If you have closed your fiscal year and have been entering transactions for a few weeks and then discover that you need to restore the previous fiscal year's information and make adjustments or corrections, here's a trick for avoiding reentering the data you've already entered for the current fiscal year:

1. Do a separate backup of your company data files to floppy disks or tape. Set these aside. (You will only need to use these if something goes wrong with the restore process in step 3.)

2. Export the journals for the dates covering the new transactions. For example, if your backups were done on January 31st and it's now March 21st, export the journals for January 31st through March 21st. (Exporting and importing data is discussed later in this chapter.)

3. Restore the previous year's files from the backups.

4. Make any adjustments or corrections to the previous year's data.

5. Close the fiscal year with the adjustments and corrections.

6. Import the journals. The journals will contain the transactions you entered subsequent to the backup.

7. Run audit reports and verify that the procedure worked and that your accounts reconcile.

Purging Information

It is not necessary to run a payroll year or fiscal year closing to purge old transactions, customers, vendors, employees, inventory, jobs, phases, cost codes, or other information. Even though it is common for many businesses to wait until year-end to purge information, you can purge information at any time using the Purge Old Transactions/Inactives option in the System submenu on the Tasks menu.

In general, to purge a transaction or record, there must be no active transactions or records linked to the item you want to purge. The item should have no outstanding balance and, where applicable, the item should be flagged as inactive.

C A U T I O N : Under no circumstances should you attempt to purge without backing up all the company data. If an error or a power failure occurs during the purge process, you could lose your company's data files! Because the purge process is inherently dangerous—you are permanently removing data from your company's data files—you should consider making two backups, one to the hard disk and one to floppy disks or tape. Do not rely exclusively on backups to the hard disk.

To start a data purge, select System from the Tasks menu, then select Purge Old Transactions/Inactives from the System submenu. The first purge guide appears (shown earlier in Figure 13-27). Follow the purge guides carefully. When you are satisfied with the entries you have made in the purge guide, Peachtree Accounting purges the selected transactions or items. (For audit purposes, you should print reports before purging any set of transactions. If you have already been printing audit reports on a regular basis, you may not need to do this.)

The purge log (described a little earlier) is also helpful for determining why a particular transaction or group of transactions was saved. The purge process has very specific rules about what to purge and not to purge, so if you see old transactions that you think should have been purged, you can use the purge log to determine why they were saved. For example, when you purge inactives from your data files, you should also make a point of purging the transactions to make sure that there are no unpurged transactions that would prevent Peachtree Accounting from purging the related inactives.

Using Action Items

One of the many powerful features in Peachtree Accounting is the ability to set action items. Action items are events that affect your business. The Action Items window is a simple personal information manager (PIM) that is integrated with Peachtree Accounting. The Action Items window lets you log business events for customers, create to-do lists, and set alerts. You can set up action items to track a variety of conditions, such as:

- Inventory below the minimum stock level
- Customer over a credit limit
- Upcoming payroll check run
- Overdue payments to a vendor

In addition to tracking specific accounting conditions, you can schedule and monitor daily events such as meetings, sales calls, and user-defined events that you can set up on your own.

Setting Action Item Options

The first step in using action items is to set the action item options. Action item options let you determine such things as the types of events you want to track and the number of days before or after the event date to start displaying the event. From the Options menu, select the Action Items/Event Log Options option. The Action Items and Event Log Options window appears with the Activities tab displayed (as shown in Figure 13-28).

The Activities tab lets you identify the types of events you want to display in the Action Items window.

Using the backups you made just prior to closing the fiscal year and purging data, you can do a temporary restore of an entire year's data to accommodate audits or to do detailed tracking of a financial question. More importantly, you can do it without overwriting your existing company files or stopping your day-to-day accounting tasks. Here's how:

1. Create a temporary directory with a name such as AUDITFIL in the PEACHW folder.

2. Using the appropriate Restore procedure, restore the company's year-end files to this directory. You must include all the .dat files and the version.txt file to this directory.

3. Start Peachtree Accounting.

4. Select Open Company from the File menu and then go to the AUDITFIL directory and open the company you've just restored. (You should see the company's name in the Company Name box along with the other company names.)

5. Double-check that this is the right company by selecting System from the Tasks menu, then selecting Change Accounting Periods from the submenu. The accounting period in the dialog box should reflect the company you've just restored.

6. As a final safety measure, open the Maintain Company Information window and change the company name to reflect that this is not the current company. For example, for the 2000 data for Big Business, you might change "Big Business, Inc." to "Big Business – 2000 Data." The purging process may take quite some time depending on the number of records to purge, the range of records to look for, and how fast your computer or network is. You may want to schedule a purge process overnight or even over a weekend. You can also purge records in smaller ranges, such as by quarters or by months (if your company has a great deal of accounting activity). Some experimentation will give you pointers on the most effective purging method to use for your company.

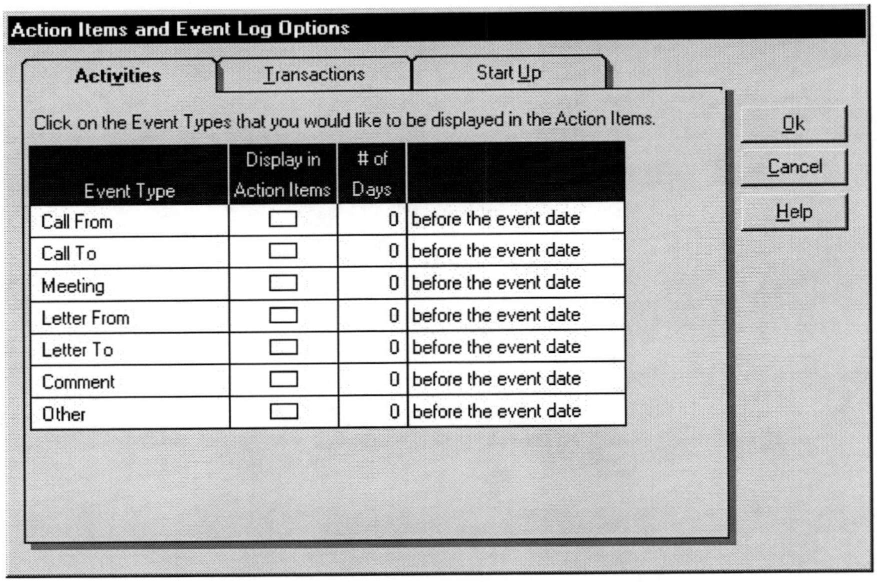

FIGURE 13-28 Action Items and Event Log Options window with the Activities tab displayed

Event Type This is the type of event you want to display in the Action Items window. This field is display-only: the event types are predefined (although you can enter additional custom events under the Other category). The events you can select for are Call From, Call To, Meeting, Letter From, Letter To, Comment, and Other.

Display in Action Items Mark this checkbox to display the corresponding item in the Action Items window. (The default is for all the items to be checked. Unless you are familiar with action items, you should simply accept the defaults.)

# of Days Enter the number of days before (or after) the date an event occurs that you want Peachtree Accounting to display the event in the Action Items window. To specify the number of days after the event, select After the Event Date from the drop-down list in the field immediately to the right of this one. (You must have checked the corresponding Display in Action Items checkbox to make an entry in this field.)

When you are satisfied with your entries, click the Transactions tab. The Transactions tab appears, as shown in Figure 13-29.

You use the Transactions tab to identify which types of transactions to create and display events for in the Action Items window, such as quotes or invoices sent, collection letters, receipts, and paychecks.

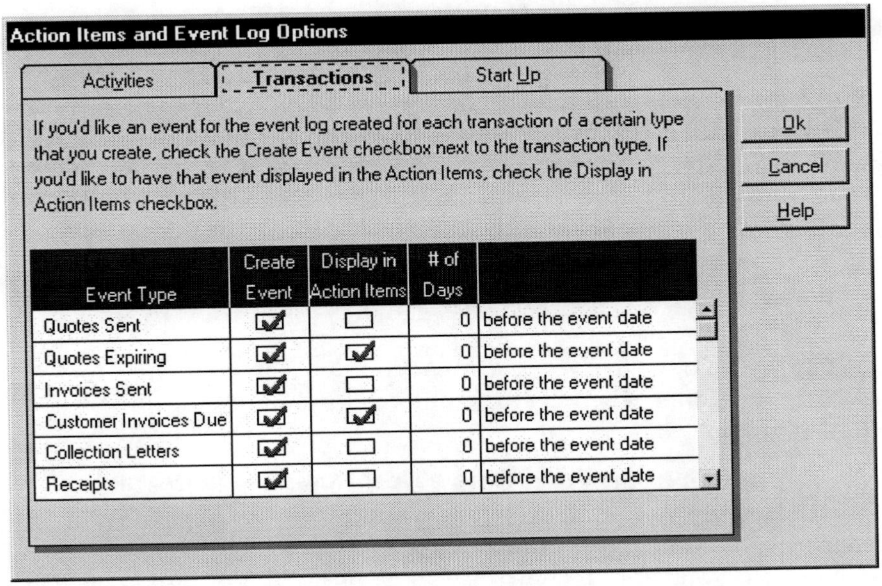

FIGURE 13-29 Action Items and Event Log Options window with the Transactions tab displayed

Event Type   There are 11 transaction event types set up in Peachtree Accounting: Quotes Sent, Quotes Expiring, Invoices Sent, Customer Invoices Due, Collection Letters, Receipts, P.O. Sent, P.O. Expiring, Vendor Invoices Due, Checks To Vendors, and Paychecks. This field is display-only.

Create Event   Mark this checkbox to create an event each time you create a transaction of this type. For example, each time a quote is set to expire, Peachtree Accounting would create an event that would let you know that the quote for a given customer is about to expire. This would let you follow up with the customer and see if they wanted to close the order.

> **T I P :** Even if you don't plan on displaying the event in the Action Items window, it's a good idea to check all the Create Event boxes. If you later decide to display the events, the events will already have been created.

Display in Action Items   Mark this checkbox to display the corresponding item in the Action Items window. You might not want to track some items if knowing about them isn't a high priority. For example, you may feel comfortable about your check processing and not want to create events for checks to vendors or paychecks. (You must have checked the corresponding Create Event checkbox to make an entry in this field.)

# of Days   Enter the number of days before (or after) the date an event occurs that you want Peachtree Accounting to display the event in the Action Items window. To specify the number of days after the event, select After the Event Date from the drop-down list in the field immediately to the right of this one. (You must have checked the corresponding Display in Action Items checkbox to make an entry in this field.)

When you are satisfied with your entries, click the Start Up tab. The Start Up tab appears, as shown in Figure 13-30.

The Start Up tab lets you set the Action Items Start Up options. Start Up options determine when the Action Items window appears automatically and how it is displayed.

Display Action Items Each Time a New Company Is Opened   Check this box to have the Action Items window appear each time you open a company's files using the File Open Company option. Bellwether Garden Supply, one of the sample companies included with Peachtree Accounting, is an example of how this feature works—the Action Items window appears every time you open the company.

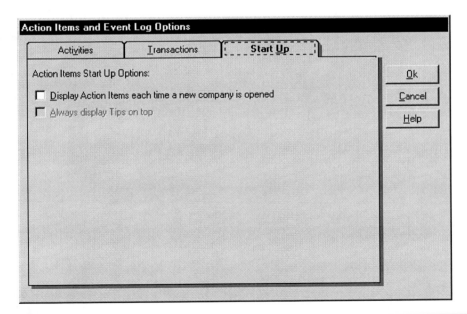

FIGURE 13-30   Action Items and Event Log Options window with the Start Up tab displayed

Always Display Tips on Top Check this option to display the Tips tab as the default tab whenever you display the Action Items window. If you leave this field unchecked, the last tab you had open in the Action Items window will appear the next time you open the window. (The Tips tab is described later in this section.)

When you are satisfied with your Action Items and Event Log options, click OK. You are now ready to enter events and to-do items.

Entering Events

Once you have set up your Action Item defaults, you can enter events and to-do items in the Action Items window. From the Tasks menu, select the Action Items option. The Action Items window appears with the Events tab displayed (as shown in Figure 13-31).

The buttons on the Action Items window change depending on the tab displayed. The buttons for the Events tab are shown in Table 13-3.

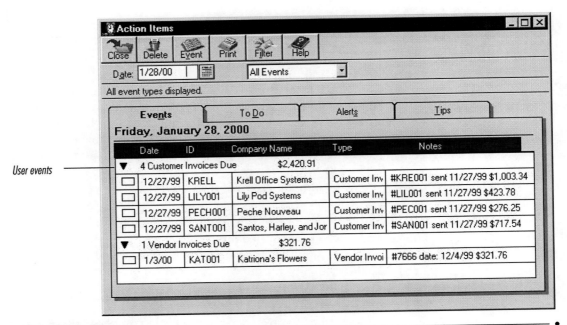

User events

| **FIGURE 13-31** | Action Items window with the Events tab displayed |

BUTTON	NAME	DESCRIPTION
Close	Close	Closes the Action Items window
Delete	Delete	Deletes the selected action item
Event	Event	Lets you create an event in the Create Event window
Print	Print	Prints the events
Filter	Filter	Sets filter criteria for action items
Help	Help	Displays the online help on this window

TABLE 13-3   Toolbar Buttons on the Action Items Window for the Events Tab

The Events tab shows the outstanding events—events you haven't checked off as completed. There are two kinds of events you can display: system events and user events. System events are generated automatically from transactions in Peachtree Accounting. User events (like those shown in Figure 13-30) are events you set up yourself. When you specified the options earlier in the Action Items and Event Log Options window, you identified which types of system and user events will be displayed in the Events tab. (Although the tabs are discussed in the order they appear on the window, you can use the tabs in any order you like.)

You can close the user or system events sections of the Events tab by double-clicking on the down arrow located on the far left of the section's header. You might close a section to simplify the view or, in this example, to see the next section. Figure 13-32 shows the Events tab with the user events section closed. (When a section is closed, the down arrow switches to a right arrow.)

To redisplay a closed section, double-click the corresponding right arrow.

You can use the Action Items – Filter Selection window to adjust the events you see in the Events tab. Clicking Filter at the top of the Action Items window displays the Action Items – Filter Selection window (shown in Figure 13-33).

User events
(closed)

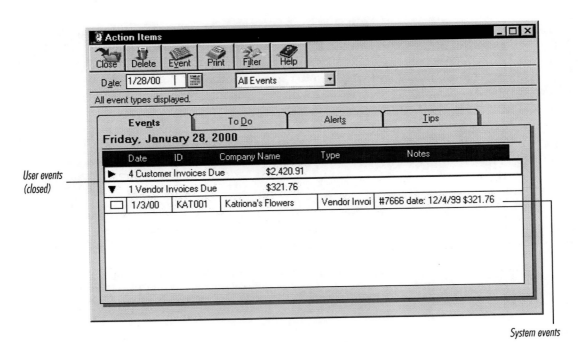

System events

FIGURE 13-32   Action Items window with the user events section closed

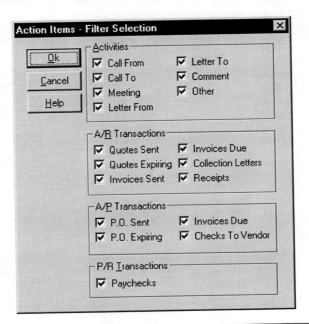

FIGURE 13-33   Action Items – Filter Selection window

The Action Items – Filter Selection window shows the complete list of events you can display in the Events tab. The Activities section at the top of the window lists the various user events you can display. The A/R Transactions, A/P Transactions, and P/R Transactions list the various system events you can display. When you are satisfied with your entries on this window, click OK to return to the Action Items window.

While system events are generated automatically, you need to set up user events on your own. To set up events, click Event in the Action Items window. The Create Event window appears (shown in Figure 13-34). You can also display the Create Event window and edit an item by double-clicking the item on the Event tab.

The Create Event window has a separate set of buttons, as shown in Table 13-4.

You create and edit user events through the Create Event window, such as for meetings, phone calls, letters, and user-defined events you set up yourself.

Type   Choose from one of three types: Customer/Prospect, Employee/Sales Rep, or Vendor. The type you choose determines which list of IDs you see in the ID field.

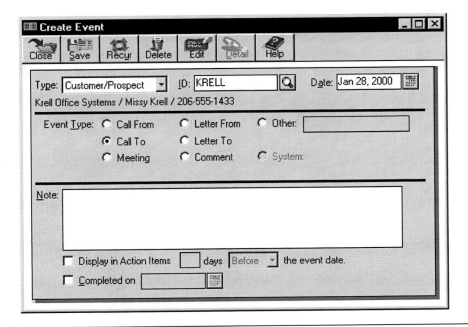

FIGURE 13-34   Create Event window

BUTTON	NAME	DESCRIPTION
Close	Close	Closes the Create Event window
Save	Save	Saves the event
Recur	Recur	Sets up recurring events
Delete	Delete	Deletes the selected event
Edit	New Records/ Edit Records	Lets you create or edit an event
Detail	Detail	Goes to appropriate transaction window to view the detail for a system event
Help	Help	Displays the online help on this window

TABLE 13-4 Toolbar Buttons on the Create Event Window

ID Select an ID from the list. The IDs you see in this field are determined by your selection in the Type field. When you select an ID, the general information appears on the line below the Type, ID, and Date fields.

Date Select the date you want for the event. Click the Calendar button or right-click in this field to display the date-selection calendar.

If you select a type, ID, and date that are already used for an event, the information appears in the window. A typical Comment event appears in Figure 13-35.

Event Type Select one of the event types. Peachtree Accounting can filter on each different type of event and display some, all, or none of these. For the Other event type, you can enter up to 14 alphanumeric characters for the event, such as DELIVER MDSE or BUILD MODEL. Although you can set up as many

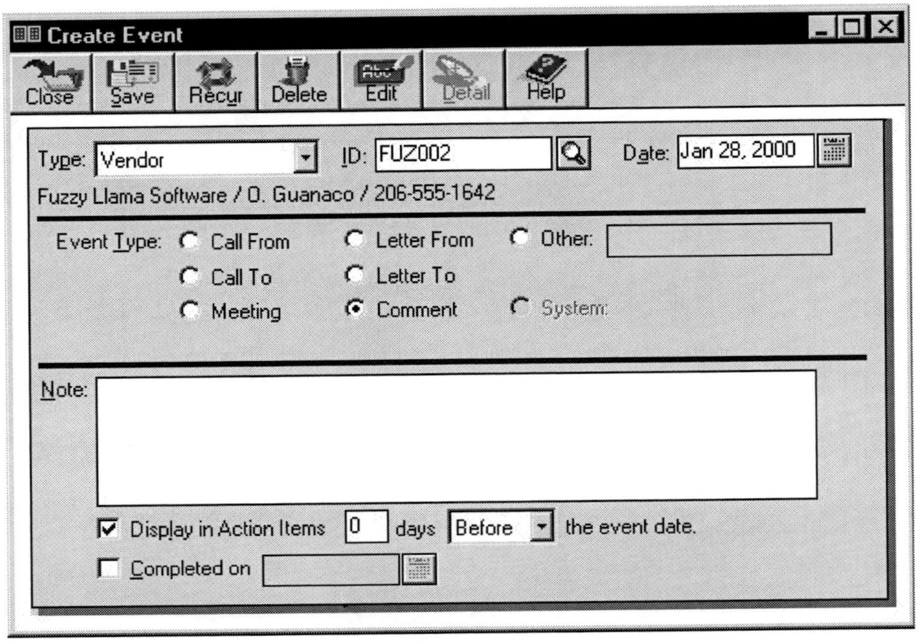

FIGURE 13-35 Create Event window with Comment event information

different events with the Other event type as you like, Peachtree Accounting classes all of them as Other for the purposes of filtering.

When you're working with a user event, System (below Other) is grayed out. When you're working with a system event, all the Event Type buttons are grayed out except for System. System events are created by Peachtree Accounting, so you cannot create them through this window; you can only edit them.

Note Enter a note about the event of up to 255 alphanumeric characters in this field.

Display in Action Items Check this box to display the item in the Action Items window. You can optionally set the event to show up a specified number of days before or after the event. To do this, enter the number of days in the days field, and select before or after the event date in the date field. If you don't check this box, the item will still show up as an event when you display the Events tab.

Completed On Check the box when the task is completed. Enter the date in the field to the right. Click the Calendar button or right-click in this field to display the date-selection calendar. Completed items are automatically removed from the Events list.

When you're satisfied with the entries in the Create Event window, click Save to save the event, and click Close to return to the Action Items window.

Editing an Event

To edit an event, click Edit Records in the Create Event window. The Contact Entry List window (the standard Edit Records window) appears, as shown in Figure 13-36.

Select the event you want to edit. Peachtree Accounting displays the event information in the Create Event window.

You can edit system events as well. When you are displaying system event information in the Create Event window, you can click Detail to display the appropriate window from Peachtree Accounting for the transaction and then make changes to the transaction information. When you are editing a system event, you can only make changes to the Note field when the event appears in the Action Items window. Other information in the system event is part of the actual transaction itself, not an event based on that transaction.

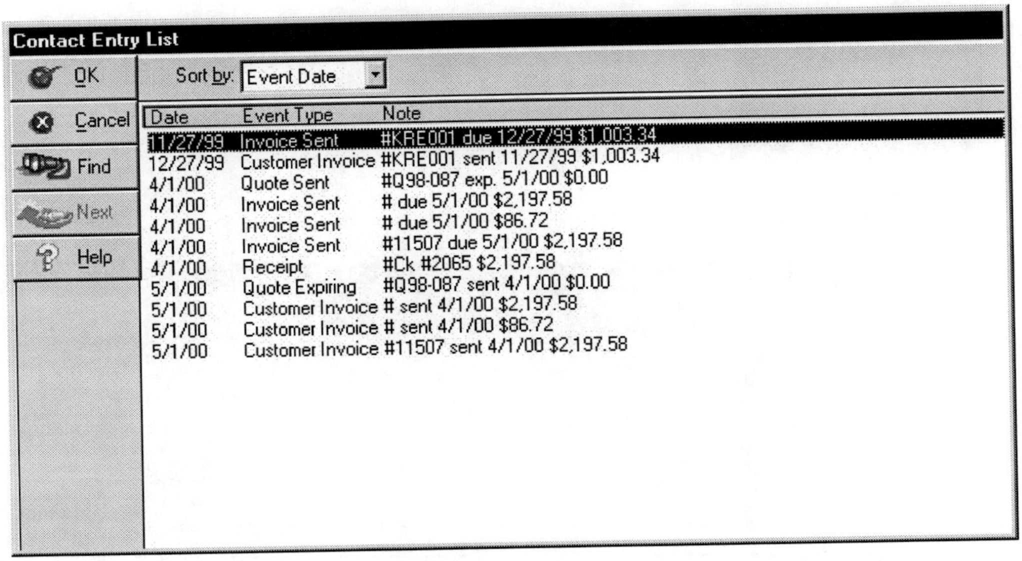

Contact Entry List

OK	Sort by: Event Date	
Cancel	Date	Event Type	Note
Find	11/27/99	Invoice Sent	#KRE001 due 12/27/99 $1,003.34
	12/27/99	Customer Invoice	#KRE001 sent 11/27/99 $1,003.34
	4/1/00	Quote Sent	#Q98-087 exp. 5/1/00 $0.00
Next	4/1/00	Invoice Sent	# due 5/1/00 $2,197.58
	4/1/00	Invoice Sent	# due 5/1/00 $86.72
Help	4/1/00	Invoice Sent	#11507 due 5/1/00 $2,197.58
	4/1/00	Receipt	#Ck #2065 $2,197.58
	5/1/00	Quote Expiring	#Q98-087 sent 4/1/00 $0.00
	5/1/00	Customer Invoice	# sent 4/1/00 $2,197.58
	5/1/00	Customer Invoice	# sent 4/1/00 $86.72
	5/1/00	Customer Invoice	#11507 sent 4/1/00 $2,197.58

FIGURE 13-36 Contact Entry List window

Creating Recurring Events

You can create recurring events for action items as you would create other recurring events, such as invoices. For example, you may want to set a reminder that the paychecks need to be run several days in advance of each payday. Start by entering the event information in the Create Event window. Then, instead of clicking Save to enter the event information, click Recur on the toolbar. The standard Create Recurring Event window appears (shown in Figure 13-37).

Events can recur daily, weekly, every two weeks, every four weeks, 15th and end of month, 1st of month and 15th, every accounting period, monthly, quarterly, twice a year, or annually.

 CAUTION: Don't click Save after you set up a recurring event because you'll duplicate the event for the current period by saving the information on the window as another event. Just click Close to close the window.

Displaying Events for Vendors, Customers, or Employees

In earlier chapters, you saw that some of the Maintain windows had a Log button. You can click this button to see the Event log for customers, vendors, or employees. When you click Log, an Event Log window appears. A typical Event Log window (from the Maintain Customer/Prospects window) appears in Figure 13-38.

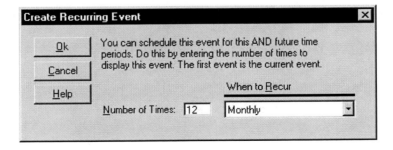

FIGURE 13-37 Create Recurring Event window

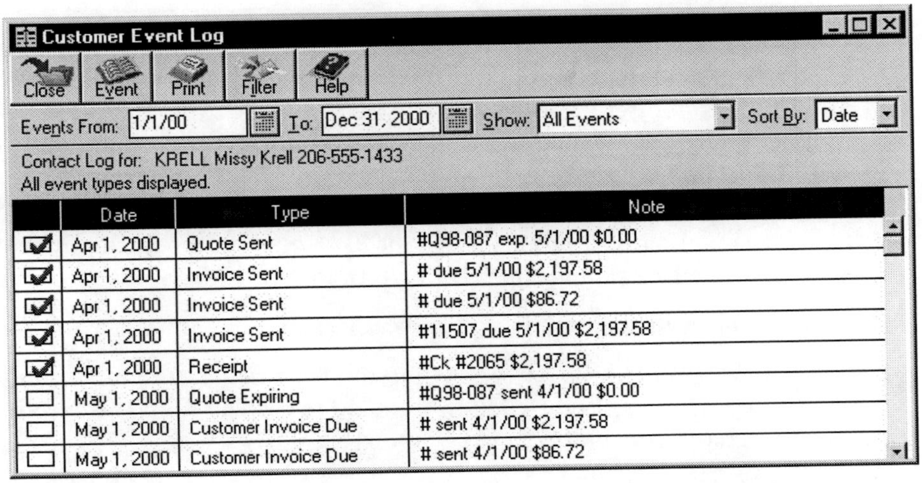

FIGURE 13-38 Customer Event Log window

From the Event Log window, you can add events for the customer, vendor, or employee by clicking Event.

Events From Enter the starting date for the events for the customer, vendor, or employee. The default for this field is the first day in the fiscal year.

To Enter the ending date for the events for the customer, vendor, or employee. The default for this field is the last day in the fiscal year.

Show Select the events you want to show from the drop-down list: completed events, uncompleted events, or all events.

Sort By Select the sorting method: type or date.

Completed (unlabeled) Click the checkbox to mark an item as completed.

Date This is the transaction date. This field is display-only.

Type This is the transaction type. This field is display-only.

Note This is the note (if any) for the transaction entered through the Create Event window in the Note field. This field is display-only.

You can also click Filter to filter the events that appear on the list. Peachtree Accounting will display the Event – Filter Selection window (not shown) to allow you to make your selections. This window is identical to the Action Items – Filter Selection window shown earlier in Figure 13-33.

Entering To-Do Items

As with other standard personal information manager programs, Peachtree Accounting lets you set up to-do items. Unlike events, to-do items are tasks that are not necessarily associated with a specific vendor, customer, or employee, such as discussing accounting questions with your tax attorney or CPA, or organizing a company move.

To view and enter to-do items, click the To Do tab in the Action Items window. The To Do tab appears, as shown in Figure 13-39.

Comp?   Check this box when you have completed the item.

Date   This defaults to the date shown in the Date field at the top of the Action Items window. You can right-click in the field to display the date-selection calendar to change the date.

Completed   Enter the date the task was completed in this field. You must have checked the Comp? box to enter a date in this field. By default, Peachtree Accounting enters the date shown in the Date field at the top of the Action

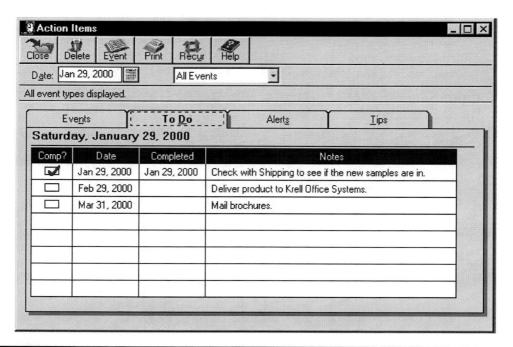

FIGURE 13-39   Action Items window with the To Do tab displayed

Items window. (Checking an item as completed is simply a way to see that it is completed. To remove an item, you must highlight the item and click Delete.)

Notes Enter up to 255 alphanumeric characters in this field to describe the to-do item.

You can use Recur to set up recurring to-do items. The recurring items appear in the tab with the appropriate date.

Setting Alerts

You've seen how to set events and to-do items. Events are not alerts; they are simply events you want to track. An alert is an event for which you have set certain criteria. When the criteria are met, Peachtree Accounting displays an alarm in the status bar at the bottom of the screen.

Shows you current alerts.	🕐	1/29/00	Period 1 - 1/1/00 to 1/31/00

Typical alerts you might set up could include:

- A customer whose latest purchase puts them over their preset credit limit
- An inventory item that falls below the minimum stock level
- A vendor to whom you haven't made a payment

To see the alerts, start by clicking the Alerts tab. The Alerts tab appears in the Action Items window (shown in Figure 13-40 with several sample alerts displayed).

The Alerts tab has one button that's different from the previous tabs, as shown here:

BUTTON	NAME	DESCRIPTION
🕐 Alert	Set Alert	Sets an alert through the Set Company Alerts window

Alert For The ID and name of the vendor, customer, or employee appears in this field. This field is display-only.

Alert Condition The conditions of the alert appear in this field. This field is display-only.

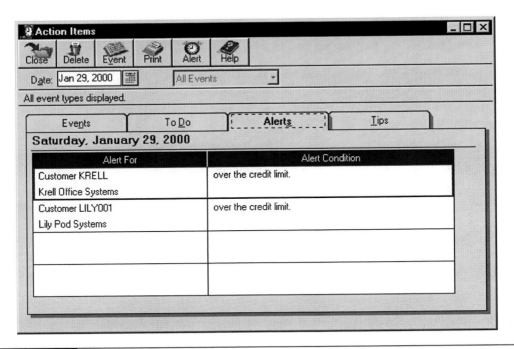

FIGURE 13-40 Alerts tab with sample alerts

The alerts you see on this tab are all the alerts that meet the criteria you've defined. Any alerts that aren't active (that is, that haven't had their alert criteria met) do not appear in this window.

Peachtree Accounting checks the criteria for all the alert conditions you have set up whenever you open a company or save or post a transaction. If the criteria for an alert are met, Peachtree Accounting displays the alarm icon in the status bar. Click this icon to display the Alerts tab in the Action Items window.

To set up alert criteria, click Alert in the toolbar. The Set Company Alerts window appears (shown in Figure 13-41 with sample alerts already entered).

Apply To   Select what you want the alert to apply to from the drop-down list: customer, vendor, employee, inventory item, or General Ledger account.

From   From the drop-down list, select the first ID in the range to set criteria for. (If you want to select a single ID, enter the ID in both the From and To fields.)

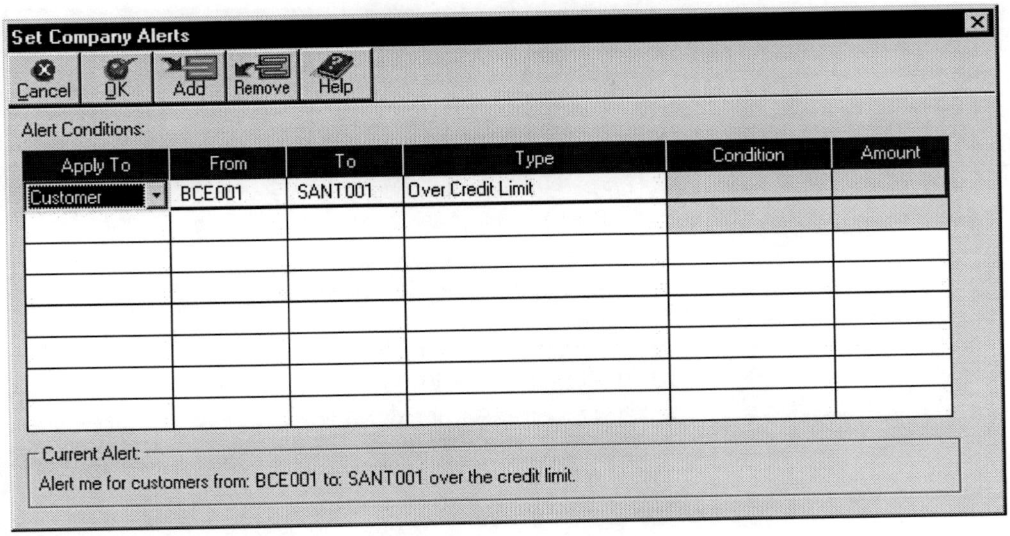

FIGURE 13-41 Set Company Alerts window

To From the drop-down list, select the last ID in the range for which you want to set criteria.

Type Select the type of criteria from the drop-down list. Peachtree Accounting defines the criteria based on your selection in the Apply To field. Table 13-5 shows the Apply To options and the types of criteria you can track for each one.

Condition Select the appropriate condition in this field, such as >= (greater than or equal to), <= (less than or equal to), > 30 days old, > Budget, and so on. The conditions available depend on the criterion you selected in the Type field. (The Condition and Amount fields are grayed if they aren't relevant for the selected type.)

Amount Enter the amount for the comparison.

Current Alert Peachtree Accounting displays a sentence describing the conditions currently set in the highlighted alert.

You can add and remove alerts with Add and Remove at the top of the Set Company Alerts window as you were able to add and remove invoices and other information in other windows shown throughout this book.

APPLY TO	CRITERIA
Customer	Over Credit Limit Sales Volume – Current Period Sales Volume – Year to Date Current Balance Outstanding Invoice Balance Outstanding Invoice Age
Vendor	Purchase Volume – Current Period Purchase Volume – Year to Date Current Balance Outstanding Invoice Balance Outstanding Invoice Age
Employee	Total Hours – Per Paycheck Total Hours – Yearly Total Gross Pay – Per Paycheck Gross Pay – Yearly Total
Inventory Item	Quantity on Hand below Minimum Stock Sales Volume – Current Period Sales Volume – Year to Date Quantity Sold – Current Period Quantity Sold – Year to Date
G/L Account	Balance – Current Period Balance – Year to Date Budget – Current Period Budget – Year to Date

TABLE 13-5   Criteria for Apply To Options

Viewing Peachtree Accounting Tips

Peachtree Accounting offers a variety of interesting tips on how to use Peachtree Accounting more effectively. To see these tips, click the Tips tab in the Action Items window. The Tips tab appears, as shown in Figure 13-42.

To see the next tip, click Next Tip at the bottom of the window.

Using Management Tools

Peachtree Accounting has four management tools to help you manage your business and analyze your financial information. The four tools in the Manager Series are the Cash Manager, the Collection Manager, the Payment Manager,

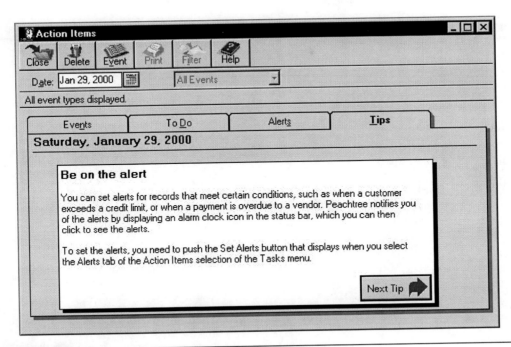

FIGURE 13-42 Action Items window with the Tips tab displayed

and the Financial Manager. Each of these provides you with graphs and tools to analyze your company's financial data and gain a better understanding of how your business is doing. You can examine data at any of four levels: the overview level, the transactions within an overview, detailed information about vendors or customers, and the actual transactions.

The following sections will show you how to use each of these tools.

Using the Cash Manager

The Cash Manager is the first and most important of the management tools. The Cash Manager helps you project cash availability. You use the Cash Manager to track cash receipts from Accounts Receivable and disbursements for Accounts Payable and Payroll.

To start the Cash Manager, select the Cash Manager option from the Analysis menu. The Cash Manager window appears, as shown in Figure 13-43. (Before you start the Cash Manager, you should make sure that all the journals have been posted.)

The Cash Manager has a separate set of buttons, as shown in Table 13-6.

BUTTON	NAME	DESCRIPTION
Close	Close	Closes the Cash Manager window
Save	Save	Saves the information as a record
Event	Event	Displays the Create Event window (discussed earlier in this chapter)
Refresh	Refresh	Refreshes the information in the window
Print	Print	Prints a report of the information in the window (varies depending on the Cash Manager window)
Numeric Graph	Numeric/Graph	Switches to numeric or graph format from spreadsheet view
S.Sheet	S.Sheet	Switches to the Cash Manager spreadsheet
Source	Source	Displays detail on a customer or vendor
Detail	Detail	Displays the appropriate transaction window to view and optionally edit the detail for a transaction
Help	Help	Displays the online help on this window

TABLE 13-6   Toolbar Buttons on the Cash Manager Window

Display   Choose Numeric to display the information in numeric form (as shown in Figure 13-43). You can also choose Graph to display information in either a column or bar graph. See the "Using the Graphic Display" section later in this chapter.

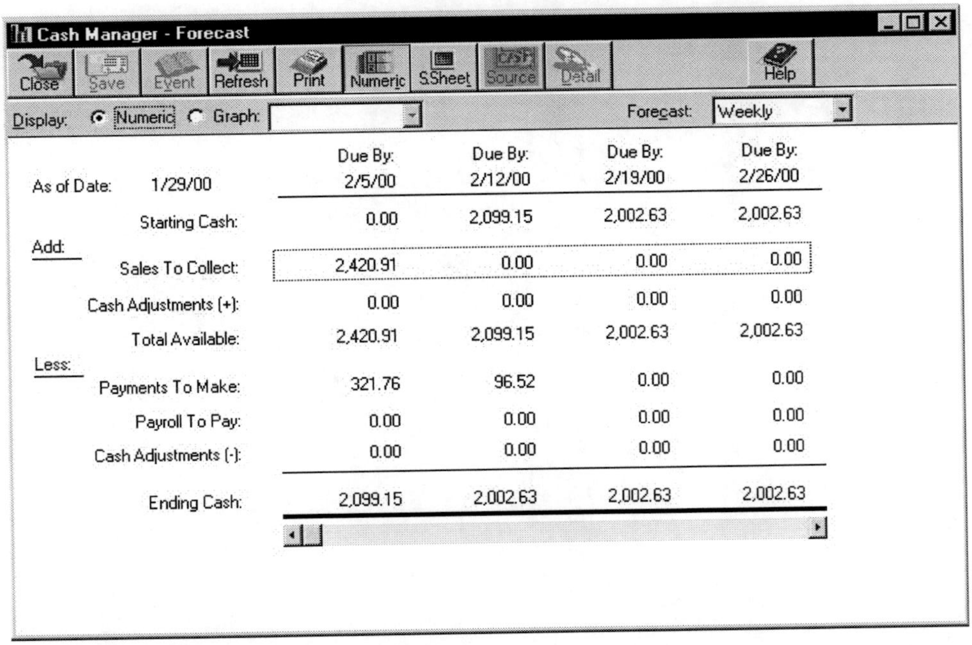

FIGURE 13-43 Cash Manager window

Forecast   Select a weekly, biweekly, or monthly display of information. The information in Figure 13-43 is in a weekly format. Figure 13-44 shows the information in monthly format.

Starting Cash   This is the starting cash for the period. This field is display-only.

Sales To Collect   This is the total Accounts Receivable for the period. Double-click the field to display the information for the period in a detail window.

Cash Adjustments (+)   The total of any positive cash adjustments you've made through the Cash Manager – Forecast window (discussed later in this section).

Total Available   This is the total of the starting cash, the sales to collect, and the cash adjustments. This field is display-only.

Payments To Make   This is the total Accounts Payable for the period. Double-click the field to display the information for the period in a detail window.

Payroll To Pay   This is the outstanding payroll for the period. Double-click the field to display the information for the period in a detail window.

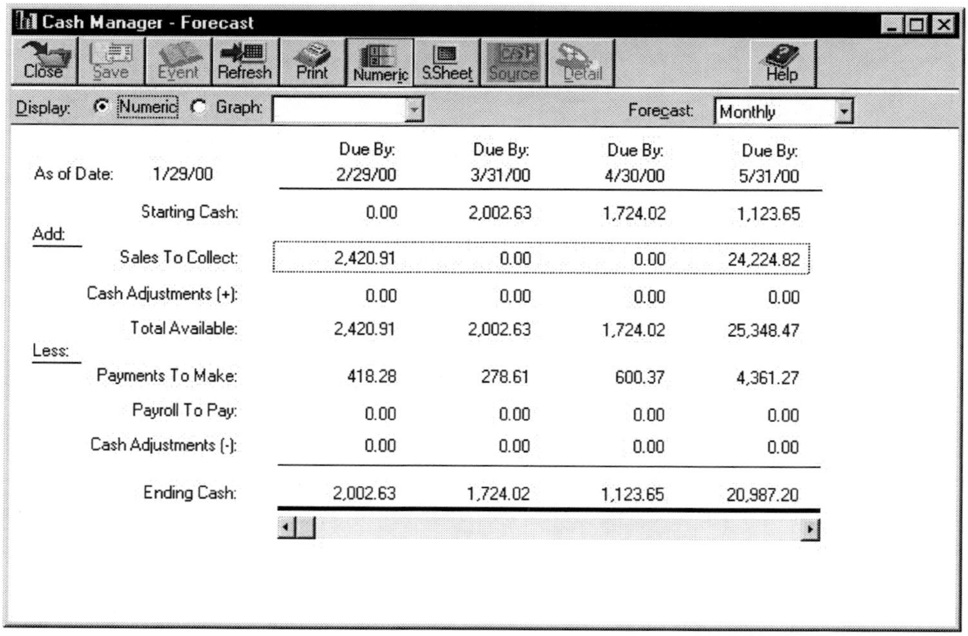

FIGURE 13-44 Cash Manager information shown in monthly numeric format

Cash Adjustments (-)   The total of any negative cash adjustments you've made through the Cash Manager – Forecast window (discussed later in this section).

Ending Cash   This is the total available cash less the outstanding payments, the payroll to pay, and any cash adjustments. This field is display-only.

Updating Cash Manager Information

Whenever you make changes to information that may affect the information displayed in the Cash Manager, you should refresh the information by clicking Refresh at the top of the window. This ensures that the forecast information displayed in the Cash Manager is complete and up to date.

When you click Refresh, the Cash Manager – Forecast Refresh window appears (shown in Figure 13-45).

As you can see from Figure 13-45, the default option will completely update the information in the Cash Manager and will overwrite any manual adjustments you've made. (Manual adjustments cover such things as orders or purchases that you know are coming in, but which haven't been entered in Peachtree Accounting yet.) If you want to update the transaction information

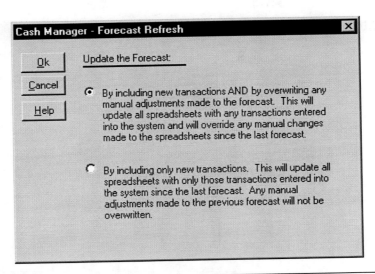

FIGURE 13-45 Cash Manager – Forecast Refresh window

but maintain the manual adjustments, select the second option in the window. You might want to keep the adjustments if you're adding a group of sales orders, but you also want to keep information on anticipated sales or expenses.

Using the Graphic Display

The information shown in the Cash Manager defaults to a numeric display. To show information in a graphic format, click the Graph radio button. You can display information in either a column or bar format (select the format from the drop-down list).

Figures 13-46 and 13-47 show graphic displays of the information you saw earlier in Figure 13-43.

The periods used in the graphic display are those specified in the Forecast field: weekly, biweekly, or monthly. If you change the period, Peachtree Accounting recalculates the graph and changes the dates at the base of the columns or bars.

If you're preparing a report and need to include information from Peachtree Accounting, you can use the built-in screen capture feature in Windows to cut and paste a copy of the graph into a word processor or other Windows application. Simply press ALT-PRINT SCREEN to copy the current screen to the Windows clipboard in a bitmap format. You can then use the Edit | Paste function from within your Windows application to paste the bitmap into a document or spreadsheet.

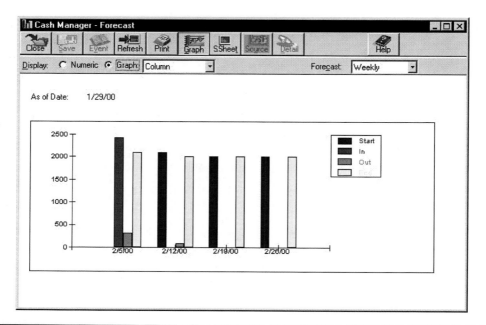

FIGURE 13-46 Cash Manager information shown in column format

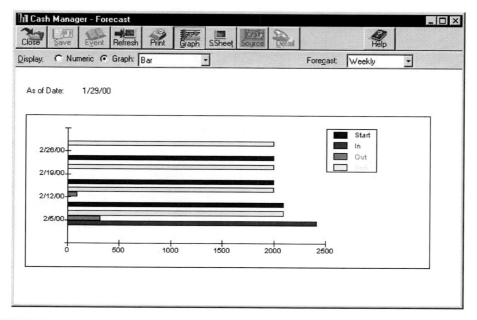

FIGURE 13-47 Cash Manager information shown in bar format

N O T E : You can use the ALT-PRINT SCREEN capture function to capture any screen and paste it into another application.

Because this function captures the entire screen, including headers, you may want to edit the bitmap to trim any extraneous information. You can use Windows Paintbrush (included with Windows) or other graphics programs to edit bitmaps.

Using the Cash Manager Spreadsheet

The first level of analysis in the Cash Manager is to use the numeric and graphic displays to view the overview information. The next level of analysis is to use the spreadsheet to view specific information and make adjustments, as well as to attach notes to transactions. To start the spreadsheet from the numeric display, double-click the row you want to view, or highlight the row and then click S.Sheet at the top of the window. (If you're in graph view, double-click anywhere on the window.) The spreadsheet appears, as shown in Figure 13-48.

Cash Manager - Forecast

Close | Save | Event | Refresh | Print | Graph | S.Sheet | Source | Detail | Help

Spreadsheet: Sales To Collect

Weekly

As of Date: 1/29/00   Actual   As Adjusted/Moved

Customer	Due By	Amount	Due By 2/5/00	Due By 2/12/00	Due By 2/19/00	Due By 2/26/00	Note
Krell Office Systems	12/27/99	1,003.34	1,003.34				NOTE
Krell Office Systems	5/1/00	2,284.30					NOTE
Lily Pod Systems	12/27/99	423.78	423.78				NOTE
Lily Pod Systems	5/1/00	21,940.52					NOTE
Peche Nouveau	12/27/99	276.25	276.25				NOTE
Santos, Harley, and Jo	12/27/99	717.54	717.54				NOTE
	Totals:		2,420.91	0.00	0.00	0.00	

FIGURE 13-48 Cash Manager – Forecast

From the spreadsheet, you can view the individual transactions that make up the totals for a category and a period, and if necessary, change their due dates as mapped in the Cash Manager. (Changes you make on the spreadsheet appear only in the Cash Manager. They do not affect the actual transaction information in the various Peachtree Accounting sections.)

Spreadsheet   This field displays the row you are currently working on. You can select a different row from the drop-down list.

Customer/Vendor/Employee   This is the name of the customer, the vendor, or the employee (depending on whether you have selected Sales To Collect, Payments To Make, or Payroll To Pay). This field is display-only.

Due By   This is the due date for the transaction. This field is display-only.

Amount   This is the amount of the transaction. This field is display-only.

Due By (Period)   The Due By (Period) fields let you disburse an amount across several periods. For example, if a customer is going to be paying part of an invoice down and the rest on delivery, you can adjust the amount across the periods for a more accurate forecast. Similarly, you can show extended payments to a vendor to accommodate your company's cash flow. You can scroll through the periods using the horizontal scroll bar just above the period totals.

Peachtree Accounting does not check the total amounts for a line item against the actual transaction total. This lets you make manual adjustments for scheduled receipts or payments that may not tie directly to the transaction, such as for extended payments, or reduced payments for amounts in question. Be sure that your amounts add up correctly.

Note   Click the Note icon to display the Edit Comment window (shown in Figure 13-49).

Enter up to 250 characters of information about the transaction or adjustment. You can press CTRL-ENTER or CTRL-J to insert a line break.

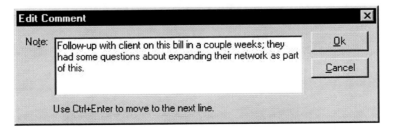

FIGURE 13-49   Edit Comment window

Totals This line shows the totals for the period. The totals are display-only.

Making Cash Adjustments

You can make adjustments to your forecasted cash flow through the Cash Manager – Forecast window. This feature is useful for entering anticipated revenues or expenses that do not currently have a transaction in Peachtree Accounting.

To enter a cash adjustment, highlight the Cash Adjustment (+) or the Cash Adjustment (-) row in the numeric view (as shown earlier in Figure 13-43) and click S.Sheet, or select the Cash Adjustment (+) or the Cash Adjustment (-) option in the Spreadsheet drop-down list in the upper-right corner on the Cash Manager spreadsheet view. The Cash Manager – Forecast window appears, as shown in Figure 13-50.

The Cash Manager – Forecast window is similar to the spreadsheet you saw earlier, except that there is no information on the spreadsheet initially. You can make entries in this window for a variety of items. For example, you could enter revenues from sales that are about to close or from anticipated rents and royalties. You could also include upcoming expenses for new equipment or for payments to consultants.

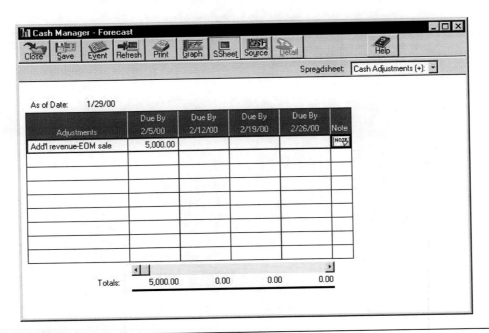

FIGURE 13-50 Cash Manager – Forecast window

C A U T I O N : If you have made cash adjustments on the spreadsheet, be sure to select the second option when you refresh the data in the Cash Manager, as discussed earlier in the "Updating Cash Manager Information" section.

Examining Cash Sources

The second level of analysis in the Cash Manager is the spreadsheet. The third level is the cash source view (which is only available for the Sales To Collect and Payments To Make categories). The cash source view lets you view the transactions for a specific customer or vendor.

To start the cash source view, either double-click a line item in the spreadsheet, or click Cash Source at the top of the Cash Manager window. The Cash Manager Detail window appears (as shown in Figure 13-51).

The Cash Manager Detail window has an additional button, which differs depending on whether you are viewing detail information for a customer or for a vendor, as shown in Table 13-7.

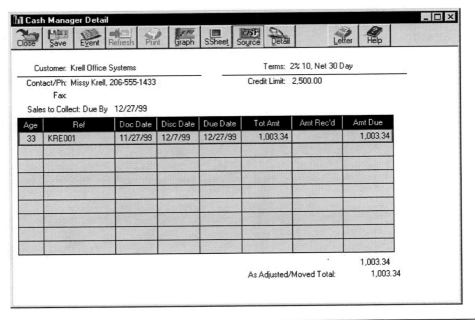

FIGURE 13-51 Cash Manager Detail window (information for a customer)

BUTTON	NAME	DESCRIPTION
Letter	Letter	Prints a collection letter (customers only)
Check	Check	Prints a check (vendors only)

TABLE 13-7 Toolbar Buttons on the Cash Manager Detail Window

The information for the customer or vendor appears at the top of the window. The transaction information in this window is display-only.

Amount to Pay   This is the total of the invoices you've checked to pay in the Pay column. (This field is for vendors only and is not shown in Figure 13-50.)

Age   This is the age of the transaction. (Aging is determined by the aging defaults you've set up in Accounts Receivable or Accounts Payable.)

Ref   This is the reference ID for the transaction.

Doc Date   This is the date the transaction was entered in Peachtree Accounting.

Disc Date   This is the last date a customer can make a discounted payment to you or that you can make a discounted payment to a vendor on the transaction.

Due Date   This is the due date for the transaction.

Tot Amt   This is the transaction amount before any discounts or finance charges are applied.

Amt Rec'd/Amt Paid   This is the amount you have received from the customer or that you have paid to the vendor.

Amt Due   This is the amount remaining to be received or paid on a transaction.

Pay   Check this box to pay the invoice. (This field is for vendors only.)

The Cash Manager Detail window lets you print collection letters to customers and checks to vendors. To print a collection letter, select Letter at the top of the window (the Letter button only appears when you are viewing customer information). The standard Print Forms: Collection Letters window appears (as shown in Figure 13-52).

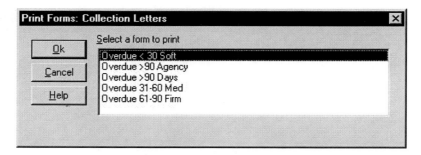

FIGURE 13-52 Print Forms: Collection Letters window

Select the appropriate collection letter. For more information on printing collection letters, see Chapter 5.

To print checks, select Check at the top of the window (the Check button only appears when you are viewing vendor information). The standard Print Forms: Disbursement Checks window appears (as shown in Figure 13-53).

Select the appropriate check. For more information on printing checks, see Chapter 6. (You cannot print checks unless you have checked the Pay box for one or more invoices.)

Viewing Transactions

The final level of analysis in the Cash Manager is the detail level. You can view and edit a transaction in the actual window in which it was originally entered. For customers, this is the Sales/Invoicing window; for vendors, this is the Purchases window.

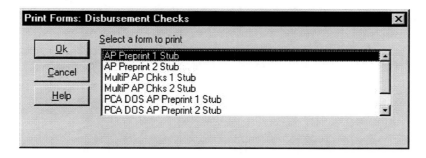

FIGURE 13-53 Print Forms: Disbursement Checks window

To view detail for a specific transaction, you can either double-click the transaction in the Cash Manager Detail window or highlight a transaction and click Detail at the top of the window. The Sales/Invoicing window or Purchases window appears, depending on the type of transaction. When you have finished viewing or editing the transaction, click Close at the top of the window. Any changes you made will not be reflected in the Cash Manager Detail window until you have refreshed the information using Refresh.

Using the Collection Manager

The Collection Manager focuses specifically on Accounts Receivable. You can use the Collection Manager to analyze your Accounts Receivable information, do detailed aging reports, and graph income.

To start the Collection Manager, select the Collection Manager option from the Analysis menu. The Collection Manager window appears, as shown in Figure 13-54. (Before you start the Collection Manager, you should make sure that all the journals have been posted.)

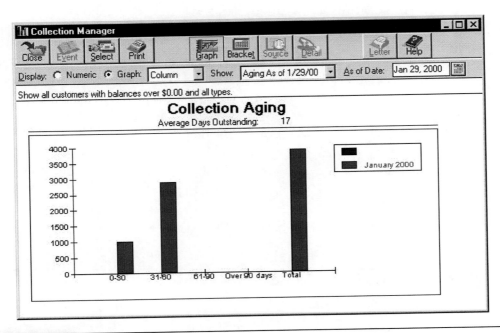

FIGURE 13-54 Collection Manager window

BUTTON	NAME	DESCRIPTION
Close	Close	Closes the Collection Manager window
Event	Event	Displays the Create Event window (discussed earlier in this chapter)
Select	Select	Selects customers to display
Print	Print	Prints a report of the information in the window (varies depending on the Collection Manager window)
Numeric Graph	Numeric/Graph	Switches to numeric or graph format from spreadsheet view
Bracket	Bracket	Lists information for an aging bracket
Source	Source	Displays information about the customer
Detail	Detail	Displays the appropriate transaction window to view and optionally edit the detail for a transaction
Letter	Letter	Prints a collection letter to a customer
Help	Help	Displays the online help on this window

TABLE 13-8 Toolbar Buttons on the Collection Manager Window

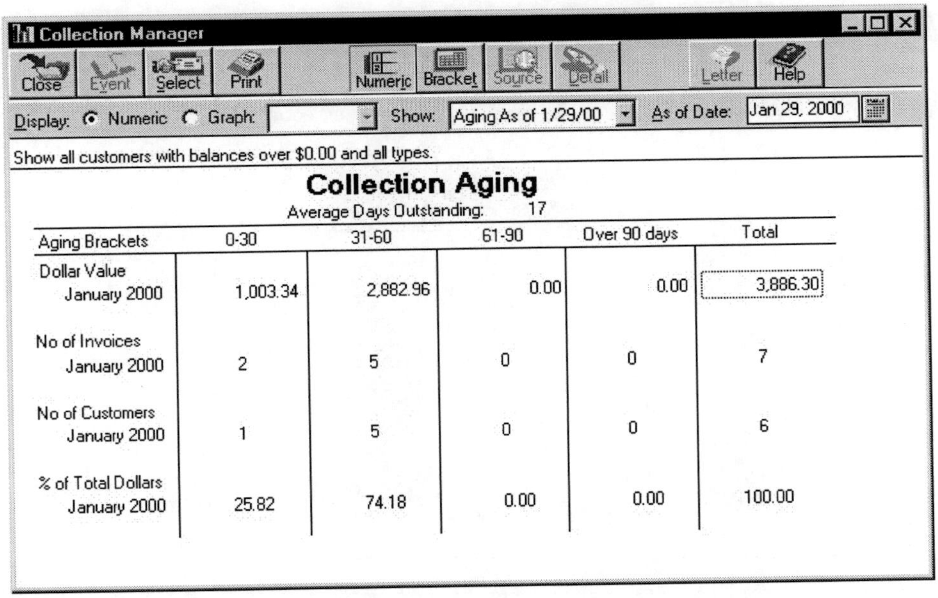

FIGURE 13-55 Collection Manager window displayed in numeric format

The Collection Manager has a separate set of buttons, as shown in Table 13-8.

Display   Choose Numeric to display the information in numeric form. The default display format for the Collection Manager window is in graph format. Figure 13-55 shows the information from Figure 13-54 displayed in a numeric format.

You can also display information in pie, column, or bar chart formats by clicking Graph and selecting the appropriate format from the list. See the "Using the Graphic Display" section later in this chapter for more information about graphs in the Collection Manager.

Show   Select the type of aging information to display. You can select the aging information as of the current system date, show the aging compared to one month ago, or the aging compared to one year ago. Figure 13-56 shows the aging compared to that of the previous month.

As of Date   Select the as-of date for the aging reports.

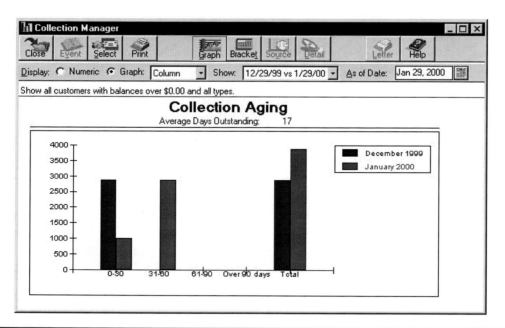

FIGURE 13-56 Current month's aging information compared to that of the previous month

 N O T E : Whenever you make changes to information that may affect the information in the Collection Manager, Peachtree Accounting automatically updates the forecast information displayed in the Collection Manager.

Using the Graphic Display

The information shown in the Collection Manager defaults to a graphic column display. There are two other graphic display formats you can use: a bar chart and a pie chart. Figure 13-57 shows a pie chart.

Pie charts showing a comparison are placed side-by-side. The comparison shown in Figure 13-56 appears in a pie chart format in Figure 13-58.

Selecting Customers in the Collection Manager

The default for the Collection Manager is to show all the customers in Peachtree Accounting. You can change the selection to show a more specific group of customers.

To select customers, click Select at the top of the window. The Collection Selections window appears (shown in Figure 13-59).

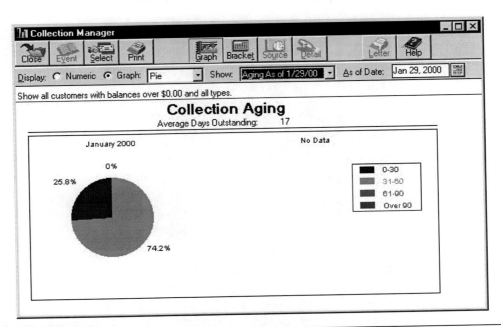

FIGURE 13-57 Collection Manager information shown in pie chart format

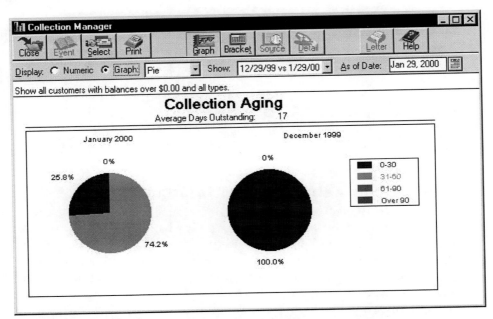

FIGURE 13-58 Current month's aging information compared to that of the previous month shown in pie chart format

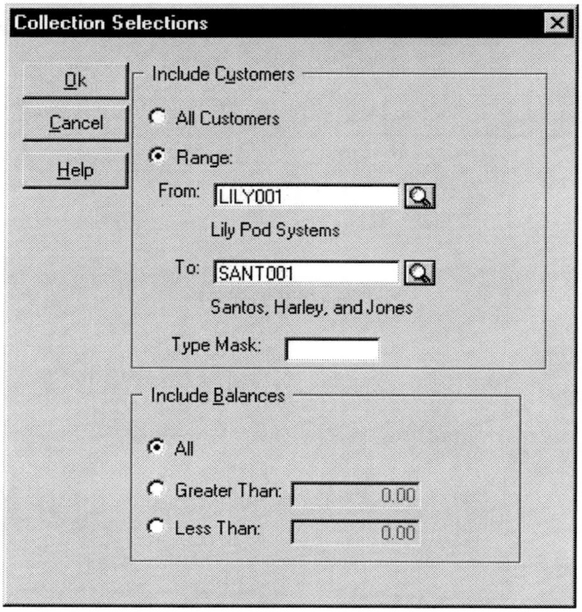

FIGURE 13-59 Collection Selections window

Include Customers Click All Customers to select all customers in Peachtree Accounting, or click Range to select a range of customers. You can also enter an optional type mask for further selection.

Include Balances Click All to include all customers. You can also select for customers with a balance greater or less than an amount you enter. After you've made your selections, click OK to close the window.

The selection information appears near the top of the Collection Manager window.

Viewing the Aging Bracket Information

The first level of analysis in the Collection Manager is to use the numeric and graphic displays of overview information. The next level of analysis is to use the bracket feature to view specific invoice information for customers in an aging bracket. To view a bracket from the numeric display, double-click the information in the Dollar Value row (the top row) for the aging bracket you want to view, or highlight the information and then click Bracket at the top of the window. (If you're in graph view, double-click anywhere on the window.) The Collection Manager window appears (shown in Figure 13-60 with a range of customers selected).

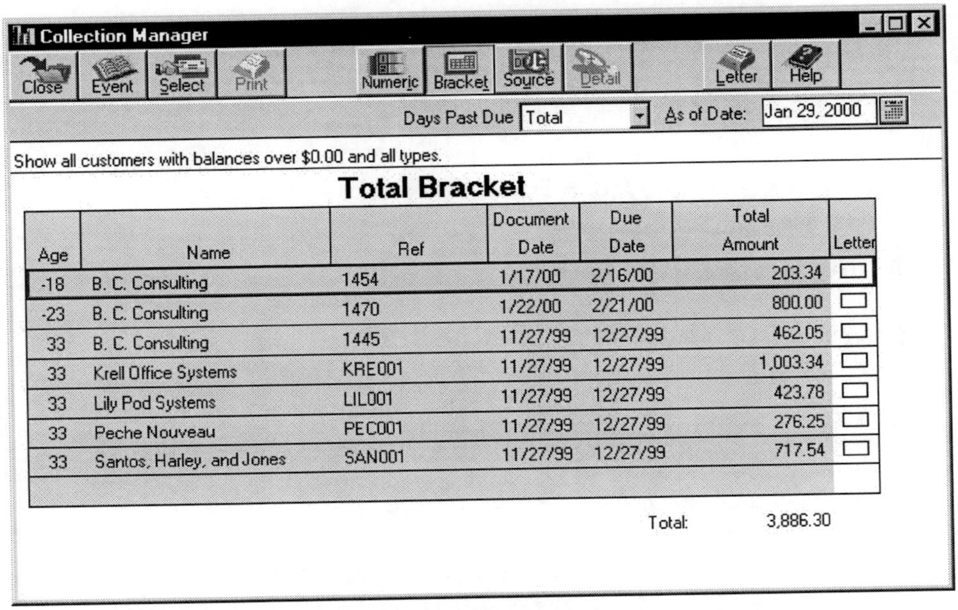

FIGURE 13-60 Collection Manager window

As you saw with the Cash Manager, you can use the spreadsheet to view the individual transactions that make up the totals for a category and a period.

Days Past Due Select the aging bracket. You can select any of the four aging brackets you've set up in Accounts Receivable, or select Total to see all aging. (If you started the Collection Manager by double-clicking on a Collection Manager graph, Peachtree Accounting automatically selects Total.)

As of Date Select the as-of date for the aging bracket.

Age This is the age of the transaction. (Aging is determined by the aging defaults you've set up in Accounts Receivable.) This field is display-only.

Name This is the customer name. This field is display-only.

Ref This is the reference ID for the transaction. This field is display-only.

Document Date This is the transaction date. This field is display-only.

Due Date This is the due date for the transaction. This field is display-only.

Total Amount This is the total amount of the transaction. This field is display-only.

Letter   Check this box to flag this transaction for a collection letter to the customer.

The Collection Manager lets you print collection letters to customers by selecting Letter at the top of the window. The standard Print Forms: Collection Letters window appears (as shown earlier in Figure 13-52). Select the appropriate collection letter. For more information on printing collection letters, see Chapter 5.

Total   This line shows the total for the period. The totals are display-only.

Examining Customer Balances

The second level of analysis in the Collection Manager is the Collection Manager window, which shows all the transactions for an aging bracket. The third level of analysis in the Collection Manager is the customer detail. The Customer Detail window shows you the transactions for a specific customer within an aging bracket.

To start customer detail view, either double-click a line item in the Collection Manager Bracket window, or click Source at the top of the window. The Customer Detail window appears (as shown in Figure 13-61).

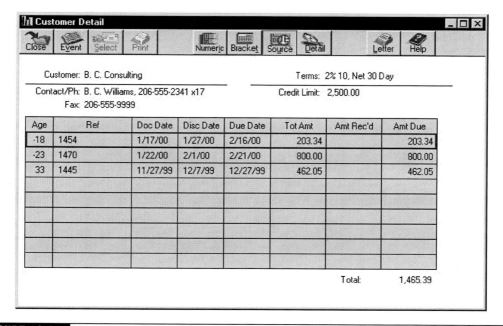

Age	Ref	Doc Date	Disc Date	Due Date	Tot Amt	Amt Rec'd	Amt Due
-18	1454	1/17/00	1/27/00	2/16/00	203.34		203.34
-23	1470	1/22/00	2/1/00	2/21/00	800.00		800.00
33	1445	11/27/99	12/7/99	12/27/99	462.05		462.05

Total: 1,465.39

FIGURE 13-61   Customer Detail window

You can print a letter for a transaction from this window by highlighting a transaction and then clicking Letter at the top of the window. The transaction information in this window is display-only.

Viewing Individual Transactions

The final level of analysis in the Collection Manager is the detail level. You can view and edit a transaction in the Sales/Invoicing window.

To view detail for a specific transaction, you can either double-click the transaction in the Customer Detail window, or highlight a transaction in the Customer Detail window and click Detail at the top of the window. The standard Sales/Invoicing window appears. When you have finished viewing or editing the transaction, click Close at the top of the Sales/Invoicing window. Any changes you make will be reflected in the Collection Manager window automatically.

Using the Payment Manager

The Payment Manager focuses specifically on Accounts Payable. You can analyze your Accounts Payable information, do detailed payables reports, and graph outflow.

To start the Payment Manager, select the Payment Manager option from the Analysis menu. The Payment Manager window appears, as shown in Figure 13-62. (Before you start the Payment Manager, you should make sure that all the journals have been posted.)

The Payment Manager's buttons (shown in Table 13-9) are similar to those for the Collection Manager.

Display   Choose Numeric to display the information in numeric form. The default display format for the Payment Manager window is graph format. Figure 13-63 shows the same information from Figure 13-62 displayed in a numeric format.

You can also display information in pie, column, or bar chart format by clicking Graph and selecting the appropriate chart format from the list. See the "Using the Graphic Display" section later in this chapter for more information about graphs in the Payment Manager.

Show   Select the type of aging information to display. You can select the aging information as of the current system date, show the aging compared to one month ago, or show the aging compared to one year ago. Figure 13-64 shows the aging compared to that of the previous month.

As of Date   Select the as-of date for the aging reports.

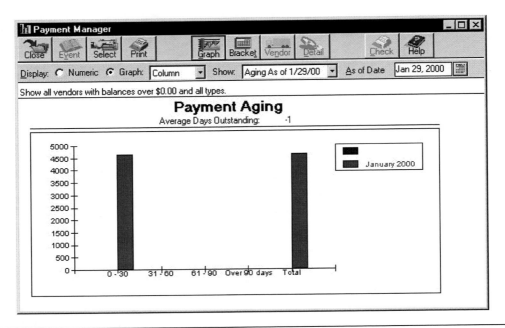

FIGURE 13-62 Payment Manager window

BUTTON	NAME	DESCRIPTION
Close	Close	Closes the Payment Manager window
Event	Event	Displays the Create Event window (discussed earlier in this chapter)
Select	Select	Selects customers to display
Print	Print	Prints a report of the information in the window (varies depending on the Payment Manager window)
Numeric Graph	Numeric/ Graph	Switches to numeric or graph format from spreadsheet view

TABLE 13-9 Toolbar Buttons on the Payment Manager Window

BUTTON	NAME	DESCRIPTION
 Bracket	Bracket	Lists information for an aging bracket
 Vendor	Vendor	Displays information about the vendor
 Detail	Detail	Displays the appropriate transaction window to view and optionally edit the detail for a transaction
 Check	Check	Prints a check to a vendor for an invoice
 Help	Help	Displays the online help on this window

TABLE 13-9 Toolbar Buttons on the Payment Manager Window (continued)

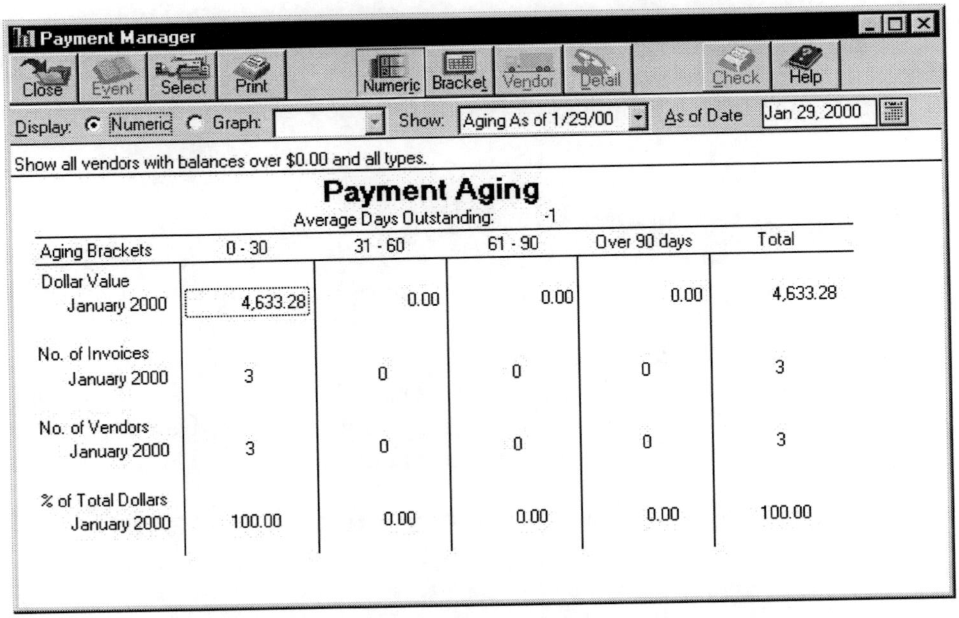

FIGURE 13-63 Payment Manager window displayed in numeric format

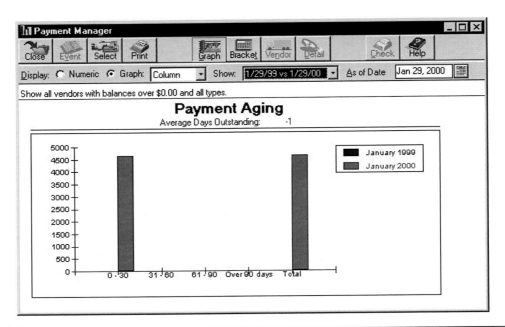

FIGURE 13-64 Current month's aging information compared to that of the previous month

> **N O T E :** Whenever you make changes to information that may affect the information in the Payment Manager, Peachtree Accounting automatically updates the forecast information displayed in the Payment Manager.

Using the Graphic Display

The information shown in the Payment Manager defaults to a graphic column display. There are two other graphic display formats you can use: a bar chart and a pie chart. Figure 13-65 shows a pie chart representation of the same data shown previously in Figure 13-62.

As with the Collection Manager, pie charts in the Payment Manager showing a comparison have two pie charts side-by-side. The comparison shown in Figure 13-64 appears in a pie chart format in Figure 13-66.

Selecting Vendors in the Payment Manager

The default for the Payment Manager is to show all the vendors in Peachtree Accounting. You can change the selection to show a more specific group of vendors.

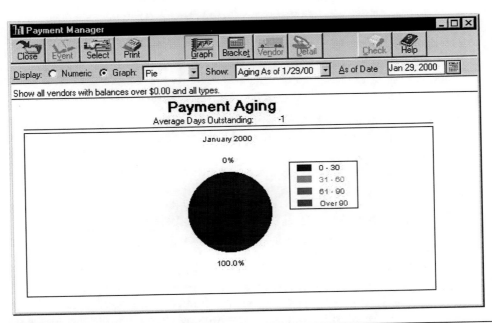

FIGURE 13-65   Payment Manager information shown in the pie chart format

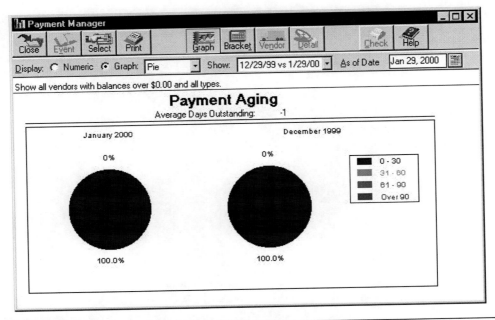

FIGURE 13-66   Current month's aging information compared to that of the previous month shown in pie chart format

To select vendors, click Select at the top of the window. The Payment Selections window appears (shown in Figure 13-67 with a range of vendors selected).

Include Vendors   Click All Vendors to select all vendors in Peachtree Accounting, or click Range to select a range of vendors. You can also enter an optional type mask for further selection.

Include Balances   Click All to include all balances. You can also select for vendors with a balance greater or less than an amount you enter. Once you've made your selections, click OK to close the window.

The selection information appears near the top of the Payment Manager window.

Viewing the Aging Bracket Information

The first level of analysis in the Payment Manager is to use the numeric and graphic displays of overview information. The next level of analysis is to use the bracket feature to view specific payment information for vendors in an aging bracket. To view a bracket from the numeric display, double-click the information in the Dollar Value row (the first row) for the aging bracket you want to view, or highlight the information and then click Bracket at the top of

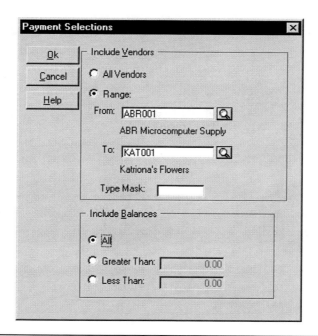

FIGURE 13-67   Payment Selections window

the window. (If you're in graph view, double-click anywhere in the window.) The Payment Manager window appears (shown in Figure 13-68).

From the spreadsheet, you can view the individual transactions that make up the totals for a category and a period.

Days Past Due   Select the aging bracket. You can select any of the four aging brackets you've set up in Accounts Payable, or select Total to see all aging. (If you started the Payment Manager by double-clicking on a Payment Manager graph, Peachtree Accounting automatically selects Total.)

As of Date   Select the as-of date for the aging bracket.

Age   This is the age of the transaction. (Aging is determined by the aging defaults you've set up in Accounts Payable.) This field is display-only.

Name   This is the vendor name. This field is display-only.

Ref   This is the reference ID for the transaction. This field is display-only.

Document Date   This is the transaction date. This field is display-only.

Due Date   This is the due date for the transaction. This field is display-only.

Total Amount   This is the total amount of the transaction. This field is display-only.

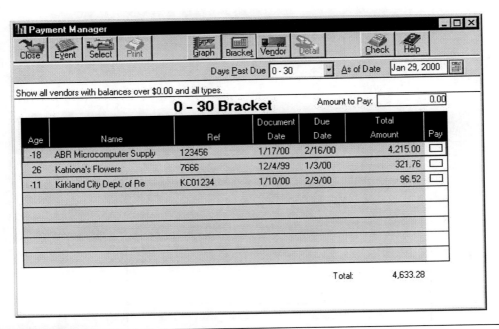

FIGURE 13-68   Payment Manager window

Pay   Check this box to flag this transaction for a check to the vendor.

The Payment Manager lets you print checks to vendors by selecting Check at the top of the window. The standard Print Forms: Disbursement Checks window appears (as shown earlier in Figure 13-53). Select the appropriate check. For more information on printing checks, see Chapter 6.

Total   This line shows the total for the period. The totals are display-only.

Examining Vendor Balances

The second level of analysis in the Payment Manager is the Payment Manager window, which shows all the transactions for an aging bracket. The third level of analysis in the Payment Manager is the vendor detail. The Vendor Detail window shows you the transactions for a specific vendor within an aging bracket.

To start vendor detail view, either double-click a line item in the Payment Manager window or click Vendor at the top of the window. The Vendor Detail window appears (as shown in Figure 13-69).

You can print a check for a transaction from this window by clicking on the pay column and then clicking Check at the top of the window. The transaction information in this window is display-only.

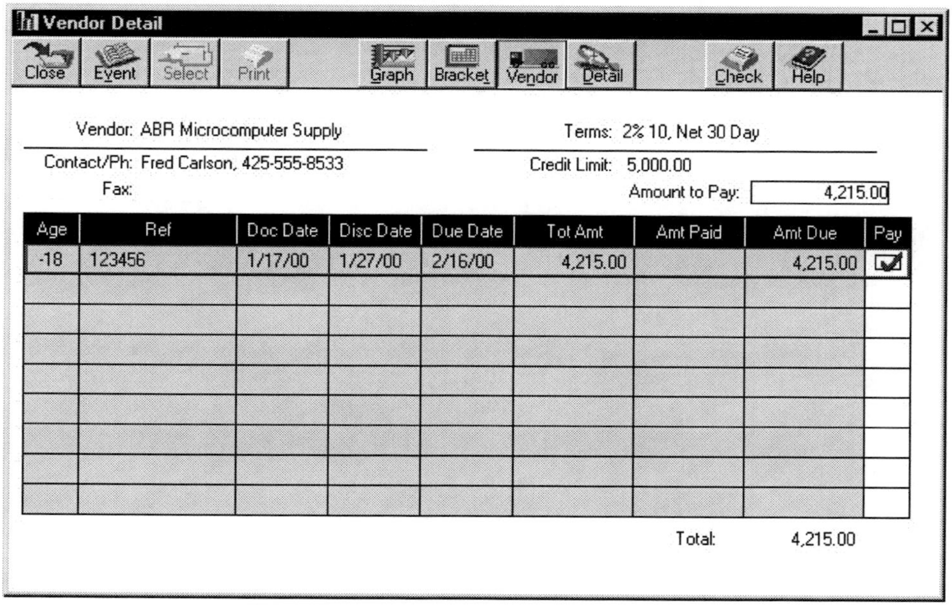

FIGURE 13-69   Vendor Detail window

Viewing Individual Transactions

The final level of analysis in the Payment Manager is the detail level. You can view and edit a transaction in the Purchases window.

To view detail for a specific transaction, you can either double-click the transaction in the Vendor Detail window or highlight a transaction in the Vendor Detail window and click Detail at the top of the window. The standard Purchases window appears. When you have finished viewing or editing the transaction, click Close at the top of the Purchases window. Any changes you make will be reflected in the Payment Manager window automatically.

Using the Financial Manager

The Financial Manager focuses specifically on the overall financial picture of how your business is performing. You can view your business in a numeric level or spreadsheet level. The numeric level displays financial data and business ratios as of a specific date. The spreadsheet level displays a comparison of financial data and business ratios. The spreadsheet level can display balances of up to 36 previous periods.

To start the Financial Manager, select the Financial Manager option from the Analysis menu. The Financial Manager window appears, as shown in Figure 13-70. (Before you start the Financial Manager, you should make sure that all the journals have been posted.)

NOTE: All calculations are rounded to two decimal places.

The Financial Manager's buttons (shown in Table 13-10) are similar to those for the Payment Manager.

Display Choose business summary or key balances.

As of Date Select the as-of date for the calculations.

Operational Analysis The Operational Analysis business summary calculates the following reports:

- Cost of sales as a percentage of sales
- Gross profit as a percentage of sales
- Net income as a percentage of sales

Resource Management   The Resource Management business summary calculates the following reports:

- Current assets
- Current liabilities
- Current ratio

Profitability   The Profitability business summary calculates the following reports:

- Return on total assets as a percentage
- Return on net worth as a percentage

Working Capital   The Working Capital business summary calculates the following reports:

- Inventory turnover
- Days accounts receivable outstanding

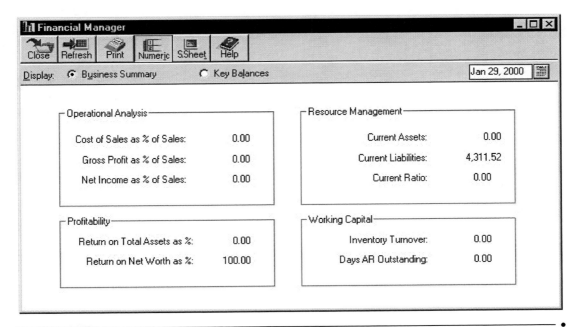

FIGURE 13-70   Financial Manager window with business summary

BUTTON	NAME	DESCRIPTION
Close	Close	Closes the Payment Manager window
Refresh	Refresh	Updates the financial data
Print	Print	Prints the displayed financial data
Numeric	Numeric	Displays account balances at a specific point in time in a numeric table
S.Sheet	S.Sheet	Switches to the Financial Manager spreadsheet
Help	Help	Displays the online help on this window

TABLE 13-10 Toolbar Buttons on the Financial Manager Window

If you select the Key Balances ratio button, the key balances and operations data from a specific date will be displayed in a numeric format as shown in Figure 13-71.

Key Balances The following Key Balance (display only) fields are displayed:

- Cash
- Accounts Receivable
- Inventory
- Accounts Payable
- Total Assets
- Total Liabilities

Operations The following Operations values (display only) are compared from the current period to year to date:

- Income

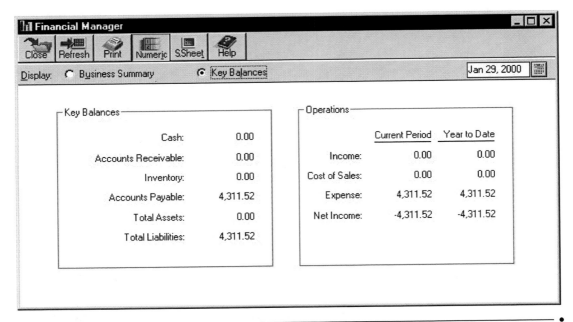

FIGURE 13-71   The Financial Manager window with key balances

- Cost of Sales
- Expense
- Net Income

Importing and Exporting Data

The final procedure covered in this chapter is importing and exporting data. Importing is the process of bringing data into Peachtree Accounting from another program. You can import data from other accounting programs, database programs, spreadsheets, or text files. Exporting is the process of writing data from Peachtree Accounting into a file that you can then import into another program. Importing is useful when you are converting from another accounting program to Peachtree Accounting. Exporting is useful for sending data from Peachtree Accounting into a database or spreadsheet so you can do additional reporting, analysis, or presentations using the data you have stored in Peachtree Accounting.

Imported and exported data is stored in a standard file format known as *comma-separated text* or, more commonly, *comma-delimited text.* In *comma-delimited text,* commas are used to separate each field (or item) of information in a single record (or line) of the text file. If the item has embedded spaces or commas, such as a customer name and address, the item is enclosed in quotes. A comma is used to represent the space for each item, even if there is no item to import or export. Each line of information in a comma-delimited file corresponds to a single record or transaction. Most databases, spreadsheets, and word processors can read and write comma-delimited files.

The information in Table 13-11 shows sample customer data and fields. This information would be put into comma-delimited format as follows:

```
"Melvin Morsmere, Ph.D.","P.O. Box 5340321",,Seattle,WA,98125,1913.84,532.15
```

You can see in this example that the fields with embedded spaces and commas are enclosed in quotes. There are comma separators functioning as placeholders for the second address line, even though there isn't any information in that field.

Importing Data into Peachtree Accounting

Importing data into Peachtree Accounting is fairly simple. You need to specify the type of information you want to import and then tell Peachtree Accounting where to find the file.

Peachtree Accounting has a number of standard import and export templates that look for data in a predefined order. Each file of data you import must have the fields in the same order as the template so Peachtree Accounting knows where to put the data. For example, the Payroll Employee List data is entered in the order Employee ID, Employee Name, Sales Rep, Employee, Inactive, address information, and so on. You can use the templates that come with Peachtree Accounting or create your own if you want. See "Creating Import/Export Templates" later in this section for more information. You

DATA	FIELDS
Melvin Morsmere, Ph.D.	name
P.O. Box 5340321	address line 1
	address line 2
Seattle, WA 98125	city, state, zip code
$1913.84	opening balance
$532.15	current liabilities

TABLE 13-11 Sample Import/Export Data

should also note that the Peachtree Accounting help files have extensive information on the field descriptions and order that will help you identify what will be imported and how. It's a good idea to print these out and examine them for the files you are about to import.

You might import data at any time while you are setting up a new company. For example, you may have a complete accounting package from which you are transferring data. In such a case, you would first set up the company header information in Peachtree Accounting and then immediately start importing data: the chart of accounts, then Accounts Receivable information, and so on. On the other hand, you may want to add a list of employees to the information in Peachtree Accounting, in which case you would only import payroll information after almost everything else had been set up. If you are not sure of how best to plan this process, check with your accountant on where and when in the process to import data.

C A U T I O N : Importing data has the potential to damage the integrity of your information in Peachtree Accounting. You should always make a backup of your company information before importing data from another source. See the "Backing Up with Peachtree Accounting" section earlier in this chapter for more information.

Some common problems to look out for when importing data are:

- Account, customer, vendor, employee, inventory, and job IDs must conform to Peachtree Accounting standards and contain no embedded spaces.
- Avoid quotation marks in description fields. The information will have a starting and ending quotation mark, so when Peachtree Accounting sees the quotation mark in the middle of the field, it assumes that's the end of the information for the field and starts trying to import the data for the next field with the remainder of the description, which is sure to cause errors. However, be sure to use starting and ending quotation marks in comma-delimited (CSV) files in any alphanumeric field that contains spaces or punctuation marks (such as names or addresses).
- Data can only be imported that falls within the two accounting years that are currently open in the company's data file.

To import data into Peachtree Accounting, choose the Select Import/Export option from the File menu. The Select Import/Export window appears, as shown in Figure 13-72.

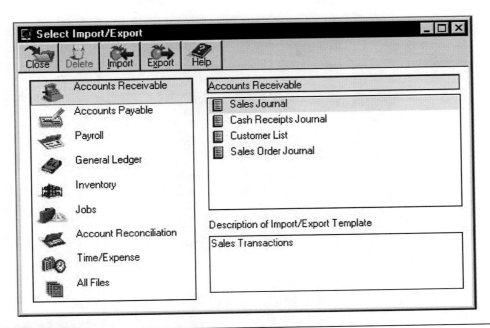

FIGURE 13-72 Select Import/Export window

Select the appropriate group and the template for the information you want to import.

NOTE: You cannot import or export Peachtree Fixed Assets information at this time.

Peachtree Accounting requires that you import data with the fields in a specific order and with the customer information preceding each record. Before you import data to Peachtree Accounting, you may want to export information from the sample client included with Peachtree Accounting to see what the file looks like. You can then match the type and order of the fields in the import data file to the type and order of the fields in the export data file.

Click Import at the top of the window to tell Peachtree Accounting you want to import information. A window appears with the Fields tab selected (shown in Figure 13-73).

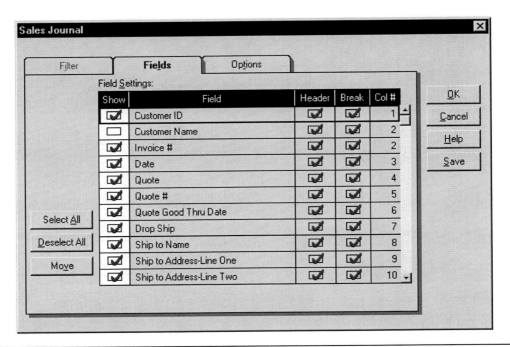

FIGURE 13-73 Fields tab for selecting fields to import

Peachtree Accounting lets you select specific fields of information to import in this window.

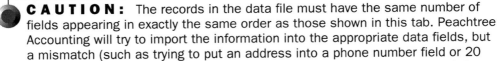

C A U T I O N : The records in the data file must have the same number of fields appearing in exactly the same order as those shown in this tab. Peachtree Accounting will try to import the information into the appropriate data fields, but a mismatch (such as trying to put an address into a phone number field or 20 characters of information into an 8-character field) will cause an error and the import will not be successful.

Show Check this box to select the information items that appear in the record. You would most commonly use this to exclude information that you don't have in your import files. Fields that are not already checked in the Show column when you first display this tab are only for export. You cannot import them through this template. However, if you are importing Customer List information, the Ship To addresses are unchecked, but you can check them to import them.

Field   This is the name of the field to be imported. This field is display-only.

Header   For import and export all field headers are selected. This field is display-only.

Break   For import/export, each field uses its own column. This field is display-only.

Col #   This is the order in which the information must appear in the record. This field is display-only. Peachtree Accounting changes the column number when you check or uncheck items (very similar to adding and removing items from report layouts, as discussed in earlier chapters) or when you change the order of items in the layout (discussed later in this section).

When you are satisfied with your entries, click the Options tab. The Options tab appears, as shown in Figure 13-74. Because you are importing data, Peachtree Accounting grays out the export options on this tab.

Import/Export File   The default import filename appears in this field. Click the button to the left of the filename to display a standard file selection box (not shown) to select another filename and location.

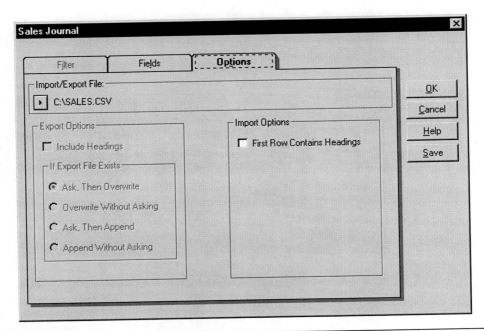

FIGURE 13-74   Options tab showing import options

First Row Contains Headings   If your comma-delimited file contains a line of heading information as the first record, check this box.

Warn If Duplicate Reference   Whenever you are importing payments, payroll, and receipts, Peachtree Accounting displays this checkbox. Checking the box tells Peachtree Accounting to warn you if a transaction you are importing has a reference number already used by another transaction. It is strongly recommended that you check this box. If you leave this box unchecked, Peachtree Accounting will append the information you are importing to the data file whether it has a duplicate reference or not. This can cause many problems when trying to reconcile your accounts.

When you are satisfied with your entries, click OK. Peachtree Accounting warns you that you should make a backup before attempting to import information and asks if you want to continue. Click Yes to start the import. Peachtree Accounting will display a progress graph on the screen as it imports the data from the file, after which it returns you to the Select Import/Export window. If you want to import several kinds of information, such as Accounts Receivable sales journals, Accounts Receivable customer lists, Accounts Payable purchases journals, and a General Ledger chart of accounts, you will need to import each group of information from a separate data file.

For information on specific field requirements in each template, refer to the Import/Export Field Definitions section in the Contents screen of the Help menu. This section contains extensive descriptions of the fields and the type of data Peachtree Accounting expects in them.

Exporting Data from Peachtree Accounting

Exporting data is very similar to importing data. From the Select Import/Export window shown earlier in Figure 13-72, select the type of information you want to export such as Accounts Receivable/Sales Journal information, then click Export at the top of the window. The Sales Journal window appears with the Filter tab displayed (as shown in Figure 13-75).

The Filter tab in the Sales Journal window is very much like the Filter tab in the Report Options window. You select the data you want to export, then click the Fields tab to display the Fields tab (shown earlier in Figure 13-73). When you export data, you should check or uncheck the Show box for the fields you want to include or exclude from the data Peachtree Accounting exports.

When you are satisfied with your entries in the Fields tab, click the Options tab. The Options tab appears, as shown in Figure 13-76. Because you are exporting data, Peachtree Accounting grays out the import options on this tab.

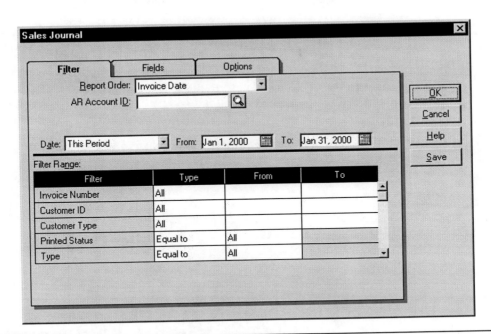

FIGURE 13-75 Sales Journal window with the Filter tab displayed

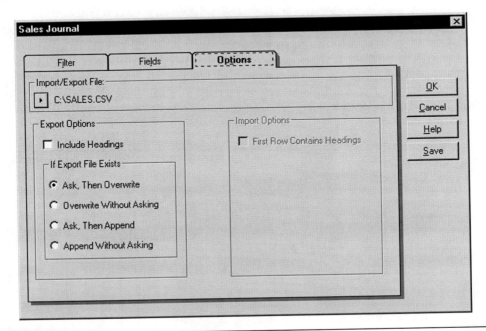

FIGURE 13-76 Options tab showing export options

Import/Export File   The default export filename appears in this field. Click the button to the left of the filename to display a standard file selection box (not shown) to enter another filename and location.

Include Headings   Check this box to include a line at the start of the file. The headings record shows the names of the fields. Header information is useful for identifying fields for mail merge and database operations.

If Export File Exists   Check the appropriate option for how you want to deal with an existing export file.

When you are satisfied with your entries, click OK. Peachtree Accounting exports the data to the file.

Peachtree Accounting will only export one type of information at a time. If you want to export several types of information, you must perform several successive exports. If the program you are exporting data for needs a single file, you should append the information from each export to the same file.

Using Peachtree Accounting with PCA, Quicken, QuickBooks, or Veritask Write-Up

Peachtree Accounting can import data from PCA, Quicken, QuickBooks, or Veritask Write-Up, and it will export data to Veritask Write-Up. Select the All Files group on the Select Import/Export window (shown earlier in Figure 13-72), then select the appropriate option from the list on the right of the window and click Import or Export. Peachtree Accounting will ask for the path name for the files and start the process. See the documentation for the specific program you are importing data from for more information on the data file format and import/export process.

 N O T E :   Only company data created in versions 4 or 5 of both QuickBooks and QuickBooks Pro for Windows can be imported.

Peachtree Accounting will also export data to electronic banking for reconciliation. Select the Account Reconciliation group on the Select Import/Export window, then select the Electronic Banking option.

Creating Import/Export Templates

The standard import/export templates included with Peachtree Accounting are fairly comprehensive. However, you may want to create a custom template that imports or exports information in a particular order or with particular fields selected.

To create a custom template, select a template from the Select Import/Export window (shown earlier in Figure 13-72) and click Import. The Import/Export Options window with the Fields tab is displayed (as shown earlier in Figure 13-73).

You can select or deselect fields by checking or unchecking the appropriate Show box. To move a field to a new position, highlight the field, click Move, and then click the field above which you want to move the first field. The column numbers change accordingly to show the order in which the fields will appear in the file.

When you are satisfied with your changes, click Save. The Save As window appears, as shown in Figure 13-77.

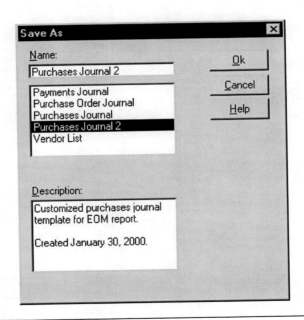

FIGURE 13-77 Save As window

Enter information in this window as follows:

Name   Enter a name for the new template. This name should reflect the name of the template upon which this template is based. Entering a name for an existing custom template will overwrite the template. (You cannot overwrite the standard templates that come with Peachtree Accounting.)

Description   Enter a description of the template. As with many other memo and description fields, you can press CTRL-J to insert a line break. It's a good idea to enter the date the template was created or modified and a brief comment about the changes to the template in this field to track changes you've made.

When you are satisfied with your entries, click OK. The new template appears in the list on the Select Import/Export window, as shown in Figure 13-78. Custom templates can be used for both importing and exporting data.

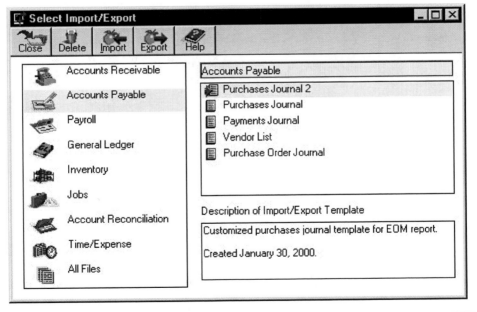

FIGURE 13-78   Select Import/Export window showing new template in list

Summary

Congratulations! With this chapter, you have completed your tour of the major components of Peachtree Accounting.

With Peachtree Accounting, you can take control of your business finances. In this book, you have seen how to set up and use Peachtree Accounting to perform all aspects of basic accounting for your business. Once your business is set up, you can break down your accounting tasks into a series of simple procedures that do not require any specialized accounting knowledge—just the ability to enter data into the right fields and windows. Peachtree Accounting then does the rest: posting information to the journals, processing, and printing reports, checks, and forms.

Keep this book handy as you work with Peachtree Accounting. It will be a resource you turn to again and again as you set up, maintain, and take charge of your company's finances.

Glossary

This is a glossary of terms and concepts you will encounter as you work with Peachtree Accounting. For a complete understanding of bookkeeping and accounting courses, you should look at any of the wide variety of accounting texts and references available at your local bookstore.

account	Identifying name and/or number for transactions, the basic building blocks of accounting.
accounting	A system of related records for all financial transactions of a person or business.
accounting period	The units of time used to divide the fiscal year.
accounts payable	The money you owe to vendors.
accounts receivable	The money owed to you by your customers.
accrual accounting	A system of accounting that recognizes revenues and expenses in the accounting period in which they are incurred, regardless of when the money comes in or goes out.
action items/event log options	Events that affect your business that are set in the Peachtree Action Items/Event Log Options window.
alert	An event for which you have set certain criteria.
assembly	An inventory item comprised of individual inventory items and sold as a unit.
assets	The resources a company uses to generate revenue.
audit trails	A feature in Peachtree Complete Accounting that lets you track each action made by a user in a log file.
backing up	Copying your data from your computer's hard disk to another portion of the hard disk, floppy disk, or tapes.
balance sheet	A snapshot summary of your company's asset, liability, and equity accounts as of a specific date or accounting period. Balance sheets always list assets first, liabilities second, and equity last. Also known as *statement of financial condition*.
batch processing	Saving transactions in a temporary file before posting them to the journals.
bookkeeping	The process of recording information on financial transactions.
cash accounting	A system of accounting that recognizes revenues and expenses when they are received or paid.

chart of accounts   The accounts for a specific company.

Close button   Button with an X in the upper-right corner of the window that closes the window and, if this is the main program window, exits the program.

closing   A financial procedure that produces final reports for a set period and, at the end of the fiscal year, resets all equity closing, cost of goods, income, and expense accounts to zero for the next fiscal year. In Peachtree Accounting, the closing process involves posting journals, printing year-end reports for the audit trail, and optionally purging transactions and changing your accounting periods for the next fiscal year. Closing the fiscal year zeros all income, expense, cost of goods, and Equity-Gets Closed account types and posts them to your retained earnings account on the balance sheet.

control menu   Drop-down menu in the upper-left corner of an individual window that allows you to restore, move, or resize the window.

conversion date   The date on which you know all your company's accounting balances so you can switch accounting systems.

cost codes   Subdivisions of phases for assigning costs or tasks.

cost of goods   Expenses incurred directly in the production of something to be sold.

costing method   Any of several different ways of determining the cost of inventory items.

credit   A transaction that decreases the balance of the debit account being credited. Also, a type of account that accumulates with a negative to offset debits (positive) for accurate account balancing.

current assets   Cash and assets that will normally be converted into cash within one year or within the company's normal operating cycle, whichever is longer. Also known as *liquid assets* or *working assets*.

current liabilities   Liabilities that mature (become payable) within one year or one operating cycle, such as accounts payable, wages payable, and taxes payable. In addition, long-term liabilities become current liabilities during the year in which they become due.

debit	A transaction that increases the balance of the debit account being debited.
deferred assets	Assets that are booked to be received in a later accounting period. See also *prepaid expenses.*
deferred expenses	Expenses that are booked to be paid for in a later accounting period. See also *prepaid expenses.*
equity	The value, less liabilities of a property or business, the net worth.
expenses	The cost of doing business (such as rent, depreciation expense, professional fees, heat, light, and so on).
exporting	Writing data from Peachtree Accounting into a file that you can then import into another program.
field	The smallest piece of information in a record, such as a name, a telephone number, an account number, or a transaction amount.
financial statements	A special kind of report that you can display on the screen or print on the printer.
fiscal year	The company's accounting year (as determined by the dates the company opens and closes the books). Fiscal years are usually but not necessarily the same as calendar years.
fixed assets	Assets with a useful life of more than one year, such as furniture, computers, software, fixtures, machinery, equipment, buildings, and vehicles.
GAAP	Short for *Generally Accepted Accounting Principles,* a set of accepted principles and practices for accounting regulated by law and precedence. Assets, liabilities, capital, income, cost of sales, and expenses are all types of GAAP account groupings.
general journal	Entries to the General Ledger that do not come in from any of the other ledgers.
general ledger	The summary of all financial activity for your company, comprised of information from Accounts Receivable, Accounts Payable, Payroll, General Journal, and Inventory.
importing	Bringing data into Peachtree Accounting from another program. You can import data from other accounting programs, database programs, spreadsheets, or text files.

inactive	In Peachtree Accounting, this identifies an account, a record, or an item that is not to be used in transactions, but will remain in the system rather than being deleted (usually due to outstanding transactions that use the record or item).
income	The remainder when you subtract expenses from revenues.
Income Received in Advance	Money received in advance of goods or services from a customer. A magazine publisher, for example, would include paid subscriptions in this category. See also *deferred income.*
job	A specific project your company is undertaking to which you want to assign expenses or income.
journal	A register in which you record every transaction that affects your firm.
liabilities	The economic obligations of a firm to outsiders.
liquid assets	See *current assets.*
long-term liabilities	Any liability not due within the current accounting period. These are sometimes referred to as *fixed liabilities* or *long-term debt*, and include such liabilities as mortgages.
masking	Creating IDs to allow filtering of specific divisions, departments, and locations when printing financial reports.
Maximize button	Button with a square in the upper-right corner of the window that expands the window to fill the desktop.
memorized transaction	A standard transaction that you can then call up and use without having to reenter the standard information, rather like a template for entries.
Minimize button	Button with an underscore character in the upper-right corner of the window that shrinks the window down to an icon-sized button on the Windows 98 Taskbar.
navigation aid	A graphic representation for navigating Peachtree Accounting features.
net income	The amount of net income from operations.
net income from operations	The net sales less cost of goods sold and operating expenses.

operating cycle — The length of time between the purchase of inventory or merchandise and the sale of the finished product.

operating expenses — Expenses not directly related to the production of something for sale, such as sales expense and general administrative expense.

phases — Subdivisions of individual stages of a project.

posting — Submitting information to your ledger(s) after entering transactions.

prepaid expenses — Expenses that are paid in advance and provide benefit over a period of time, such as insurance or rent paid in advance. Also known as *deferred expenses* or *deferred assets*.

purging — Clearing old transactions, records, and other information.

real-time processing — To post transactions directly to the journals when you save them.

record — A single transaction or complete information unit stored in Peachtree Accounting, such as an accounting transaction, or a customer, job, or employee record.

recurring transaction — A transaction that repeats at regular intervals with the same transaction information.

retained earnings — The accumulated net income retained by the firm. The overall profit (or loss) of a company, including the equity.

return on assets — The result of dividing net income by total assets.

revenue — Income or proceeds from business activities (such as rental or sales income).

sales tax authority — A taxing agency able to levy taxes, such as federal, state, county, and city agencies.

sales tax codes — A tax rate from one to five sales tax authorities.

statement of financial condition — See *balance sheet*.

statements — A summary of invoiced amounts over time.

status bar — The status bar in Peachtree Accounting shows information about the field you are working with, the current date, and the current accounting period.

stockholders' equity   The amount owners pay for their investment in capital stock in a company. The sum of stockholders' equity and retained earnings represents the owners' value in the company.

title bar   A line at the top of a window containing the name of the company you're working with, the name of the window, or other information.

transaction   Any business operation that has a financial impact.

trial balance   A listing of all account balances to ensure that credits precisely offset debits.

vendor   A person or company you owe money to.

what's this   Changes your mouse pointer to a question mark. Then click anywhere for context sensitive help to be displayed.

wizard   Walks you through new company setup, payroll setup, and purge guide.

working assets   See *current assets*.

Index

Sense Networking of Seattle (oz.net) the <u>top-rated</u> ISP in Washington State from 1995 to 1997 (c|net ISP listings) offering unlimited dialup access from $20 per month, and full 128k dual-channel ISDN for only $40 per month!

For full details on getting an account through the best Internet Service Provider in Western Washington, call one of the distributors listed below:

VISUAL
Internet Services Group

```
voice: 253.946.9426
  fax: 253.941.9084
  bbs: 253.529.3734
  www: http://www.oz.net/visual
```

Home
Grown
Systems

```
voice: 206.329.8070
  www: http://www.oz.net/hgs
```

Mention this publication, and your first month's service is free!

Peachtree Support

Get the service you deserve
from Peachtree's premier support center.

Whether you have a technical problem

or a quick question, need help setting up your system,

or want a local area network installed, PSI's Peachtree

certified staff is available to help you.

PSC

Authorized Peachtree
Support Center

Perfect Systems, Inc.
Helping you Build a Better Business
1-800-783-2399 or (206) 270-9080
Fax: (206) 324-2882
e-mail: psinc@halcyon.com
http://www.halcyon.com/psinc/

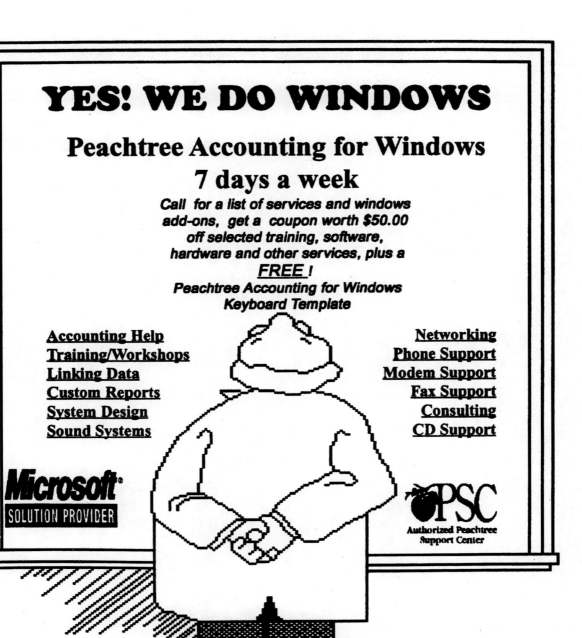

2602257

Made in the USA